GODS AND HEROES
OF THE EUROPEAN
BRONZE AGE

GODS AND HEROES OF THE EUROPEAN BRONZE AGE

Katie Demakopoulou, Christiane Eluère
Jørgen Jensen, Albrecht Jockenhövel, Jean-Pierre Mohen

THAMES AND HUDSON

Patronage

Council of Europe, Strasbourg

25ᵗʰ Council of Europe Art Exhibition

Published on the occasion of the exhibition
Gods and Heroes of the Bronze Age
Europe at the Time of Ulysses

This catalogue is published to accompany the exhibition
Guder og Helte i Bronzealderen. Europa på Odysseus' tid
from December 19, 1998, to April 5, 1999, at the
National Museum of Denmark, Copenhagen,
Götter und Helden der Bronzezeit.
Europa im Zeitalter des Odysseus
from May 13 to August 22, 1999, at the Kunst- und
Ausstellungshalle der Bundesrepublik Deutschland,
Bonn, Germany
L'Europe au temps d'Ulysse.
Dieux et Héros à l'Age du bronze
from September 28, 1999, to January 9, 2000,
at the Galeries nationales du Grand Palais, Paris, and
Θεοί και Ήρωες της Εποχής του Χαλκού.
Η Ευρώπη στις ρίζες του Οδυσσέα.
(Gods and Heroes of Bronze Age Europe.
The roots of Ulysses)
from February 11 to May 7, 2000, at the National
Archaeological Museum, Athens

First published in Great Britain in 1999 by Thames and
Hudson Ltd. London

First published in hardback in the United States
of America in 1999 by Thames and Hudson Inc.,
500 Fifth Avenue, New York. New York 10110

British Library Cataloguing-in-Publication Data
A catalogue record for this book is available from the
British Library

Library of Congress Catolog Card Number 98-74860

ISBN 0-500-01915-0

Printed in Germany

Foreword by the Secretary General of the Council of Europe

Over the past half century the Council of Europe has organised approximately every other year an exhibition displaying the greatest treasures of European art and culture. Most of the main artistic currents from the early times up to the present day and many aspects of the intricate interplay between art and civilisation have been covered. The aim is not only to increase awareness and appreciation of this priceless heritage, but also to stimulate the feeling that our legacy is as shared as our destiny.

Each of the exhibitions held in the series quite naturally has something that is distinctively European about it, but perhaps never so much as this one devoted to the Bronze Age. For it was at that time, at the distant dawn of European history, even before people in this part of the world began to write down their myths and legends, their stories and their travels, that Europe can first be distinguished as an emerging entity. The exhibits from so many different areas which figure in this catalogue indeed bear witness to a unique and lively civilisation stretching across the entire continent.

It is both moving and apposite in these times of strife and fratricidal wars to remind ourselves of this indubitable fact of a common origin. Recognition of this and the body of values which have been gradually become our jointly held heritage are the very foundations on which the work of the Council of Europe is built and from which it constantly draws inspiration. Diversity is doubtless a richness but it is not by stressing our differences that we shall improve the lot of our children. So now and again it is refreshing and healthy to recall what unites us all and from long ago.

We are consequently deeply indebted to all those who have striven so hard over many years to give us this beautiful and informative exhibition. It comes as the crowning event in the Campaign for Archaeology organised by the Council of Europe and relayed with resounding success in our member countries and illustrates our faith in the idea that better knowledge and appreciation of our past belong to the necessary preconditions for a peaceful future.

Daniel Tarschys

NATIONALMUSEET

National Museum of Denmark, Copenhagen, Denmark

Kunst- und Ausstellungshalle der Bundesrepublik Deutschland, Bonn, Germany

m Réunion
des Musées
Nationaux

• • • • • • • • • •

Association Française d'Action Artistique **A F A A**
Ministère des Affaires Étrangères

Galeries nationales du Grand Palais, Paris, France

National Archaeological Museum, Athens, Greece

Directors' Preface

Gods and Heroes of the Bronze Age, the 25th exhibition initiated by the Council of Europe, will augment the range of cultural activities in four European cities: Copenhagen, Bonn, Paris and Athens. The exhibition seeks to bring to life one of our most important prehistoric epochs, a period in which the peoples of this continent experienced profound transformations and innovations. The traces of this development are visible to the present day in numerous European lands – in Greece, for example, at the sites of Knossos and Mycenae (closely associated with Troy in Asia Minor as well), in Portugal at the fortified settlement of Zambujal, in England at the sanctuary of Stonehenge, or in the countless burial mounds of central Europe extending to Maïkop in the Caucasus.

The 237 objects shown in the exhibition derive from famous as well as less spectacular archaeological sites in twenty-three European countries. They manifest the spread of the new technique of bronze metallurgy in the 3rd millennium BC and the concurrent development of new levels of craftsmanship, the result of an influx of raw materials from ever greater distances and the growth of trade in luxury goods. The achievements of this period include work not only of bronze, but also of gold, silver, glass and faience, amber and ivory. All of this conveys the impression of a period of splendid wealth: one is almost tempted to call it a "Golden Age". Yet this same period, which was to last two millennia, also experienced its share of social conflict and war.

The special significance of the European Bronze Age also lies in the birth of Greek linear writing at the middle of the 2nd millennium BC, an occurrence that was to herald the beginning of European history.

The Trojan War and the Return of Ulysses number among the most important events of the Bronze Age of which we possess knowledge, thanks to an effective oral tradition that was doubtless recorded very early. The Homeric myths, rooted in the European Bronze Age, still speak to us today and provide evidence of a cultural legacy handed down over centuries.

The five sections of the exhibition focus on elements from this period of history that have exerted a decisive influence on western civilisation:

1) Adventurers and Travellers of the Bronze Age
2) The Heroes in their Palaces
3) The Heroes: Life and Death
4) The World of the Gods
5) The Awakening of Europe

An exhibition bringing together extraordinary pieces from the most important museums in Europe was considered the most appropriate way to adequately convey both the originality and the homogeneity of the European Bronze Age, visible in lines of communication extending from east to west and from north to south. Thus gold from Crete and the royal graves of Mycenae appears alongside comparable treasures from central and northern Europe, such as the famous "sun chariot" from Trundholm in Denmark, a symbol of the close association of the precious metal with the worship of the divine sun. In the war-like society of the heroes, the shining bronze of swords, helmets and of armour such as those from Marmesse signifies both the light of the sun and a kind of supernatural authority. The great stelai of hewn stone from the Iberian Peninsula, Italy, France and Germany show these same heroes, ceremonially arrayed in their weapons.

While at first glance the gods may appear to be under-represented, two iconographic themes serve to spectacularly invoke their presence: the motif of the bull, found everywhere in the Mediterranean and to which the horned helmets from Viksø (Denmark) also allude, and that of the bird. The bird appears on the altars of Knossos and of Mycenae and a number of votive chariots from central and northern Europe, as well as on large drinking vessels of the Nordic Bronze Age, doubtless dedicated to the gods. The bird motif was widespread throughout all of Europe in the 2nd millennium BC and signified both travel and return, for it probably recalled the migrating birds that announced the arrival of spring and the renewal of the sun.

The exhibition *Gods and Heroes of the Bronze Age* seeks to explore the conditions under which European history was born – at a time when the modern Europe is in the process of creation, building on foundations which, though as yet little known, are not far removed from those of its origins and myths.

Steen Hvass
National Museum of Denmark, Copenhagen

Wenzel Jacob
Kunst- und Ausstellungshalle der Bundesrepublik
Deutschland, Bonn

Françoise Cachin
Réunion des musées nationaux, Paris

Jean Digne
Association Française d'Action Artistique, Paris

Yannis Tzedakis
Ministry of Culture, General Directorate of Antiquities,
Athens

Contents

CHAPTER 3
The Heroes: Life and Death
Editor: Jørgen Jensen

CHAPTER 4
The World of the Gods in the Bronze Age
Editor: Christiane Eluère

CHAPTER 5
The Birth of Europe
Editor: Katie Demakopoulou

Cut-out relief in the shape of a Tripartite Shrine, Mycenae Argolid, ▷
Greece, Late Bronze Age, second half of 16th century BC
(Cat. No. 75)

Jarlshof

Haga ▲
Mälar ▲
Hallunda

Migdale

North

Tanum ▲

Sea

Fårdal ▲
Brudevælte

Traprain Law

Drunkendult ▲
Rathtinaun ▲

Trundholm ▲ ▲ Viksø Kivik
Egtved ▲ Skallerup ▲ ▲ Simrishamn
Voldtofte ▲ ▲ Ystad
Grevensvænge

Scarborough ▲

Barrybeg ▲
Moyarta ▲
Dowris ▲

Roos Carr ▲

Bornhöved ▲
Wismar ▲
Peckatel ▲
Granzirl
Melz
Seddin ▲

Ückeritz

Wierz

Banie

Bis

Eberswalde ▲

G

Mold ▲

Mount Gabriel ▲

Fengate ▲
Wilburton ▲

Moordorf

Bargeroosterveld ▲

Stade ▲

Sögel

Harpstedt ▲ Dohnsen

Elbe

Oder

Łęk

Bush Barrow ▲
Gwithian ▲ Stonehenge ▲ ▲ Wilsford

Hove

Helmsdorf ▲
Neunheiligen ▲ ▲ Dieskau
Leubingen

Marszow

Gevelinghausen ▲

Rhine

Schwarza ▲
Gehülz

Únětice (Aunjetitz)

Vela
Lovčič
Blučin
Vět

Knovíz

ATLANTIC OCEAN

Plainseau ▲

Fritzdorf ▲

Adlerberg ▲

Acholshausen ▲

Ezelsdorf ▲ Milavče

La Motta ▲
Plougrescant ▲

Aulnay-aux-
Planches

Schifferstadt ▲

Baierdorf

Kelheim ▲

Tréboul ▲

Fort
Harrouard

Haguenau ▲

Straubing
Poing ▲ Gemeinlebarn ▲
Lochham Hart a.d. Alz ▲ Sauer

Saint-Brieuc-
des-Iffs ▲

Cannes-
Ecluse ▲

Rixheim ▲

Bad Buchau

Riegsee ▲ Mitterberg ▲

brunn

Nantes ▲

St. Germain
du Plain ▲

Mörigen ▲

Sankt Moritz ▲

Kesz

Coulon ▲ Avanton ▲

Larnaud ▲

Val Camonica ▲

Fiave ▲

Po

Vénat ▲

Rongères ▲

Le Bourget-du-Lac

Polada ▲ Peschiera ▲

Škocjan ▲

Bay of
Biscay

St. Denis de Pile ▲

Rhone

La Côte-
St.-André ▲

Fontanella

Frattasine

Bismantova ▲

Monte Bego ▲

Hio ▲

Nîmes ▲

Pianello

Huerta de Arriba ▲

Douro

Duero

Ebro

Tolfa ▲

Allumiere ▲

Filitosa ▲

Pragança ▲

Tajo

Tejo

Solana de Cabañas ▲

Sant'Antine ▲ ▲ Ozieri

Pertosa

Guadiana

Alamo ▲

Fuente
Álamo ▲ Villena ▲
de Murcia

Huelva

Arrubiu ▲
Barumini ▲

Lipari ▲

Mediterranean Sea

El Argar ▲

Thapsos

Pantalica

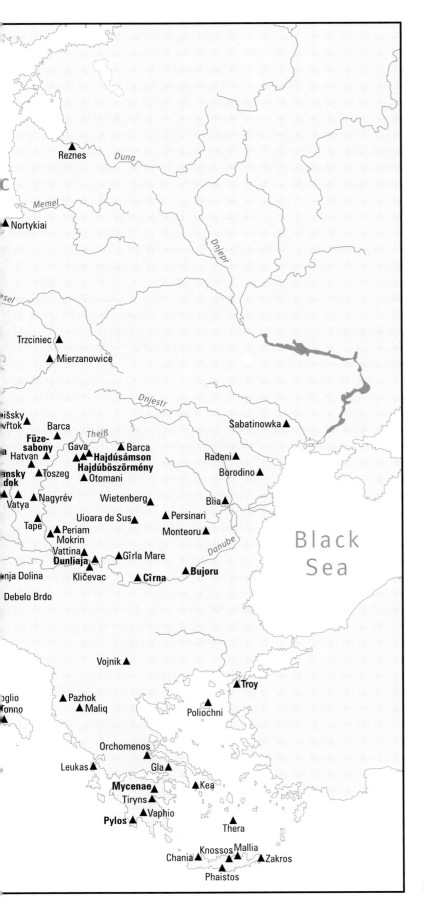

Map of the principal Bronze Age sites in Europe

Introduction
Gods and Heroes of the Bronze Age. Europe at the Time of Ulysses

Katie Demakopoulou, Christiane Eluère, Jørgen Jensen, Albrecht Jockenhövel, Jean-Pierre Mohen

The project that explored the Bronze Age in Europe as "The first Golden Age" and that was realised between 1994 and 1996 on the initiative of the European Council, generated a variety of events, exhibitions and scholarly conferences throughout Europe. The goal was to present the concept of a culturally unified Europe to a broad public. Indeed, northern and southern Europe shared much – Baltic amber, for example, and numerous symbols such as the waterfowl, the sun and the chariot – as did eastern and western Europe as well – with their horses and their tin. A Europe joined by cultural affinities began to take shape. Yet despite this relative unity we cannot ignore the social, religious and economic differences that during the Bronze Age separated the three major ecological zones of Europe – the arid Mediterranean region, the forest-covered expanse of central Europe and the cold North, a region of lakes, forests and mountains.

Reliable indicators about the duration of the Bronze Age have been found in the historical calendars of the ancient Orient and ancient Egypt, now supplemented by data acquired through scientific methods, including radio-carbon dating and dendrochronology. Thus we know that the period characterised by the steady rise of metal processing in Europe, known as the Chalcolithic or Copper Age, was a preliminary technological phase which preceded the Bronze Age, named after that alloy of copper and tin. This Copper Age began spectacularly about the close of the 5th millennium BC with the gold-rich "Princes' Graves" of Varna (on the Bulgarian Black Sea coast). At that time, many regions of Europe, particularly in the north and west, were still inhabited by farming communities in which the use of metals was unknown. During this era, with its hierarchically structured societies frequently at war, we recognise features whose appearance herald the advent of the Bronze Age.

The Copper Age culture did not gain a foothold in mid-central Europe until the 4th millennium BC. The "Ice Man" discovered near Hauslabjoch in the high Alps of the Tyrol and dated to about 3300 BC lived during this period. Metallurgy did not appear in western Europe until later, however. By contrast, metallurgical development began in the Aegean areas about the middle of the 5th millennium BC.

The Bronze Age proper began in the eastern Mediterranean region as early as the first half of the 3rd millennium BC, roughly concurrent with the founding of the first city of Troy (Troy I). Advanced civilisations were already established in the Cyclades and on the island of Crete at this time, while in the area of northeastern Aegean (Poliochni on Lemnos and elsewhere) social and cultural changes along with metallurgical innovations are observed.

The first Minoan palaces were erected on the island of Crete towards the end of the 3rd millennium BC. Their fall has often been linked to the disastrous eruption of the Thera volcano at about the end of the 16th century (in the conventional dating system), although no firm proof has been found for this claim. From the beginning in the 15th century BC, the rulers of the Mycenaean culture, whose people spoke an early dialect of Greek, gradually gained cultural and political dominion over the Greek mainland as well as the Aegean including Crete and influenced Cyprus and the coastal areas of Asia Minor. The first advanced culture on the European mainland, the Mycenaean civilisation exerted a range of cultural influences of varying intensity from its Aegean powerbase.

The reminiscences of the ancient Greeks date back to this period and are documented in Homer's epics the *Iliad* and the *Odyssey*, which focus on the events and heroes of the Trojan Wars. Agamemnon, King of Mycenae, was the Greek leader, the people's prince of the Achaean heroes, during the ten-year siege of Troy. Ulysses returned to his homeland on the island of Ithaca after ten years of wandering and adventure. The wars glorified in Homer's epics were dated by ancient Greek and Latin authors at about 1300 BC.

The epics of Homer, Europe's oldest literary legacy, were composed about 750 BC – that is during an early phase of the Iron Age in Greece. They extend back well

into the Mycenaean Bronze Age and provide valuable insights into Bronze Age life. Archaeological studies and above all the clay tablets with the Linear B script bear witness to the archaic character of the Homeric epic poems. For the Greeks, the *Iliad* and the *Odyssey* were richly traditional books full of recollections of a lost world, but the epics also promulgated the gods of Olympus and their mythology, a body of lore that has had a profound impact on western culture to this day.

The distribution of closely related items of archaeological evidence over a vast area tells us a great deal about European unity during the Bronze Age – round shields, swords, vessels decorated with sun and bird motifs. Can the sun chariot of Trundholm, a product of the Early Bronze Age in northern Europe, be related to the image of Apollo standing in a chariot? Was the homeland of the legendary Hyperboreans located in central or northern Europe?

The objective of the present exhibition is to illuminate the development of Europe from its Bronze Age roots. Essential elements of western culture and thought can be traced to their origins in Homer's texts. Yet the archaeological discoveries from the Bronze Age, a world familiar to Ulysses, must not distract our attention completely from the first written historical references found in Egypt and the Near East. The lists of the names and deeds of the Pharaohs and the Mesopotamian kings also provide important data on the European Bronze Age. The Linear B tablets discovered in Greece and Crete and deciphered in 1952 as well as the later Homeric poems serve as particularly valuable aids in our efforts to resolve specific linguistic, social, cultural and economic questions.

Nevertheless, most of the available evidence for Bronze Age culture in Europe is pre-historic – "silent" documents which must be taught to speak using the tools of archaeological research. For the most part, such artefacts have been either uncovered in the course of systematic archaeological excavations or located with the use of modern technology, for example identified through aerial photography. Once discovered, such traces and remains are ordinarily found to be fragmentary or to have undergone physical and chemical alteration. Thanks to new scientific procedures, it has been possible to identify finds, restore entire objects and even reconstruct important segments of the everyday life of the period, including cultural activities, burial rites and similar. With respect to craft technologies, a thorough analysis of component and raw materials provides valuable information about their geological origins as well as the techniques used in processing and fashioning such items.

Knowledge about settlement units and their topographic distribution is gained from the systematic study of habitation sites, cemeteries, complete burial chambers and landscapes. It was in such settlements that the "peoples" of ancient Europe, about whom we learn from the reports of the first geographers and historians of the early Iron Age, developed – the Greeks, the Etruscans, the Scythians, the Celts and the Thracians, to name only a few. The dynamism of European history that is evident even in this early phase is difficult to describe on the basis of archaeological findings, which tend to focus upon statistical relationships. It is nevertheless an undeniable factor, as the collapse of the Minoan and Mycenaean civilisations clearly illustrates.

The History of Bronze Age Scholarship in Europe

Like all other scholarly disciplines, Bronze Age archaeological research looks back upon a history of its own. That history is of particular interest in that it bears the indelible imprint of individual champions of romantic ideals who, like Heinrich Schliemann, attempted to use the accounts of Homer as exact historical sources.

The Bronze Age was first identified in scientific terms as an archaeological, "pre-historic" era by the Danish scholar Christian Jürgensen Thomsen (1788–1865). Thomsen, the son of a wealthy shipping magnate, was appointed Secretary of the Royal Antiquities Commission in 1816 – an institution which later developed into the National Museum in Copenhagen. In the process of establishing order in the museum's extensive prehistoric collection – one of the largest in Europe at the time – he developed the "three-period system" based upon the subdivision of human prehistory into three eras (the Stone, Bronze and Iron Ages) in 1836. His system, now generally

◁ 1 Wheeled bronze cauldron, Peckatel, Mecklenburg, Germany
Middle Bronze Age (Cat. No. 178)

2   Christian Jürgensen Thomsen (1788–1865). Painting by
      J. V. Gertner, Copenhagen 1848, The National Museum of Denmark

3   Heinrich Schliemann (1822–1890). Painting by Sydney Hodges,
      London 1877, Museum für Vor- und Frühgeschichte, Berlin

accepted by students of the ancient world, was confirmed at practically the same time by German researchers (G.C.F. Lisch of Mecklenburg; J.F. Danneil of Salzwedel in the province of Altmark).

   This first generation of prehistorians was followed by a second, of which Jens Jacob Asmussen Worsaae (1821–1887) and Heinrich Schliemann (1822–1890) were perhaps the most noteworthy figures. Worsaae was a student and colleague of Thomsen's and eventually his successor. He served as Director of the National Museum in Copenhagen from 1865, and was also the founder of the Danish National Record of Ancient Monuments, a defender of the three-period system in Europe and ultimately one of the greatest prehistorians of his time. Worsaae, however, sought the origins of the Bronze Age in India.

   Proof of the existence of the Bronze Age as a genuine historical epoch was actually provided by an amateur archaeologist – Heinrich Schliemann, son of a pastor from Mecklenburg and himself a successful businessman. Schliemann accepted Homer's epics at face value as a reliable source of information on the topography of the locations mentioned in the Homeric tales, including Troy, Mycenae and Pylos amongst others. His goal was to find Troy, Homer's Ilios, and he did indeed find it on a hill called Hissarlik in western Turkey, a site that is still under exploration today.

   Schliemann had to overcome many difficulties in the academic world, and it is no secret that he faced considerable problems of his own making. Yet despite the deficiencies of Schliemann's exploratory methods, many of which could hardly have been avoided at the time, we must concede today that he laid the essential groundwork for the archaeological study of the Mycenaean civilisation. Many of his hypotheses have

4   Arthur Evans standing in the North
Entrance of the Palace of Minos at Knossos

The third generation of Bronze Age archaeologists is represented in the exemplary work of Oscar Montelius (1843–1921) of Sweden and Arthur Evans (1851–1941) of England. Montelius developed a method of typology that made it possible to classify bronze artefacts on a relative chronological scale. The model is based upon a subdivision of the northern European Bronze Age into six distinct periods (Periods I–VI) and was originally proposed for application to central and western Europe as well; it is still accepted today. In studies published in several monumental works, Montelius explored the cultures of pre-classical Greece and Italy in the hopes of finding points of reference for an absolute chronology for central and northern Europe.

Arthur Evans began digging in search of evidence of Minoan culture on the island of Crete in 1900. Beginning that year, he undertook annual research expeditions to Knossos, the presumed site of the palace of King Minos, as mentioned in Homer. His four-volume work entitled *The Palace of Minos at Knossos*, published in London between 1921 and 1935, is still regarded as an authoritative source of information on Minoan culture. Evans' studies also covered the Aegean region, Egypt and the Near East. He also served as Keeper of the Ashmolean Museum at Oxford.

Today, research on the Bronze Age in Europe still relies upon the framework established by these famous scholars. Bronze Age chronology has been refined in many regions of Europe, making it possible to synchronise the discreet phases of the Bronze Age and to identify correlations with historical periods in the advanced civilisations of southern Europe, Egypt and the Near East. Thus the foundation has also been laid for research in the fields of Bronze Age society, economy, technology, religion and cult activities and environmental questions, areas in which scholarly efforts have increased in recent years. Studies of this kind offer invaluable insights into the complex lost world of the European Bronze Age.

been confirmed. Schliemann donated his "Collection of Trojan Antiquities" to the city of Berlin and was made an honorary citizen of that city in 1881. In 1945 the golden treasures of Troy, including the "Treasure of Priam", were taken to Moscow and placed in the Pushkin Museum, a fact that did not come to light until 1993. They are a major focus of interest in the context of the current debate on art theft and the spoils of war, an issue that has little to do with Schliemann's spectacular discoveries, however.

Bibliography: Dani & Mohen 1996; Emlyn-Jones et al 1992; Hänsel 1997; Jensen 1992; Müller-Karpe 1980; Randsborg 1996; Demakopoulou 1990.

From: GODS + HEROES OF THE EUROPEAN BRONZE AGE p10

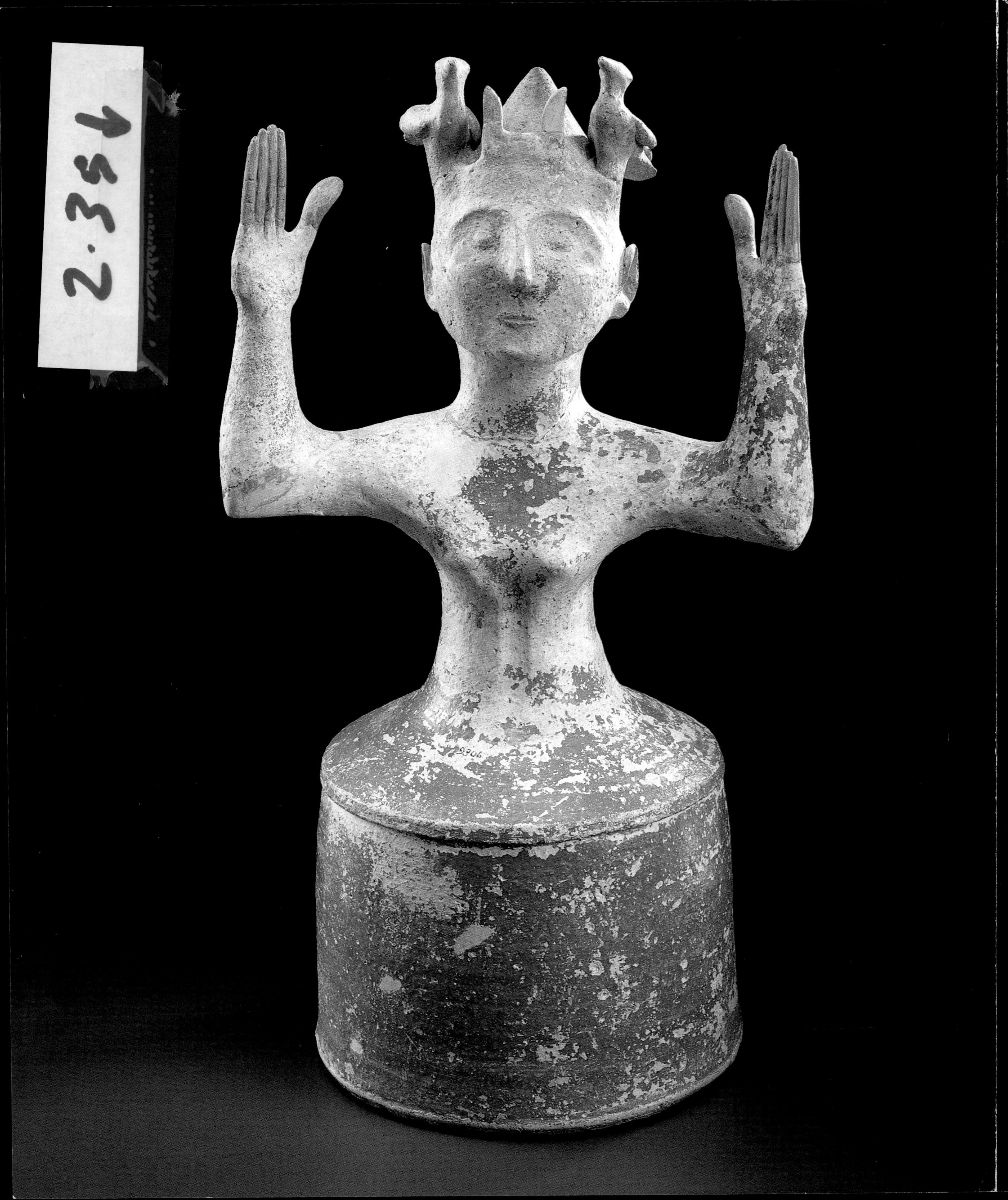

Written Sources and Archaeology: Homer, Linear B Script and Archaeology

Katie Demakopoulou, Christiane Eluère, Jørgen Jensen, Albrecht Jockenhövel, Jean-Pierre Mohen

Scholars have for long faced the question of whether his two great epics, the *Iliad* and the *Odyssey*, can truly be seen as historical sources on pre-Homeric culture, the period we know as the Bronze Age. The issue remains a controversial one, and the answers provided by scholars – historians, linguists and archaeologists alike – have varied greatly. In the view of the well-known British historian Moses I. Finley (writing in 1956), Homer can be assessed only within the context of his time, the 8th century BC, the period during which the two epics were written. Thus, writes Finley, Homer's perspective from the early Iron Age in Greece is of limited value to an evaluation of the earlier Bronze Age.

Yet archaeologists have since compiled a substantial body of facts which show that the world described in Homer's epics is indeed to a certain extent a pre-Archaic one. A number of passages in Homer, including references to material culture and Mycenaean civilisation (the description of the boar's tusk helmet, for example) support this contention. It is evident now that the Trojan War was not merely a figment of Homer's literary imagination based upon orally transmitted Bronze Age ballads and legends but could actually have occurred, as Bronze Age written accounts by the Hittites concerning warfare on their western borders clearly suggest. Armed conflict of this kind could indeed provide an explanation for the destruction of Level VI of the city of Troy by fire, for which reliable archaeological evidence has been gathered.

Classical philologists are now virtually unanimous in their acceptance of the view that Homer wrote his two epics during the latter half of the 8th century BC and that the *Iliad* is the older of the two. Homer's deliberate archaisation of his accounts is seen as the poet's attempt to embed the events in a long tradition by shifting the Trojan Wars far back in time and into the cultural context of the Bronze Age. Homer's successors appear to have recognised this themselves. Herodotus, the "father of historiography", believed that Homer had lived during the 9th century BC, four centuries before his own time. Hesiod, writing in about 700 BC, not long after Homer, set the Trojan Wars in the Bronze Age. Thucydides dates the arrival of the Dorians in Greece eighty years after the fall of Troy and thus no later than 1196 BC. In the *Suda*, a Byzantine lexicon from the 10th century AD, we read that Troy was captured 410 years before the first Olympiad, i.e. in the year 1154 BC.

Thus the struggle for the possession of Troy celebrated in literature is dated during the era of Mycenaean civilisation. Hittite texts referring to a land called "Ahhiyawa", which many scholars equate with Mycenaean Greece, and possibly to Mycenaean kings and other persons allude to late 14th century BC events that could be related to wars at Troy and to the Mycenaean expansion into the Aegean and Asia Minor.

It is entirely conceivable, though virtually impossible to prove, that the evidence of extensive fire damage found in Troy Level VI (the only level worthy of consideration, from a chronological standpoint) is the consequence of an attack by Mycenaean Greeks, known as the Achaeans. However, the fire may also have been caused by an earthquake mentioned in the Hittite sources. Although this question cannot be resolved here, it remains clear that the time frame of the Trojan Wars cited in the *Iliad* can indeed be corroborated on the basis of archaeological evidence.

Archaeologists continue to uncover evidence and finds from both Mycenaean and post-Mycenaean civilisation, that is objects from the so-called "Dark Ages" of early Greek history, which suggest comparisons with information found in Homer and in some cases even serve to illustrate certain Homeric statements. Archaeology is accordingly in a better position today to support the theory that the *Iliad* and the *Odyssey* actually incorporate several distinct chronological segments. In her dual – literary and archaeological – interpretation (1992), E. S. Sherratt recently reworked this "stratigraphic" scheme

◁ 1 Figure of Goddess with upraised arms, Gazi, Crete, Greece Late Bronze Age (Cat. No. 67)

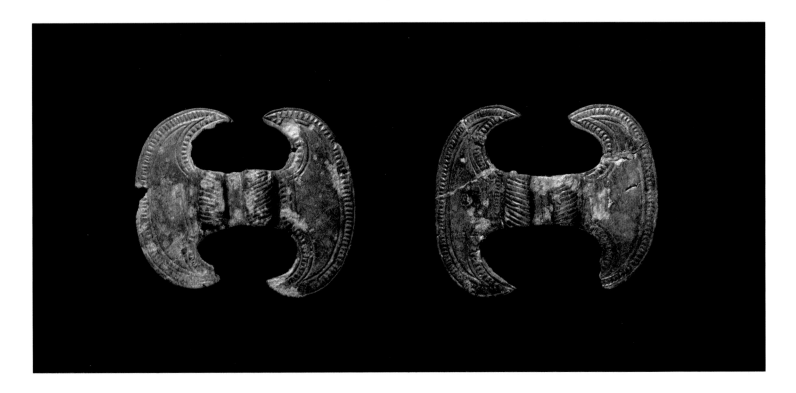

covering the period from the 16th to the late 8th century BC. In the course of the various palatial layers (16th–13th centuries BC), the story set in the Peloponnese, the heartland of Mycenaean civilisation, appears to draw to a close at much the same time as the Trojan War. Iron, found here for the first time, still played an insignificant role. Warriors wore helmets adorned with boar's tusks, carried long swords and lances and were protected by a broad tower shield that concealed the entire body and in some cases by bronze armour extending down to the knee (Dendra-type armour). These soldiers were equipped for close combat, for noble man-to-man battles into which they rode, or were driven, in two-wheeled chariots of war. Their living quarters were the early Mycenaean palaces, complex structures with stairs and flat roofs.

The post-palatial "layer" (from the 12th to the early 8th centuries BC) is even more clearly distinguished by its dynamic character. This was the period of Phoenician influence and lively maritime trade. Iron was now in common use. Cremation had become the most prevalent burial ritual. Warriors carried a small round shield, a

3   Double-Axe shaped objects, Lundsbakke, Værløse, Zealand, Denmark, Early Bronze Age (Cat. No. 180)

sword, two lances or spears and wore a horned helmet. Soldiers fought in columns, an early form of the phalanx, to ward off frontal attacks by their enemies. Palaces were rather simple structures with slanting roofs and rooms at ground level.

The last "layer" is from the 8th century BC and coincides roughly with the composition of Homer's heroic epics. Warriors now fought on foot, protected by helmets, round shields with large bosses in the form of Gorgon's heads, short cuirasses and greaves. They carried two lances into battle. No longer did they live in palaces, but in simple houses with foundation plans familiar to us from other settlements of the same period.

Despite the undeniable historical character of Homer's epics, we should keep in mind that they are, nonetheless, and will remain works of fiction.

Accordingly the intent underlying this exhibition is to offer a view of Homer's world, as his poems unfold it before our eyes and in our minds, by the presentation of archaeological relics from the Bronze Age in Europe. Ulysses traversed vast areas of the Mediterranean (and

◁ 2   Votive Double-Axe, Arkalochori Cave, Crete, Greece
Late Bronze Age (Cat. No. 74)

perhaps of the Atlantic as well) in the course of his legendary journeying, reaching both familiar and unfamiliar shores. And so it is surely of interest to view a representative collection of ancient objects from both the European Bronze Age, with its roots in the European Copper Age and the earliest phase of its Iron Age (the 2nd and early 1st millennia BC) and thus to call to mind the Bronze Age world of Homer's heroes.

Homer's heroes were the kings and nobles of Mycenaean and pre-classical Greece. Regardless of the size of a given ruler's domain, his position in society was always a very special one. The world of the nobles is illustrated by the precious objects they owned and exchanged amongst themselves and by their residences, the palaces. It is not at all difficult, therefore, to assign the luxurious graves of the Mycenaean civilisation – the Shaft Graves of Mycenae, the tholoi of Mycenae, Pylos or Orchomenos and the chambered tombs of Dendra, for example – to this particular social class. They disappeared with the demise of the Mycenaean civilisation in the 12th century BC, the first of the "dark centuries" of Greek history. We do not often find richly furnished graves again until Homer's time, the 8th century BC (in Argos, for example). However, the recently discovered nobleman's grave at the Heröon in Lefkandi, dating from the 11th or 10th centuries BC, together with the rich clan graves about it clearly remind us of the large gap in historical sources that separates these periods.

Outside the Aegean region, archaeologists have uncovered finds from all phases of the Bronze Age – most notably richly-furnished burial sites and objects of great value – which we may presumably associate with nobles, chieftains or "kings" – that is, with the uppermost social class in the respective societies. Certain Bronze Age objects share important features with others found at locations quite far away, a circumstance which suggests that direct or indirect contacts among the European elite may have been much closer that we have generally supposed. Ulysses, the ancient explorer, assumes a symbolic role as an intermediary between the noble courts of Europe, and thus his name appears in the title of this exhibition.

Due to the nature of the available archaeological evidence, it is impossible to present more than a fragmentary picture of the European world of the Bronze Age, and we are compelled to accept the presence of significant gaps. For this reason, the exhibition focuses primarily on the uppermost class of society and the world of the Bronze Age nobility. The presentation encompasses five major themes:

The Bronze Age image of the world
The hero as prince
Death and the hero
Bronze Age religion
The earliest written documents in European history

The exhibits selected illustrate these themes and place them in the appropriate prehistoric context.

Bibliography: Carter & Morris 1995; Duchêne 1995; Emlyn-Jones et al 1992; Finley 1956, 1967, 1970; Rowlands 1980; E. S. Sherratt 1992; *Ulisse* 1996.

4   Shield of Herzsprung type, Nackhälla, Halland, Sweden
    Late Bronze Age (Cat. No. 151)

Chronological Table

B.C.	Egypt	Aegean – Mainland Greece	Aegean – Crete	Aegean – Cyclades	Central Europe		Northern Europe	
500	Late Period (26. Dyn. ff.)	Classic Age			Late Hallstatt Culture	Ha D	Pre Roman Iron Age	
600		Late Archaic Age						Period VI
700	Third Intermediate Period (21. – 25. Dyn.)	Early Archaic Age			Early Hallstatt Culture	Ha C	Late Bronze Age	
		Late Geometric Period						
800		Middle Geometric Period						
900		Early Geometric Period			Final Bronze Age	Ha B 2/3		Period V
		Protogeometric Period						
1000		Submycenaean	Subminoan			Ha B 1		Period IV
1100		LH III C	LM III C		Later Bronze Age	Ha A 2	Middle Bronze Age	
1200	New Kingdom (18. – 20. Dyn.)	LH III B 1-2	LM III B	LC III		Ha A 1		Period III
1300						Bz D		
		LH III A 2	LM III A2			Bz C 2		
1400		LH III A 1	LM III A1		Middle Bronze Age	Bz C 1		Period II
		LH II B	LM II	LC II				
1500		LH II A	LM I B			Bz B	Early Bronze Age	
	Second Intermediate Period (13. – 17. Dyn.)	LH I	LM I A	LC I				
1600		MH late				Bz A 2		Period I B
1700			MM III A-B	MC late				Period I A
			MM II B					
1800	Middle Kingdom (11. und 12. Dyn.)	MH mature	MM II A	MC early	Early Bronze Age			LN II
			MM I B					
1900	First Intermediate Period (9. und 10. Dyn.)					Bz A 1	Late Neolithic	
2000		MH early	MM I A					
2100				EC III				LN I
2200		EH III	EM III					
2300								
2400	Old Kingdom (3. – 8. Dyn.)					Bell Beaker Culture		
2500					Final Neolithic			
2600		EH II	EM II	EC II		Corded Ware Culture	Middle Neolithic B	Single Grave Culture
2700								
2800								
2900	Early Dynastic (1. und 2. Dyn.)				Later Neolithic	Horgen/Cham/Wartberg	Middle Neolithic A	Late Funnel Beaker Culture
3000		EH I	EM I	EC I				

B.C.

B.C.	Iberian Peninsule	Great Britain		France		Italy
500						
600	Tartessian Period	Iron Age	Llynfawr	Hallstatt	Early Hallstatt Culture	Orientalizing Period
700						
800	Orientalizing Period Late Bronze Age III		Ewart Park	Late Bronze Age III B	III Atlantic	II Villanova I Villanova
900			Wilberton Wallington	Late Bronze Age III A		III Protovillanova Late Bronze Age II
1000	Late Bronze Age II	Deverell Rimbury	Penard II	Late Bronze Age II B	II Atlantic	
1100			Penard I	Late Bronze Age II A		I
1200	Late Bronze Age I		Taunton	Late Bronze Age I	I Atlantic	Younger Bronze Age
1300			Acton Park			
1400	El Argar B 2	Wessex II		Breton Tumuli Middle Bronze Age	Bignan Tréboul	Middle Bronze Age
1500			Arreton			
1600						
1700	El Argar B 1	Wessex I	Colleonard			
1800				Early Bronze Age		Early Bronze Age
1900	El Argar A					
2000						
2100						
2200						
2300			Migdale			
2400						
2500						
2600						
2700						
2800						
2900						
3000						

Chapter 1
Adventurers, Artisans and Travellers

Editor: Jean-Pierre Mohen

◁ "Frying-Pan", Syros, Cyclades, Greece
Early Bronze Age (Cat. No. 14)

Adventurers, Artisans and Travellers

Jean-Pierre Mohen

After the discovery of the remains of the man known as "Ötzi" near the top of Tyrol's Similaun Glacier in 1991, a number of different hypotheses have been proposed regarding this man from the ice, who lived about 3300 BC (see Leitner, pp. 24 ff.). Successive theories saw him as a wanderer, an artisan or a traveller. With regard to the first view, he possessed weapons and tools that would have ensured him a certain degree of self-sufficiency on his way to some quiet, secluded mountain refuge. His remains were found on a route leading to the herds grazing on the high meadows at an elevation of 3200 meters, a trail also used by hunters of eagle, mouflon and bear. The artisan theory is supported by the presence of mineral traces in his hair, which suggested that the man from the ice may have been in search of the valuable ores that had become so important at the start of the Copper Age – as his shafted hatchet bears witness. As a wanderer, he carried a birch-bark satchel found in pieces at the time of discovery. What had it contained? During those times, travellers were often peddlers, people who brought fine flints, a rare stone or medicinal substances of one sort or another – like the two pieces of birch fungus he had with him. But the traveller could also have been a pilgrim on his way to the sacred mountain region that extends across the Alps from the valley of Val Camonica to Monte Bego.

"Ötzi" provides valuable evidence of the fact that the Alpine region was being opened up. The higher areas were exposed during the warm seasons to the increasingly frequent presence of humanity passing through on religious or commercial missions. The high Alpine peaks became centres of a pastoral economy, and their passes were heavily travelled. Raw materials and finished products transported along such routes have since been found in settlements and burial sites. Commercial traffic was soon brought under organised control, yet the tradition of smuggling offers a revealing look back at the climate of profit-seeking and aggression in which this new overland trade was pursued.

The world of the sea is easily as dangerous as that of the mountains. The great ships portrayed by miniature models or painted on vases and frescoed walls were true ocean-going transports. They regularly carried rich cargoes as those being shipped at the end of the Bronze Age and recovered off Cape Gelidonya or at Ulu Burun, off the southern Turkish coast. Homer's *Odyssey* illustrates the perils of sea voyages with stories of sea monsters and storms. The mountain smugglers had their counterparts in the pirates of the high-seas. The shipping routes were well known at the time. The course taken by the Ulu Burun vessel, a ship measuring between fifteen and seventeen metres in length, has been reconstructed on the basis of the products it contained. The ship set sail from Egypt, as evidenced by the ring and a scarab bearing inscriptions connecting them with Queen Nefertiti. This royal gift may have been meant for a Cretan or Mycenaean king – along with its cargo consisting of ingots of copper, tin, and cobalt-blue glass; and amphorae filled with olives, glass beads and the dye-stuff orpiment. Nearly one hundred of these amphorae contained the aromatic resin of the turpentine bush, which was undoubtedly intended for use in the production of perfume. Ceramic products from "Canaan" support the assumption that the ship from Egypt had stopped for supplies in Syrian Palestine and was on a westerly course towards Mycenaean Greece and Crete, before its likely return to Egypt. The voyage took place during the period of the 18th Egyptian Dynasty, perhaps – to be more precise – to the Amarna period (1352–1333 BC). The feverish activity of the Mediterranean ports, full of warships and freighters, is rendered masterfully in one of the frescoes of Thera.

We know of other wrecks dating from this period. Although the ship found off Dover in southern England had broken up, the 9.5 metre section recovered probably represents two-thirds of the original vessel. And what is to be said of the dozens of pictures chipped into the cliffs of Sweden and Norway (see Capelle, pp. 153 ff. and Cat. No. 77), which show very Mediterranean details of construction for certain sailing vessels?

Ships undoubtedly represented the most effective and prestigious means of transportation for people in the lands of the high North, yet the pictures do not always tell us what they carried – with the exception of the probably mythical warriors brandishing their battle-axes and huge lances. Nevertheless, we have reliable knowledge of their relations with the South.

The thousands of drawings scratched into the Norwegian and Swedish rocks clearly indicate that in those countries hunters armed with bows and arrows as well as wandering traders travelled not only by ship but on skis as too. With respect to the carts and wagons depicted in the cliff drawings, of which miniature models bearing symbolic motifs have been found (Cat. Nos. 176–178), they may well have been intended more for show than for any utilitarian purpose. Such a conclusion is supported by the virtual absence of paved roads in northern and central Europe. The concept is illustrated in a fresco in Thera showing a dignified lady seated on a horse-drawn wagon.

Even if such vehicles were not suited for long journeys, yet ships, mules, horses and people themselves travelled throughout Europe, distributing the valuable products needed by artisans and their clients. The extensive economic region they created represented a significant expansion of horizons typical of the Chalcolithic and the Bronze Age. Still in widespread demand were quality stones – like Mediterranean obsidian, the green Alpine stone used to make polished axe heads, and others of dolerite from Plussulia on the coast of Brittany, and flint from Grimes Graves (England), Spiennes (Belgium), Hardivilliers (Somme), Jablines (Seine and Marne) and Krzemionki Gatovski (Poland), the best material for sharp axes or long blades. Distribution of these is reported several hundreds of kilometres off from their point of extraction. Today, many materials are being found at sites located at great distances from their places of origin. The famous honey flint from Grand Pressigny south of Tours (Indre and Loire), the raw material used in the production of knife blades, was being processed intensively at the end of the 3rd millennium BC and delivered to the Netherlands and, in large quantities, to the lake villages of the subalpine region. A material like amber must have been of great appeal to all segments of the population during the Bronze Age. Beads and pendants of it were widely distributed – from areas around the Baltic, the source of the raw material as chemical analysis has recorded, as far south as Greece (Kakovatos and Mycenae,

Cat. No. 84) and Crete. Several finds, such as that from Fort-Harrouard in Sorel-Moussel (Eure and Loire), indicate that amber was exported in rough lumps and processed as needed at the point of delivery. As has also been established, the Mycenaean technique when processing elephant tusks imported from the East was the same (see Poursat, pp. 164 ff.).

The information available to us relates primarily to the material remains that survive, yet certain substances exist, such as the aromatic resin of the turpentine bush contained in the amphorae of the Ulu Burun wreck, to show that perfumes were also produced by subtle means of manufacture from high quality imported goods. Also noteworthy in this context are textiles and furs; wood for construction purposes from Lebanon and beads of Egyptian faience, widely imitated throughout Europe. Specialised craftsmen now began to appear, among them such as the makers of hard stone seals (at the workshop at Malia on the island of Crete) or the craftsmen who created the painted ceramics in Minoan palatial workshops.

One of the most important factors in the growth and spread of commercial relations during the Chalcolithic and the Bronze Age was the development of metallurgy and the goldsmith's art, which focused primarily on the production of prestigious objects, weapons and jewellery. Clearly the mines from which these materials came were rarely near the sites at which such objects were given their final form. Workshops were established primarily in cities, such as Enkomi (Cyprus) or in densely populated areas (sites fortified to varying degrees in central and west Europe, such as Runnymede on the banks of the Thames, Fort-Harrouard in Sorel-Moussel or Velem-Szent-Vid in western Hungary) which appear from all the evidence to have been under the control of central political or economic powers. In this context, we learn from the inscribed tablets discovered in Pylos (Greece) that this relatively modest 13th-century Mycenaean kingdom employed 400 artisans to work bronze for the prestige of the king and his army. This number gives us an idea of the dynamics that characterised these "Homeric" societies, but it also documents the existence of regular trade with distant lands for the purpose of acquiring supplies of copper and tin.

The bearer of a copper ingot – the so-called "oxhide" type (Cat. Nos. 19, 20) – is an iconographic theme found in Egyptian frescoes and on the "tripod stands" made of bronze from Cyprus. As for the tin, it most probably came from the West (Cornwall in England and southern Brittany), although little is known about how it was passed on to the workshops of the bronzesmiths.

The "Homeric" world of the Bronze Age owes its dynamic economic condition to the establishment of long-distance exchange trade on a European scale. Trading links were created by trading societies that were much more flexible than had been previously assumed.

Advocates of a more linear scheme of development, anthropologists of the 19th and early 20th centuries such as Morgan theorised that human society developed in successive stages from a hunting culture to animal husbandry, farming and finally urban culture. Today's prehistorians, pursuing a more realistic approach that has been expanded on the basis of numerous recent discoveries, emphasise the variety of adaptations conceived of by human societies in response to their various ecological environments. This ethnographic diversity manifests itself – during the same time-period – in the birth of the city-states in the Near East, the Aegean palatial centres, the farming communities in central and western Europe, the ascendancy of pastoral societies in eastern Europe, Siberia and even the Sahara, and the expansion of hunting-stockbreeding cultures in northern Europe. We must come to realise that these adaptive economies coexisted and established relationships with one another that often involved significant degrees of dependence. Thus, the nomadic herders of western Asia appear to have had a kind of osmotic exchange with agriculturists settled in the same coastal region or in areas supplied by rivers, thus forming a single, homogeneous economic system. The nomadic or semi-nomadic way of life of the herding peoples has often been contrasted with the settled lifestyle of farmers and city-dwellers. Yet it is important here as well to differentiate carefully in assessing these contrasts. We must understand, for example, that migrations of herds affected human populations only during certain seasons of the year and, due to the influence of traditional migration patterns, only in well-limited areas. The mountain grazing and pasturing economy introduced around the mid 4th millennium BC belongs to this category. Conversely, semi-nomadic groups of artisans and "itinerant

merchants" emerged alongside the settled farming and urban cultures and pursued routes of their own (one of which has been reconstructed in the East Mediterranean basin on the basis of information gained from the study of the ship's cargo from Ulu Burun off Anatolia in the 14th century BC). The industrial dimensions of certain activities, such as the exploitation of flint and copper ores or the production of ceramics (Mycenaean ceramics) led to concentrations of specialised artisans plying their skills in relative safety in close proximity to the traders entrusted with the sale and distribution of their products. The balance established among the various communities depended upon their relative population figures. When concentrations of several thousands of people formed at a given location, population density began to play an important role.

According to Andrew Sherratt (1996), the Aegean palatial system comprised a rigidly structured one, a function of both the permanence of their stone buildings and the relatively small size of their territories. In contrast, the agricultural system of central and western Europe during the Bronze Age proved to be more flexible: farms were distributed over wider expanses of territory. Houses were constructed of wood, with loam-and-straw walls and straw roofs, which meant that they were ordinarily rebuilt within the span of a single generation. Furthermore, farming culture was oriented towards self-sufficiency and diversified to encompass the breeding of domestic animals. Major turns in the course of societal development may have resulted from abrupt climatic changes. Worsening climatic conditions near the end of the Bronze Age in the Cheviot Hills (England) would have led to a shrinking in population numbers and thus to a regrouping of the population in fortified settlements (see Jockenhövel, pp. 71ff.). Entire population groups migrated from around Neuchâtel in Switzerland in the wake of sudden floods that rendered the lake-villages uninhabitable around 850 BC (see Pétrequin, p. 70).

A number of cultural innovations contributed equally to profound changes in society. Such include the introduction of the yoke plough, and of oxen as traction animals, the use of manure to renew the fertility of the soil, as well as the introduction of alcoholic beverages, such as mead, which was soon followed by wine in the southern regions. Other such factors were the introduction and use of horses in the East (see Dietz, pp. 83 f.) for combat and prestige purposes, the proliferation of both offensive and defensive weapons (see Jensen, pp. 88 ff.) and the appearance of writing on the European continent in Greece. These new developments, documented by archaeologists, are entirely in keeping with the image in Bronze Age times of the world boiling with new ideas, of which the Homeric texts grant us but a distant literary remembrance.

Bibliography: Dani & Mohen 1996; Forbes 1964–72; Gale 1991; Müller-Karpe 1980.

Ötzi – The Man in the Ice

Walter Leitner

1991 was a milestone year in the history of prehistoric archaeology. At an elevation of 3200 metres, melting glacial ice in the Ötztal Alps (Austria/Italy) exposed the mummified body of a man, thus triggering a world-wide sensation. The find was entirely coincidental and due primarily to meteorological influences. Successive years of mild temperatures had resulted in appreciable shrinking of Alpine glaciers. In this particular year, the precipitation of dust from the Sahara region caused further warming of the ice's surface by reducing the reflection of sunlight.

The Discovery and Recovery of the Ice-Man

Erika and Helmut Simon, mountain climbers from Nuremberg, discovered the Ice-Man at 1.30 in the afternoon on September 19th, 1991. Only his head and shoulders protruded from the rock crevice filled with a mixture of ice and water. Ötzi lay face down on a large, flat stone; his face concealed. Totally astonished by their unexpected discovery, the two climbers took a photograph and then hurried to the nearby Similaun Glacier travellers' aid station to report their find to the stationmaster. After taking a brief look at the site, the stationmaster immediately

notified the local authorities and called up the police and the mountain rescue team. A variety of wooden implements, scraps of fur and string, and a metal hatchet were discovered in the immediate vicinity of the body. Since it was not clear at first whether the site was located in Austrian or Italian territory, the Institute for Forensic Medicine of the University of Innsbruck initially took charge of recovery operations. It was later determined that the site was actually 92.6 metres beyond the borderline separating Austria from Italy and thus located in the autonomous province of Bolzano, Italy. At first, the discovery of the Ice-Man was not regarded as an archaeological issue, and the recovery operations reflected that fact. The original objective was to determine the cause of death and the identity of the man, assumed at the time to have been a

2   Melting ice exposed the mummy, which was discovered by mountaineers on September 19th 1991.

mountain climber killed – albeit quite long ago – in an accident. The body had been mummified and ideally preserved in its bed of ice. A number of suppositions were ventured with respect to its age, but it was not until the remains had been brought to Innsbruck and archaeologists were consulted that the secret came to the surface. It was Professor Dr. Konrad Spindler of the Institut für Ur- und Frühgeschichte who first confirmed the unmistakably prehistoric origin of the Ice-Man on the basis of an analysis of all of the evidence found.

1   The site of the discovery of the "Ice-Man" (circle in red) in the Ötztal Alps (elevation 3200 metres).

Conservation and Restoration

Once it had become clear how unique this find really was, specialists began work on the development of a method for conserving the body of the Ice-Man for the purposes of a long-term research program. Having established the typical natural climatic conditions prevailing in glacial ice, the conservation team stored the body at 6° C and nearly 100 per cent relative humidity in a refrigeration unit at the University's Institute of Anatomy. From that point on, the mummified body was no longer available for public viewing. Medical examinations were planned carefully and limited for the most part to twenty-five minutes per month.

The various items of equipment found with the body and the remains of the man's clothing required special conservation and restoration measures. These were undertaken by the Römisch-Germanisches Zentralmuseum in Mainz, whose staff completed its excellent work on this delicate assignment in four years.

An Interdisciplinary Research Project

The broad-based program of studies carried out on the complex Ice-Man find could only be accomplished within the framework of a world-wide interdisciplinary research project. More than sixty academic institutions with some 150 qualified scholars applied to participate in the project. The medical and scientific disciplines were heavily represented in the research work. One of the most impatiently awaited outcomes of the studies related to the issue of precise dating. Samples of bone, tissue and residual botanical material were sent to Great Britain, Sweden, France and the USA for the purpose of establishing a reliable chronological assessment on the basis of Carbon-14 dating. The outcome was a sensation in itself. We now know that the Ice-Man must have lived sometime during the period between 3350 and 3100 BC.

The Mummy

The body is the oldest and most completely preserved undessicated mummy known to exist. It is 1.6 metres in height and weighs 13.5 kg. With the exception of a wound in the hip region, the corpse is virtually undamaged. The moderate depressions in the face are attributable to ice pressure and the position of the body in

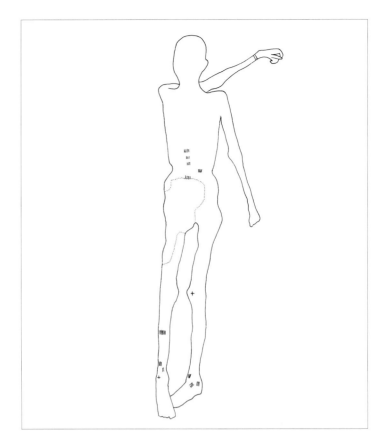

3 The 3500-year-old body found on the glacier was naturally preserved and largely undamaged. Tattoos were found in several places on the body – the oldest such markings known to exist.

the rocky crevice. X-rays and computer topography revealed several anatomical peculiarities and pathological processes. The wisdom teeth and the 12th pair of ribs are missing. A serial rib fracture and a cystic growth on one of the little toes were diagnosed. All of the internal organs have undergone shrinking and displacement caused by the natural dehydration process. Signs of degenerative arthritic processes were ascertained in the joint areas. The peculiarities of the mummy include a number of linear tattoos localized primarily in the area of the ankles and knees and on the calves and loins. These are the oldest verifiable signs of this type. Presumably made for the purpose of treating rheumatic disorders, the markings correspond to an early form of acupuncture.

Clothing

The Ice-Man was ideally dressed for a journey into the Alps. He wore shoes, leg coverings, a loincloth, a coat, a cloak and a cap, consisting variously of fur, leather and   25 grass material. The furs and skins were processed primarily from the hides of red deer, bear, goat, mountain goat and cow. This gives us a highly informative picture of the previously little-known dress of late Stone Age man in the Alpine regions. On the other hand, Ötzi's clothing may represent a special mode of dress suited to his particular needs.

Equipment

The Ice-Man was diversely equipped. The first distinction to be made is that between weapons and tools. Ötzi's tools included flint implements in the form of a knife, a sharp blade, a drill and a scraper; a bone awl, an antler point set in a retouching tool of lime-wood. The shafted copper axe occupies a special category of its own and presumably served as both a weapon and a tool.

The yew bow-stave (1.825 metres in length) is a particularly effective long-distance weapon. Fourteen arrow shafts, of which two are armed with stone points, form part of the ensemble. Four longer antler points may also have served as parts of yet another long-distance weapon – a wooden sling.

Among the items in the category of "containers" are a quiver for the arrows, two cylindrical birchbark satchels, a small bag hung at the waist and a wooden back-frame.

The Ice-Man also had kindling materials and pieces of tinder for use in making fire. He also had a small "first-aid" kit with chunks of fungus containing a medicinal substance which would enable him to treat wounds.

Who was the Man in the Ice?

We shall never have a definite answer to this question. Although the scientific findings point to several different models for interpretation, all of them must remain in the realm of hypothesis.

The story begins with the autumnal journey of an old, rather sickly man into the high Alps. Bearing a heavy load and totally exhausted, he reaches the highest ridge in the mountain range. An oncoming storm forces him to seek refuge in a protected crevice in the rocks. He falls asleep and freezes to death. Snow and ice preserve his body and all of his possessions for thousands of years.

But what drove this man into the mountains?

4   The preserved items of clothing, weapons and tools provide new insight into the modes of dress and equipment used by late Stone Age inhabitants of the Alps.

He has often been seen as a shepherd leading his herds of goats or sheep to their summer grazing areas. Yet no such animal hairs were found in his clothing. His bow and arrow suggest that he may have been a hunter, although the weapons were unfinished and therefore not ready for use. Some scholars have pointed to a possible function as a trader, a warrior or even a shaman, yet no proof is available for such suppositions. In general, his valuable metal axe is seen as an indication of high-standing in his own society.

With respect to his origin, comparisons with similar types of implements as well as the botanical evidence found with the body point to the Etschtal region south of the Alps as his homeland. Further studies of the archaeological environment in this Alpine region will be needed before new insights can be gained.

Six years after his discovery, the Ice-Man was transferred from Innsbruck to Bolzano, where the entire complex is on exhibit at the Tyrol Archaeological Museum. A four-metre-high stone pyramid placed at the site of the find serves as a memorial to one of the most significant archaeological discoveries of the 20th century.

Archaeometry and Research Methods

Jean-Pierre Mohen

Our knowledge of the Bronze Age in Europe is based upon a wide range of scientific studies of archaeological finds. The developments of the past thirty years – in physical and chemical analysis, in the morphological identification of mineral and organic residues and remains, in statistical surveys, all techniques associated with what is known today as the field of "archaeometry" – have all, alongside other scholarly sources and in the absence of adequate textual material, made it possible to acquire new knowledge, to clarify relationships linking available items of evidence and to reconstruct an image of domestic, economic and social systems. Trained archaeologists prefer working on site, excavating remains of past human life and interpreting new insights as parts of an as yet unsolved puzzle. Yet the goal of every archaeologist is to explore the anthropology of the past, within its limited historical scope, and to study living conditions, relationships with the natural environment, systems of belief and customs within discreet geographical regions. Beyond this, research on the Bronze Age in Europe is focused especially upon the issue of the extent to which the historical and cultural developments of the era shaped the foundations of western civilisation.

Several of the scientific methods employed in Bronze Age research are described below. Excavation techniques have been modernised. Digging operations on land benefit from the use of aircraft and aerial photography which permit searching and locating on an extensive scale. Underwater studies have taken on greater importance as new technical aids, such as independent diving apparatus, have made it possible to discover and investigate previously unexplored wrecks, particularly those like the Bronze Age ships lost off Cape Gelidonya and near Ulu Burun on the coast of Anatolia.

Many research aids can be employed at the excavation sites themselves for the identification of human and animal bones, seeds, charcoal, pollen, grains, and acid and phosphate concentrations in the soil. Entire landscapes are surveyed and, as in the case of those in the vicinity of the Minoan palaces, material collected is subjected to microscopic and spectroscopic analysis in the laboratory. Analyses of amber have documented the distribution of this fossil resin throughout Europe. Faience beads were originally thought to have been produced in Egypt; only later was it determined that they were produced locally, and particularly in central Europe. Studies of recently discovered "Mycenaean" ceramics in Italy reveal the presence of products both imported from Greece and locally manufactured imitations, thus proving beyond a doubt that this Mediterranean region had been colonised at least six or seven centuries prior to the emergence of the culture of Magna Graeca.

Another ambitious programme of analytical study undertaken in the Mediterranean region is that based on the natural occurrence of lead isotopes in copper and bronze objects (Gale 1991). Maps illustrating patterns of distribution suggest several specific Mediterranean islands and Lavrion as sources of the metal-deposits with such occurrences. This allows the reconstruction of economic and political relationships. Orpiment, a complex sulphur/arsenic compound, found in an amphora in the Ulu Burun wreck was intended as a dark-red dye. Fragments of terebinth resin were discovered in a hundred or so other amphorae contained in the same wreck; these were presumably intended for use in perfume production.

Of the analytical techniques rendered more difficult by the need for absolute purity in the sample, the DNA studies have provided some of the most useful findings that permit the charting of change amongst persons from extensive burial sites – in the establishment of the frequency and extent of endogamy and exogamy, genetically transmitted illnesses and "family" character traits.

Scientific research methods have been equally helpful in the clarification of dating issues, although not all of the results have been completely satisfactory. Thanks to "gifts" from Egypt and the Near East that were brought into the European Mediterranean region, comparisons of historical chronologies, such as that of the Pharaohs with the relative ones of the early historical period, have gained in importance. The C-14 or radiocarbon dating method used to determine the age of organic material (the radioactive components of which are known to have a half-life of 10,000 years) has been improved to the extent that since 1950 – and to an even greater degree since 1980 – it is possible to achieve a more precise dating of even the smallest samples with the use of the mass-spectrometer. Dendrochronology, based upon the study of growth rings in preserved timber, has recorded in the last few years considerable advances in many parts of Europe, including Scandinavia (see Christensen, pp. 110ff.) southern Germany, Switzerland, northern Italy and the eastern Mediterranean region. Dendrochronological calculations are exact to within a single year. The careful application of the three chronological systems discussed thus far – the historical, the physical-chemical and the dendrochronological – has provided important information about the relative time frame encompassed in the development of the Bronze Age.

A summary of the balance of opinion gained with respect to the absolute Bronze Age chronology was presented at the Verona conference in 1996 and published in Copenhagen. This report provides refinements on the form of the radioactive C-14 curve, which is not as naturally regular as had been supposed; and makes corrections to the roughly-dated life spans of certain Pharaohs; it also correlates the southern, historical chronologies with those of continental and northern Europe according to uniform criteria. Thus, progress achieved in chronological studies has solidified our understanding of the period in question and is thus to be regarded in an entirely positive light. Yet difficulties nevertheless arise as soon as we start to investigate specific events. The eruption of the Thera volcano and the dating of events in the archaeological history of the Minoan palace culture is a good example of such a matter. The date of 1530 BC has been proposed by Foster and Ritner (1996) – within the reign of the Egyptian king Ahmose, yet calculations based upon C-14 dating point to the 17th or the early 16th century BC, while calibration according to the dendrochronological scale produces even earlier dates (1736–1705 BC). If we accept this chronological revision, then we are forced first to alter the dates assigned to the associated ceramics; thence the timing of historical events and ultimately that of the demise of the Minoan civilisation itself, so as to maintain that correlation with the volcanic eruption, as had been established on the basis of intensive stratigraphical studies on Thera.

Another date regarded as historical is that given to the Trojan War as described in Homer's *Iliad*. These events would correspond to the destruction of that city known as Troy VI, which was surrounded by a Cyclopean wall. The conventional date is the middle of the 14th century BC. According to Stuart Manning, however, the war must be pushed back at least as far as the 15th century BC. At the same time Manning poses the question of how these events affected the other Mycenaean cities. As a result, no conflicting evidence contained in the available archaeological material has to be taken into consideration.

Scientific research has brought a precision to numerous archaeological positions with respect to the Bronze Age and thus has made a significant contribution to our understanding of the phenomenon of the birth of European history.

Bibliography: Gale 1991; Harding 1984; Randsborg 1996; Renfrew & Bahn 1991; Tite 1972.

Interaction between the Carpathian Region and the Eastern Mediterranean during the mid-2nd Millennium BC

Václav Furmánek

In the era of its great flowering, the Mycenaean and Minoan civilisation represented one of the true cultural high points in world history – certainly a goal unachievable for the peoples of Europe at the time. Social and economic life had advanced to a level at which the ancient Mycenaean and Minoan population was able to assimilate and adapt all of the positive impulses that came from Asia Minor, the Near East and Egypt.

Yet the accomplishments of Minoan-Mycenaean culture did not remain confined to the islands and the mainland of Greece, but spread westward and northward to the Apennine and Iberian peninsulas, to the British Isles, into western, central and northern Europe and even to the Balkan peninsula and the Carpathian region. In fact, the Balkan peninsula and the Carpathians were clos-

1 Detail of the stone wall at the settlement of Spišský Štvrtok (Otomani culture; Slovakia)

est to the Mycenaean world. Archaeological sources provide substantial evidence that the civilised South and the barbarian North were well aware of each other's existence. For inhabitants of the southern regions, the barbarian North was a wild and primitive country, yet also the area from which amber and perhaps gold and other precious materials could be obtained. Those in the north were strongly attracted to the south as a region of warmth, sunshine, wealth and prosperity. The question is

2 Ceramic ritual chariot from Nižná Myšľa (Slovakia). (The four wheels are lost.)

whether relations between the two regions were merely random, isolated contacts or instead represented regular and deliberate interaction.

Archaeological evidence from the advanced northern Balkan and Carpathian cultures at the end of the Early and the beginning of the Middle Bronze Age give us an impression of the nature and extent of Mycenaean influence on the general character of these cultures. Stone architecture and internal urban structures in the permanent settlements point to southern models. The particular characteristics of burial rituals, as seen both in Early Bronze Age princely grave-mounds (Leubingen, Łęki Małe, see Cat. No. 159) and in the use of burial urns for example, are unmistakable signs of eastern Mediterranean influences. Yet imitation went much further. The

29

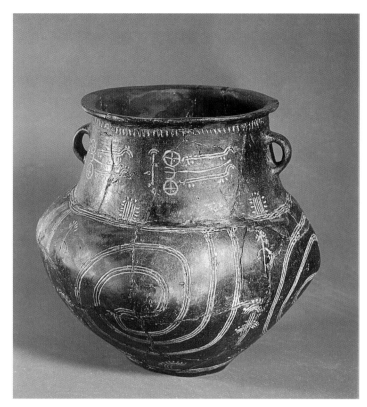

3 Amphora with wagon scene, from Vel'ké Raškovce, Slovakia (Suciul de Sus culture), Middle Bronze Age, c. 1300 BC (Cat. No. 124)

126–128). The former were employed in commercial exchanges and long-distance trade, the latter in warfare. The use of two-wheeled chariots in battle and for magnificent religious ceremonies is assessed on the basis of analogies with Mycenaean culture. This was one of the elements that linked the Aegean and Carpathian milieux together. The wagon and the wheel were appropriated for religious purposes. Unmistakable evidence of this is found not only in model chariots and preserved remains of harnesses but also most notably in the scene depicted on an amphora from the Suciul de Sus culture of Vel'ké Raškovce in eastern Slovakia (Cat. No. 124). Of course such finds have been made in the Carpathians as well – specifically in the Siebenbürgen region – and their Mycenaean origins are generally beyond dispute. Such items include gold discs with spiral ornamentation, swords, so-called Transylvanian rapiers, daggers made of precious metals (Cat. No. 99), embossed metal vessels and other items. A number of other artefacts, regarded until recently as royal gifts, are now being interpreted quite differently (Gánovce) or dated to a different period (Vel'ka Lomnica).

oldest epigraphic images found on ceramic objects from the Vattina culture no longer represent isolated cases in barbarian Europe. Similar "written" symbols have recently been discovered in the course of a detailed study of ceramic materials from the permanent settlement of the Otomani culture in Barca. Symbols of this kind have always offered irrefutable evidence of contacts, of attempts to imitate or of progress towards the so-called "globalisation" of mankind.

It has been determined that the spiral-based ornamentation applied to bronze, antler and bone objects originated in the eastern Mediterranean region. Bone and antler components of harnesses decorated in this manner represent a tight Carpathian grouping characterised by a narrowly defined style in the 16th and 15th centuries BC (Cat. No. 125). Certain motifs from Minoan and Mycenaean sealstones were also adapted in the Carpathian region in the form of various types of bronze pendants.

The social and economic flowering of the mid 2nd millennium BC was accelerated by the development of heavy two-axle and light single-axle wagons (Cat. Nos.

4 Sealstone from Mochlos (Crete) and a horned bronze pendant from Včelince (Slovakia)

It is an unfortunate historical fact that during the 15th century BC, at the threshold between the Early and the Middle Bronze Age, interaction between the eastern Mediterranean region and central Europe began to wane. The advanced cultures of the Carpathian region and central Europe declined, and centuries passed before the old level of economic and social development was achieved and complex North-South interaction once again became significant.

30

Two Skilled and Prestigious Inventions:
Metallurgy and the Goldsmith's Art

Jean-Pierre Mohen

Metallurgy and the goldsmith's art appeared together in Europe during the Copper and Bronze Ages and thus lie within the focus of interest here. Both of these achievements soon began to play an important contributing role in the development of increasingly more hierarchical societies in which objects made of metal – especially weapons, axes and daggers – were used as symbols of power. Beginning in the 2nd millennium BC, defensive weapons, helmets, breastplates, leg armour and chariots of war were presented in ceremonial parades as a prelude to battle. Homer's description of Achilles' shield offers a fine example of the exploitation of technical skill in the interest of social prestige.

Even the very oldest evidence of metal processing and goldsmithing discovered in Europe to date – the finds uncovered at the burial grounds of Varna (Bulgaria) and dated to roughly 4300 BC – show all of the essential characteristics of metallurgy. Represented here are the two most important metals, copper and gold, and a number of other valuable materials: polished greenstone axes, flint blades more than thirty centimetres in length, numerous shells – dentalia and spondyli. Among these treasures are items of copper and gold, products of pyrotechnology. The use of fire had been mastered long before. Although it had been employed in the production of lime in Lepinski Vir (Serbia) as early as the 7th millennium BC, yet it was not until the appearance of the kiln, first used by potters and later by metallurgists, that the control of fire in working materials took on a crucial role. The potter's kiln consumed oxygen and achieved temperatures of 550°–700° C during the firing process. Some of the vessels produced, along with many types of beads made during this period, were glazed in Near Eastern and Egyptian workshops. Both malachite and copper minerals played a role in the development of such glazes. Several scholars are convinced that a connection existed between the crafts of ceramics and metallurgy. Metallurgy is indeed a multi-disciplinary activity that begins with prospecting for native metals – for example, gold and other minerals (including copper) on the Sinai Peninsula, in Anatolia, in the Balkan region (the mines of Ai Bunar in Bulgaria and Rudna Glava in Serbia), in the Mitterberg region, in the Alps, in southern France and on the island of Corsica, in the Rio Tinto region of southern Spain, in Wales and in Ireland (Mount Gabriel).

Metals and rocks more or less rich in ore were mined with picks made of stone or antler and shovels shaped from the shoulder blades of cattle. Ore, usually in an oxide form, was crushed and then processed in a special smelting oven which could be heated, in reducing conditions, to temperatures of more than 1000° C (copper melts at 1083° C).

The first metals

The first small copper objects appear in the regions between eastern Anatolia and Iran in the 8th and 7th millennia BC. Nearly forty such pieces, including awls, hooks, wire, beads and small amounts of leaf, have been recovered in Cayönü Tepesi. Are they products of the native copper located quite near the site at Ergani Maden? Evidence of exposure to high temperatures would suggest that metallurgical processing had reached an advanced stage. It rapidly spread into Europe, where first traces of its use have been discovered in Bulgaria and Greece.

The example of Troy I, located at the western border of Anatolia opposite the European mainland, tells us a great deal about the high value placed upon local copper as well as gold and silver and bears witness at the same time to contacts with the Balkan region, as is particularly evident in the grave-goods at Varna dating from the early 5th millennium BC.

The copper mines of Rudna Glava in Serbia were worked during this period. Miners brought out copper oxide, copper carbonate (azurite and malachite). The spread of copper axes indicates a mastery of metallurgical technology in this region that appears to have been at least as dynamic as that of Anatolia and Mesopotamia (Susa). The small lead objects of the same period found at Çatal Hüyük raise the question of whether an accompanying cupellation process may have been used. Lead was one of the first metals used in the Aegean region, particularly in Siphnos, and lead objects from succeeding periods have been discovered in western Europe as far as Spain. The production centres in the Near and Middle East developed hand in hand with the rise of kingdoms; their graves were furnished in splendour with vessels and ornaments of silver and gold. This is true of Ur in Mesopotamia around 3000 BC and, a few centuries later, of Alaça Hüyük in Anatolia and Maïkop in the northern Caucasus.

During the Copper Age down into the middle of the 3rd millennium BC, literally tons of copper objects were produced in central and, to a lesser extent, western Europe – a veritable heyday of metallurgy that declined as the Bronze Age began. How is this profound change to be explained? Copper daggers and axes, precious objects and jewellery made of gold and vessels of silver were regarded by society as symbols of prestige and personal power, an attitude expressed in the lavishly furnished graves of individuals. Yet the prince or king who commanded these attributes of power and protected their production was unfamiliar with the secrets of metallurgists and goldsmiths. He was obliged to invite these highly specialised artisans to come to him – people whom we know not from their workshops (none of which have yet been discovered), but from their graves, a fact that lends support to the conviction that their occupation was held in great esteem and of high symbolic value. More than thirty discoveries from all over Europe are associated with such figures: only certain components, never complete panoplies. Among these items, for example, crucibles, parts of moulds, a stone hammer and similar items. It is clear, in any event, that the dead metallurgist took neither metal ingots nor finished pieces with him to the grave –

1 Metal-working tools, Génelard, Saône-et-Loire, France, Late Bronze Age, c. 1000 BC (Cat. No. 102)

nothing, in fact, that would have signified the economic importance of his trade.

Only his expertise was important, and that was recognised even beyond the worldly context. Does that mean that he preserved the secrets of metallurgy at this higher level?

Metallurgy and Goldsmithing in the Bronze Age

Bronze is a compound consisting of copper and another metal – arsenic, tin or lead. The "classical" bronze contains roughly ten per cent tin and represents, on the one hand, a technological innovation (more fluid in its cast and with greater hardness when cooled). At the same time it must also be seen as a major economic accomplishment, since tin was virtually non-existent in Mesopotamia, Egypt and the Mediterranean (with the exception of minor deposits in Anatolia, Italy and Spain) and thus had to be imported from distant areas. Where, then, did the tin come from for the mid 3rd millennium bronzes found in the royal graves at Ur and in the city of Susa? Whence the earliest significant products of the goldsmith's art – symbols of the first major empires?

The most popular hypotheses argue for an origin in the Far East, perhaps as distant as Malaysia. Staging posts did exist; Egypt appears to have played a particularly important role in the development of metal processing techniques in the 3rd and 2nd millennia BC. Many hundreds of tons of metal are known to have been processed there. The artisans were directly subordinate to the rulers and engaged in the service of the great sacred temples. The most important centres for metallurgy and goldsmithing were located in Thebes (under the aegis of the Amun Temple) and at Memphis (closely associated with the shrines of Ptah and Sokar, the patron gods of bronze artisans). Ingots of copper and tin were available in the region of the Nile delta, like those recovered from the Ulu Burun shipwreck (14th century BC). They supplied the casting operations in Avaris/Tell el-Dab'a, which produced metals for the weapons-makers of Ramesses in Piramesse/Qantir. According to calculations, the gold in the graves of Tutankhamun (d. 1237 BC), of Ramesses II (d. 1237 BC), and those at Tanis (11th–10th centuries BC) amounts to a total of 1000 tons, all of which came from lower Nubia. At the same time another 570 tons were obtained from Lower Egypt. The prestige of the rulers of the great dynasties is expressed not only in monumental architecture but also in bronze statues and golden jewellery, items which were also presented as gifts to noble correspondents in Mediterranean Europe. Interest in western European cultures was quickened in response to the discovery of extensive deposits of casserite (tin oxide) in Cornwall in England and southern Brittany in the early 2nd millennium BC. Tin mining in the "Isles of the Cassiterides" provided the seminal impulse for the growth of metallurgy in western Europe and on the European continent as a whole – areas which now began to compete with the Near and Middle East. In the Mediterranean region itself the significant copper wealth of Cyprus, the "isle of copper", was then exploited. However, opinion has it that the raw material in ingot form circulated readily to feed other centres of production, where items were manufactured on demand. And much the same can be said of the goldsmiths' operations.

The diverse spectrum of techniques ranging from casting, raising/sinking to soldering was now fully developed. The hammer and anvil were employed to give small tools their final form, as can be seen in the finds from Génelard (Saône and Loire), which also include punches, chisels/gravers and angle squares used to produce traces and repoussé decoration (Cat. No. 102).

Goldsmiths developed techniques of their own, such as granulation or filigree. Gold surfacing techniques took off – from the application of often very thin leaf to pressure welding.

Bronze metallurgists and goldsmiths of the Bronze Age plied their trade in workshops concentrated in urban centres (at Enkomi, Cyprus, or the Greek city of Pylos, for example) or in other sufficiently densely populated areas such as fortified settlements in central Europe. They would have required the support of government sufficiently centralised to afford protection to the routes by which the supplies came in and over which the finished products were distributed.

The Emergence of Iron Metallurgy

The spread of iron began during the latter half of the 2nd millennium BC under conditions about which we still know very little. The technology was new and required specialised knowledge and a great deal of skill. It was not yet possible to smelt iron mined from underground deposits, for example. By reducing iron ore in furnaces heated to temperatures as high as 1500° C, metallurgists were able to produce a spongy mass that had to be worked intensively with a hammer in order to separate off the slag and recover the fragments of pure iron. These were then transformed into bar-ingots through hammer-welding in the smith's forge. Still soft, the metal was then reheated in a charcoal fire; it needed yet further hot-working with the hammer, so that it became impregnated with some 1.7 per cent of carbon, which converts iron to a steel – the only metal capable of competing with bronze for weapons and tools alike.

We do not know where iron was used for the first time. Several prestige objects made of iron, such as a needle from Alaça (2400–2100 BC) or the blade of a dagger from the grave of Tutankhamun (1353 BC), were hammered up from meteoritic iron, which, thanks to its high nickel content, is very hard. Other Bronze Age iron objects appear to have been made starting from some natural iron mineral. These include the dagger blade from Alaça (2400–2100 BC), a tool found in the Cheops pyramid at Giza (2560–2240 BC) and a dagger from the central European Otomani culture (c. 1500 BC).

Rich in iron minerals, the sands of the south-eastern coast of the Black Sea were undoubtedly initially in demand as a flux in order to facilitate the smelting of copper-bearing ores. Attention was attracted to the resulting presence of pieces of iron fragments quite early on, beginning in the 3rd millennium BC. It is likely that the early Armenians became acquainted with the new metal in this way. The Hittites developed iron processing into a veritable "Iron Age" during the 2nd millennium BC. Around 1200/1100 BC the Egyptians took up the use of iron, followed by the Greeks. Investigations undertaken in the Kerameikos cemetery of Athens have shown how iron progressively replaced bronze for weapons, tools and the auxiliary items of dress (such as fibulae or garment clasps). Evidence for iron in western Europe dates to the 8th century BC and is found a little later still in northern Europe and the British Isles.

The production of iron, although a tricky process, was by now widespread. Iron ores were and are much commoner than those of copper. Every rural settlement had its forge, where iron ingots were processed. Iron becomes much more broadly integrated into society than did bronze, which retains its aristocratic character to this day.

Bibliography: Eluère 1982, 1987; Eluère & Mohen 1991; Gale 1991; Maddin 1988; Mohen 1990, 1991; Muhly 1973; Tylecote 1987.

Shipwrecks in the Eastern Mediterranean

Katie Demakopoulou

Finds from underwater excavations in various parts of the Aegean and the Eastern Mediterranean have significantly enriched our knowledge of the movement of goods and ideas between East and West in the Bronze Age, especially during the final phase of this period. Our information comes mainly from cargoes of wrecked ships that were transporting raw materials and other commodities from one place to another (Ill. 1).

Communications and exchanges of goods with distant regions began as early as the 3rd millennium BC. With the passage of time, commercial contacts intensified by way of the sea routes linking the harbours of the Syro-Palestinian coast and Cyprus with Crete, the Argolid and other areas of the Aegean, as well as with sites in the Central Mediterranean: Southern Italy, the Aeolian islands, Sicily and Sardinia. This led to the development of organised trade, which reached its peak in the Aegean in the Late Bronze Age, especially the 14th and 13th centuries BC. In the wrecks of ships carrying a wide variety of commodities have been found large quantities of raw materials and other items, which are not usually discovered in such abundance in excavations conducted on dry land.

1   The Mediterranean Sea, showing the sites of the shipwrecks (after Dickinson 1994, 235, fig. 7.1, with some additions)

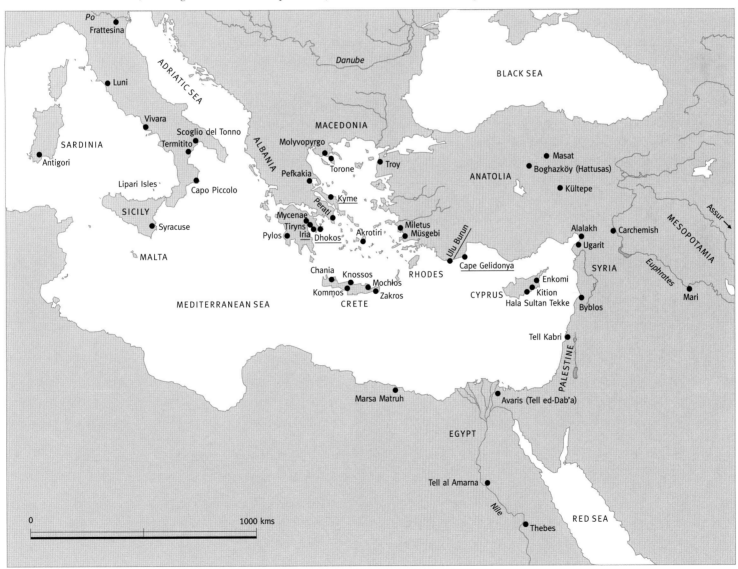

The earliest shipwreck in the Mediterranean is that of a ship that sank during the first half of the 3rd millennium BC near the island of Dokos, between Hydra and the coast of the Argolid. Excavation of this wreck brought to light the ship's cargo, consisting of about one thousand clay vases of the Early Helladic II period (c. 2900–2400 BC). This material from the Dokos shipwreck is the largest known closed pottery group of the Early Helladic II period in Greece, and contains not only storage vessels, but also fine-ware types. The vases in question are pithoi, amphoras, basins, jugs, askoi, bowls and sauceboats. The bowls form the largest group in numerical terms. There are about two hundred sauceboats, which are divided into three types. In addition to the pottery, the ship's cargo also included many andesite millstones, which seem to have been trade objects. The storage vessels probably contained agricultural produce, but the fine-ware vases, especially the bowls and the sauceboats, were probably items for sale in various places, or special orders. The Dokos wreck demonstrates the existence of exchanges and trade in the Aegean as early as the Early Bronze Age. This is also attested by the dissemination of certain works of art, such as Cycladic figurines, and other objects, to many areas of the Aegean during this period.

A clear picture of the commodities that were moved over long distances by trade in the Mediterranean is given by the cargoes of two Late Bronze Age ships found wrecked off the southwest coast of Asia Minor, one near Cape Gelidonya and the other at Ulu Burun near Kaş. The cargoes contained raw materials, ready-made, finished objects, probably specially made for export, and other luxury items.

The ship that sank off Cape Gelidonya towards the end of the 13th century BC appears to have set sail from a port on the Syro-Palestinian coast, and to have called in at Cyprus. Its cargo, which was not very large, included quantities of raw materials and other objects. There were many copper and tin ingots, several agricultural tools, craftsman's tools, and other implements and weapons. Pieces of scrap bronze were also found on this ship, on which there seems to have been a workshop for metal objects. The purpose of the ship's voyage was probably to exchange finished metal products for scrap metal, and to repair other metal objects during its spells in different ports.

The ship wrecked at Ulu Burun was larger, about fifteen to sixteen meter long, and its cargo contained a far greater range and number of commodities. Indeed, it is one of the largest assemblage of ancient trade goods yet discovered in the Mediterranean. This ship, too, probably set out from the Syro-Palestinian coast. Its sinking is dated around 1300 BC according to recent dendrochronological evidence, about a century earlier than the wreck of the other ship at Cape Gelidonya. The Ulu Burun ship was carrying a mixed cargo from Egyptian, Near Eastern, Cypriot and European sources. The objects found included ten tons of copper in ox-hide ingots, a substantial amount of tin also in ingot form, dozens of ingots of cobalt-blue glass, logs of Egyptian ebony, hippopotamus and elephant ivory, ostrich eggshells, murex opercula and tortoise shells. A great number of "Canaanite" storage and transport jars contained terebinth resin, used for the manufacture of perfume; others held spices and foodstuffs, including coriander, safflower, figs, grapes, sumac, almonds, pomegranates and olives.

Swords of Syrian and Mycenaean types were also retrieved, as well as other weapons and tools, a few Mycenaean vases and a quantity of Cypriot pottery vessels which were packed in large pithoi for safe shipment. Goods from areas of Northern Europe, such as Baltic amber, were also found. Some jewellery and precious objects of Near Eastern origin were recovered, too, which may have belonged to the captain or to a wealthy passenger. However, the most important recovery were a set of two or three boxwood tablets or diptychs, perhaps the ship's log or a traveller's diary, most probably of Near Eastern origin. Twenty-four stone anchors and some musical instruments found in the ship seem to be from the same source.

Generally speaking, the overall picture presented by the Ulu Burun shipwreck reveals the itinerary of a merchant ship, which set sail from an eastern port, transporting a large cargo of various commodities to remote harbours in the Eastern and Western Mediterranean. The discovery of Cypriot and "Canaanite" pottery at Kommos in South Crete, at Marsa Matruh in West Egypt and on Sardinia lends support to this view.

Evidence for two other Late Bronze Age shipwrecks have also been located in the Aegean, attesting to the

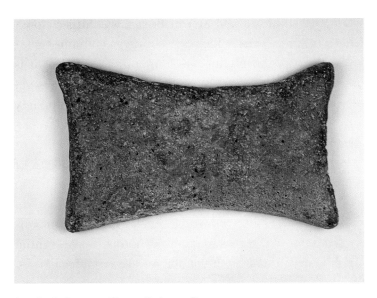

2 Ox-hide ingot, Kyme, Euboea, Greece
Late Bronze Age (Cat.No. 19)

existence of organised trade between the East, Cyprus and the Aegean. One was found near Kyme in Euboea. A chance find brought to light seventeen ox-hide copper ingots (Cat. No. 19), which must have come from a ship-wreck that has not so far been identified or investigated. It must be noted that the Kyme wreck is dated to the beginning of the Late Bronze Age, in the 16th or 15th centuries BC. Of the same date and again from off the Turkish coast (the Bay of Antalya) is a ship that as yet has not been properly investigated, but is known to be carrying copper ingots.

Another wreck in the Aegean reveals the important role played by Cyprus in East-West trade. This wreck has been found and recently investigated near Cape Iria in the Argolid. It is dated to the end of the 13th century BC. In contrast with the cargoes of the wrecks found at Ulu Burun, Gelidonya and Kyme, there were no copper ingots or other metal item in the ship wrecked at Iria. Its cargo, however, contained an impressive pottery group consisting of Cypriot pithoi and storage jugs, Minoan storage stirrup jars, pithoid jars of Helladic type, and also some Mycenaean vases of the LH IIIB period. Precisely what these vases contained during the ship's final, fatal voyage, is unknown. That they were used as basic transport containers for liquids (mainly oil and wine) in the Cypriot and Creto-Mycenaean trade, however, is not disputed. The cargo found in the Iria wreck makes it likely that the ship was of Cypriot origin, and its position suggests it was following a major trade route that linked Cyprus, Crete and the Argolid – undoubtedly part of a wider network of communications and commercial contacts.

The shipwrecks of the Eastern Mediterranean found to date, together with the pottery and other objects of Aegean, Cypriot and Near Eastern origin discovered at various sites in the Eastern and Western Mediterranean, have provided important evidence for contacts and commercial exchanges, which had begun already in the Early Bronze Age. During the second half of the 2nd millennium BC it is clear that an organised, long-distance trade was established. This trade involved not only the countries of the Eastern Mediterranean, but also the Aegean world and parts of the rest of Europe. The finds reveal that a wide network of contacts and commercial exchanges evolved from one end of the Mediterranean to the other, in which Cyprus and Sardinia, with the Aegean between them, played leading roles. The purpose of this trade was mainly the movement of metals, such as copper and tin, though it also included other raw materials and finished products.

Bibliography: Bass 1967, 1986, 1991, 1998; Kilian 1993; Dickinson 1994; Papathanasopoulos et al 1995; Pennas et al 1995.

North-South Exchanges of Raw Materials

Anthony F. Harding

In a Bronze Age context, it is natural to imagine that the only materials of importance that were moved from place to place were metals: copper, tin and gold. Important though these undoubtedly were, they were by no means the only materials that were moved. Some, such as amber, were rare and exotic, and used solely for ornaments or amulets; others, such as salt, were truly mundane in that their use and purpose was intimately bound up with the continuance of everyday life, the survival of humans and animals. Abundant and detailed evidence recovered in recent years reveals an elaborate set of mechanisms and technologies for the movement of many materials across large distances of the Bronze Age world.

Copper

The starting point for any discussion of the transport of metals must be the places at which the ores occur, and the evidence for their extraction and distribution. A great deal of information has become available in recent years about the mining of copper from a number of well-preserved and prolific sources. What is less clear is the extent to which it is possible to show that copper was moved from one place to another. The identification of copper types by the "signatures" brought about by characteristic impurity or trace element patterns has made some progress, but many difficulties have been encountered in tying finished artefacts down to particular ore sources. Thus while recent work on the traces of prehistoric mining has been spectacularly successful in France, Britain, Ireland, Spain, Slovakia, Yugoslavia and Austria, little is known for certain about the distribution of the products of these mines over more than short distances.

2   Malachite, one of the most commonly occurring ores of copper.

1   The copper mines on Great Ormes Head, north Wales.
The picture shows the entrances to shafts originally dug in the Bronze Age.

Nevertheless, the composition of British Middle and Late Bronze Age metalwork suggests that an Alpine source was being used, in preference to local Welsh, Scottish or Irish sources which were the main suppliers in the Early Bronze Age. Similarly, in the south Scandinavian area, where there are no copper deposits, one might expect that the ores of the Harz Mountains of Thuringia would be the natural suppliers, but in the earliest part of the Bronze Age a series of imported objects from central Europe (principally the Carpathian Basin) indicate that supplies very likely came from the Alpine and Carpathian ore sources. Another striking example is provided by the finds of ring ingots (*Ösenhalsringe*) which are distributed across a wide area of Europe from the Alps almost to the Baltic coast. Circumstantial evidence suggests that these objects were manufactured in Austria or Moravia from Alpine copper, and moved in ingot form across these hundreds of kilometres, even if some authorities favour a votive explanation for these finds.

Tin

Bronze is an alloy of copper, usually utilising tin added in proportions of around 5–10%. This means that bronze-using cultures and civilisations must have had

3 Cassiterite (tin ore). Tin was extracted both in this form and as "placer" deposits in streams.

access to significant amounts of tin. The location of the tin sources used in antiquity remains one of the great puzzles of the ancient world – though recent discoveries are making some progress towards solving this particular mystery.

Tin occurs naturally in rather few locations. In Europe, these are Cornwall, Brittany, parts of Spain, Etruria and the Erzgebirge of southern Saxony, though in the case of the latter there has been debate as to whether the technology available in the Bronze Age would have been capable of exploiting the source. There is some tin in Turkey, but since Near Eastern cities seem to have

imported tin from the East, it is perhaps more likely that distant Afghanistan was the preferred supplier. Recent finds of tin ingots, most notably on the shipwreck from Ulu Burun near Kas on the south coast of Turkey, demonstrate that tin was moved about, and in considerable quantities. At present it is not known whether the sources of the Northwest (Cornwall, Brittany) could have supplied the Mediterranean civilisations, though it is very likely that Cornish tin was moved to the Continent, potentially reaching far across Europe. The definitive solution to this problem must await new analytical programmes that are now in prospect.

Gold

Today, most European gold sources are worked out and gold is considered a rarity. Gold actually occurs widely in Europe and in the Bronze Age it must have been available in some quantity. As with copper, attempts have

4 Gold cup, Wachtberg-Fritzdorf, Rhein-Sieg-Kreis, Nordrhein-Westfalen, Germany (Cat. No. 201)

been made to tie down the different gold sources by analytical means, with limited success; new work now under way should assist in solving this problem.

Particularly prolific sources of gold are those in Ireland, Spain and Transylvania. Analytical evidence suggests that much of the gold of western continental Europe, especially in north Germany and southern Scandinavia, came from Ireland. There has been much speculation that the gold of Mycenaean Greece, and possibly of Crete as well, came from the Transylvanian sources, but this is not proven. Since the goldsmiths of Egypt and the Near East undoubtedly utilised sources closer at hand than those of Rumania, it is equally possible the Greece did as well.

5   Amber cup, Hove, Sussex, England
Wessex Culture, 18th–17th centuries BC (Cat. No. 85)

Amber

One of the most intriguing substances to have been used in later prehistory was amber, the resin of extinct species of pine, deposited over geological time-scales in various parts of the world (Cat. No. 81). In a European context, the most abundant sources of amber are those labelled "Baltic", of Tertiary Age, but other, smaller, sources are found in Rumania and Sicily. Fortunately, a

well-established analytical technique– infra-red spectroscopy– is able to distinguish between different ambers, and in particular to identify Baltic amber by its characteristic signature in infra-red spectra. A long-standing programme of analysis has shown that almost all of the amber found in Minoan and Mycenaean Greece, and much of that found in Bronze Age Italy and the Balkans, is of Baltic origin. This may not mean that the amber actually came exclusively from the shores of the Baltic, because amber of this type is found quite widely in northern Europe, even on the east coast of England and in Ukraine. It does, however, prove beyond doubt that the inhabitants of Late Bronze Age Greece, especially those of the Shaft Graves of Mycenae and comparable rich societies in the west of the Peloponnese, were plugged in to vast exchange networks which were able to bring them exotic materials, of which amber was just one. Whatever its precise point of origin, transportation from the north or west seems to be certain. Consideration of the specific forms of bead that were manufactured, notably the "spacer plates", strongly suggests that a particular connection existed between southern England, southern Germany and Greece; it may be that these areas acted as some kind of intermediary in the movement of amber from north to south.

Salt

A little-understood commodity which was nevertheless of enormous importance in ancient as in modern times is salt. Salt deposits, in the form of brine springs or (more rarely) rock salt, are found widely though unevenly in Europe. The evidence of salt production and distribution in historical times, for instance in Africa, indicates how extensive the movement of salt in cake form might be. In practice, the study of Bronze Age salt-working is in its infancy, though in an Iron Age context there is much excellent information from Austria. Good evidence comes from central Germany (the Halle region), and the characteristic finds of materials for salt production (briquetage– clay trays and pedestals for the evaporation of salt water) are increasingly turning up in Bronze Age contexts in western and central Europe. Presumably southern cultures have had ample access to salt, since there are many salt lagoons along Mediterranean shores, though no bri-

6 Jet necklace, Blindmill, Rothie, Aberdeenshire, Scotland
Early Bronze Age (Cat. No. 86)

7 Bronze Age rock carvings at Frännarp, south Sweden, showing wheeled vehicles such as must have been used to transport raw materials and other goods overland.

quetage has yet turned up in Bronze Age Italy or Greece. It is, however, perfectly possible that salt cakes were moved northwards from the south to the mountainous interior of the Balkans or central Europe.

Other Materials

Little is known about the transport of other materials, though clay, wood and stone were as crucial for Bronze Age societies as for Neolithic or Iron Ages ones. The Ulu Burun ship contained a piece of ebony, indicating that wood could be moved about for special purposes. Wood for ship-building, for instance, might have had to be brought from considerable distances– though we have no indication that there was a specific south-north or north-south movement of wood. Likewise, the best potting clay was limited in distribution, and could have been moved to those areas where specialist potters needed it (though it is often more likely that the potters would have lived near the clays, the pots being moved instead).

Means of Transport

All of these movements imply that effective means of transport existed, in north-south as well as other directions. Open-sea craft are known in depictions from the Aegean area and Egypt, and the Turkish shipwrecks indicate something of what was possible. Boats that survive in the north are log canoes, not capable of open-sea voyages, but the depictions on Scandinavian rock art of what are taken to be skin-covered vessels of considerable size indicate that longer journeys were undertaken. Such boats would probably have been capable of carrying most of the commodities discussed here, just as the Ulu Burun ship was. Smaller craft, including canoes, were used for river and lake transport.

On land, there is evidence for carts and wagons, though little is known about roads. Paved roads did not exist in the Bronze Age, so the transport of materials must have been a long and arduous process, restricted by weather conditions. Nevertheless, materials *did* travel; the obstacles *were* overcome; and smiths and other craftsmen were supplied with the materials necessary for the production of the splendid artefacts and art objects that constitute "Europe's first Golden Age".

Hoards and Atlantic Shipwrecks

Stuart Needham

The discovery of a hoard of bronze or gold objects dating to the Bronze Age, say 3000 or more years old, immediately invites some wonderment. On learning of its antiquity it is natural to visualise the producers and users of the objects as relatively primitive, and these items as relatively valuable to them. We can puzzle over the circumstances of their burial and the failure of anyone to retrieve them. These are understandable reactions, but they do no more than scratch the surface of the potential importance of hoards, both to the original owners and, indeed, to us as a means of understanding the past.

Hoards are known in their many thousands across the continent of Europe, and yet archaeologists deduce that those recorded in the recent century or two are probably only a tiny faction of those originally buried and unretrieved. We get glimpses of the considerable volume of metal circulating by the later Bronze Age from large finds, such as the 91 kg of the Isleham hoard, England, 65 kg retrieved from the sea-bed at Langdon Bay, in the English channel, or 75 kg at Vénat, France; but in some regions there are even weighty hoards as early as the Early Bronze Age, for example 150 kg and 85 kg respectively at Mauthausen and Munchen-Luitpoldpark respectively, in southern Germany, or 69 kg at Bennewitz bei Halle, Saxo-Thuringia. Discoveries and exploration of contemporary copper mines have added further weight to the scale of the metal supply. Although a hazardous exercise when based on the voids where ores once lay, calculations suggest large outputs of metal over time.

Before proceeding, we need to address the question what is a hoard? Strictly defined it is a group of objects, which was deliberately concealed on a single occasion (cf. Cat. Nos. 103, 104, 119–121). We take as evidence of single-event deposition that objects lay in very close proximity in the ground, i.e. they were seemingly buried in the same hole or niche. This is not infallible reasoning, since a buried deposit might act as a repository intended to be opened periodically to extract or add material. Even where this did not happen, a "closed" hoard does not guarantee that some objects had not previously been part of earlier buried hoards. Hoards were not the only context in which metalwork and other valuables were deliberately removed from circulation and use. The richness of grave furnishings in many cultures during the European Bronze Age (see elsewhere in this volume) illustrates one obvious alternative context. But there is also the major phenomenon of deposits placed in open water or marshy ground, a dominant theme in certain parts of Europe, and rarer deposits in inaccessible caves and fissures.

So how did the thousands of hoards and indeed single bronze objects found in every part of the continent come to be left there? This deceptively simple question lies at the centre of a long running debate about which hoards were intended to be retrieved, and which were deposited in perpetuity, with no intention by the depositors to retrieve. The people who lived their lives three to four thousand years ago, being pre-literate, could only leave for posterity a series of ambiguous signs and symbols, and their intentions cannot easily be read from the archaeological evidence. Bronze deposits do, however, offer many important clues about the circumstances of deposition and the prior histories of the contained objects.

The depositor's intentions might always of course be thwarted by illegal recovery, i.e. theft, or by unforeseen events such as the death or flight of the individuals concerned. These factors alone are sufficient to cloud the issue, but there are other areas of uncertainty. For example, if cult objects normally on view at special sanctuaries came to be buried during a period of instability, the character of the objects would throw little light on the particular cause of deposition. Equally troublesome for interpretation is the possibility that the two opposing intentions (to retrieve or not to retrieve) that seem so cut-and-dried, were much less so; that the decision to retrieve buried valuables may have been under frequent review by the depositor in accordance with changes in the local political and economic scene.

Hoards have the capacity to give us insights into many facets of the Bronze Age world. This potential stems in part from the intrinsic characteristics of the objects included. This is an obvious point since the types deposited together will normally have belonged to a similar period and culture of use. It is this feature of contempo-

43

raneity within associations that has been exploited by archaeologists for the past century to construct a chronology for the European Bronze Age. Associated objects can also sometimes be united by their context of use, for example, the tool-kit or adornment of a single person, or the trophies won in combat. Furthermore, the objects themselves will yield much information on the technology by which they were produced, while certain combinations might throw light on the way that production was organised.

There is, however, a quite other range of insights which depend instead on our interpretation of hoarding. For example, differences in the combination of objects brought together for burial might betray important cultural boundaries, or suggest some ranking within one cultural group. There might be indications of changing preoccupations as to which objects best symbolised the group or the individual of importance represented. Then there are deductions regarding cultural interactions, drawn for example from the presence or absence of specific types imported from other regions.

The movement of metal around the continent is of central importance because of the restricted sources of copper and tin. The identification of types that have been transported from one zone to another helps build up the picture of the distribution network. However, the scope for recycling bronze was undoubtedly recognised in the Bronze Age, and this means, firstly, that the tangible evidence of contacts may not survive and, secondly, that the metal locked up in an object will frequently have had a much longer history than the life-span of the object. Analysis of the composition of the metal, although prone to difficulties in interpretation, helps us to understand distribution patterns, and ultimately perhaps to relate the metal in circulation to ore bodies.

It is clear that by one process or another, metal was being moved around on a scale that allowed large quantities to be amassed in certain zones. Contrary to logic, perhaps, this does not necessarily mean that large quantities were moved in single acts of transportation. What we perceive most easily from the archaeological finds is the gross scale of movement; more difficult to adduce is the extent to which this might be the product of many small-scale transactions. It is easy to forget that the net effect is the product of many generations of social interaction and,

potentially, a steady, osmotic flow of wealth that may be stored as much as used. The question of the organisation and scale of "trade" in metals across Europe is still under active debate.

There may have been some circumstances which encouraged the movement of large consignments of bronze. A prime case is that of transportation to foreign shores, since the sea presented a zone of impedance to normal land interactions. To make a passage of any great distance required skill and knowledge; it probably also required awaiting favourable weather; these factors would be an inducement not to conduct transactions in a piecemeal fashion, but instead to accumulate material for wholesale or simultaneous transactions.

The best evidence yet in northern waters for such a process comes from the sea-bed at Langdon Bay, just outside Dover harbour, England. A total of at least 360 objects of bronze have been retrieved from a limited zone in fairly shallow water. Although some are heavily eroded by three thousand years of tidal action, the great majority are recognisable as Bronze Age implements, indeed datable to a single phase of the Bronze Age, to c. 1300–1150 BC. In fact it is possible to argue that the material belongs to the earlier part of this period. The currents surging through the straits of Dover had also ensured that no remnants of a boat survived and we are left to deduce from the character of the bronzes the probability that they represent the spilt cargo of a cross-channel voyager which came to grief below the cliffs of Dover.

While many other finds of bronzes from off the coastlines of Europe, from estuaries and indeed from rivers might be speculated to derive from wrecked ships, none are certain. The river finds at least are generally subject to an alternative interpretation in which they are viewed as ritual deposits offered to water deities. Some other contexts, however, have given us boats and portions of boats belonging to the Bronze Age. The most famous site is that of North Ferriby on the Humber estuary, eastern England, where the remains of four boats have been excavated. Another classic find was made recently at Dover, Kent, at a depth of seven metres below the town's pavements. These, with the 19th century AD find at Brigg, Lincolnshire, and further fragments elsewhere, all demonstrate a very specific boat-building technology in

1   Hoard of bronze vessels, Dresden Dobritz, Saxony, Germany, Late Bronze Age (Cat. No. 210)

which shaped planks were butted together, lashed with yew withies and caulked with moss along the seams; "cleats" projecting from the planks allowed the insertion of linking stays. This boat building tradition was already underway by the earlier half of the 2nd millennium BC, and while their exact capabilities might be a matter for debate, there can be little doubt that a much more sophisticated technology had been developed to cater for the increasing demands made on water-borne transportation.

Whatever mechanisms in detail were operating, the movement of metal, as well as other commodities, was vital to sustain Bronze Age life-styles. Whatever the scale of movement, transactions required planning and an infra-structure of complex social relations between the myriad social groups. Control over stock-piles of metal objects would have been an essential aspect of the process, allowing elites to monitor any surplus locally, and indeed to prepare for critical transactions, either with living communities, or with the gods.

The widespread and long-lived phenomenon of depositing hoards of bronze and, less frequently, gold, in Europe suggests some common underlying needs in soci-

ety. On the practical level, it has long been recognised that the ground offered relative security at a time when strong-rooms and locks did not exist. However, with interpretation increasingly steering towards most hoard deposits having had some form of ritual purpose, then the common ground in explanation may largely lie in belief structures. In actuality it is believed that hoards served many and varied reasons relating to social competition, commemorative events such as notable battles or marriages, or the sacrifice of material in supplication to deities. Only by detailed analysis of the diverse combinations of objects and burial context across the many regions of Europe can we advance particular interpretations of particular sets of hoards. Despite this undoubted diversity, however, it is possible to offer a general all-embracing definition. Thus we might understand hoards and hoarding as a means of regulating and circumscribing the movement of metal, a movement that takes place at different levels between different territories, between different classes within a social group, and between the living world and that of the spirits and gods.

45

The Journey as a Rite of Initation

María Luisa Ruiz-Gálvez Priego

Ulysses, the Greek hero whose name appears in the title of this exhibition, symbolises and epitomises the adventurer, the voyager to the ends of the earth, the discoverer of new lands and peoples. The meaning of the epic narrative is more symbolic than real, however. It describes the rites of initiation the hero must pass in order to become a leader, trials in which he must demonstrate skill, intelligence and the ability to overcome unexpected dangers and learn from his encounters with different peoples and other worlds (Helms 1988). Other heroic legends provide accounts of comparable initiations – the journey of Jason and the Argonauts to Colchis; the story of Perseus, who slays the dreaded Gorgon and thus rescues Andromeda; the travels of Theseus, who survives the attacks of robbers and monsters on his way to Athens and later enters the labyrinth of the Minotaur.

This image of the hero as adventurer confronted with dangers in strange, mysterious lands and rewarded for his boldness and courage with new skills and knowledge is the product of a static, ethnocentric view of the world that is particularly characteristic of settled farmers. Such people view the outside world from a secure vantage point behind their fences, walls or other protective barriers which separate field from forest and cultivated land from untamed nature. And from this centre of the world, as every human sees himself to be, he categorises the elements of his environment: good or evil, civilised or barbaric, safe or dangerous, familiar or mysterious, normal or monstrous, depending upon their degree of conformity (or non-conformity) with his own personal perceptions and *Weltanschauung*. The farther we wander from our own personal world centre, the more strange and mysterious the beings and landscapes we encounter appear (Helms 1988). That is why the Han dynasty referred to itself as the "Middle Kingdom". Firmly believing themselves to occupy the centre of the universe, they regarded all other peoples as barbarians. It is this fundamental attitude which forms the typical settled farmer's prejudices towards and mistrust of people in travelling occupations – shepherds, gypsies, peddlers, actors, wandering smiths, etc. All of this is clearly reflected in the myth of the "Wandering Jew" (Zumthor 1994).

An explanation for this restricted view of the world lies in the extreme difficulty of travel in pre-industrial times, when practically every journey was a strenuous and hazardous undertaking. It took the nobleman Ruy Gonzalez de Clavijo three years – from 1403 to 1406 – to complete the trip from Alcalá de Henares to Samarkand and back on his mission to carry a message from the King of Castile to the Great Khan Timur. Chaunu (1984) has calculated that a European dignitary had less than a thirty-per-cent chance of returning to his point of departure from a journey to the Far East. And if nobles fared no better than this, how much less mobile would the "simple man travelling on foot" have been? Many ancient and medieval myths can be explained with reference to news received from "other worlds", reports filtered and distorted by the time they reached European ears. Thus the unicorn, whose horn was thought to have both medicinal and aphrodisiac powers, was nothing more than a hybrid of rhinoceros and narwhal. The Sirens, the very embodiment of the attractions and the dangers of seafaring, are seals, plain and simple, of which one species can still be found in the Mediterranean today. Underlying the myth of "Prester John", whose spirit appeared in Columbus' dreams, is a distorted report of the existence of Coptic Christians in Ethiopia.

Just as the medieval alchemist was regarded as a kind of sorcerer and therefore as a dangerous person, so must Bronze and Iron-Age man have looked upon the bronze and iron metallurgists with a mixture of wonder and fright. After all, these artisans possessed magic powers with which to transform solid matter into liquid and convert the liquids to quite different solid materials again. This combination of fear and fascination explains why the smith often appears as a god in myths, although frequently described as lame, deformed, grotesque or as a betrayed husband. This is clearly a case of an attempt to combat fear with ridicule.

This narrow view of the world was also the basis for the common practice of assigning magical or curative properties to certain products of nature simply because they came from far away and thus appeared strange and mysterious. Accordingly, amber is attributed healing powers in the *Lapidary* of King Alphonso X the Learned of Castile, a 13th century AD work in which the scientific traditions of Greece, Egypt and the Orient are treated. There, people are advised to wear amber as jewellery to be hung around the neck to heal glandular swelling, hydrophobia, eye disorders and heart disease (Folch 1986). Jet was believed to ward off magic spells and the "evil eye". Thus natural products from foreign lands and objects made or processed in unfamiliar, apparently mysterious ways became prestige items. Their possession and the very fact of being associated with foreigners who possessed, obtained or produced such things was also equated with a share of the power (Brumfiel & Earle 1987). Then as now, the control of "know-how" – the knowledge of the elite – brought prestige and power within one's own society. This explains why iron was regarded as a precious rather than a utilitarian metal prior to the introduction of iron technology and why Arab coins were treasured and hoarded as precious objects in the Viking settlements of the 11th century AD (Gaimster 1991). Silver coins and amber from the Balkan region are still viewed as valuable components of dowries for women in North Africa today. Gold was admired for its brilliant lustre and its warm, sunlike colour. Regarded as divinities and representatives of the sun, the Ashanti kings of Ghana held a monopoly on gold (V.V.A.A. 1957), and in the Indian court ceremonies of Columbia (upon which the legends of El Dorado are based) the coronation ritual called for the body of the new ruler to be covered with gold dust. This ceremony was preceded by rites of initiation for the future chieftain, which began with a period of fasting and seclusion in a cave. Having completed this trial, the young man would go to Lake Guatavita to undergo initiation (Willis 1994).

Similar rituals, involving seclusion in darkness and enforced silence or, in some cases, the use of narcotics, were also employed as initiation tests and as a precondition for advancement to positions of political or religious leadership. These are comparable to those undergone by Jesus and Buddha: Jesus fasted for forty days and nights in the desert and withstood the temptations of the devil (Matthew 4:1), while Buddha set out as a wanderer in search of enlightenment and resisted the temptations of the demon Mâra (V.V.A.A. 1957). Unlike the travels of Ulysses, these were journeys of the soul. In a state of trance, the subject entered the most distant regions of his own subconscious. Yet like the physical journeys of Ulysses and others, the difficulty involved in travels into the psyche was how to find one's way back. In both cases, however, that is the real test of the mental and spiritual strength of a potential leader. He who returns from a mental journey has also gained experience and wisdom.

The significance of certain resins such as incense and myrrh, both of which were traded over long distances in ancient times and reached central and western Europe during the 12th century AD (Artzy 1992), lay in their euphoria-inducing properties (Sherratt 1992) and consequently in their capacity to promote communication with the gods. That is why we frequently find salve containers and incense burners in the graves of princes – as symbols of the journey to the hereafter and the ascent of the deceased to the status of a hero or divinity. And that is also why they were used in coronation ceremonies for kings and rites of ordination for priests (Exodus 30:22). A good example of the symbolic meanings allocated to exotic objects and materials in societies which had no written language and thus relied upon images to record and communicate information is found in the gifts brought by the "Wise Men from the East" to the infant Jesus in Bethlehem: gold for the king, incense for the god and myrrh for the man-child (Matthew 2:11). Near the end of the 3rd millennium BC, the abandonment of bronze in favour of silver as the "common currency" in the foreign trade of the Mesopotamian states produced a reorientation of long-distance trading routes and the incorporation of the Aegean into the world system (Sherratt A. and S. 1991). Gradually, the remaining regions of Europe were integrated into the extensive trading complex that involved the exchange of rare raw materials, new technologies, specialised knowledge and even human beings as well. In spite of the many difficulties in communication, symbolic codes were also developed as shared cultural cargo that we still encounter today.

Bibliography: Artzy 1992; Brunfiel & Earle 1987; Chaunu 1984; Folch 1986; Gaimster 1991; Helms 1988; Sherratt 1992; Sherratt A & S 1991; V.V.A.A. 1957; Willis 1994; Zumthor 1994.

Crises in Western European Metal Supply During the Late Bronze Age: From Bronze to Iron

Lothar Sperber

The production of iron presumably originated as a by-product of copper metallurgy, i.e. through the processing of sulphide copper ores that either contain iron themselves or are smelted with substantial admixtures of iron ore. Accordingly, isolated evidence of the existence of smelted and forged iron is documented in the Near East from the 3rd millennium BC, and in central Europe since about 1700 BC. Yet it was not until first the shortages of copper and tin resulting from rising consumption made these metals expensive in the advanced cultures of the Near East and the Aegean, and then, about 1200 BC, the "flood of Sea Peoples" significantly disrupted the supply of metals within the eastern Mediterranean that a shift to iron in the production of weapons and tools began. By 1000 BC it was in widespread use for such purposes. By this time, iron technology had spread from Greece across the central Danube region and into western central Europe, where iron was initially used only sporadically and in small quantities as a decorative metal and for the production of small implements. Neither iron nor the earliest forms of steel were harder than bronze, and they required more work to process. Thus as long as a reliable supply of copper, tin and old bronze was available, there was no particular reason to abandon bronze.

Nevertheless, the gradual shift away from bronze over the course of several hundred years in western central Europe was already in progress by the 11th century BC. The cause was the general shortage of the preferred source of copper smelted from chalcopyrite ore and the necessity of replacing it with "grey ore", which was technically more difficult to process. An increase in the use of copper derived from "grey ore" has been documented in analytical studies for England, northern and central France, south-western Germany, Switzerland, northern Tyrol, Salzburg, southern Bavaria, Bohemia and southern Scandinavia and is known to have begun in all of these regions by about 1100 BC or soon thereafter. This

chronological congruence over such an extensive geographical area also indicates that the supply of copper within this broad region was organised systematically and that the supply of new copper (and not only of grey-ore copper) came primarily from a very few major deposits. We might imagine this arrangement as a metals circulation system into which new copper was introduced (for the most part from the large mining complexes in the northern Alps and probably in central Germany as well), but in which processed bronze, or used metal, predominated. New copper tended to drift towards the tin-mining regions of north-western Europe, central Germany and Bohemia, where tin (to simplify somewhat) was presumably paid for primarily in copper. In this way, grey-ore copper originally mined in the Alps or central Germany eventually moved in large quantities to areas as distant as northern France and England.

In a certain sense, chalcopyrite and "grey ore" represent the two poles between which Bronze Age copper production shifted in central Europe. Chalcopyrite ore yielded a grade of copper low in accompanying elements (Cat. No. 87), whereas the copper gained from "grey ore" had high concentrations of antimony, arsenic, silver and often nickel as well. With respect to its appearance, "grey ore", with its grey or dull coloration (hence the name), is easily distinguishable from brightly coloured chalcopyrite ores. Similarly, bronze-yellow copper derived from "grey ore" contrasts markedly with the reddish copper yielded by chalcopyrites. During the first phase of the Early Bronze Age (21st–19th centuries BC), the early experimental stage of bronze metallurgy, grey-ore copper was employed in massive quantities as an alternative to tin bronze, with which metallurgists had been familiar in principle for some time. Yet the smelting of "grey ore" had already begun to decline in the more recent Early Bronze Age and was abandoned completely in about 1600 BC for a period of some five hundred years.

The rejection of grey-ore copper was presumably a consequence of the fact that the high consistency of the copper and tin alloy – and thus the desired quality of bronze employed both as a cast *and* wrought alloy in processes developed (using copper from chalcopyrite ore) during the more recent Early Bronze Age could not be achieved with grey-ore copper. Its light bronze colour was easily confused (as analyses have shown) with that of proper tin bronze; such grey-ore copper was subject to considerable fluctuation in its tin concentration, which generally tended to be much lower than in a true tin-bronze probably because Bronze Age artisans assumed the existence of a much higher tin concentration in what was in fact raw copper and/or recycled bronze and accordingly regarded it as unnecessary to do more than compensate for the loss of tin routinely expected during the (s)melting process. Furthermore, grey-ore copper is

soon (about 1020 BC) followed by the collapse of chalcopyrite ore mining operations in the Salzburg and Kitzbühel areas, a circumstance that is reflected in the abrupt shift from the dominance of chalcopyrite copper processing to the equally predominant use of grey-ore copper in the neighbouring regions. The Salzburg and Kitzbühel mines did not stand alone. Together with the copper mining operations in the lower Inn Valley (northern Tyrol) and in southern Bavaria, Salzburg and the northern Austrian piedmont region, they had formed a

1   Antimony tetrahedrite, from Schwaz in the Inn Valley of the North Tyrol (left) and chalcopyrite from Mitterberg (Salzburg); both pieces are approximately 7 cm across.

2   Antimony tetrahedrite, from the Early Bronze Age settlement of Wiesing-Buchberg in the Inn Valley of the North Tyrol, 20th century BC; approximately 5 cm across.

relatively brittle, due to its often high antimony content, and thus less amenable to processing.

    In short, "grey ore" and grey-ore copper came to be regarded as less desirable than chalcopyrite ores and their derived copper, once bronze metallurgy had developed to maturity. Thus the widespread emergence of grey-ore copper as the material of choice after 1100 BC can be explained as a response to necessity – the fact that deposits of chalcopyrite ores of suitable quality and availability for mining were no longer sufficient to cover the rising demand for copper or were indeed already nearing depletion. This development can be traced directly, for example, in the discontinuation of mining in one of the most important Bronze Age chalcopyrite mines – the main shaft of the Mitterberg in Salzburg – which was

kind of alliance with respect to the mining, distribution and processing of copper, a union that began to dissolve as mining ceased in Salzburg and Kitzbühel.

    The end of the mining boom in the lower Inn Valley of northern Tyrol that came later was heralded first by migrations as early as the 11th century BC. The "concentrations" of settlements in the southern Bavarian piedmont region (including the area around Munich) which had emerged during the heyday of Alpine copper mining began to disintegrate in the 11th century BC. The region's flourishing metalworking trade, whose swords and knives had set standards for the entire region of southern Germany and even into Switzerland and eastern France, stagnated. Leadership in the development of new metal forms shifted to the north-western Alpine piedmont.   49

3 "Heidenzechen" at Eiblschrofen near Schwaz in the Inn Valley of the North Tyrol: probably a prehistoric copper mine (open-cast).

Recent analytical studies of metals have cast new light on these events. Despite the presence of rich deposits of "grey ore" in the lower Inn Valley in northern Tyrol, mining operations focused exclusively on chalcopyrite ore during the middle and early Late Bronze Ages. Systematic grey-ore mining did not begin until the late 12th century BC, from which point it grew steadily. It was not until the end of the copper boom in northern Tyrol around the mid 10th century BC, however, that grey-ore copper from the lower Inn Valley was accepted as a worthy material in its own right. Until then, it had always (and not only in northern Tyrol) been alloyed with chalcopyrite copper. If we assume that the shift in favour of grey-ore copper was triggered by the increasing depletion of chalcopyrite ore deposits in northern Tyrol, then it is clear that *large-scale* copper mining operations in the lower Inn Valley made sense only in conjunction with copper production in Salzburg and Kitzbühel. Without the chalcopyrite copper produced there, the grey-ore copper mined in the lower Inn Valley was marketable only to a limited extent. Thus the demise of the Salzburg and Kitzbühel (chalcopyrite) copper mines also led (during the period between 980 and 950 BC) to the decline of the once massive copper production operations in the lower Inn Valley of northern Tyrol. Like the Salzburg and Kitzbühel mining complexes, northern Tyrol was relegated to the status of a minor producer in a regional context.

Comparable to the metallurgical union comprised of Salzburg, northern Tyrol and southern Bavaria was another regional alliance that encompassed northern and western Switzerland and the copper mining regions of their Alpine hinterland, which extended from Montafon through Graubünden to Valais. Although little research has been done on Bronze Age copper mining in this region, V. Rychner's study on metal analyses offers a useful survey of the copper supply system in northern and western Switzerland. The increasing instability of supply after the 11th century BC is reflected here in multiple shifts of resources, the last and most decisive having occurred around or shortly after 900 BC, as the previously steady supply of new copper from the mines in the Alpine hinterland apparently ebbed substantially, forcing Swiss bronze artisans to rely predominantly upon recycled material and thus upon massive imports of metal from neighbouring regions.

By the beginning of the 9th century BC all of the northern Alpine copper mining areas – from the Salzburg Pinzgau to Valais in western Switzerland – had ceased to function as *major producers* of copper. The extensive copper-supply network that stretched from the Alps to the North Sea, which relied *primarily* upon the large mining areas for its infusions of new copper, began to fall apart. Local or regional supply systems began to form, drawing on numerous and widely distributed mining operations of small scale and only regional importance. The total quantity of metal in circulation appears to have diminished in the process. Evidence for this is provided, alongside other sources of information, by findings which show that no grey-ore copper from central Europe reached the tin-mining areas of north-western Europe after 900 BC, although such copper remained predominant in western central Europe. At the same time it is possible that the return flow of northern European tin was also disrupted. Appreciable shortages of copper, bronze and tin began to appear after the mid 9th century BC, at least to the extent verifiable on the basis of well documented finds in northern and western Switzerland. Here, and in other regions dependent upon tin from north-western Europe, we recognise the emergence of another technical crisis: the deterioration of the quality of the alloy used to make weapons, tools and sheet products as a result of the increasing lead concentrations in bronze, a development that becomes evident after 900 BC and is probably attributable to the use of tin naturally containing lead. The increasingly noticeable effects of lead produce greater heat-brittleness in bronze, making it difficult or impossible to work-harden metal for weapons and tools and also reducing the general workability of the metal in processing. Bronze Age casters and smiths were surely well aware of the negative effects of lead, as their efforts to obtain low-lead or lead-free alloys for heavy-duty products and materials, particularly for sword blades and hammered items, clearly indicate. Yet the trend was apparently irreversible. Analyses of bronze objects from Swiss lakeside settlements of the latter half of the 9th century BC show that the use of tin with high concentrations of lead ultimately impaired alloy consistency. It had become very difficult to produce bronze of an assured high quality.

Given the constraints imposed by problems in the supply of copper and bronze and the deterioration of quality in such metals as were available, the use of iron now became more attractive from both a technical and an economic standpoint. The first swords and spear points made of iron or soft steel were produced – with an astounding command of iron technology – during the latter half of the 9th century BC. And from that point on the use of iron increased steadily until, in the early 8th century BC, bronze was abandoned completely as a material for the production of weapons, tools and cutting implements.

The above remarks are based to a significant extent upon unpublished papers by the author and a study fund-

4 Evidence of Late Bronze Age copper smelting, seen during excavation at Flinstbach (Rosenheim) at the mouth of the Inn Valley (11th century BC). Numerous whole and broken furnace ingots of copper, with a total weight of more than one hundred kg, have been recovered; all were smelted from antimony tetrahedrite ores mined in the lower Inn Valley. Here one of the plano-convex ingots has been completely exposed.

ed by the Volkswagen-Foundation on the production and marketing of Alpine copper in Salzburg, northern Tyrol and southern Bavaria during the Middle and Late Bronze Ages which was carried out by K.-P. Martinek, St. Möslein, E. Pernicka, L. Sperber and St. Winghart, and which is to be published in 1999.

Chapter 2

The Heroes and their Palaces
Editor: Albrecht Jockenhövel

◁ Head of warrior, Spata, Attica, Greece
Late Bronze Age (Cat. No. 47)

The Image of Bronze Age Man

Albrecht Jockenhövel

The images people of the Bronze Age in Europe created of themselves are consistently small in format and executed with little emphasis on naturalistic depiction. Even the golden masks from Grave Circle A at Mycenae, in which Heinrich Schliemann believed in his eagerness to have discovered the faces of Agamemnon, Cassandra and Eurymedon, the Homeric heroes murdered by Clytemnestra and Aigisthos, are not genuine portraits, although some individual characteristics are evident in the facial features of the male masks. In our efforts to recreate a living image of the people of the Bronze Age we are forced to rely upon corpses preserved in peat bogs, the remains of

bodies recovered from burial and cremation sites and other such evidence, which often provides information about living circumstances such as diseases (see Schultz, pp. 73ff.) as well. Remains of textile clothing and decorative metal items also give us a certain impression of Bronze Age modes of dress (see Schumacher-Matthäus, pp. 79ff.).

The Early Bronze Age marble idols with their highly schematic forms (especially in the so-called "violin idols", Cat. No. 16) found on the Cyclades, an island group in the Aegean, represent, on the one hand, the culmination of developments in the abstract articulation of late Stone Age statues; at the same time, they illustrate the turning point towards a more natural depiction of the human body, as is particularly evident in the rarer figures of the flute and harp players. These idols were ordinarily placed in graves and are viewed by many scholars as images of divinities. (Cat. Nos. 17, 18)

A large number of clay and metal figures from the Minoan and Mycenaean cultures have been identified. Among the three-dimensional anthropomorphic idols made of clay by the Mycenaeans we can distinguish between two significant types, known as "psi" and "phi" figurines – both fairly schematic (Cat. Nos. 64, 66). The "psi" figures are characterised by raised arms, a gesture explained as a symbol of divine epiphany. The Minoans were more concerned at times in achieving a more naturalistic impression; an early example is the dagger-bearing figure from Petsofas, fixed in an attitude of adoration (Cat. No. 45). Later examples in bronze and in ivory, in particular, are capable of portraying anatomical details such as musculature and veining. Life-sized Bronze Age images of divinities are virtually unknown. Such figures were presumably made of perishable materials like wood.

Few bronze figures have been preserved in regions beyond the boundaries of the Aegean. Only the island of Sardinia witnessed an astonishing proliferation of small figures, in most cases representations of fully-armed and armoured warriors (see Lo Schiavo, pp. 123f.). The most noteworthy treasure preserved from the Nordic Bronze Age is the unique ensemble of the "Sun chariot of Trundholm", the largest sculpture produced in non-Aegean

1   Male figurine, Amorgos,
    Cyclades, Greece
    Early Bronze Age
    (Cat. No. 18)

2   Female figurine, Naxos,
    Cyclades, Greece
    Early Bronze Age
    (Cat. No. 17)

3   Piriform jar, Prosymna, Argolid, Greece   ▷
    Late Bronze Age (Cat. No. 27)

54

4   Cult object, Balkåkra, Scania, Sweden
     Early Bronze Age (Cat. No. 130)

Europe during the Bronze Age (Cat. No. 175, see Mohen, pp. 20ff.). The placement of clay statues in graves was common practice along the lower reaches of the Danube during the Middle Bronze Age (Cat. No. 111). The decorations on these pieces give us some idea of traditional modes of dress in the region.

Bronze Age Man and his Lifestyles

The Homeric kings lived in palaces. Telemachus visited the ageing Nestor, King of Pylos, and admired the magnificent architecture and interior furnishings of his palace. Significant portions of "Nestor's Palace" have been reconstructed in the course of excavations undertaken by Carl Blegen above the Bay of Pylos, where the adjacent harbour – a basin whose water level could be controlled – was discovered quite recently. Research at the less well-preserved palace complexes of Mycenae and Tiryns has provided additional clues regarding the basic scheme upon which these residences were built (see Demakopoulou, pp. 66ff.). The plan was based upon the principle of ascent towards the ruler, beginning at the point of entry through a heavily-armoured entrance gate (cf. the heraldic Lion Gate of Mycenae) and leading along corridors, up stairways and through anterooms before opening into the central palace hall – the megaron, with its central fireplace and throne positioned to one side. The impression gained by the visitor called to the ruler's pres-

ence is heightened by numerous frescoes in which the marine world is displayed in images of dolphins, squids and the like – motifs that also appear in ceramics of the period (Cat. Nos. 26, 27).

The world of the palaces, of royal residences, disappeared along with Mycenaean culture itself. The recently discovered hall-like longhouse of Lefkandi (dating from the 10th century BC) gives us an impression of the appearance of rulers' houses during the pre-Homeric "Dark Ages".

Structurally comparable residential architecture is practically unknown outside the Aegean region (see Kovács, p. 65, Jockenhövel, pp. 71f. and Oliveira Jorge, pp. 60ff.). Only a very few individual structures of noteworthy size and furnishings are attributable to Bronze Age rulers, among them the stone structure in Pantalica on the island of Sicily. Central European Bronze Age architecture pales in comparison to that of the Aegean palaces. Even given the limitations imposed by the current state of research, it is worth noting that no clearly identifiable residential areas or palatial houses inhabited by the undoubtedly existent upper class, the warrior nobility, have been found in the building structures themselves. As things now stand, the significant distinctions between the various "classes" of Bronze Age society, often clearly discernible in graves, are impossible to establish in the "world of the living". Although no satisfactory explanation for this has yet been found, it is possible that the elite distinguished itself primarily on the basis of individual ability and prestige or, in other words, through its charisma (Max Weber). Their elevated position had to be reaffirmed again and again; it could not, or did not need to be, emphasised in permanent architecture, for it is apparent that acquired status (even ruling status) was not hereditary among the "barbaric" chieftains and could not be passed from generation to generation.

The climatic conditions that prevailed during the European Bronze Age, accompanied in many cases by drastic changes in secular society, inhibited the growth of highly stable social and economic structures in European populations beyond the boundaries of the Aegean region. The history of the Bronze Age "pile-built" settlements set very near bodies of water (see Pétrequin, pp. 70ff.) provides eloquent testimony to this fact.

Precious goods made of gold, bronze, tin, amber and glass as well as other valuable materials, including ivory imported from the Mediterranean region, have been found in many Bronze Age settlements in central, northern and western Europe. Wide-ranging contacts within the framework of regional patterns of distribution offered opportunities for trade in raw materials and finished products. Such goods were also acquired, as in the case of the Homeric heroes, in the course of plundering raids or as gifts in ritual exchanges between guests and hosts. Precious gifts symbolised alliances among Bronze Age chieftains or larger groups. Women were also exchanged, as evidenced by the appearance of "foreign" modes of dress in some areas, for the purpose of sealing personal or political pacts.

Men and Women

The Bronze Age male upper class is characterised by the warrior's weaponry and armour. Although weaponry evolved rapidly throughout the Bronze Age, the central representative figure of Early Bronze Age society was the dagger-bearing warrior (Cat. Nos. 159–163), who was replaced by the sword-wielding fighter beginning in the Middle Bronze Age (Cat. Nos. 166–168). These armed figures have been identified all over Europe – either in richly furnished graves or as images in rock paintings (see Capelle, pp. 153ff.) and on stelaei (see Oliveira Jorge, pp. 114ff. and 137ff.). Magnificently outfitted women stood at the side of the warrior class, although their equivalence in rank is frequently impossible to demonstrate (Cat. No. 106). The Bronze Age hierarchy that distinguished between the male and female worlds is also reflected in corresponding patterns of furnishings discovered in settlement sites (Cat. Nos. 114–118).

Vehicles and Horses: Technical and Social Innovation in Europe

The Mycenaean warrior heroes rode into battle in two-wheeled, horse-drawn chariots. Henceforth, vehicles and horses – the latter did not appear until quite late in the Bronze Age – would become symbols of an aristocratic lifestyle in Europe, both during the lifetimes of rulers and chieftains and on their final journey to the hereafter (see Dietz, pp. 83f., and Pare, pp. 125f.). Models of

5   Model of a group of dancers, Palaikastro, Crete, Greece
    Late Bronze Age (Cat. No. 40)

wagons, preserved metal parts from large wooden wagons, bronze wheels (Cat. Nos. 126–128) and harnesses (Cat. No. 129) are frequently found in richly-furnished graves and settlement sites, but also played a role in sacrificial rituals.

The Pastimes of Bronze Age Lords: Hunting, Games, Music and Dance

Aside from warfare, hunting played a major role in the life of the Bronze Age aristocracy. The lion hunt was of considerable social significance among Mycenaean rulers, much as it was among the great kings of Assyria. The dangerous wild boar was also a popular prey of hunters, not least as a source of the valuable boar's tusks used to decorate Mycenaean helmets (Cat. No. 49). Between twenty and thirty boars had to be killed in order to accumulate enough tusks for one helmet. As we learn from Homer, these precious helmets were passed down from generation to generation. Although such helmets were unknown in central Europe, boar's tusks were regarded as precious items there as well and often worn as trophies in intricately worked necklaces or amulets (Cat. Nos. 109, 110).

57

6 Acrobat-figurine, Grevensvænge, Denmark, Late Bronze Age (Cat. No. 136)

8 Bird-shaped rattles, several findspots, Poland, Late Bronze Age (Cat. No. 141)

7 Knife with hilt in form of female figure, Beringstedt, Schleswig-Holstein, Germany, Late Bronze Age (Cat. No. 112)

The furnishings of aristocratic kitchens included, among other things, clay fire dogs and bronze roasting spits and fleshhooks. Noteworthy items of tableware were the gold and bronze vessels such as buckets (Cat. Nos. 213, 211), large cauldrons (Cat. No. 210), cups (Cat. Nos. 210, 213), sieves and basins. A number of Bronze Age drinking horns made of bronze (Cat. No. 212), clay and of horn itself have been preserved. Many implements and vessels, particularly those decorated with symbolic elements such as bird motifs or comparable symbolic adornments, were presumably used in religious rites as well, as in the case of the golden hats (see Menghin and Springer, pp. 172ff. and Cat. Nos. 204–207). Metal keys, the oldest known to exist in Europe, were employed to safeguard property – to lock doors or chests, for example.

Games (especially those played with dice carved from bone), music and dance were the forms of entertainment most preferred by Bronze Age rulers and their entourages. Depicted in a fresco from "Nestor's Palace" near Pylos is a man playing a lute, perhaps as an accompaniment to a Mycenaean heroic ballad. A diverse range of musical instruments was produced during the European Bronze Age. Of particular interest are the remarkable bronze lurs, the trumpets found only in Bronze Age northern Europe (Cat. Nos 132, 133), and a type of horn pre-

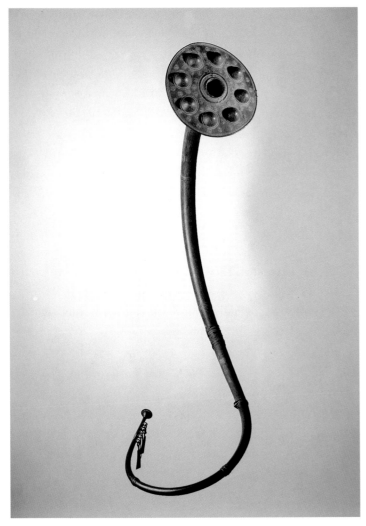

9   Lur, Brudevælte, Lynge, Zealand, Denmark
    Late Bronze Age (Cat. No. 132)

10   Lur, Brudevælte, Lynge, Zealand, Denmark
     Late Bronze Age (Cat. No. 133)

served only in Ireland (Cat. Nos. 134, 135). Also quite popular in the Lausitz culture of eastern central Europe were bird-shaped clay rattles filled with pellets (Cat. Nos. 140, 141). Highly unique are the two objects, presumably drums, found in Hasfalva (Cat. No. 130) and Balkåkra (Cat. No. 131), whose virtually identical manufacturing techniques clearly identify them as products of the same workshop. Bronze cymbals, known as "tintinnabula" (Cat. No. 139), and clapper plates are as much a part of the inventory of Bronze Age musical instruments as the singular Hochborn sistrum (Cat. No. 138) and a variety of flutes (Cat. No. 137), including panpipes.

Depictions of groups of figures such as those found on the piece modelled in clay from Palaikastro (Crete,

Cat. No. 40) and shown on the belt plate from Roga (Mecklenburg, Germany, Cat. No. 185) document the popularity of the round dance during the Bronze Age, while comparable items from Grevensvaenge (Denmark, Cat. No. 136) show figures performing acrobatic leaps, akin perhaps to the bull-leaping games of the Minoan culture. War dances are depicted in the rock paintings of the late Nordic Bronze Age and the early Iron Age in Val Camonica (northern Italy). However, music and dance, the twin Muses, were not merely forms of worldly amusement during the Bronze Age but also served as essential elements of magic and religious ceremonial rites.

Bronze Age Settlements and Territories on the Iberian Peninsula: New Considerations

Susana Oliveira Jorge

The 1st millennium BC witnessed the establishment of many settlements on the Iberian Peninsula. Surrounded by walls of many different types and characterised by varying degrees of permanence, these settlements formed a diverse range of ecosystems determined by their specific economic and social characteristics. Thus the term "fortified settlement" takes on a variety of meanings during this period. The only consistently observed feature is their general architecture. All of the settlements in question were enclosed by stone constructions of varying degrees of permanence, visibility and scale. The size of inhabited areas was smaller than it had been during the 4th millennium BC and was generally restricted to the space enclosed by the surrounding wall.

The first question that arises relates to the purpose of such stone walls. We believe that they make sense only within the context of functions which themselves relate to the larger framework that is observable in this broad geographical territory. Quite apart from their purpose as protective barriers in particular historical situations, the walls that enclosed settlements such as Los Millares (Almeria), Zambujal (Estremadura) or Castelo Velho (Trás-os-Montes and Alto Douro) (Ill. 1) must be seen as communication facilities erected in support of particular territorial structures and meant to identify communities. Indeed, a closer examination of the regions in which such walled settlements are located reveals the presence of a common characteristic: a new approach to the appropriation of land and, accordingly, the need for new forms of representation.

After the end of the 4th millennium BC we observe the appearance of durable agrarian facilities and practices (which admittedly involved widely differing applications of technology and human labour) wherever such "fortified settlements" emerge. These facilities and practices include irrigation systems (e.g. in the south-eastern region of the peninsula) (Gilman & Thornes 1985; Chap-

man 1991) or other forms of intensive cultivation such as the practice of allowing fields to lie fallow for brief periods. All such facilities imply the uninterrupted occupation of a given settled area over a long period of time, and we are reminded of the chronological lifetimes of settlements like Los Millares, Zambujal, Castelo Velho and others (Ill. 2 and 3). Thus one cannot separate these agricultural facilities from the trend towards systematic, long-term claims to dominion over land in territories whose boundaries were becoming much more clearly identifiable in both conceptual and geographic terms. The transition from the 4th to the 3th millennium BC was accompanied by the transition from undefined territories to generally smaller ones with both real and cognitively perceived boundaries, in which dichotomies such as inside/outside and internal/external became increasingly relevant.

Dominion over these new territories by largely non-hierarchical and politically decentralised groups required a much more obvious identification of boundaries, an unmistakable partitioning of space. The new form of rule demanded a different definition of power, which in turn implied a corresponding perception of territorial hegemony. Like the shrines with "stelai" of the Cabezo da Mina type (see Chapter IV of this catalogue), the walled settle-

1 Location of some of the finds mentioned in the text: 1 = Cabezo da Mina; 2 = Castelo Velho; 3 = Bouça do Frade; 4 = Zambujal; 5 = El Acequión (of the Motillas group); 6 = Los Millares; 7 = El Argar.

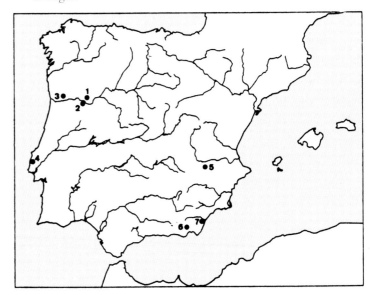

ments of the 3rd millennium reproduced – regardless of the network of contextual relationships that linked them together – a new sense of identity at the local level, new individual and collective perceptions of social life. During the Copper Age, walled settlements and cult sites were the clearest expression of this new form of territorial dominion.

The El Argar Culture and Beyond

Traditionally, archaeologists concerned with the early and middle phases of the Bronze Age have distinguished between the Southeast, where the so-called "Argaric Culture" (Lull 1983) flourished, from the other parts of the Iberian Peninsula, which were supposedly occupied by less complex groups characterised by Copper Age traditions (Chapman 1991; Barceló 1991; Díaz-Andreu 1993; García-Sanjuán 1994).

According to this view, Argaric society showed a high degree of complexity, as expressed in the permanent features of a large number of settlements, of which several reveal the presence of decidedly proto-urban characteristics. Within these settlements we recognise areas and structures specialised in different types of production – of a metallurgical nature – and the existence of hierarchically organised burial sites in which at least five distinct social classes can be identified. In summary, it can be said that by imposing hierarchical structures (which also extended to areas with complementary resources) upon the population, Argaric society achieved an advanced level of economic intensity and specialisation as well as a high degree of regional integration and interdependence.

In contrast to the "complexity" of the Southeast, the rest of the peninsula remained in cultural semi-darkness. If we look for the classical indicators of complexity beyond the boundaries of the south-eastern region we encounter the following general situation. During the Early and Middle Bronze Ages, many walled settlements with Copper Age traditions continued to survive in a number of areas distant from the Southeast. Several specific examples have been discussed in publications: the settlement of Castelo Velho in the Douro Valley (Oliveira Jorge S. 1993), in the Portuguese part of the Estremadura at Zambujal (Phase V) (Sangmeister & Schubart 1981); various walled settlements from this period are

2   Aerial photo showing the Copper and Bronze Age settlements of Castelo Velho (V. N. de Foz Côa, Portugal)

also found to the south of the northern Meseta (Fabián García 1993). Located along the upper Guadalquivir is the Early Bronze Age settlement of Peñalosa (Contreras Cortés 1995) – one of the few places in which we find features of the Argaric periphery. The Motillas group (Martin et al 1993; Fernández-Posse et al 1996) in La Mancha may also be viewed within the context of the Argaric realm. Yet once we leave the regions bordering on the Southeast, whose walled constructions can be explained with reference to their proximity to Argaric society, and turn our attention to the largely unpublished finds of other areas, we discover that permanent settlements existed in practically every part of the Peninsula, although they were fewer in number than during the preceding period.

Aside from the signs of complexity mentioned above, we encounter other expressions of territorial hegemony. These include stelai from the religious sites or burial grounds in the western part of the Peninsula; burial sites   61 evidencing a certain degree of architectural complexity, such as the older graves of Atalaia (Alentejo) (Schubart 1975; García-Sanjuán 1994) or the monument of Outeiro de Gregos 1 in the province of Douro litoral (Oliveira Jorge S. 1989); grave treasures suggesting a certain degree of wealth in the vicinity of Montelavar-Ferradeira; cliffs bearing engraved depictions of weapons in the Northwest, seen within the context of "Galician-Portuguese art" (Peña Santos & Rey García 1993) and hoards containing metal and other types of artefacts. This panorama essentially refutes the supposed dichotomy between the Southeast and the other regions of the Peninsula.

Yet what does distinguish Argaric society from the other societies on the Peninsula during this period are the relatively enclosed structure of its barter-trade network and the presence of clearly defined social categories.

The overall archaeology of the El Argar period suggests the existence of fixed groups practising "prestige economy" under the influence of the barter-trade system in a climate of strong competition. In contrast, the other regions, particularly those bordering on the Atlantic, were populated by societies which produced, processed and marketed metal – regardless of the extent to which they were hierarchically structured – perhaps even within the larger framework of interregional barter-trade zones. This barter system promoted the circulation of prototype metal products along the European Atlantic coast and led to increasing differentiation in the use of these metal objects. Thus the availability of such metal objects contributed to the tendency to abandon original communal symbolism and encouraged the shift away from the traditional economy towards the early mercantile phase (Sherratt 1993) that would characterise the Late Bronze Age. Regardless of the relative capacities of their elites for leadership, many societies on the Iberian Peninsula appear to have been far more open and permeable than those in the Southeast. In our opinion, however, this difference relates less to the dominance of "social complexity" than to principles of social organisation that deserve scrutiny from an entirely different perspective.

Late Bronze Age Territories

A discussion of Late Bronze Age settlements on the Iberian Peninsula would be incomplete without an examination of the complex problem of stability and/or the duration of territorial dominion.

In approaching the peninsula as a whole, we recognise major regional differences in living conditions and settlement population density. Yet settlements which offered natural protection, particularly those with defensive fortifications, were in the minority. Most settlements of the Late Bronze Age were open and consisted of houses built with apparent disregard for permanence (Oliveira Jorge S. 1990). One example is the settlement of Bouça do Frade in northern Portugal, where we find evidence of mining activity (Oliveira Jorge S. 1988) (Ill. 1). Furthermore, it has been shown that a number of settlements in

3   Fortification of the upper area of Castelo Velho with the western entrance, viewed from within.

which evidence of intensive metallurgical production has been found were characterised by buildings of relatively unstable construction.

On the other hand, we undoubtedly face a deficiency in research with respect to forms of territorial dominion and the identification of territorial boundaries in Late Bronze Age societies. The generally observable tendency towards buildings constructed for short-term durability coexists alongside evidence of specialised production activities associated with just such building structures. And that is not in line with the instability and the nomadic lifestyle postulated for Late Bronze Age populations by many scholars.

4 Detail from the wall enclosing the upper area of Castelo Velho (after restoration) with the outer bastion.

It seems reasonable to relate the "fortified settlements" of the Late Bronze Age with the entirely new phenomenon of territorialisation on the Iberian Peninsula. Unlike the walled settlements of the Copper Age, Late Bronze Age fortifications were not communication facilities erected in support of isolated colonisation movements and for the purpose of enhancing social identification. In order to comprehend the diversity of function that characterised these fortifications we need to examine some of the new scenarios of territorial dominion.

It is now a generally accepted fact that the settlements and "stelai" or menhirs of the Late Bronze Age document the emergence of hereditary forms of rule in societies dispersed over broad segments of territory on the Peninsula.

According to a study published by E. Galán Domingo (1993), the stelai found in the Southwest served as visible landscape signs referring to routes of communication that linked the south-western interior with its more southerly fringe areas. Thus the stelai represent territorial markers; they appeared at a time in which neighbouring groups preparing to establish settlements posed a threat to the already settled inhabitants of the Southwest. The latter groups, Galán suggests, erected these monuments (particularly on the fringes of their politically organised settlement areas – that is, where the potential for conflict was greatest) in order to strengthen community solidarity and to spread the word that a given area belonged to a specific group and/or a specific territory. Galán is of the opinion that the images on the stelai do not refer to actual objects within their effective reach but are instead to be interpreted metaphorically, rather than realistically. He believes that their respective meanings took shape as they would in language and that their forms referred to original objects located a considerable distance away. These forms, he writes, had special meanings which only members of groups with the same system of identification were capable of understanding.

This interpretation of the stelai is compatible with another basic idea – namely, that during this era the Iberian Peninsula represented the western fringe of a centre located in the eastern Mediterranean region and thus formed part of a larger interactive system – centre-periphery-fringe – a view shared by Sherratt (1993; 63

Galán Domingo 1993) as well. According to this theory, elements expressive of formal links to the Mediterranean world (images engraved in stelai, grave treasures or metal artefacts in settlements) are to be viewed as local products of interregional barter-trade systems that linked the Mediterranean, the Atlantic coast and central Europe together.

If we accept the plausible assumption that all local products represent transformations of the original meanings of their corresponding prototypes, it becomes clear that they can hardly be interpreted in the absence of a prior contextual analysis of the societies in question. The territories of the Late Bronze Age, themselves the products of significant transcultural interactions, reveal a difficult history of identification. Indeed, beginning in the 1st millennium BC, changing patterns of coexistence or alternation between different stages of barter-trade economies, coupled with the evolution of new forms of accumulation and means of demonstrating wealth, contributed to the destruction of the social and political structures of many social groups on the Iberian Peninsula.

Bibliography: Barceló 1991; Chapman 1991; Contreras Cortés 1995; Díaz-Andreu 1993; Galán Domingo 1993; Fábian García 1993; Fernández-Posse et al 1996; García-Sanjuán 1994; Gilman & Thornes 1985; Oliveira Jorge S. 1988, Oliveira Jorge V.1989.
Oliveira Jorge S. 1990, 1993, 1998; Lull 1983; Martin et al 1993; Peña Santos & Rey García 1993; Sangmeister & Schubart 1981; Schubart 1975; Sherratt 1993.

1   Turkeve-Terehalom, plan of house from level 4 (unpublished)

2   Turkeve-Terehalom, reconstruction of a house from level 4 (unpublished)

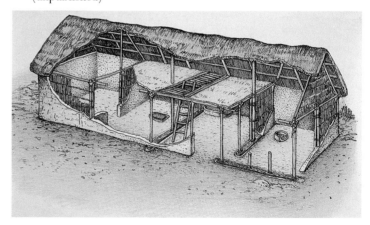

Tell Settlement in the Danube Region

Tibor Kovács

The stratified settlements in the Danube region, whose investigation was begun in the 1870s, were first considered, after L. Pigorini, the Central and Eastern European variants of the *terramare* settlements of Italy. This mistake was only corrected a few decades later when V. G. Childe noted the Near Eastern origins of this distinctive prehistoric settlement type. Even though the stratified settlements of Eastern Europe and the Lower Danube region can hardly be equated with the classical tells of Asia Minor – such as Alaca Hüyük, Demirci Hüyük and Poliochni, yet these settlements do share one definite feature with the genuine tells. Namely, that following the destruction or decay of buildings, their remains were levelled and the new buildings were erected over the old ones in the same spot. Thus the internal disposition of streets and houses remained virtually unchanged for long generations. It was only the settlement mound, the tell itself, which grew in height. Any actual changes in settlement layout, as observed for example at Békés, Tószeg and Jászdózsa, can be usually attributed to cultural and/or ethnic changes. The tell as a characteristic settlement form was a distinguishing feature of a sedentary way of life: one founded on an economy of grain cultivation and animal husbandry which had evolved in the ancient Near East. This permanent basis for the peasant culture which came to dominate the pattern of life of the inhabitants of the Danube region was spread less through migrations than through the agency of diffusion. It would appear that both in the Late Neolithic and in the Early Bronze Age, the tell settlements in the Danube and the Tisza region usually evolved in areas where favourable environmental conditions were combined with a socio-economic stability; the last factor developed as a consequence of ethnic population movements. Together they permitted the emergence and floreat of this southern-style economy.

The core area of European Bronze Age tells (and the so-called "tell cultures") lay in the Carpathian Basin and the area bordering it to the south: in the first half of the 2nd millennium BC this region was occupied by the Nagyrév, Hatvan, Otomani, Porjámos, Vatin, Vatya, Füzesabony and Madárovce cultures.

These tells, often occupied during several successive cultural periods (Vèsztö, Vinča, Gomolava, Malé Kosihy), usually evolved at the "ecological centre" of a small region where environmental conditions were the most favourable. They may be found situated at readily-defensible river bends (Békés, Socodor, Vèsztö), on loess plateaus along the Maros and the Danube (Pecica, Bölcske, Dunaújváros), and in the mountain uplands (Pákozd, Szécsény). Houses were one- or two-roomed. Most were timber-framed and daubed with clay, although log cabins built entirely of wood are also known (for example at Békés). Floors were sometimes covered with rushwork matting; occasionally they even had a wooden substructure (as at Jászdózsa, Tiszafüred and Barca). Such a tell settlement, often divided into an "acropolis" and a "town", acted as the major centre of a given culture. Accordingly they invariably played an important role in trade (Tószeg), were often important centres of metalworking (Možorin, Dunaújváros, Tiszafüred, Nitriansky Hrádok, Barca) and they often functioned as cult centres. This last is shown by the presence of bothroi (Berettyó Újfalú), of a sanctuary (Salač), or of models of wagons and of human or animal statuettes. Representations of humans, animals and weapons have been found on these sites (Füzesabony, Tószeg, Pákozd).

Extending over an area of 0.5 to 1.5 hectares and often accumulating several metres of cultural deposits (Békés: 3.1 m, Jászdózsa: 5.4 m, Tószeg: originally 8 m), these tell and tell-like settlements are one of the most important sources of information about the Bronze Age in this region. Potentially the tells of the Danube region were the predecessors to towns with stone-built houses. However, traces indicating such a development have so far only been uncovered at Spišský Štvrtok and at Velím (from a later period).

Bibliography: Kovács & Stanczik 1988; Meier-Arendt 1992; Tasic 1984.

Aegean Palaces

Katie Demakopoulou

The earliest monumental buildings, which probably served as administrative centres or as the residence of the local ruler, made their appearance in the Aegean during the second phase of the Early Bronze Age (c. 2900–2400 BC), when Central Greece and the Peloponnese were on the verge of developing an advanced civilisation. The major achievements of this period, which reveal the existence of a complex social and political organisation, lay in the spheres of architecture, with the erection of monumental buildings known as "corridor houses" in Boeotia, parts of the Peloponnese and Aegina; of administration, with the use of seals and archives in which to keep them; and of innovations in the storing of produce. All these achievements vanish, however, at the end of the Early Helladic II period, to be followed by a period of cultural regression, which ended in Mainland Greece at the beginning of the Mycenaean Age in 1600 BC.

True palaces, as centres of a strong, central authority, first appeared in Crete at the beginning of the Middle Bronze Age. The Palace Period in Crete and Mainland Greece, is divided into three phases: the First Palace Period, during which the first palaces were built in Crete (c. 2000–1700 BC); the Second Palace Period, in which newer, more splendid palaces were erected in Crete (c. 1700–1450 BC); and the Third Palace Period, which is associated with the construction and functioning of palaces on Mainland Greece (c. 1450–1200 BC).

The first palaces in Crete were erected on sites later occupied by the second palaces. They were fairly large, with a ground floor and upper storeys, and were carefully constructed. The walls were built of rubble and mudbrick and strengthened with timbers. The facades were reinforced with large dressed blocks of stone and, in long walls, use was made at intervals of orthostats, i.e. slabs set vertically. The walls and floors of rooms were decorated with paintings, which made their appearance as early as this First Palace Period.

The large palace complexes of Crete during the Second Palace Period were erected at Knossos (Ill. 1), Phaistos, Mallia and Zakros. They were much larger than the first palaces, and a greater variety of materials can now be observed, including coloured stones, gypsum and sandstone. The basic plan consists of a large number of halls, rooms and corridors set around a central courtyard, which is usually oriented north-south. The main facade was on the West, and in front of it there was another courtyard, presumably for public gatherings. The palace buildings may have a basement, ground floor and upper storeys. The ground floor was devoted to groups of rooms that will have been used as storerooms and workshops, though some of them were ceremonial rooms. The more spacious, formal suites, however, were on the upper storeys.

The main architectural features of these unique Minoan palaces are "polythyra" (multiple pier-and-door partitions), ceremonial halls, "lustral basins", monumental staircases, columns used in porches or porticoes, and the construction of a drainage system. Many of the rooms, particularly those of a formal nature, were decorated with magnificent wall-paintings depicting figured scenes.

The Minoan palaces were undoubtedly the residences of ruling families. However, the most formal rooms in the palaces were probably intended for religious or ceremonial purposes, or as reception rooms for visitors.

1   View of the Palace at Knossos

2–3 Plaques, "Town Mosaic", Knossos, Crete, Greece. Middle Bronze Age (Cat. Nos. 35–36)

The Cretan palaces were destroyed by an unknown cause, perhaps an earthquake or a war, about the middle of the 15ᵗʰ century BC, with the exception of the palace at Knossos, where a Mycenaean dynasty, which probably ruled the whole of Crete, established itself shortly afterwards.

In the Third Palace Period, palace complexes modelled on the Minoan palaces were constructed in Mycenaean Greece. The earliest buildings having the character of palaces appeared towards the end of the 15ᵗʰ century BC in the Menelaion in Lakonia, at Tiryns, at Nichoria in Messenia and at Phylakopi on Melos. True palace complexes, however, were only built later. The best preserved of them are those at Mycenae, Tiryns and Pylos. There were also palaces at other Mycenaean centres, however, such as Thebes, Orchomenos, the Athenian Acropolis, and Midea. Most of these were built within imposing fortified citadels (Ill. 4).

The design of Mycenaean palaces differed considerably from the Minoan, though there were several points of similarity in the overall conception, building materials, and construction methods. The main area was the "megaron" approached through a porch and an anteroom; this sizeable throne-room featured in its centre a circular hearth surrounded by four columns supporting the roof. Like other ceremonial rooms of the palace, it was lavishly adorned with wall-paintings (Ill. 5). In turn the megaron, which overlooked an inner courtyard, was surrounded by a large number of different-sized rooms, communication between which was secured by corridors, smaller courtyards, entrances and staircases that gave access to the upper storeys. At Pylos and Tiryns, a second, smaller megaron existed. There were also bathrooms, guest rooms and the residential quarters of the ruling family, probably on the upper storeys. Yet other rooms served as workshops and storerooms: some were intended

4   Aerial view of the acropolis at Mycenae with the palace on the summit of the hill.

for administration and the palace archives, which, in the case of Pylos, were located immediately inside the main entrance (Ill. 6).

The Mycenaean palace complexes were equipped with a drainage system, like the Cretan palaces. Though not as extensive and imposing as their models, they covered a fairly large area, and their overall appearance, with their structural volume and richly decorated interiors, was designed to show visitors the political and religious power of the ruler – the *wanax* of the Linear B tablets, who gave his name to the palace or *wanaktoron*.

The Mycenaean palaces were destroyed around the end of the 13th century BC. The causes of the destruction have not yet been fully elucidated, though some of the palaces were apparently struck by devastating earthquakes. In any event, their destruction led to the collapse of the palace economy and the palace system of government in the Aegean. In spite of the fact that a partial recovery has been detected in the Aegean in the Postpalatial Period, the decline of palatial power ushered in the end of the Mycenaean civilisation about two centuries later.

Bibliography: Cadogan 1976; Demakopoulou 1988; Dickinson 1994; Graham 1987; Iakovidis 1983; Kilian 1987, 1988.

5   Reconstruction of the throne room of the Palace at Pylos
    (Piet de Jong).

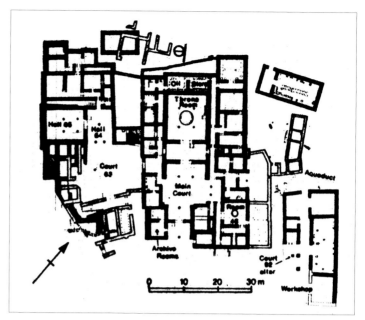

6   Plan of the Palace at Pylos (after Dickinson 1994, 156, Fig. 5.31).

Settlements in Wetland Areas

Pierre Pétrequin

The settlements established on moist ground throughout Europe serve as a remarkable example of adaptation to spongy, mechanically unstable soils subject to flooding. They are familiar as hamlets or villages with parallel streets and rectangular houses arranged in rows in the formerly swampy regions of the Po Valley (Italy) and on the banks of lakes to the northwest of the Alps. Thorough studies have been made at the community of Cortaillod (Switzerland), of the homes and grain storage structures built around a central square in the upper Swabian peat moors, in the Zurich area, of the rows of rectangular houses erected in shallow water both at Fiavè (Italy) and to the south of Lake Garda, and of the large round structures built on the man-made islands and the crannogs of Scotland and Ireland. For Bronze Age farmers, the distance thus created between their homes and fields was an expression of their concern for their own security, and this was all the more true in cases where villages were separated from solid ground by broad bands of swamp or even rivers or streams. The gap could only be negotiated with animal-drawn wagons or by driving flocks of smaller animals over a single path or bridge constructed of planks laid upon pairs of piles. This same concern is reflected in the presence of other enclosures, palisades or even wooden protective walls erected around the villages. The idea was to gather as many people as possible within the village area. In some cases, such as the town of Biskupin (Poland), as many as 105 small, virtually identical houses were built on a scant hectare of land.

Yet the social need for security required that planners and builders take the soft, floodable ground into account. During the Bronze Age, people in every region of Europe knew how to deal with the problems of wet ground, fluctuating water levels and weak mechanical soil stability. In some places, piles were driven deep into the underlying limestone (Chalain, France); in others, the ends of the supporting piles were rammed into holes in platforms made of broad planks (Zug-Sumpf, Switzerland); elsewhere, entire houses were built upon piles with floors mounted above the high-water mark (Fiavè, Italy).

The correlation between these elevated villages and the dry periods of the Bronze Age is quite evident, at least with respect to the region north of the Alps. These villages were frequently flooded and abandoned, particularly between the 15th and 12th centuries BC, during periods of extreme cold or glacial melting. Given these very difficult conditions, the construction of moist-ground settlements during the era of popular migrations between the 18th and 15th centuries BC and then again from the 11th to the 9th centuries BC appears an entirely reasonable measure.

Bronze Age Fortresses in Europe: Territorial Security

Albrecht Jockenhövel

No structures comparable to the palaces of the Minoan-Mycenaean culture are found outside of the Aegean region. In many areas of non-Aegean Europe, settlements are typically defensive in character and structured to offer protection against the weapons of war. Most of the core settlements of central Europe during the Bronze Age consisted of dense networks of fortifications comprised of walls, gateways and surrounding moats or trenches. Yet we recognise regional differences here as well, for this form of settlement was, with but a few exceptions, virtually unknown in the Nordic regions and on the British Isles during the Bronze Age.

Fortified settlements do not appear in central Europe during all phases of the Bronze Age but instead are concentrated within certain "fortress-building periods". The first of these began at the transition point between the Early and Middle Bronze Ages, the second at the threshold to the Late Bronze Age and the third at the end of the Bronze Age. Evidently, this ebb and flow of fortress construction relates to specific social, economic and environmental circumstances and the changes they underwent during given periods.

The size of these fortifications also varies over time. While the early fortified settlements were relatively small, encompassing no more than three hectares of enclosed space, the more recent ones are significantly larger, with enclosed spaces measuring thirty hectares and more. Unfortunately, no major excavations have been undertaken in such settlements, and thus their exact function remains to be determined. Slovakian archaeologists have succeeded in describing the diverse functions of the fortresses in that country. Some have been identified as seats of rulers and religious centres, while others were presumably established to meet the needs of specific types of artisan trades, such as pottery manufacture, bone and horn processing or metallurgy.

Fortified settlements were quite rare during the central European tumulus culture of the Bronze Age. It was not until the dawn of the Late Bronze Age, at the beginning of the Urnfield period, that such settlements began to appear in large numbers all over Europe – from the Rumanian Carpathian region to eastern France, from the Alps to the northern rim of the German Mittelgebirge mountain region, into the flatlands of north-eastern Germany and from there into the Lusatian culture of eastern Germany and Poland.

Fortresses are ordinarily found in naturally favourable defensive positions – on island refuges, on elevated ground rising from a plain or on spurs of land surrounded by rivers. In the lake landscapes of eastern Germany and Poland they are frequently located on hills above the high-water mark or on small peninsulas. Fea-

1 View of the Bullenheim Mountain (Lower and Central Franconia). The entire facade was supported by a wall of wood, earth and stone that has since collapsed: Late Bronze Age.

2 On Tafle Mountain, near Klentnice (Moravia), a large fortified settlement existed in the Late Bronze Age.

71

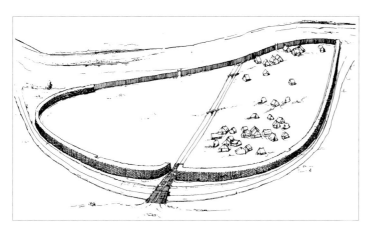

3   Reconstruction of the Early Bronze Age settlement of Nitriansky Hrádok (southwest Slovakia), giving an idea of the size and interior structure of a typical fortified site (15th–14th centuries BC)

tures of the local terrain determined the course of the ring-shaped or segmented (often artistically designed) protective walls of stone, earth and wood, which have since collapsed to form the ramparts we see today. Although a few exceptional settlements encompassed up to a hundred hectares, most enclosed spaces of about thirty hectares.

Nearly all of the fortresses erected during the Bronze Age contain abundant and often valuable archaeological material. Evidence of concentrated construction is often found, suggesting large numbers of inhabitants and extended periods of occupation. Consequently, such fortresses, built by the hands of many labourers, are no longer regarded as castles of refuge to which people retreated only in times of crisis but as continuously inhabited settlements.

It has not yet been possible to identify housing structures within those occupied by the Bronze Age elite. Presumably, no such structures existed – in contrast to the richly furnished graves which characterise the burial places of the upper class. Significant metal treasures have been uncovered in many fortresses – on Mount Bullenheim (Mittelfranken, Germany), for example, and in Blucina (southern Moravia). More than a dozen of such hoards have been found. Such accumulations of wealth apparently served both profane and religious purposes.

Such fortified settlements were also accompanied by "suburbs" of associated non-fortified agrarian settlements. As early "urban centres", they offered protection to the local settled communities, which may be compared to "tribes" in terms of their organisational structure. The territory they protected generally encompassed between fifty and one hundred and fifty square kilometres.

Fortresses disappeared in many parts of central Europe around the dawn of the Iron Age. Although the exact causes for this have not yet been determined, it is likely that a long-term deterioration of climatic conditions culminating in a period of cold, wet weather near the end of the Bronze Age was a significant contributing factor. Scholars also attribute the end of the northern Alpine "pile-built settlements" to the same climatic change (see Pétrequin, p. 70).

 Bibliography: Chropovsky & Hermann 1982; Jockenhövel 1990.

Bronze Age Man

Michael Schultz

Since time immemorial, man has lived with the dangers posed by his environment and faced the constant threat of illness and disease. Man's perpetual battle with illness has had a determining influence on the development of human cultures, although traditional archaeological research has uncovered little hard evidence of that fact. Now, palaeopathology, the medical study of archaeological skeletal finds, has made it possible to examine the role played by disease in the course of human development from the prehistoric era to the early phase of the historical period. The primary objective of palaeopathological research is to explore the type and nature of a particular disease, its origins and incidence and its distribution within a given prehistoric or historical population. In addition, the results of palaeopathological studies provide information about the conditions under which prehistoric and ancient man – and thus Bronze Age man as well – lived. We learn about the effects of nutrition, of living and working circumstances, of geographic and climatic influences, of sanitary facilities and hygienic practices on the health of the people of a given era (Schultz 1982).

Palaeopathology

Modern palaeopathology, a relatively young discipline, is actually an interdisciplinary research field which relies to an increasing extent upon innovative technologies. Methods and techniques employed in palaeopathological research (radiology, ordinary light and scanning electron microscopy, endoscopy, molecular biology) make it possible – given a sufficient degree of experience in their application – to arrive at very precise diagnoses. However, our knowledge of the aetiology (the study of the causes of disease) and epidemiology (the study of the incidence and spread of disease within a population) of the diseases that plagued prehistoric and early historical man is still rudimentary. For this reason, and due to differences in the condition of human skeletal finds resulting from variations in soil conditions, our palaeopathological knowledge about the diseases of Bronze Age man is still quite limited and restricted geographically to central Europe and parts of the Near East (e.g. eastern Turkey and Egypt).

The Physical Appearance of Bronze Age Man

The external morphological appearance of Bronze Age man was by no means uniform. We already recognise distinctions among the Early Bronze Age populations of central and eastern Europe. Even more marked were the morphological differences between central Europeans and peoples of the Near East during the Bronze Age. Studies of body height have shown, for example, that the average height of Early Bronze Age males in the region now known as lower Austria (Windl et al 1988) was between 169 and 171 cm, while that of women ranged from 159 to 161 cm. Thus the average values for height during the Early Bronze Age were only slightly less than those calculated for populations living in the same regions during the later Iron Age and the early Middle Ages.

Childhood Diseases

It is a generally accepted fact that childhood and old age are the two phases in the life of a human being when the immune system does not yet – or no longer – function at full capacity. Particularly sensitive to this deficiency are infants and very young children, especially at the point of transition from mother's milk to cereals and eventually to adult nourishment. Manifestations of malnutrition may appear during this phase, and these often produce immune-system deficiency. In such cases, children are highly susceptible to infectious diseases. Seasonal vitamin shortages may have similar consequences. Comparative population studies have shown that childhood disease serves as a highly sensitive indicator of the quality of life at a given point in time (Schultz 1994). Negative reactions to the transition from mother's milk to solid foods, malnutrition and the incidence of acute infectious diseases were probably the most important factors contributing to the relatively high infant and child mortality rates (between 40 and 60 per cent) that characterised the Bronze Age.

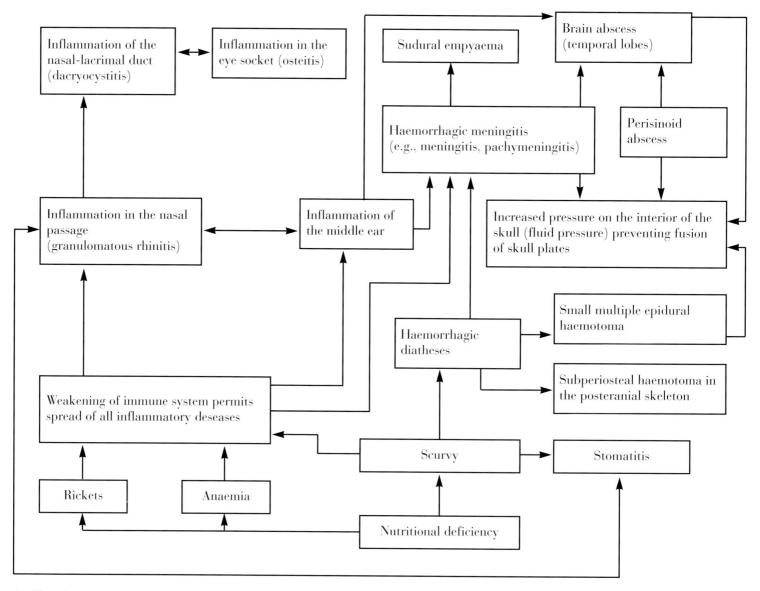

1   Flow chart. Aetiological relationships between various symptoms seen on the skeleton of a three- to four-years old
child; Middle Bronze Age (Lidar Hüyük, east Turkey).

The Aetiology of Childhood Diseases

The interplay of the factors cited above can be illustrated on the basis of an example (Ill. 1). The remains of a child from the Middle Bronze Age (c. 1800–1500 BC) were discovered at Lidar Höyük, a large tell settlement on the upper Euphrates (in what is now Turkey). The child was between three and four years old and had obviously suffered from severe malnutrition. The palaeopathological examination of the child's skeleton revealed signs of anaemia, scurvy (chronic vitamin C deficiency) and rickets (chronic vitamin D deficiency). The latter disease appears rarely in regions with high exposure to sunlight, since the effects of ultra-violet rays in the human organism ordinarily produces vitamin D from components already existing in the body. Where chronic vitamin D deficiency nevertheless appears in regions exposed to high levels of sunlight, other factors besides simple malnutrition must be taken into consideration (e.g. genetic factors, unusual long-term negative climatic trends). Given the deficiency disorders identified, this particular child's

74

immune system must have been severely impaired. This condition presumably favoured the development of a middle-ear infection, which in turn expanded as a form of mastoiditis well into the mastoid process and probably contributed to the formation of cystic inflammations in the nasal cavity and the paranasal sinuses (e.g. the sinus maxillaris). Side effects produced by the middle-ear infection – following the penetration of pus into the cranial cavity – included meningeal reactions (e.g. meningitis, subdural empyaema, cerebral abscess, perisinouos infection). The chronic vitamin C deficiency had increased the propensity for haemorrhaging, so that the meningitis produced minor intrusions of blood into the space between the vault of the skull and the dura mater or hard cerebral membrane (epidural haematoma). The increased accumulation of fluid triggered by the inflammatory process generated a substantial rise in intercranial pressure. As a result, the surface of the brain was pressed with considerable force against the interior surface of the cranial dome (brain-pressure symptoms). The inflammation in the nasal cavity spread via the ductus nasolacrimalis (nasal tear duct) into the orbita (eye-sockets). The child presumably died of generalised sepsis (blood poisoning) or meningitis.

The Epidemiology of Childhood Diseases

Significant insights with respect to a reconstruction of general health patterns and living conditions during the Early Bronze Age were provided by the palaeopathological examination of skeletons of children discovered in what is now Slovakia. The Slovakian archaeologist J. Bátora uncovered several hundred skeletons at the burial grounds of Jelšovce in the north-western Carpathian region, and these were examined from an anthropological perspective by J. Jakab. The skeletal finds presented here originated in the Nitra culture (c. 2200–1900 BC) and the Únětice culture (c. 1900–1700 BC). The palaeopathological examination of all of the children's skeletons from the Nitra and Únětice periods produced very interesting findings and cast revealing light upon the conditions under which these two different cultures lived (Schultz et al 1998). The group from the older Nitra population comprised 55 individuals, that from the younger Únětice culture a total of 45.

Nutritional Deficiency Disorders in Early Bronze Age Children

Signs of nutritional deficiency disorders were found in 53.2 per cent of the Nitra-period children and 61.9 per cent of the children from the Únětice culture. Anaemia was diagnosed in 17 per cent of the Nitra children and 38.7 of those from the Únětice group. Evidence of scurvy (chronic vitamin C deficiency, see Ill. 2 C) was found in 12.8 per cent of Nitra children and 21.4 per cent of the Únětice skeletons examined. Signs of rickets (chronic vitamin D deficiency) appeared in 2.1 per cent of Nitra and 7.1 of Únětice children. On the basis of the skeletons studied, the incidence of all three nutritional deficiency disorders was found to be much higher in the Únětice group. This clearly suggests a marked change in conditions, most notably those affecting nutrition, in the more recent culture of the Early Bronze Age in the Carpathian region.

Infectious Diseases among Children in Central Europe during the Early Bronze Age

Only those diseases most frequently identified in children of Early Bronze Age populations are cited in the following remarks. Signs of meningeal inflammation (e.g. meningitis) appeared in 11.6 per cent of skeletons from the Nitra culture. The figure rises to 20.7 per cent for the Únětice group. Not a single case of osteomyelitis was found in either group. Evidence of middle-ear infection and/or mastoiditis appeared in 11.6 per cent of the Nitra skeletons and 12.5 per cent of the Únětice children. No cases of sinusitis maxillaris were diagnosed among the children of the Nitra culture, while 15.8 per cent of the Únětice children showed signs of that disorder. As in the case of nutritional deficiency disorders, the children of the Únětice culture showed a significantly greater incidence of infectious disease in all cases.

Dental and Periodontal Disorders in Early Bronze Age Children

As a rule, tooth disorders and afflictions of the gums and supporting structures were relatively rare among children. Caries was identified in only 7.7 per cent of the Nitra population and 20 per cent of the skeletons from the Aunjetitz group. Periodontal disorders appeared

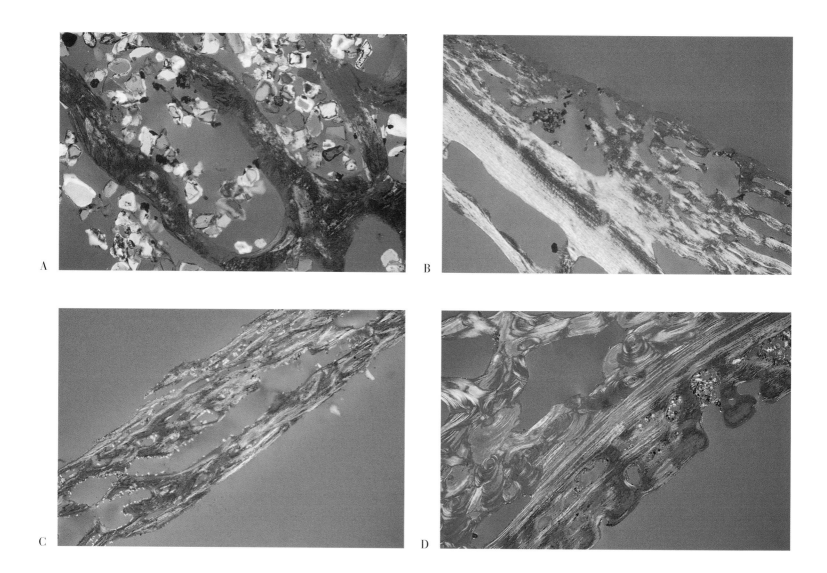

2 All photographs show: Sections of bone (50 µm) taken from child's skeleton retrieved in excavation.
Viewed under a microscope with polarised illumination using a quartz. Magnification 25 x.

A   Anaemia. Swollen surface of the skull with characteristic formation of the so-called "hair-on-end phenomen": parallel arrangement of vertical bone growth (with sand cristals).

B   Scurvy (chronic deficiency of vitamin C). Several layers of ossi-
fied material (following internal blood clotting. e. g. haemotoma)
on the external surface of the skull.

C   Rickets (chronic deficiency of vitamin C). Characteristic structures of the laminae and the diploe.

D   Inflammatory haemorrhagic meningitis. Internal surface ot the
skull vault (healing stage).

in 25.6 per cent of Nitra children; the figure rises to 45.8 per cent for the Aunjetitz culture. In many cases, gingival (gum) inflammation can be attributed to the accumulation of dental calculus, and only a very weak correlation is apparent among Early Bronze Age children. In this regard it should be noted, however, that at least a portion of the dental calculus accumulated during the lifetimes of these children could have been lost post-mortem – that is, after burial in the ground or in the course of cleaning procedures performed on the skeletal remains after exhumation. Only 2.6 per cent of the Nitra population showed evidence of dental calculus formation, while plaque was detected in 32 per cent of the children from the Aunjetitz group. The Aunjetitz population also showed a considerably higher incidence of dental and periodontal disorders than the Nitra population.

Surgery and Injuries to the Cranium

Skulls showing evidence of surgical opening (cranial trepanation) have been found in many European burial areas from the Bronze Age. It should be noted that 90 per cent of such cases represent deliberate surgical interventions and that no surgery was performed on the brain in any of them. Many of the trepanned skulls show signs of a previous cranial trauma. In such cases, the cranium was obviously opened in order to "let out the evil spirit" or to provide a drain in the presence of epidural haemorrhaging (between the skull and the hard cerebral membrane) and thus to relieve potentially fatal intercranial pressure. Other indications are also conceivable, however (e.g. chronic headache, symptoms of neurological dysfunction in the area of the head). Thus the majority of cases of trepanation identified were undertaken as treatment for a pathological process. Given the state of medical knowledge at the time, injury or perforation of the hard cerebral membrane would inevitably have led to the death of the individual. In prehistoric and early historical times, four different techniques for opening the skull were known (scraping, round-cut, drilling and incision techniques). Of these, the scraping technique appears to have been the least dangerous, as the survival rate of 73 per cent indicates (as compared to the survival rate of 50 per cent following operations using the cranial trepanation technique developed in ancient Greece, see

Teschler-Nicola & Schultz 1985). This method called for the opening of the skin of the head with a sharp blade (e.g. an obsidian blade). The skin was retracted, after which the skull was scraped with a tool (a scraper or knife made of flint, copper or bronze) until the hard membrane encasing the brain was exposed.

Good examples of cranial trepanation have been identified among the Early Bronze Age population of İkiztepe, a rich harbour settlement on the southern coast of the Black Sea in northern Anatolia (Schultz 1995). Of a total of 302 skulls examined, at least five showed definite traces of surgery (using the scraping, round-cut and incision techniques). A sixth is regarded as uncertain. This corresponds to an unusually high rate of two per cent. Five of the individuals treated surgically were men. All six skulls also showed evidence of the effects of violence in the form of a cranial trauma caused by impact with a blunt (stone, club, etc.) or bladed (axe, hatchet) object. Of the 302 skulls studied, nineteen showed evidence of cranial trauma. The high percentage (6.3) as well as the type and position of the injuries to the cranium point to the likelihood of warfare as the cause of injury or death. These findings are confirmed by the archaeological evidence uncovered at the site. The wealthy Early Bronze Age settlement of İkiztepe was burned to the ground at least five times during wars. Interesting in this context is the survival rate of the six persons who received surgical treatment. Only two died during or immediately following surgery (possibly from other injuries no longer determinable today, due to the incomplete condition of the skeletal remains). The other four individuals lived for many years after their operations.

Summary and Conclusions

The methods and techniques of palaeopathology enable us to reconstruct a relatively reliable picture of the living conditions of Bronze Age man, including the physical disorders and diseases that prevailed during the period. In many cases, it has been possible to make precise diagnoses and even to reveal entire medical histories, as the impressive example of the child from Lidar Hüyük during the Middle Bronze Age (1800–1500 BC) shows. Of particular interest for the study of Bronze Age living conditions are the spectrum and incidence of childhood diseases, as is demonstrated in the case of the Jelšovce populations. The Nitra-period population (2200–1900 BC) evidently lived under considerably more favourable circumstances than the population of the Únětice culture (1900–1700 BC). Living conditions obviously deteriorated markedly within only a few centuries and possibly within as short a span as 200–300 years. This is reflected not only in the rising incidence of nutritional disorders but in the rate of infectious diseases as well. The causes underlying these changes have not all been identified at this time. Under discussion are an increase in population and an associated change in the biotope (e.g. environmental destruction caused by man). Of special interest from the standpoint of medical history are the evidence of cranial surgery (trepanation) and the analysis of the reasons why it was performed. In many cases, these operations were undertaken as deliberate life-saving measures following cranial trauma. The example of the Early Bronze Age population of İkiztepe (2600–2400 BC) illustrates this quite vividly.

Bibliography: Schultz 1982, 1994, 1995; Schultz et al 1998; Teschler-Nicola & Schultz 1985; Windl et al 1988.

Clothing and Jewellery

Gisela Schumacher-Matthäus

Clothing has always been a necessity, as the human body needs protection – and this holds true for most parts of Europe during the Bronze Age, even during the warm summer months. Depending upon the stage to which a given culture has advanced, clothing is also an expression of sophistication and may be used to demonstrate social status. And the same can be said of jewellery as well.

The patchiness of our knowledge about Bronze Age modes of dress is primarily the consequence of a lack of

2   Figurines from a Bronze Age burial site at Cîrna in Rumania

1   Clothing worn by a young woman from Egtved, Jutland, Denmark
     Early Bronze Age, c. 1400 BC

archaeological evidence. Only under very favourable soil conditions can organic materials such as fabrics or leather be conserved. While isolated fragments of textiles document the existence of fabric production, they say nothing about whether and in what manner they may have been used for clothing.

The Late Neolithic "Ice-Man", known as "Ötzi", who died on the Hauslabjoch in southern Tyrol about 5000 years ago,[1] represents a fortunate coincidental find. He wore leggings, a loin cloth and leather shoes, a sleeveless coat and a fur cap as well as a cloak made of woven grass.

With respect to the Bronze Age, we must continue to rely exclusively upon the finds uncovered in Danish burial mounds[2] for information about original items of clothing (Ill. 1). The woman from Borum Eshøj wore a close-fitting blouse and a long pleated skirt made of wool; a sixteen to eighteen year old woman buried in Egtved was dressed in a blouse (made of a piece of woollen material) and a short skirt made of woollen cords. The man from Trindhøj wore a belted apron, a cloak and a cap.

Other finds provide additional information. Finds at both gravesites and settlements of the Zuto-Brdo/Gîrla-Mare culture that occupied the lower reaches of the Danube included clay statuettes with carved decorations which offer clues about clothing and jewellery (Ill. 2).[3] Most of the figurines represent women; only a very few are of men. It is possible to observe differences within this

79

3   Saffron-gatherers depicted on a fresco in Akrotiri on the island of Thera, 16th century BC

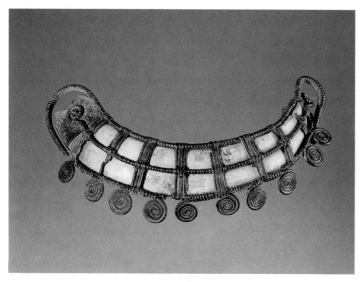

4   Boar's tusk mounted in a frame of wire, La Colombine, Yonne, France, Late Bronze Age (Cat. No. 110)

apparently homogenous region by means of clothing and traditional modes of dress. Thus we find statuettes with and without head scarves. Only to the east of the Iron Gate do we recognise what appears to be the figure of a hunter. The wide variety of costume components with their embroidered elements is complemented by neck and breast jewellery, pendants and sewn-on pieces – items of jewellery found in gravesites and hoards.

Figurines made of clay, bronze and faience, ivory carvings and sealstones from the Minoan and Mycenaean cultural region supplement what knowledge we have.[4] Such evidence does not concern everyday clothing, however. Flounced skirts and open, bolero-style jackets that leave the breast exposed – a style of dress found in palaces and shrines – are indicators of a mode of dress appropriate to religious or courtly settings. Information about the colours of such garments is provided by wall paintings from Knossos, Haghia Triada, Pseira, Mycenae, Pylos, Tiryns and most notably in Akrotiri on the island of Thera (Ill. 3).[5] Less evidence of male forms of dress is found, however. Men often wore only a kilt or loin cloth; longer garments made of fabric or skin generally characterise priests or other dignitaries.

Statements about jewellery can be made for practically all Bronze Age cultures.[6] Ordinarily fashioned from precious metal and bronze, jewellery provides valuable information about regional peculiarities and social status (Ill. 4). Graves, statuettes and wall paintings offer information about the manner in which such items were worn and their gender-specific use (women's graves are generally more elaborately furnished than men's).

In general, it can be said that jewellery for the neck in the form of heavy rings or chains (often with beads made of different metals), armbands/bracelets, rings, earrings and leg jewellery (anklets, spirals) all appear in a range of regional variations; hybrid forms are seldom encountered (Cat.Nos. 106, 108).

The technique of bronze casting enabled artisans to develop a broad spectrum of forms. Magnificent necklaces, diadems and bronze belts ordinarily identify per-

5   Hoard with female ornaments, Wierzchowo, Szecinek, Koszalin, Poland, Late Bronze Age (Cat. No. 121)   ▷

sons of high rank. After centuries in the ground, these pieces of jewellery are now covered with a green patina, and their visual appearance has altered significantly. Originally, they would have looked more like bright, shiny gold.

We obtain valuable clues about fabric strengths and for items used as clothing fasteners (pins, clasps and belts); these – although primarily functional – also have an undeniable decorative function.

1 Josef Winiger, 'Die Bekleidung des Eismannes und die Anfänge der Weberei nördlich der Alpen', in C. Spindler et al (eds.), *Der Mann im Eis. Neue Funde und Ergebnisse*, Vol. 2 (Vienna/New York, 1995), pp. 119–187.

2 Hans Chr. Broholm, Margarethe Hald, *Costumes of the Bronze Age in Denmark* (Copenhagen, 1940); also *Bronzealderens Dragt* (Copenhagen, 1961).

3 Zagorka Letica, 'Antropormorfne Figurine Bronzanog Doba v Jugoslavije', Dissertationes et monographiae 16 (Belgrade, 1973); Gisela Schumacher-Matthäus, 'Studien zu bronzezeitlichen Schmucktrachten im Karpatenbecken', *Marburger Studien zu Vor- und Frühgeschichte* 6, Mainz, 1985, pp. 6–26; Monica Chicideanu-Sandor, Ion Chicideanu, 'Contributions to the Study of the Gîrla Mare Anthropomorphic Statuettes', Dacia (Bukarest), 1990, NS 34, pp. 53–75.

4 Arthur Evans, The Palace of Minos, 4 vols. (London: 1921–1935); Effi Sapouna-Sakellerakis, 'Die frühen Menschenfiguren auf Kreta und in der Ägäis', *Prähistorische Bronzefunde (PBF)*, Vol. 1, 5, Stuttgart, 1995; Friedrich Matz, Ingo Pini, *Corpus der minoischen und mykenischen Siegel (CMS)*, pp. 1964 ff.

5 Sara A. Immerwahr, Aegean Painting in the Bronze Age (Pennsylvania, 1990); Christos Doumas, Die Wandmalerei von Thera, German edition (Munich, 1995).

6 For a general overview see Hermann Müller-Karpe, *Handbuch der Vorgeschichte. Bronzezeit*, Vol. 4 (Munich, 1980).

Bibliography: Broholm & Hald 1940; Chicideanu-Sandor & Chicideanu 1990; Doumas 1995; Evans 1921–1935; Immerwahr 1990; Letica 1973; Müller-Karpe 1980; Pini 1964; Schumacher-Matthäus 1985; Sapouna-Sakellarakis 1995; Winiger 1995; Jensen 1998b.

Horses in the Bronze Age

Ute Luise Dietz

It has still not been determined with certainty where and when the horse was first domesticated, although this presumably took place on the grass plains of Eurasia near the end of the Stone Age. Horses were in widespread use in Europe in the 3rd millennium BC. Although first husbanded as a source of meat, indications of taboos on the consumption of horseflesh during the Late Bronze Age suggest that the horse soon acquired a special status among domesticated animals. Horsepower was initially employed to pull wagons; vague references to ridden horses are the subject of considerable dispute. The first wheeled vehicles were heavy, four-wheeled carts fitted with massive disc wheels and pulled by oxen (Cat. No. 122). The ox's head is lower than its withers, and yokes were often fastened firmly to its horns; thus these animals could apply their full weight to the yoke and manage heavier loads than horses, whose necks took the strain.

The first depictions of equestrian teams from Sumer (in the middle of the 3rd millennium BC) show wagons with heavy disc wheels and four long-eared equids (probably onager hybrids) hitched before them. These massive disc wheels were soon replaced by lighter models with open sections and eventually (near the end of the 3rd millennium) by spoked wheels that combined adequate stability with minimum weight. These developments may have taken place on the Eurasian steppes and in eastern Anatolia at about the same time.

With the introduction of horses and lighter wagons to exploit the potential for increased speed, it became necessary to steer from a position in or on the wagon. The diversity of harness systems developed is reflected in the numerous different types of disc, plate and bar bits which have been preserved from the period (Cat. Nos. 123, 125, 129). By the end of the Bronze Age the snaffle harness with its relatively simple headgear was in widespread use.

Ownership of a war chariot was an expensive and time-consuming proposition. Horses suited for teamwork had to be selected, trained and exercised regularly, fed and given adequate water. The chariot itself required a

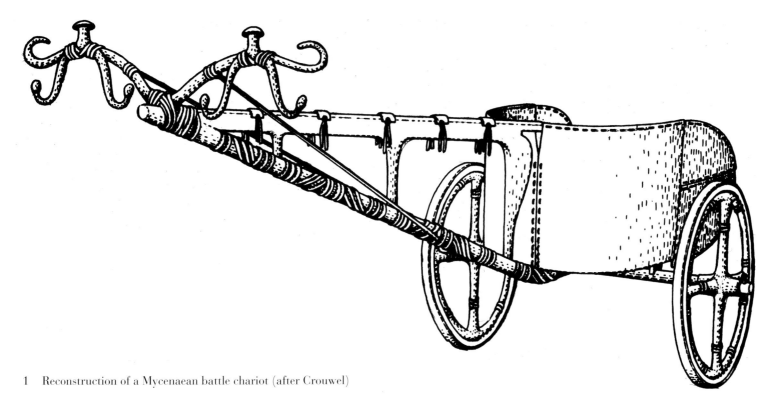

1   Reconstruction of a Mycenaean battle chariot (after Crouwel)

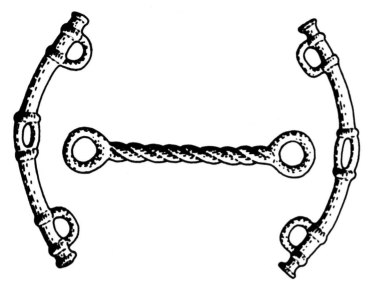

3   Complete snaffle bit consisting of a mouthpiece and cheek-bars
from Wallerfangen, Saar, Germany

great deal of care, since the component parts consisted almost exclusively of organic material and were subject to extreme wear and tear. While the large-scale use of war chariots in chariot cavalry units was possible on the arid plains of the Near East, such light, two-wheeled wagons were used only to a limited extent in Bronze Age Europe (Cat. No. 126). Because of the difficult ground conditions in the wet lowlands and on forested slopes, ox-drawn wagons remained the vehicle of choice for the transport of goods.

We have sufficient evidence of the use of light vehicles for parades, excursions and races in Mycenaean Greece. The role of chariots in warfare was restricted to impressive careering rides along the battle lines, as fighting was still done on foot. Indications have been found of the husbanding of horses as well as the use of spoked wheels in other regions of Europe as well. Beginning in the Middle Bronze Age and particularly in the Late Bronze Age, the horse and the wheel are found frequently as decorative motifs on religious objects and everyday implements (Cat. No. 124). Teams of horses pulling two- and four-wheeled wagons are depicted in rock paintings in northern and southern Europe. Such lighter wagons, however, were probably used as prestige objects – symbolising contact with the "civilised world" but serving no practical function beyond their roles within the sphere of religion and mythology. The Sumerians knew of the

"chariots of the gods", and the figure of Helios driving a team of horses is familiar from Greek mythology. The "Sun Chariot" from Trundholm in Denmark, with its single horse drawing a six-wheeled wagon bearing a gold-plated bronze disc, may perhaps be viewed within this same conceptual context (Cat. No. 175). The so-called "cauldrons on wheels" were presumably used for ritual purposes; their religious significance is underscored by the images of waterfowl mounted atop them (Cat. Nos. 176–178).

The earliest mounted warriors appeared during the 1st millennium BC. Illustrations from Near Eastern sources show warriors riding horses hitched to reins held by a "driver" in a chariot. The campaigns of the Cimmerians and the Scythians into Asia Minor marked the end of the era of the great armies of chariots. By that time, however, wagons and teams of horses had become important items in grave furnishings for members of the upper class. The charioteer, in whose honour the construction of the wagon and the erection of a burial monument (ordinarily a burial mound) was dedicated, was ranked noticeably above the mere horse-rider.

3   Reconstruction of a Late Bronze Age bridle with stirrup bars
(after the example from Crailsheim)

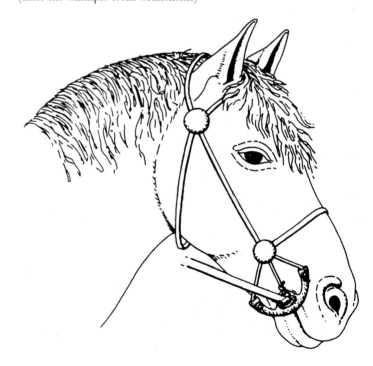

The Boar's Tusk and Bronze Setting from Karlsruhe-Neureut

Rolf-Heiner Behrends

In early 1988 the Karlsruhe office of the Bureau of Historical Monuments of the German state of Baden-Württemberg was notified of the discovery of two unique bronze objects: a complex chain necklace and breastpiece of bronze and a boar's tusk mounted in a setting made of bronze wire (Cat. No. 109). Both pieces were recovered. Further research revealed that they had come to light in the course of gravel-excavation operations in the community of Neureut in the north-western part of the city of Karlsruhe.

It was no longer possible to determine the depth at which the finds had been deposited. The location itself was isolated to the extent that its approximate position could be identified. According to the available information, both items came from a former arm of the Rhine River that dried out at an unknown time. It appears likely that the two pieces lay relatively close together, and the absence of patina suggests that they had been deposited in open water. Thus they belong to the category of river finds and are to be regarded as consecrated offerings. The possibility that other such objects have been lost in the course of quarrying operations cannot be ruled out.

The boar's tusk is roughly twenty centimetres long. The enamel is absent on most of the exposed side and may have been split off when struck by the mechanical shovel. The most severe damage to the bronze setting is visible here as well. The interior surface is much better preserved. The base of the tooth is covered by a sleeve of bronze plate into which several windings of the bronze-wire setting have been inserted, as the x-rays investigations show. The pattern described by the wires is rather

1   Boar's tusk, Karlsruhe-Neureuth, Rheinbett, Germany
Middle Bronze Age (Cat. No. 109)

complicated and indicative of an advanced level of technical skill. Some of the thicker wires are themselves wrapped with finer ones.

Pendants in the form of "doves' tails" of bronze plate were attached to loops of wire on the underside; seventeen of these have been preserved. The holes show appreciable signs of wear, suggesting that the piece may have been worn for a long period of time. No clues as to the manner in which the object was worn are visible on the piece itself. Finds from sites located in central France point to the possibility that such items may have been worn at the waist (Cat. No. 110).

The French finds also provide vague clues as to the chronological origin of the Karlsruhe piece, for they have been assigned to the early Urnfield period. However, the wire settings found in France are much simpler; and the "doves' tails" pendants on the Karlsruhe find suggest a somewhat later origin. It is possible, therefore, that this decorative object can be dated to the early or even middle Urnfield period.

Bibliography: Behrends 1993.

Chapter 3
The Heroes: Life and Death

Editor: Jørgen Jensen

◁ Horned helmet, Viksø, Frederiksborg, Zealand, Denmark
Late Bronze Age, 11th–10th centuries BC (Cat. No. 190)

The Heroes: Life and Death

Jørgen Jensen

Warrior Heroes of the Aegean

In his epic poems, Homer repeatedly describes the fascination and enthusiasm of Bronze Age man for the weaponry and armour in which the warrior heroes arrayed themselves. In the nineteenth book of the *Iliad*, for example, he describes the departure of Achilles after the death of his friend Patroclus:

"And Automedon grasped in his hand the bright lash, that fitted it well, and leapt upon the car; and behind him stepped Achilles harnessed for fight, gleaming in his armour like the bright Hyperion." (*Iliad* XIX. 395 ff. trans. A.T. Murray, London 1925.)

A faint echo of the splendid weaponry used by the Mycenaean kings and heroes to demonstrate their power and standing still resonates in the poetry of Homer. While the Homeric epics primarily describe the infantry-based warfare that developed during the 13th century BC at the time of the collapse of the Mycenaean culture, they still preserve the memory of essential elements of Mycenaean military strategy, such as the two-wheeled chariot. The Linear B tablets reveal to us the immense resources required by the rulers to maintain a force (possibly hundreds strong) of light-running chariots in their great palaces. A large staff of officials oversaw the upkeep of the chariot-yard and attended to spare wheels, axles, vehicle bodies, men and horses. From pictorial representations, including those on the stelai over the Shaft Graves at Mycenae, we know that the chariot was a status symbol of the elite. Yet it was also an instrument of war and a key resource of the army.

The heroes' armaments – their shields, for example – are also documented in poems, inscriptions and archaeological finds. Until around 1200 BC, warriors used either a large, "figure-of-eight" shield (Cat. No. 51) that covered the entire body or a somewhat smaller, though still nearly man-sized, rectangular "tower" shield. Shields were first and foremost defensive weapons, offering the warrior little opportunity to fight freely with his arms. In battle, shields were presumably used in combination with long thrusting-spears, with which the enemy could be cut

down at close quarters. Over the course of time, a shorter javelin was also developed, a weapon that could be hurled at its target from a certain distance.

Many notable warriors wore helmets of boar's tusks (Ill. 1). This item bears witness to the high rank of the warrior in question. The tusks of about forty boars were needed to produce a helmet of this type. Presumably a Mycenaean invention, boar's-tusk helmets were worn already in the 16th century BC and are illustrated in vase painting and frescoes (Cat. No. 50) as well as in smaller works of ivory (Cat. No. 47). The boar's-tusk helmet was a head-covering reserved only for the most distinguished warriors. During the Trojan War, Odysseus' head was adorned with such a helmet:

"… and about his head he set a helm wrought of hide, and with many a tight-stretched thong was it made stiff within, while without the white teeth of a boar of gleaming tusks were set thick on this side and that, well

2   Hoard of weapons, Hajdúsámson, Hungary
    Middle Bronze Age, 16th–15th centuries BC (Cat. No. 104)   ▷

1   Boar's tusk helmet, Spata – Chamber Tomb, Attica, Greece
    Late Bronze Age, LH IIIB, 13th century BC (Cat. No. 49)

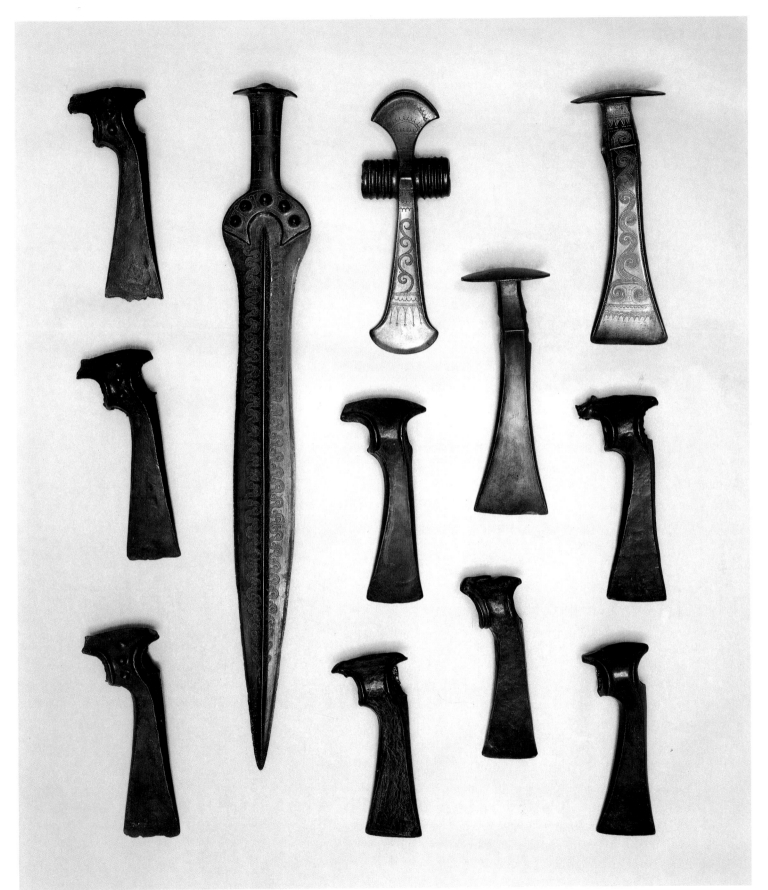

3 The Warrior Vase from Mycenae, c. 1200 BC

and cunningly, and within was fixed a lining of felt."
(*Iliad* X.261ff; trans. A.T. Murray, London 1925)

    Warriors of particular prominence sometimes wore
metal armour and greaves of bronze, armaments probably produced for chariot fighters. Yet it was above all the
sword or dagger (Cat. Nos. 56, 58) that constituted the
hero's *insignia dignitatis*. No other weapon more clearly

proclaimed the authority of the ruler. The artistically-
designed hilt was made of costly materials, while the
blade itself was often decorated with splendid inlays, so-

4 Armour, Petit Marais, Marmesse, Haute Marne, France ▷
Late Bronze Age, 9ᵗʰ–8ᵗʰ centuries BC (Cat. No. 147)

90

91

called "painting in metal" (Cat. No. 56). This kind of display weapon was reserved only for the most distinguished of warriors.

It is above all after their death, however, that we encounter the warrior heroes in their full splendour. In the Shaft Graves of Mycenae they were buried amidst their rich possessions: the faces of dead rulers were covered with gold masks, while around the body lay swords and daggers decorated with hunting and fighting scenes in gold and silver inlay. Drinking vessels of gold and silver (Cat. No. 44), vases of rock-crystal and containers of gold and ivory are also found, as well as hundreds of gold disks decorated with rosettes, spirals and animal motifs, which could be attached to clothing.

This almost exorbitant display of splendour continued until about 1300 BC. The famous "Warrior Vase" from Mycenae shows the appearance of warriors during the last phase of this magnificent Bronze Age culture. The vase depicts six bearded warriors with horned helmets, possibly marching to battle. Their body-armour extends to the waist, with a skirt of leather strips below. They wear greaves of leather or bronze and carry a lance as well as a light, round shield with a semicircular bite taken out at the lower edge. A new type of foot soldier is represented here, one whose equipment very likely reflects the changes in fighting technique that occurred during the transition to the last, catastrophic period of Mycenaean civilsation. At that time, the warrior heroes of the Aegean fought with weapons resembling those used in large parts of the European continent (Cat. No. 48).

This striking similarity will be considered in more detail later. First of all, however, let us look to the North, where a comparable aristocratic culture developed in the expanses of central and northern Europe over the course of the 2nd millennium BC.

The Early Bronze Age

Around the turn of the 2nd millennium BC, human society changed in its nature almost everywhere north of the Alps. At the same time, the circulation of copper and bronze increased between the various communities. Even regions far from natural sources of metal were incorporated into the bronze-reliant culture. The increased demand for metal brought with it a change in the expression of power, wealth and status. In metal-rich areas, there now appeared powerful personages who were interred in giant burial mounds after their death. Their rich grave goods consisted of bronze weapons and other precious objects, often fashioned of exotic materials such as gold and amber.

In transalpine Europe, a change in the position of the individual in society had occurred already in the 3rd millennium BC. All societies consist of both individuals and social groups, and in the funerary cult of the Stone Age, it was above all the social groups that left their mark, for example in the construction of the great megalithic graves. In the course of the 3rd millennium, however, an individualising tendency emerged, resulting in increased individual burial. With the beginning of the Bronze Age proper, objects of metal and other precious materials such as amber begin to be used as grave goods, thus reflecting the social position of the deceased during their lifetime.

Around the year 2000 BC, metal was used in three major regions of Europe: to the south-east in the central European and Carpathian region; in the Atlantic region, particularly in areas rich in metal such as Brittany and Wessex (see Briard, p. 102 and Cat. Nos. 160, 162, 163); and to the north in central Germany with the so-called Únětice culture (see Vandkilde, pp. 103 ff. and Cat. No. 103). The prosperity of the Únětice culture was based on rich resources of gold, copper, tin and salt, which led to the development of important centres of metalwork. The influence of the powerful Únětice groups is felt in Ireland, Brittany, England and the Baltic region, while influences from the Atlantic region are discernible in central Europe as well.

Although the basis of wealth differed from area to area, the symbols of power in individual regions were strikingly similar, a result of the fact that transalpine Europe had developed into a coherent trading system. Bronze was the common medium of exchange, and in large parts of the continent a way of life had developed in which the production and exchange of prestige goods played an essential role. Even areas poor in metal such as the Baltic region were now incorporated into this common bronze-based culture. The cultural participation of the Baltic was probably due to its possession of amber (Cat.

Nos. 81–83), a resource that appeared with increasing frequency in the regions south of the Baltic.

Around the beginning of the 2nd millennium BC, daggers, halberds and axes appear in many areas of Europe, objects whose archaeological context always testifies to the high status of their owners. Halberds, for example, are found from the Iberian Peninsula to Hungary, from Ireland to Italy, and from Scandinavia to the Balkan Peninsula. They were weapons with an "international" character and were always used in a ceremonial context, whether in Ireland, Germany, Denmark or Brittany. In most regions, moreover, objects such as these served to emphasise the social position of the elite.

Around 1700 BC, the centres of cultural development shifted. The centre of the Únětice culture dissolved, possibly due to the collapse of copper production from the Harz region in central Germany, which occurred simultaneously with a marked growth of production in the Carpathian region. In the centuries that followed, the Carpathian basin came to dominate a wide-ranging network of contacts extending as far north as southern Scandinavia and northern Germany.

The Middle Bronze Age

In the period after 1700 BC, a large, unified cultural complex developed north of the Alps, a society which, unlike that of the Early Bronze Age, was marked not by prominent concentrations of power, but by the growth of an aristocratic lifestyle. The warrior graves constitute the clearest expression of this development. The northern regions (southern Scandinavia) now belonged completely to the European Bronze Age culture. In both the North and the South, the cult of the dead called for the display and burial of powerful men in barrow mounds, their finest weapons accompanying them as grave goods on their journey to the afterlife (see Boos, pp. 106 f. and Jensen, pp. 88 ff. and Cat. Nos. 166–168, 105, 107).

Within this large, transalpine area, an important innovation in weapons production took place during this period, a development originating in the south-eastern parts of the continent. Swords and spears were now used simultaneously. One of the first swords to be introduced to central Europe was the splendid solid-hilted sword of the Hajdúsámson type (Cat. No. 104). These weapons,

produced in the Carpathian region, spread as far north as southern Scandinavia, where they were imitated by local bronze casters. The spread of these early swords provided the impetus for local development in many places. To the North in southern Scandinavia and northern Germany, for example, swords with spiral-ornamented hilts began to be produced (Cat. No. 105), while swords with octagonal hilts were preferred further south in places such as southern Germany.

The sword was a symbol of power and dignity; at the same time, however, it was also the warrior's most important weapon. In evaluating the quality of a sword, two factors were of crucial importance: the correct positioning of the centre of gravity, and a well-executed juncture between hilt and blade. To fashion the perfect sword was a true challenge for the bronze caster. A mould of stone or clay was used for the casting; subsequently, the cast product was worked again and the hilt possibly covered in wood, horn or bone. A wooden sheath (Cat. No. 166), sometimes with metal fittings, was also provided for the sword. The best swords were probably made in specialised workshops, possibly by intinerant craftsmen.

Two sword types can be distinguished: the solid-hilted sword and the flanged-hilt sword. The older, relatively short sword had a broad blade, particularly well-suited for slashing. Later, the blades became longer and narrower and thus could also be used as thrusting weapons. Toward the end of the Bronze Age, the swords became broader again, indicating that they were now once again used as slashing weapons.

Swords have been found in numerous warriors' graves throughout all of northern Europe, evidence of the central role played by warriors in these societies (cf. Cat. Nos. 166–168). The most richly equipped of such graves, moreover, lie at the junctions of a network of trade routes covering the entire continent of Europe, by means of which different societies exchanged sought-after materials such as gold, copper, tin and amber. Certain elements from the Aegean region also made their way to central and northern Europe via this network, where they appear sporadically; these include articles such as drinking vessels of an originally Mycenaean character, which now served to represent the status of the dead warrior, or fold-

6   Figurine of a kneeling warrior, Grevensvænge, Rønnebæk,
    Zealand, Denmark
    Late Bronze Age, 10th–9th centuries BC (Cat. No 189)

7   Crested-helmet, Blainville-la-Grande, Meurthe-et-Moselle,   ▷
    France, Late Bronze Age, 12th–9th centuries BC (Cat. No. 153)

ing stools known from northern German and Danish oak coffin-graves from the 14th century BC, doubtless modelled after examples from the Aegean. Finally, the occurrence of four-spoked wheels also bears witness to the adoption of Aegean technology.

The first spoked wheels appear around 1600 BC in the Carpathian basin (Cat. No. 126). Somewhat later, about 1400 BC, they also appear in Scandinavia, for example in cultic context on the Sun Chariot from Trundholm in Denmark (Cat. No. 175). The pictorial representation of a chariot in a chieftain's grave in Kivik in southern Sweden dates from approximately the same period. In these Nordic areas, chariots were not used in war; rather, they were employed – in particular the spoked wheel – in the context of cultic ritual and as a status symbol.

The Late Bronze Age

By the 13th century BC, the Mycenaean civilisation had passed its zenith and was now approaching its end in a period of crisis and genuine collapse. Comparable crises affected large parts of the eastern Mediterranean and persisted for a number of generations. In Anatolia, the Hittite empire was crumbling, while economic and political crisis prevailed in Egypt as well. Finally, around 1200 BC, the Mycenaean civilisation collapsed. There followed a so-called "Dark Age" that was to last more than three hundred years.

We know much more about the symptoms than the causes of the crises in the eastern Mediterranean. For the Bronze Age cultures on the European continent, however, one of the effects was the spread of a number of specialised crafts that had previously been monopolised by the palaces in the Aegean area, a development that manifested itself in the weapons of the warrior elite of central and northern Europe.

In Greece, the upheavals of the 13th century BC brought with them extensive alterations in military technique. The undoubtedly numerous military conflicts of that period were now marked by the emergence of a mobile infantry with standard weaponry for mid-distance fighting. It is precisely this type of warrior that is shown on the "Warrior Vase" from Mycenae. These new soldiers – or at any rate their aristocratic commanders – were armed with weapons of ever better quality. In the course of the 9th

and 8th centuries BC, defensive weapons continued to develop – in particular helmets, amour and greaves.

As mentioned above, the new weapons and fighting techniques in the Mediterranean were of tremendous significance for the entire European continent. After 1300 BC, weapons found in the western part of the Middle East, the Aegean area, and central and northern Europe begin to show remarkable similarities, most likely due to communication as well as to undoubtedly frequent military conflicts between the elites of individual regions. The influence, however, was mutual, as is clearly seen in wide-ranging areas such as northern and central Italy, Croatia and Serbia, parts of southern Germany, Austria, Hungary, Transylvania, Moravia and Slovakia. Richly-appointed warrior graves bear witness to the exchange of cultural elements and craft techniques between central Europe and areas such as the eastern Mediterranean.

As a result, central European warriors were now able to array themselves in bronze armour, as is shown for example in a lavishly equipped warrior grave in Čaka in Slovakia. This grave contained armour of beaten bronze, produced locally after an Aegean model. Metal armour had been known in the Middle East since the 15th century BC and possibly before. It was soon adopted by the Greek warrior heroes, and by the 13th century BC these costly weapons of defence are found in the east Alpine and Carpathian regions as well. A few centuries later, they also appear in western Europe, as exemplified by the fine armour of Fillinges, St. Germain du Plain and Marmesse (Cat. Nos. 146–148), presumably produced as late as the 8th century BC, likewise after Mediterranean models.

In a few cases, the armour included greaves of bronze (Cat. Nos. 156–157). In the Mycenaean period, chariot-drivers had used greaves at a very early point in time; among the infantry, however, they were apparently introduced only in the course of the 13th century BC. Greaves were also used north of the Alps during this same period, though they were not as widespread as body armour.

Like armour, metal helmets were also an invention of the Middle East that spread throughout the Aegean area in the late Mycenaean period, also appearing in central and northern Europe in the 13th century BC. A variety of different helmet types are known: cap helmets, bell helmets and crested helmets and others. Previously, warriors had used headgear such as thick felt hoods to protect them from blows. Hoods of this type are known from Danish oak coffin-graves. A relatively large number of bronze helmets have been found north of the Alps. These can be divided into two groups, east and west of a line extending from Hamburg to Salzburg and then southward to the Adriatic Sea. To the east of this line are found the so-called bell helmets, including the example from Sehlsdorf in Mecklenburg (Cat. No. 154). West of the line appear crested helmets of the type represented by the helmet from Blainville-la-Grande in eastern France (Cat. No. 153). In the 8th century BC, richly decorated cap and crested helmets appear with particular frequency in Italy.

The horned bronze helmets of Viksø in Denmark (Cat. No. 190) represent a special type. These two Danish helmets are unique archaeological finds, yet related pieces must have existed in places such as Sardinia, where they appear on small bronze statuettes. Statuettes with horned helmets are also known from other regions of the Mediterranean, including Syria and Cyprus.

Toward the end of the 13th century BC, the round shield came into use in Greece, though it was presumably employed much earlier north of the Alps. Shields of this type, made of wood with metal fittings, are known from the rich warrior grave in Hagenau (see Boos, pp. 106f.). Later, the shields were made of bronze. Two types of shields are known: round shields and oval, so-called notched-shields (Cat. Nos. 149–152). Numerous round shields have been found in England and Scotland, but they also occur in Ireland, Denmark, and central Germany. The notched-shields are found in Denmark, Sweden, northern Germany and Bohemia; examples made of leather and wood appear in Ireland as well. In southern France and the Iberian Peninsula, they are shown on stelai along with other weapons, indicating their use by a warrior elite (see Oliveira Jorge, pp. 114ff. and 137ff., Cat. Nos. 173, 174). They may have been introduced by Phoenician merchants from the eastern Mediterranean.

While most of the weapons mentioned up to this point originated in the eastern Mediterranean, the sword represents an exception. Since the beginning of the Middle Bronze Age, the sword had numbered among the most important weapons of the European warrior. A special, flanged-hilt sword type was widely used in central and northern Europe after the 15th century (cf. Cat. No. 168). A late variation of this sword shows up in the period around 1200 BC, not only in Greece (Cat. No. 48), but also on Cyprus, in the Middle East and in Egypt. This sword type was apparently developed in the Carpathian basin and spread from here to the south, presumably due to its superiority to the Aegean swords as a weapon of attack. Examples of this foreign sword type have been found at Mycenae and other Aegean sites.

After the 13th century BC, the culture of the warrior hero – a way of life that had reached its zenith in the Mycenaean civilisation – was increasingly reflected in the weaponry of transalpine Europe, though in a fashion adapted to local conditions in central and northern Europe. Proof of this phenomenon is the use of the chariot as a cult object and symbol of power.

The two-wheeled chariot, first and foremost a status symbol of the Mycenaean rulers, appears in isolated instances in the region north of the Alps (Cat. No. 126). Here, however, the development soon took its own course with the emergence of a four-wheeled chariot pulled by two horses in the 13th and 12th centuries BC (Cat. No. 127, 128). In the centuries that followed, this chariot was used for ceremonial rather than military purposes; nevertheless, along with weapons and drinking vessels, it retained its significance as a status symbol of the warrior elite, a group which gained increasing prominence in northern Europe in the Bronze Age and flourished in particular at the beginning of the Iron Age in the middle of the 1st millennium BC (see Pare, pp. 125 f., and Thrane, pp. 127 ff.).

8   Shield, Sørup, Eskilstrup, Maribo, Denmark
Late Bronze Age, 11th–10th centuries BC (Cat. No. 149)

Bibliography: Ahlberg 1971; Bader 1990; Borchhardt 1972; Catling 1956; Chenorkian 1989; Clarke et al. 1985; Clausing 1997; Coles 1962; Gedl 1980; Goetze 1984; Gräslund 1967; Hencken 1959, 1971; Hüttel 1982; Kossack 1974; von Merhart 1969; Mohen 1987; Müller-Karpe 1974; Pare 1992; Paulík 1968; Sandars 1985; Schauer 1975, 1978, 1980, 1982, 1984a, 1986; Treue 1986.

Funeral Architecture and Burial Customs in the Aegean

Katie Demakopoulou

The funeral architecture and burial customs of the Bronze Age Aegean, as known from excavations of funerary monuments and cemeteries, provide important evidence for the social dimension of this period. Despite the variability observable in burial methods, there is, generally speaking, considerable similarity in the approaches to death adopted by the inhabitants of the different regions of the Prehistoric Aegean. Moreover, many of the tomb types and burial customs found in the Aegean in the Neolithic Period continue into the Bronze Age.

From the beginning of the Bronze Age, the most common form of burial was inhumation; cremations remain exceptional until almost the end of this period, when the practice gradually increased. The body of the dead person was normally placed in the grave in a contracted position or, more rarely and more particularly during the Late Bronze Age, in a supine posture. The contracted position may in some cases have had a ritual significance, but may also have been due merely to lack of space. The dead were usually accompanied by offerings, the quality of which ranged from very poor to highly luxurious depending on the social status of the occupant of the grave. Offerings were not normally placed in graves of infants and young children. The remains are often found in graves of rituals involving the consumption of food or drink by the relatives of the deceased, either during or

1 View of Grave Circle A at Mycenae, 16th century BC

after the burial. Finds made during excavations reveal that other ceremonies in honour of the dead were also held in cemeteries. In family tombs, space was created for new burials. Fires were often lit inside the tombs in order to fumigate them, or for some other ritual purpose. In order to make room for new burials, relatives did not shrink from gathering the bones in pits or piling them up at the edges of the tomb – or even throwing them out. They also removed many of the grave offerings. After the flesh had decomposed, the dead apparently no longer inspired respect in the living, except perhaps in a very few cases. No evidence, however, exists to suggest that there was a true cult of the dead.

Graves were either isolated or organised in cemeteries, sometimes within the settlements (intramural), and sometime outside them (extramural). Already at the beginning of the Bronze Age, large organised cemeteries are found in the Cyclades and Crete. In the *Cyclades*, the graves of the Early Cycladic period are normally cists of rectangular or trapezoidal shapes, built of stones or made of upright slabs. Both small and large cemeteries containing this kind of grave have been found on most of the Cycladic islands. The most important is that at Chalandriani on Syros, in which there are more than 650 graves. The graves contained one or more bodies and normally either just a few or a large number of offerings. These took the form of clay or stone vases, metal objects, jewellery, weapons and the famous Cycladic figurines (Cat. Nos. 14–18). This kind of grave continued to be found in the Cyclades until the end of the Bronze Age, though the passage of time saw the appearance of more elaborate built graves and also rock-cut tombs.

In *Crete* are to be found large, extensive cemeteries and also some rich funerary material, especially from the Early and Middle Bronze Age. At the beginning of the Bronze Age two predominant kinds of built grave monuments are known: circular tombs and rectangular "house tombs". These were invariably family tombs intended for repeated use. They occur in organised cemeteries, the best-known of which is that of Phourni at Archanes, and also those at Mallia, Palaikastro, Zakros and Mochlos. The tombs of Mochlos were so large and elaborate, and were so richly furnished with offerings of gold jewellery (Cat. Nos. 7, 10) and other precious objects, that they

appear to have been intended for an elite group. The tombs of Archanes also contained a wealth of grave offerings. In addition to these two kinds of funeral monuments there were also individual burials in cist graves or simple pits. These were not family graves and usually contained only one body.

In Middle Bronze Age Crete, during the period of the First Palaces, a structure was erected within the area of the cemetery at Mallia at Chrysolakkos: famous for the valuable finds it yielded, it is thought to be a royal ossuary. During the period of the Second Palaces, in the Late Bronze Age, fewer tombs are known in Crete than in earlier periods. Chamber tombs in the region of Knossos

2   Gold cup, Mycenae – Grave Circle A, Shaft Grave V, Argolid, Greece, Late Bronze Age (Cat. No. 44)

contain a wealth of offerings, and the earlier cemeteries at Mochlos and Archanes continued to be used. In the Late Minoan cemeteries on Crete, however, burials were predominantly in terracotta coffins (*larnakes*), a form based on footed rectangular chests of wood.

In *Mainland Greece*, large organised cemeteries with cist graves, rock-cut tombs and simple pit graves dating from the Early Bronze Age have been found at

3   Entrance of the "Treasury of Atreus" at Mycenae, 14ᵗʰ century BC

Manika on Euboea and at Aghios Kosmas in Attica. The tombs here contained multiple burials and a wealth of offerings, some of which were imports from the Cyclades. Smaller cemeteries or individual cist graves are known from Thebes, Tiryns, Elis, Perachora and Aghios Stephanos. Most of these contained a variety of objects as offerings.

Graves with rich offerings dating from the second phase of the Early Bronze Age have been found on Leukas (Cat. No. 5) and at Thebes. The Thyreatis treasure, an ensemble of gold jewellery now in the Berlin Museum, probably comes from a tomb dating to this period.

Large cemeteries of Middle Bronze Age date have been found throughout Mainland Greece: they comprise cist graves, simple pit graves and often burials in pithoi. One of the largest and best known is the cemetery of Asine, the graves of which contained a wealth of offerings. Tumuli were also created that covered large numbers of individual burials in cists, pits or pithoi. These tumuli have been found mainly in Messenia, though they turn up too in Attica and the Argolid.

Towards the end of the Middle Bronze Age, tombs in Greece became more elaborate and had richer offerings, revealing an increasing degree of social stratification and the emergence of aristocratic and ruling families. The most famous of these tombs are the shaft graves at Mycenae, which cover the period from the late 17ᵗʰ to the early 15ᵗʰ centuries BC. These took the form of large rectangular shafts cut in the bedrock, which were enclosed within two Grave Circles: Circle A inside the acropolis at Mycenae (Ill. 1), and Circle B a little way outside it. From the treasures they contained came what are considered to be the richest and most important grave groups found to date in the Prehistoric Aegean (Cat. Nos. 42, 44, 56–58, 75). Similar shaft graves, which did not, however, contain the same wealth of offerings, have been found at Argos, at Thebes and on Aegina. That on Aegina is thought to be the earliest and dates from the second phase of the Middle Bronze Age.

The most important monuments of Mycenaean funeral architecture, however, are the tholos tombs, which are found all over Greece from the South Peloponnese to Thessaly and Epiros. They are thought to be royal tombs, and are associated with the seats of rulers at Mycenae, Tiryns, Midea (Dendra), Pylos, Vapheio and Orchomenos, to cite just the better-known examples. The tholos tombs have an approach passage (the *dromos*), an entrance, and a chamber which is invariably circular in shape. The chamber is built of stone blocks, often dressed, and is corbelled – that is with the stones laid in circular courses whose diameter gradually decreases towards the top, thereby creating the characteristic bee-hive shape of the tomb. The most famous of these tombs, which are models of their structural type and monumental appearance, are the Tholos tomb at Orchomenos ("Treasury of Minyas") and the "Treasury of Atreus" at Mycenae (Ill. 3), both dating from the Late Mycenaean period (14th century BC). The decorated walls and ceiling of the side rooms in both these monuments, and the lavishly adorned facade of the latter, indicate the luxurious nature of their construction. The enormous lintels and the height of the tholos are also impressive achievements of Mycenaean technology.

Simpler funeral architecture is represented by the chamber tombs that were dug into the soft rock in hillsides. These are widely found in the Aegean, Crete and even Asia Minor to the East and Sicily to the West during the mature Mycenaean period, and indicate the extent of the Mycenaean penetration of the periphery of their world. The chamber tombs are also approached by a *dromos* sloping downwards and leading to the burial chamber, of rectangular or elliptical shape with a low, arched roof. Burial pits were cut into the floor of the chamber and there were niches in the walls or benches along them, to receive bodies and offerings. These were family tombs, used for multiple burials over a long period of time. They are usually part of large, extensive cemeteries, of which the best known and richest are in the Argolid. A famous cemetery is that at Tanagra in Boeotia, where the tombs contained several terracotta coffins (*larnakes*) with pictorial scenes, in which the procession to the grave is shown, with ritual lamenting by female mourners, as on Attic Geometric vases (Cat. No. 59).

Cist graves continued to be used alongside the chamber tombs, and many are found within chamber tomb cemeteries. The evidence yielded by the construc-

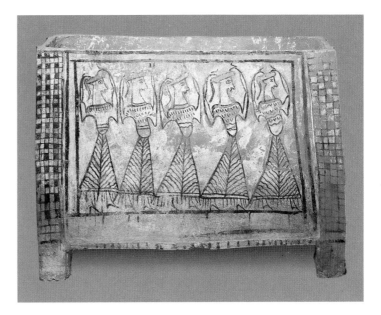

4   Larnax, Tanagra – Chamber Tomb 6, Boeotia, Greece
Late Bronze Age, LH IIIB, 13th century BC (Cat. No. 59)

tion of the chamber tombs and from the large quantities of offerings found in them, such as stone and clay vases, precious vessels, jewellery, weapons, figurines, seals and ivory objects (Cat. Nos. 26, 27, 30, 31, 34, 47, 49, 52, 53, 55, 63–65, 69, 84), all reveals a complex social structure. Chamber tombs appear to have been destined for the ordinary urban population of the Mycenaean world, though some of them – including those at Mycenae, Dendra and elsewhere – contained valuable offerings comparable to material found in the royal tombs. Tombs of this category continued to be constructed until the end of the Mycenaean Civilisation, at which point simple cist and pit graves in large cemeteries (Kerameikos, Salamis, Argos and elsewhere) became the predominant type.

Bibliography: Cavanagh/Mee 1998: Dickinson 1994: Hägg/Nordquist 1990: Kilian 1988: Laffineur 1987: Pelon 1976.

The Princes of the Atlantic

Jacques Briard

From the end of the 3rd millennium BC, the presence of copper, tin and gold encouraged the development of metallurgy in western Europe, particularly in the British Isles and Brittany. The exploitation of mines and the control of the exchange of manufactured products gave rise to societies ruled by elites who used prestige objects to demonstrate their status. The first "aristocracies" emerged in Great Britain from the rural societies at the time of the Beaker culture. Individual graves contained copper daggers, bell-beakers and amber jewellery as well as gold-studded archers' wrist-guards. The development of symbols of power and of prestige goods is evidenced by golden half-moons of the Irish type (so-called *lunulae*) and copper halberds as well as by a number of gold cups such as the one from Rillaton. The Early Bronze Age saw the formation of genuine chiefdoms on both sides of the English Channel, those of Wessex in Great Britain and that of the Armorican tumuli in Brittany.

In Wessex, axes and daggers of bronze or arsenic-rich copper, golden appliqués, and even a stone sceptre with mounts of bone and ivory – goods that most certainly constituted symbols of power – have been found in graves such as Bush Barrow (Wilsford). Yet the elite of this society was not exclusively male: one of the graves at Normanton belonged to a princess who was buried with her woollen dresses and bronze weapons, amber disks set in gold, and an extraordinary miniature halberd with a blade of amber and a golden shaft. Bowls were also carved of jet, such as those from Farway Down. Ceramic production consisted of "incense cups" and "Food Vessels". Typical of the finds from female burials in cists are fluted beads of faience and of blue glass paste, made in imitation of Egyptian models. During the same period, the monument at Stonehenge received its final form with the great outer circle of trilithons. The axe and dagger marks on some of the uprights date to the Early Bronze Age, an epoch which also saw the emergence of new structures of land division in agricultural territories, of a type studied particularly in the region around Dartmoor.

In Brittany, about thirty large tumuli bear witness to the division of territory between the "Armorican princes". Their impressive graves, such as that of La Motta near Lannion, contained axes and daggers of copper and bronze, gold and amber jewellery and fine arrowheads of flint, likewise objects of prestige (Cat. No. 163). Small silver cups found in the tumuli of Saint Fiacre in Melrand and of Saint-Adrien suggest a connection to the Iberian Peninsula, a supposition confirmed by the exist-

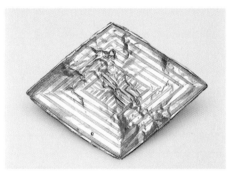

Grave gifts from Clandon barrow, Winterborne St. Martin, Dorset, Great Britain, Wessex culture, 18th century BC
(Cat. No. 160)

ence in both regions of large flange-hilted swords. In addition to the large main tumuli, more modest graves have also been found (some containing beads of glass paste), as well as groups of cists and even extremely impoverished burial sites. The existing megalithic graves were reused, converted into individual graves and sometimes – as at Saint-Just – completely "made over" and transformed by Bronze Age peoples who had adopted other rites than that of the Neolithic mother goddess, cults in which the sun, the horse, the wheel and the warrior played a central role.

The Princely Burials of the Únětice Culture

Helle Vandkilde

The first period of the Early Bronze Age in central Europe was technically speaking a stone age with limited use of metals in most regions. It is only with the second period of the Early Bronze Age, around 2000 BC, that the use of copper objects and knowledge of metallurgy became widespread and wholly integrated into social life. This emergence of a true metal age in central Europe may be connected to the discovery of sulphide copper in the mining-fields of the Alps and in the central German-Bohemian borderland, and particularly it may relate to new technical abilities to utilise such complex ores. At the same time, alloying with tin became markedly more com-

mon. Still a scarce resource in central Europe, however, tin was merely added in highly variable amounts to some 30–70% of the artefacts. An unquestionable Bronze Age with a standard tin-bronze alloy did not occur until the final phase of the Early Bronze Age, c. 1700 BC. Whereas our knowledge of the techniques of early metallurgy has increased considerably during the last decades, our understanding of its social context has not been extended correspondingly.

Archaeological evidence – i.e. material culture in its funerary, sacrificial and domestic contexts – generally hints at increasing social distinction during the Early Bronze Age. This seems to accompany rather closely the expanding use of metals and innovations in metallurgy. Around 2000 BC the social situation became especially complex with the appearance of differential and sometimes lavish presentation of wealth and social power in funerary and/or sacrificial domains. Regional variations,

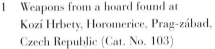

1   Weapons from a hoard found at Kozí Hrbety, Horoměřice, Prag-zábad, Czech Republic (Cat. No. 103)

however, existed, and two contrasting units in regard to social organisation resided along the Danube below the copper-rich eastern Alps and in Saxo-Thuringia at the middle Elbe-Saale surrounded by hills with abundant ores of copper, tin and gold. The material expressions, the degree and forms of social inequality evidently differed markedly between these two central regions; yet it is difficult to put exact social labels on their differences.

Social hierarchy was definitely on overt display in Únětician Saxo-Thuringia from 2000 till 1700 BC. This region, and particularly the area around the modern town Halle, literally stood out against the remainder of central Europe: metal riches in extravagant quantities were offered as gifts to the gods in sacred places, thus forming part of what must have been important ritual and social events (Cat. No. 103). Wealth and social authority were displayed mainly through such sacrificial performances, whereas funerary activities were generally of quite unpretentious character. A few personal metal items, or frequently only pottery, accompanied the deceased, who was buried among kin in a flat grave cemetery.

Against this traditional and modest funerary background, a small assemblage of six or seven giant burial mounds with richly equipped interments in massive wooden grave chambers is a complete surprise. A few mature males from high-ranking families were obviously glorified in death, and social distance from people buried in an ordinary manner was demonstrated in every possible way. It seems that these men must have held outstanding and highly privileged positions in society, and the hierarchical nature of late Únětician society in Saxo-Thuringia can hardly be doubted. The vast amount of work invested in the construction, and the abundant equipment and rich adornment of the body establish the interred persons as heads of social and political life. Their personal equipment finds striking parallels in the weapons, implements and ornaments offered to the gods, and this would suggest that they may also have been religious leaders.

The tombs at Leubingen (near Sömmerda) and Helmsdorf (near Hettstedt) were excellently preserved, and they are also the best known of these princely burials. Excavation took place in 1877 and 1906–1907, but the publications are splendid for their time. Dendrochrono-logy has recently informed us that the oak wood for the chambers was felled 1942/1900 BC and 1840/1800 BC, respectively. Similarities in construction and content confirm that the whole group of princely graves was built in the first centuries of the 2nd millennium BC.

The mound at Leubingen is thirty-four meter in diameter, and it exceeds eight meter in height. Inside the earthen mound, an enormous central cairn of overlapping stone slabs covered a triangular-sectioned, or tent-shaped, timber-built chamber, approximately four by two meter at ground level. A layer of thatch covered the chamber roofing. On the floor lay the extended body of a mature male looking towards the open northern end of the chamber, and across his hips at a right angle was another and slighter body of an adolescent or perhaps a child. The status of this second individual is unknown, but the mature male is obviously the primary person, and the objects found in the chamber seem to belong to him. At the left side of his feet was a globular storage jar, rusticated on its lower half, and placed in a stone setting. At the right side of his feet and legs several objects were carefully arranged in small groups: a large serpentine pickaxe and a whetstone for metalworking. In addition there was a series of bronze weapons and tools: a halberd with wooden haft, three small triangular dagger blades, two flanged axes, and three chisels. To the right side of his arm were placed gold jewellery: two large dress pins of the eyelet type, one spiral bead, a massive armring, and two spiral rings for the hair or the finger.

The splendour of the huge burial mounds at the middle Elbe-Saale is unique in central Europe at this time. An unexpected and very thought-provoking echo, however, appears far towards the northeast at Łęki Małe (Koscian) at the river Warta in Poznan (Cat. No. 159). Eleven burial mounds were here situated in a row along a river valley – four of them are still visible. Together with the neighbouring fortified settlement of Bruszczewo, they represent a Únětician community in an otherwise foreign cultural environment, perhaps a trading post in the transfer of metals. The smallest mound – twenty-four meter in diameter – was excavated in 1953. The bipartite primary grave of wood, stones and clay contained two burials. A male body was equipped with a metal-hilted halberd, large triangular dagger blade, flanged axe and a spiral-

2   Stele (detail). Anderlingen. Lower Saxony. Germany. Early Bronze Age (Cat. No. 172)

headed dress pin – all of bronze, and a gold spiral; a female body had two massive bronze rings around her ankles. Further, there were five pots and remains of wooden artefacts. A secondary grave towards the west in the mound contained an interment with a metal-hilted dagger, flanged axe, chisel, two eyelet dress pins, two amber beads, three gold spiral rings, and five pots. Radiocarbon dates confirm that the burials at Łęki Małe are contemporary with the princely burials in Saxo-Thuringia, and similarities in material expressions and

funerary rituals strongly suggest intensive communication on elite level between these two remote regions – perhaps amplified by kinship ties.

Bibliography: Becker et al 1989a; von Brunn 1959; Clarke et al 1985; Coles & Harding 1979; Fischer 1956; Gedl 1980; Grössler 1908; Hachmann 1972; Höfer 1906; Jahn 1950; Machnik 1977; Matthias 1976; Müller 1982; Müller-Karpe 1980; Otto 1958; Shennan 1993, 1994; Simon 1990b; Schmidt & Nitzschke 1980; Vandkilde 1996; Zich 1996.

The Chieftain's Grave of Hagenau and Related Warrior Graves

Andreas Boos

The chieftain's grave of Hagenau near Regenstauf in the county of Regensburg (Upper Palatinate), opened by a grave robber in 1975, contains the richest collection of weaponry of any Bronze Age warrior grave in southern central Europe. Apart from a later cremation burial dating from the Hallstatt period, the tumulus, located within a larger Bronze and Iron Age necropolis, contained a stone tomb chamber with a skeleton oriented south-north and numerous grave goods. Despite the amateurish excavation, the relatedness of the ensemble is beyond question.

The individual grave goods consist of the following (Ill. 1): a long and a short flange-hilted sword, a flange-hilted dagger, a median-winged axe, four socketed arrowheads, a splendid pin, a hook probably belonging to a sword belt, two spirals of gold wire, a pair of armlets and a pair of bracelets, three awls or tattoo needles, a razor, a stone blade (of tabular chert), and a large cylindrical-necked vessel with knobs and indentations, as well as thirteen smaller and thirty larger decorative pins with hollowed-knob heads.

While most of the forms are typical of Bronze Age burial mounds in Bohemia and Upper Palatinate, the

1 Grave of a chieftain, Hagenau, Upper Palatinate, Germany, Middle Bronze Age (Cat. No. 168)

large clay vessel, the early metal belt hook, and above all the 52-centimetre-long pin, its disk ornamented with protruding sticks, are pieces of striking singularity. The pin combines the ribbed type originating in eastern France and south-western Germany with the Bohemian and lower-Austrian style of disk decoration. In its capacity as the most progressive item of the grave goods, the pin dates the essentially late-Middle Bronze Age ensemble to the transition between the stages Br C2 and Br D1, i.e. to the period around 1300 BC.

Even more than the gold spirals, which were widespread in Bohemia, it is the extraordinarily extensive collection of weaponry that identifies the deceased as a chieftain or a prince. The long sword of the Asenkofen type was broken into four parts already at its interment, while the short sword, probably reworked from a longer specimen of the same type, was intact. Dagger and axe complete the set of offensive weapons of a high-ranking warrior; the arrowheads identify him as an archer as well. The forty-three decorative pins may represent the fittings of a wooden shield, which was probably deposited on or under the vessel.

With its extensive collection of weaponry, the chieftain's grave of Hagenau represents a group of rich warrior graves of the Middle and Late Bronze Age in southern central Europe. Typical of these graves is the inclusion of the sword, paired in the stage Br C1 with the dagger and axe (or at least with one of the two). By the time of stage Br C2, daggers or axes as parts of the weaponry are less frequent, and in Br D such occurs only rarely. Instead, the spear comes to be included as an additional weapon; the knife as a hunting tool: tendencies that are confirmed, particularly with respect to the knife, in the Early Urnfield period (Ha A). By stage Br D, cremation burial appears as frequently as does inhumation, the burial practice that had been common up to that point. Both funerary rites are still regularly associated with burial mounds at the beginning of the Urnfield period proper.

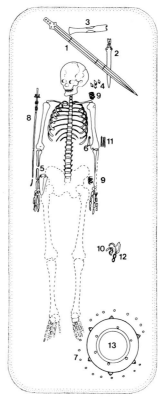

2 The Hagenau grave, Germany. 1. larger flange-hilted sword; 2. shorter flangehilted sword; 3. flanged axe; 4. arrowheads; 5. flange-hilted dagger; 6. belt-hook; 7. decorative nails; 8. gold pin; 9. gold spiral armlets; 10. gold bracelets; 11. tattoo needles; 12. razor; 13. clay vessel.
Scale: c. 1:12 (Reconstruction after H. Böhmer).

Although the swords also served as status symbols, the presence of additional equipment with weapons underlines the particular military orientation of the rich warriors and chiefs that established themselves at the intersections and junctions of the main traffic and trade routes, itineraries that shifted over the course of time. These chiefs controlled and regulated the exchange of goods, thus opening themselves up to a wide range of influences and wielding an economic power capable of affording extraordinary, culturally progressive goods.

Bibliography: Rieckhoff 1990; Schaich 1989; Stary 1980.

Oak Coffin-Graves of the Northern European Bronze Age

Jørgen Jensen

In the Early Bronze Age, c. 1700–1100 BC, funerary ritual in northern Germany and southern Scandinavia called for the burial of the dead in coffins of hollowed-out oak trunks. After interment, a burial mound, constructed of grass sod, was erected over the coffin. On the average, the mounds had a diameter of twenty metres and a height of three to four. Burial mounds with a diameter of over thirty metres were also erected, however, while a few were even larger. In Denmark alone, around 40,000 burial mounds are known from the Early Bronze Age.

In the vast majority of cases, the organic material decayed in its entirety within a short time after its interment. Occasionally, however, special natural and chemical conditions in the interior of the mound ensured the survival of the oak coffin and its contents to the present day. These oak coffins, over 3000 years old, are among the most notable finds from the Nordic Bronze Age, and nearly all of them are now held in the Danish National Museum in Copenhagen.

1   In Denmark, around 40,000 burial mounds have survived from the Early and Middle Bronze Age. Nearly all were erected within a relatively short period of time, between 1500 and 1100 BC.

In a few extraordinary cases, the core of the grave mound, ccontained a large quantity of water. The anaerobic conditions resulting from this situation caused the formation of a ferrous layer around the core of the mound, sealing its interior and preventing the decay of the oak coffin.

In the course of the 19th century, Danish archaeologists excavated a number of very well-preserved oak coffins from the Bronze Age. Many of these were found in the southern part of Jutland, near the border of

2   Folding stool from the oak coffin-grave in the burial mound Guldhøj, south Jutland, (Denmark), dated by dendrochronology to the period around 1381 BC. The folding stool is made of ash wood and originally had a seat of otter's fur. The stool was modelled after Egyptian or eastern Aegean examples.

Schleswig-Holstein. The most famous burial mounds in this region are Guldhøj, Store Kongehøj (Cat. No. 166) and Trindhøj. Here, a large number of very well-preserved men's graves were found. The dead were interred in their everyday clothes: clad in a cap, jerkin, and a round hood, they received rich grave gifts of weapons and jewellery. Occasionally other items were included as well, such as carved wooden bowls ornamented with tin or a folding stool with a seat of otter's fur. Folding stools of a similar form are also known from the eastern Mediterranean.

3 The oak coffin grave from the burial mound Borum Eshøj (Denmark). The deceased was a 20 to 22 year-old man. Dendrochronological dating methods have shown that the grave was constructed c. 1345 BC.

In the 20th century, as well, oak coffin-graves from the Bronze Age have been discovered with the help of modern excavation methods. In 1921, an extraordinarily well-preserved woman's grave was uncovered at Egtved in east Jutland. The coffin, 2.5 m long, contained the remains of a sixteen to eighteen years old girl. The body was clothed in a blouse of sheep's wool with half-length sleeves and a cord skirt, likewise of wool. Her hair was cut short; around her waist was a belt with a bronze buckle, and her wrists were adorned with bracelets. At her feet

was a small container of bark which formerly contained a fermented beverage, probably a kind of diluted mead. In addition, the coffin also contained a small bundle of cloth with the cremated remains of a six to eight years old child.

In 1936, another female grave was uncovered at Skrydstrup in south Jutland. In this case the coffin had decayed, although the body and clothing of a young girl were still very well preserved. The girl died at the age of sixteen to eighteen years. Her long, light blond hair was arranged in a complicated coiffure and covered with a net of horsehair. Her upper body was clad in a blouse with half-length, embroidered sleeves. A piece of cloth woven of sheep's wool and sewn together extended from her middle to her feet. The manner in which this "skirt" was originally worn is uncertain. The length of fabric could be wound around the body $2^{1}/_{2}$ times and extended from the armpits to the feet. At the foot of the coffin, scraps of fabric in which the feet were wrapped were also found, as well as the remains of a pair of leather sandals. The only jewellery worn by the deceased was a pair of golden earrings, while a comb of horn was tucked into her belt.

In recent years, dendrochronological methods – i.e., the counting of annual rings of the oak trunks – have been used to date the oak coffin-graves (see Christensen, pp. 110 ff.). In a few cases, even the outermost cambium of the tree was preserved, so that the date of the tree's felling could be determined with precision. By this method, the burial of the Egtved girl could be dated to the summer of the year 1370 BC. Dendrochronological dating indicates that almost all the other oak coffin-graves were likewise interred in the 14th century BC. To this day, we still have no explanation for the fact that the Danish and north German oak coffin-graves of the Bronze Age all stem from this relatively short period. Nonetheless, the precise dating has revealed the important fact that the oak coffin-graves of the Nordic Bronze Age originated during the same period when the Mycenaean palaces were flourishing in Greece.

Bibliography: Boye 1896, 1986; Breuning-Madsen 1997; Broholm & Hald 1935, 1939, 1940; Jensen 1998; Randsborg 1996; Thomsen 1929.

Tree-ring Dating of Bronze Age Oak Coffins from Denmark

Kjeld Christensen

In recent decades, the use of scientific methods has yielded new information concerning the Bronze Age oak coffins found in Denmark (see Jensen, pp. 108 f.). In many cases, dendrochronology – a method of dating based on the annual rings in tree trunks – has been successfully employed to determine the exact age of the oak coffins. As an oak tree grows, a new ring forms every year. The width of the ring is dependent on climatic conditions during the year in question – good years produce wide rings, bad years narrow ones. In an area with uniform growth conditions, all trees of the same species show the same sequence of broad and narrow rings. These variations in growth form a pattern for the entire lifetime of a tree, one that is unique and linked exclusively to a specific time-span. Thus the ring-width profiles of different trees can be compared with one another and dated on the basis of the annual ring pattern. With the help of specimens from living trees, timber from old houses, wood from archaeological excavations, etc., a composite ring-width profile can be constructed – a so-called "master chronology" that extends ever further into the past. This chronology, in turn, is used to date wood whose age is unknown.

Although the custom of burying the dead in hollowed-out oak trunks was widespread in large parts of northern Europe, the majority of well-preserved Bronze Age oak coffins have been found in Denmark, most of them within a fairly limited geographical area (see map). At present, the Danish master chronology goes back only to around the time of the birth of Christ. In Germany, however, the master chronologies for oak-wood extend as far back as 7000 to 8000 years, providing an effective means of dating wood from prehistoric sites. A number of years ago, a co-operative effort with the Danish museums was initiated by Germany to date the Bronze Age oak coffins. Around twenty-five oak coffins were analysed; as the diagram and date list show, however, final results were obtained for only eighteen examples from thirteen different burial mounds.

Since the coffins were found in different states of preservation, the year the trees were felled could be determined only with varying degrees of precision. Presumably the coffins were stripped of bark before burial, since no bark was visible on any of them. On many of the coffins, however, the sapwood (the outermost, living part of the wood) was preserved, and in a number of cases it could be shown with great probability that the bark ring (the annual ring directly below the bark) had survived as well. For these coffins, the year the tree was felled could be established with precision (accuracy level A in the date list). In cases where only part of the sapwood was preserved, the year of felling could be determined within a few years (B). Frequently, however, the sapwood was missing in its entirety, even when, according to the reports, it had still been preserved at the time of excavation. In cases where it could be shown that the less resistant sapwood had decayed only in modern times, and that the most recent surviving annual ring was located on the boundary between the heartwood and the sapwood, the year of felling could still be determined with a fair amount of accuracy (C: ± c. 10 years). In cases where all of the sapwood and possibly even part of the heartwood were missing, however, the dating was even less certain (D).

As the diagram shows, the oldest oak coffins were buried c. 1400 BC or shortly thereafter, while the youngest – whose year of felling is unfortunately very uncertain – date from 1300–1250 BC. Thus it would appear that all the coffins analysed were produced within a span of only 150 years. Even more surprising, however, is the fact that the trees used for most of the oak coffins – fifteen of the eighteen examples analysed, from ten of the thirteen burial mounds – were felled between 1410 and 1360 BC, i.e. within a period of only 50 years. Only three coffins were unquestionably produced at a later date. In a few cases, several oak coffins from the same burial mound were analysed. Three coffins from the Guldhøj burial mound could be dated to the year 1389 BC, indicating that all three were buried the same year; the coffins from Graves A and C were even manufactured from the same tree trunk. The burial mound Borum Eshøj contained two coffins that might have been produced in the same year, c. 1351 BC; since the sapwood was missing from the coffin in Grave B, however, it is also possible that the oaks were felled in different years. Of the three coffins preserved from the burial mound of Trindhøj, that of Grave C was dated to around the year 1347 BC; the others may have originated at about the same time, though Coffin A is most likely a few years older, and Coffin B a few years younger, than Coffin C.

It is surprising that the majority of the Bronze Age oak coffins date to a period of only fifty years, although the custom of burying the dead in hollowed-out oak trunks prevailed for at least six centuries. The reason for this is unknown, as is the explanation for the fact that although the burial ritual was widespread in large parts of northern Europe, most of the coffins have been found in a limited area in Denmark. These uncertainties, however, do not alter the remarkable inference that some of the people buried in the dated coffins may have known each other during their lifetimes. The possibility seems nearly indubitable when we consider the men in the burial mounds at Barde and Muldbjerg, for example, which were interred within eight years and sixteen km of each other, and the men of Hennekesdam and Trindhøj, Grave C, buried about twelve km from each other, and probably interred within a year of each other. All of them, moreover, could have met the Egtved girl dressed in her cord skirt and belt buckle. Thus the dating method of dendrochronology helps to bring us closer to the lives and activities of prehistoric peoples.

Bibliography: Christensen & Jensen 1991; Glob 1974; Haupt 1987; Jensen 1998b; Randsborg 1996; Schweingruber 1983; Vandkilde et al. 1996.

Map: The map shows the location of the burial mounds where the coffins were found.

Diagram: Each bar represents a coffin (a tree) and marks its annual rings. In cases where the coffin (tree trunk) was not preserved in its entirety, the estimated missing annual rings towards the pith and the bark are indicated.

List: The numbers of the coffins (see diagram and map) as well as the names of the sites and the years of felling are shown, along with the degree of accuracy in dating.

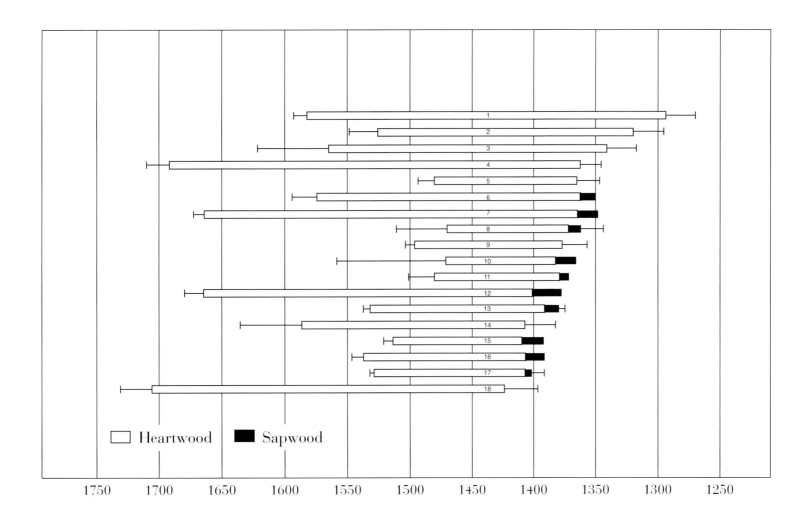

Tree-ring dating of oak coffins from the Early Bronze Age

1. Nybøl — Felled after c. 1268 BC — (D)
2. Nøragerhøj — Felled after c. 1295 BC — (C)
3. Rønhøj — Felled c. 1315 BC — (C)
4. Trindhøj, Grave B — Felled after c. 1333 BC — (D)
5. Borum Eshøj, Grave B — Felled c. 1345 BC — (C)
6. Trindhøj, Grave C — Felled 1347 BC — (A?)
7. Hennekesdam, Jels — Felled 1348 BC — (A)
8. Borum Eshøj, Grave A — Felled c. 1351 BC — (B)
9. Trindhøj, Grave A — Felled after c. 1356 BC — (D)
10. Muldbjerg — Felled 1365 BC — (A)
11. Storhøj, Egtved — Felled 1370 BC — (A)
12. Storehøj, Barde — Felled 1373 BC — (A)
13. Lille Dragshøj — Felled c. 1373 BC — (B)
14. Fladshøj — Felled after c. 1377 BC — (D)
15. Guldhøj, Grave C — Felled 1389 BC — (A)
16. Guldhøj, Grave A — Felled 1389 BC — (A)
17. Guldhøj, Grave B — Felled c. 1389 BC — (B)
18. Mølhøj — Felled after c. 1396 BC — (D)

(A) Probable year of felling, determined with precision (bark ring apparently preserved)

(B) Approximate year of felling, ± a few years (part of the sapwood preserved)

(C) Presumed year of felling, uncertain (most recent surviving annual ring probably close to sapwood)

(D) Earliest possible year of felling, uncertain (only heartwood preserved, distance to sapwood uncertain)

113

Bronze Age Stelai and Menhirs of the Iberian Peninsula: Discourses of Power

Susana Oliveira Jorge

The Stelai of the Alentejo-Algarve Region

In the Middle Bronze Age in the southwest of the Iberian Peninsula (c. 1700–1300/1200 BC), stelai with sculptural decoration appeared in the Alentejo-Algarve region (Ill. 1, 2). These monuments, whose style represents a break with the stelai and menhirs of Chalcolithic tradition (see Oliveira Jorge, pp. 137ff.), consist of slabs or monoliths without unequivocally anthropomorphic contours, on which reliefs, or more rarely engravings, of weapons are executed. These depictions are always located outside the explicit representation of the human body (Ill. 2). Swords, halberds and axes predominate among the weapons, as well as a number of more enigmatic representations, such as the so-called "anchor-shaped object".

1   Distribution in the Iberian Peninsula of the Bronze Age stelai/
    menhir statues mentioned in the text
    ■ Stele of Longroiva
    ▲ Sculpted stelai of the Alentejo type
    ○ Engraved stelai of the Estremadura type
    ● Menhir statues from Trás-os-Montes

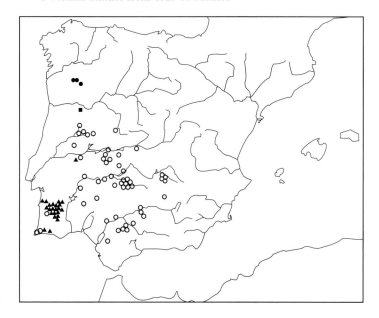

These slabs or monoliths, which are usually interpreted as gravestones (Gomes & Monteiro 1977, 309), may also have been erected in connection with burial mounds to symbolise the social position of the persons interred there.

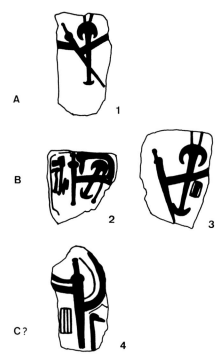

2   Schematic reproduction of the sculpted stelai of the Alentejo type
    (Typology – A, B, C: according to Gomes and Monteiro 1977;
    Gomes 1995. Drawings after M. Almagro Basch 1966).
    1. Herdada de Defesa, Santiago do Cacém (Setúbal). Height 116 cm.
    2. Assento, Santa Vitória (Beja). Height 93 cm.
    3. Pedreirinha, Santa Vitória (Beja). Height 90 cm.
    4. Trigaxes I (Beja). Height 72 cm.

According to Gomes and Monteiro (1977) and Gomes (1995), iconographic analysis of the stelai of the "Alentejo type" reveals a twofold "matrix" for the categorisation of the objects. The first group (Group A) consists of the sizeable "stelai" with the "anchor-shaped object" in the middle, either alone (Ill. 4) or in combination with a long sword and/or halberd of the "Montejícar type" (Gomes 1995, 135) (Ill. 2 A). According to Gomes, this group is the older one (c. 1600–1500 BC) and is more widespread.

The second group (Group B) (Ill. 2 B) is marked by the simultaneous depiction of a number of weapons on the same piece: in addition to swords and halberds, already seen in the first group, there also appear axes, gouges and other artefacts. The "anchor-shaped object" now tends to become lost in the overall composition (Ill. 5). Gomes (1995, 135) dates this group to the period between 1500 and 1300 BC and confines it to a part of the Alentejo, the region around Beja.

Gomes (1994; 1995) distinguishes a third group as well (Ill. 2 C), comprised of smaller-scale "stelai" characterised by a kind of hegemony of sword representations. The sword appears by itself or in combination with other objects of symbolic character (such as halberds, a pair of sandals) depicted in engraving or relief. This group occurs in the same region as Group B, though in a later phase (1300–1200/1100 BC).

According to the development suggested by Gomes, the increasing significance of the sword, which superseded the original symbol of the "anchor-shaped object", demonstrates the "growing importance of politico-military functions [...] toward the end of the second stage of the Bronze Age in the southwest" (Gomes 1995, 135).

Regarding the set of stelai described above, two brief remarks should be made:

1. Too little is known of the archaeological context of the stelai of the Alentejo type to attempt an exact chronology or even suggest a developmental scheme based on internal attributes. We know that they date to the Middle Bronze Age in the southwest, but there is no archaeological evidence for the sequence of the individual groups. In any case, even if the typological groups do represent some form of diachronic development, the same scheme would by no means hold true for the entire area in which the stelai are found. Regional differences would have exerted a decisive influence on the presence or absence of particular artefacts as well the greater or lesser frequency of their depiction.

Furthermore, it is necessary to explain the nature and "symbolic weight" of the "anchor-shaped object", which in particular contexts or ritual scenarios may have possessed a significance the same as or even greater than that of the weapons. In any event, "weapon" and "anchor-shaped object" are metaphorical representations: their specific meaning establishes itself as in a language, while their form evokes a highly contextual range of references that vary over space and time. For this reason, attempts to construct a typological or even social development on the basis of the greater or lesser "visibility" of these symbols appear at the very least to be problematic.

2. The stelai do in fact suggest a certain departure from Chalcolithic tradition:

• As a rule, the monoliths or slabs do not show even the suggestion of anthropomorphic contours. Here the "stele" of Tapada de Moita (Portalegre) (Jorge Oliveira 1986) (Ill. 6) constitutes an exception: the upper part of the stone is worked in a way that seems intended to emphasise the "shoulders". The sword and "anchor-shaped object" are held by straps that cross the "shoulders" in a manner reminiscent of the authentic menhir statues described by D'Anna (1998). Tapada da Moita thus represents the intersection of two sculptural conceptions: on the one hand, a menhir statue with the suggestion of anthropomorphic contours, and on the other a "panoply-stele" (Gomes & Monteiro 1977, 305) on which only weapons are depicted.

• Despite the absence of explicitly anthropomorphic contours in the great majority of these pieces, their compositional structure is characterised by an obvious ambiguity: the weapons and "anchor-shaped object" are held by or combined with straps that cross on the sculpturally worked face in a manner that subtly suggests an anthropomorphic "attitude". Despite this structural subtlety, which may represent an element of the original conception, the overemphasis on the depiction of particular objects at the expense of the representation of the human is unmistakable, as if the most important thing were to demonstrate the possession of certain artefacts. In this way the privileged status of the owners is implied, persons who were buried in grave mounds in the vicinity of these physical manifestations of power in funerary context. The desire to demonstrate such possession is also evident in the composition of the stelai, which is largely standardised. This group is in fact the most formally homogeneous ensemble of stelai/menhirs on the Peninsula.

The Longroiva Stele

A well-known monument is the "stele" of Longroiva (Guarda) (Ill. 7), dating from the Early to Middle

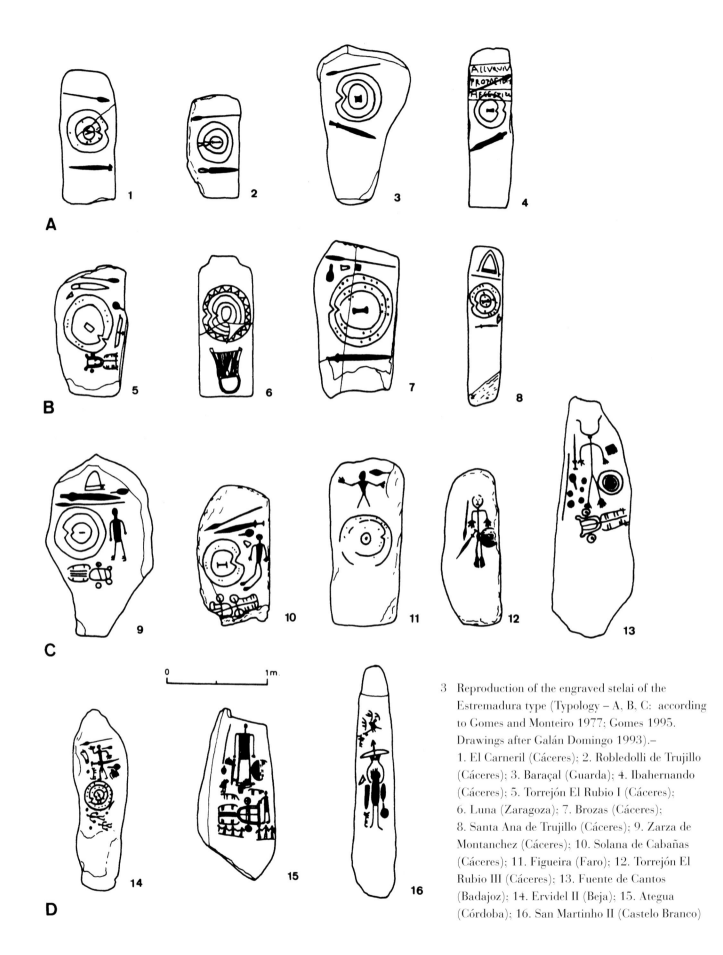

3 Reproduction of the engraved stelai of the Estremadura type (Typology – A, B, C: according to Gomes and Monteiro 1977; Gomes 1995. Drawings after Galán Domingo 1993).–
1. El Carneril (Cáceres); 2. Robledolli de Trujillo (Cáceres); 3. Baraçal (Guarda); 4. Ibahernando (Cáceres); 5. Torrejón El Rubio I (Cáceres); 6. Luna (Zaragoza); 7. Brozas (Cáceres); 8. Santa Ana de Trujillo (Cáceres); 9. Zarza de Montanchez (Cáceres); 10. Solana de Cabañas (Cáceres); 11. Figueira (Faro); 12. Torrejón El Rubio III (Cáceres); 13. Fuente de Cantos (Badajoz); 14. Ervidel II (Beja); 15. Ategua (Córdoba); 16. San Martinho II (Castelo Branco)

Bronze Age in the northern Iberian Peninsula (2000–1300 BC?). It was found in the valley of a west-bank tributary of the Douro in northern Portugal. Unfortunately, the archaeological context of the find is unknown. Nonetheless, it is clear that it is more or less contemporary with (and possibly somewhat older than) a sculptural tradition markedly different from that of the Alentejo stelai.

The Longroiva stele consists of a large block of granite whose top is worked in such a way that the upper outline of the piece corresponds to the head of the anthropomorphic figure engraved over the entire front side. The compositional structure of the smoothest side of the block is dominated by the engraved figure of a man. The face is indicated by means of eyes, nose, and mouth, as well as perhaps an ear. The body, clad in a kind of tunic, is rectangular and terminates in the lower part of the stele with four vertical strokes which represent legs. The figure may have worn a beard, behind which the representation of a very long neck can be discerned as can a necklace with a semicircular pendant. The figure holds a variety of weapons, all which are typologically identifiable: a halberd of the "Carrapatas" type, attributed to the Early Bronze Age in this region, a bow and a dagger with a triangular blade (V. and S. Oliveira Jorge 1993). The fact that the projection of the block coincides with the head of the human figure confirms the supposition that the block as a whole is meant to represent a particular person, as with a true menhir statue. Indeed, despite the legibility of only one of its sides, the so-called "stele" of Longroiva presents an indubitably anthropomorphic outline, a fact that distinguishes it from the engraved stelai or slabs of the Alentejo type and confirms its resemblance to the heterogeneous group of menhir statues on the Iberian Peninsula.

It should be noted that in the same area where the stele of Longroiva was found, though admittedly on the eastern bank of the Douro, a significant number of stelai/menhirs of "Mediterranean affiliation" were also found, dating to the late Neolithic or Chalcolithic periods (see Oliveira Jorge, pp. 137ff.). These small-scale pieces, which show no weapons, may have been the regional forerunners of stelai like that of Longroiva. Despite its uniqueness of form, Longroiva probably belongs to the realm of large stelai/menhirs showing an armed male personage (Almagro-Gorbea 1993). Viewed from a distance, this monument could indeed have "embodied" a socially prominent person (V. and S. Oliveira Jorge 1993, 38). On the regional level, Longroiva appears to signify a break; with respect to sculptural conception of power representation.

The Engraved Stelai of the Late Bronze Age

In the Late Bronze Age (mid 2nd millennium–9th century BC), engraved stelai meant to stand upright in the ground appear especially in the Spanish regions of Estremadura and western Andalusia (Ill. 1, 3). These monuments may have represented territorial "markers" along the roads connecting the southwest hinterland with its southern periphery (S. Oliveira Jorge 1998). Unlike the stelai of Longroiva or Tapada da Moita, or even those of the Alentejo type from the Early and Middle Bronze Age, the outline of these pieces betrays no anthropomorphic intention whatsoever. Moreover, in their conception, they display nothing that might even subtly suggest the identification of the block as a whole with the representation of a human figure. In these slabs, in other words, the side that is engraved functions merely as the bearer of a relatively autonomous composition (Ill. 3), showing artefacts either individually or in combination with anthropomorphic representations. According to Gomes and Monteiro (1977) and Gomes (1995), these pieces can be typologically divided into five groups, which according to the authors bear witness to a cultural development over time.

Type A (Ill. 3) consists of pieces showing at the centre a round shield with a V-shaped notch, crowned by a rod-like lance; below the shield is a sword. This type is found predominantly in the Spanish provinces of Cáceres and Badajoz, although examples have also been discovered in the Beira Alta (Ill. 3, no. 3). Gomes (1995) dates these pieces to the 12th–11th centuries BC.

Type B (Ill. 3) combines the above-mentioned representations of weapons with depictions of helmets (Ill. 3, No. 8), lyres (Ill. 3, No. 6), bows, wagons, mirrors, combs and angled fibulas (Ill. 3, No. 5 & 7), artefacts that suggest a "Mediterranean influence". This type is found in the same area as the preceding one, though it also extends

4   Stele from Alfarrobeira (Silves).
    Height: 1.70 m

5   Stele from Santa Vitória (Beja).
    Height: 0.95 m

6   Stele from Moita (Castelo de Vide).
    Height: 2.14 m

further toward the south. According to Gomes (1995), it originated in the 10th century BC.

Type C (Ill. 3) is marked by the representation of a human figure which tends to dominate the compositional structure, even when it is associated with weapons and other objects such as wagons, mirrors or helmets (Ill. 3, Nos. 9–13). The larger or smaller size of the human figure and its (relative) centring in the sculpturally worked area of the engraved surface reflects a whole range of compositional variants within this type, which is widespread in southern Andalusia and the Algarve. Gomes (1995) dates it to the 10th–9th centuries BC.

Type D (Ill. 3) comprises slabs with human representations (warriors?) in the centre of the composition. As in Ervidel II (Ill. 3, No. 14; Fig. 8), the figures are accom-

panied by engravings of a whole panoply of weapons and other objects related to a "proto-orientalising" sphere; they are found in Granada, the Alentejo or the Beira Baixa (Ill. 3, Nos. 14–16). According to Gomes (1995), these objects stem from the 9th–8th centuries BC.

This evolutionary scheme associates the occurrence of a human figure (the "Warrior") with the increasing representation of weapons and artefacts of Mediterranean origin, thus expressing the social standing of a leader in terms of his relation to long-distance trade with the Mediterranean world. According to Gomes, the stelai of this final phase served a "memorial function" in the context of "early state-like societies" (Gomes 1995).

A few brief remarks should be made concerning this evolutionary model:

7   Stele from Longroiva (Guarde).
Height: 2.40 m

8   Stele from Ervidel II (Beja).
Height: 1.75 m

9   Menhir statue from Bouça
(Mirandela). Height: 2.45 m

1. Here too, and for the same general reasons formulated with respect to the Alentejo stelai, serious questions must be raised concerning the proposed developmental chronology. This last appears to represent nothing more than a theoretical construction that still remains to be proven.

2. Without doubt, the presence of human figures in the groups C and D constitutes a significant formal distinction. The groups A and B show only weapons and other objects, as if the crucial aim – as already observed with regard to the Alentejo stelai – were above all to demonstrate possession of or familiarity with certain artefacts. The inclusion of human figures in the groups C and D, however, is not intended to fill out the entire sculptural area of the slab in an unambiguous way. The human fig-

ure, whether centred or not, shares the area set aside for displaying the composition with a large number of symbols. On the other hand, in view of the relative size of the human figures and some of the artefacts (mostly shields and weapons), we are confronted with a compositional structure that has been largely codified and abstracted and in which it is not easy to recognise "narrative scenes". Viewed in this way, the stelai of the "Estremadura type", particularly those with human figures, show an extraordinarily developed level of metaphorical communication, which is difficult to decipher. Unlike the stele of Longroiva (Ill. 7), for example, which clearly depicts a "warrior" with his weapons and adornment, on the Estremadura stelai we find symbols that could be meant to represent a human figure, some weapons and yet other

119

objects – cases in which, in our opinion, it is impossible to establish concrete references such as "warrior with shield, sword and mirror".

3. As already noted in another chapter of this catalogue (see Oliveira Jorge, pp. 137ff.), the study by Galán Domingo (1993) presents a number of interesting ideas on this corpus. First and foremost, the author argues that the routes marked by the stelai were used for the transport of subsistence goods rather than metalic artefacts such as those engraved on the stelai. Secondly, Galán Domingo emphasises that the stelai served above all to manifest social prestige, and thus are not directly associated with the exchange of goods in the area in question. Accordingly, the monuments serve to display status without reference to the actual social paraphernalia of the groups they represent. The objects engraved on the stelai were not handled directly by those who built the monuments, though they might have known corresponding prototypes through their contacts with groups that produced and/or traded the objects. In this way, the representations on the stelai make no direct reference to real objects in their social sphere. Accordingly, the representations are to be viewed as metaphorical and not realistic. Their meaning was established as with a language, their outer form reproducing the original object only in a distant and indirect way. The form was "translated" into a permanent symbol that bore a specific meaning legible only to the groups that belonged to the same identification system (Oliveira Jorge, 1998, 165).

Three Menhir Statues from the Northwest

Entirely different from the stelai of the Estremadura type are the menhir statues from Faiões, Chaves or Bouça (Ill. 1, 4). These monuments belong to the regional Late Bronze Age in the northwest of the Peninsula (V. and S. Oliveira Jorge 1993) and consist of granite monoliths set upright into the ground in order to be visible from afar

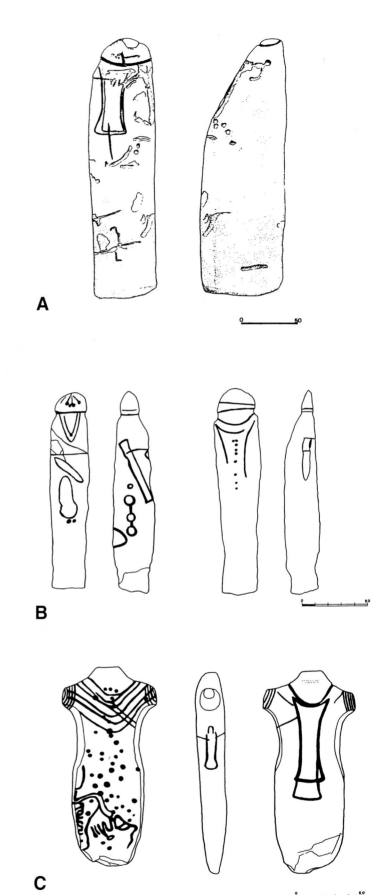

10 Schematic reproduction of the menhir statues from Trás-os-Montes

A. Bouça (reproduction after Sanches and Almeida, 1987)
B. Chaves (reproduction after Oliveira Jorge and Almeida, 1980)
C. Faiões (reproduction after Almeida and Oliveira Jorge, 1979)

(Ill. 10). Here, anthropomorphic outlines are either suggested (Chaves and Bouça) or pronounced (Faiões); the monuments are created in such a way as to be "legible" on all four sides, even if in some cases (as with Bouça) they were engraved only on one side (Ill. 10).

The menhir statue from Bouça (Mirandela) (Sanches & Oliveira Jorge, V. 1987) (Ill. 9) was found in the vicinity of a river valley; the exact archaeological context is unknown. It is a great monolith with four sides, approximately 2.45 m high. It possesses an unambiguously phallic character with an upper circle (urethra?) and a lower one (possibly the outline of the glans penis). On the polished front side, only a few cup-marks are engraved. The back shows a representation found on all three of the pieces mentioned, a vertical motif consisting of a rectangle with a trapezoidal base, perhaps meant to depict a piece of clothing ("stola") connected with a special social status.

The phallic menhir of Chaves (Oliveira Jorge & Almeida 1980) was found in the bed of the Tâmega, a tributary of the Douro, and may represent an older piece that was reused in the Late Bronze Age. It is 1.65 m high and made of granite (Ill. 10 B). At the top, the tip of a phallus is portrayed, which, on the basis of various engraved attributes, may also be identified with the head of the honoured person. These comprise a sword of considerable length, shown on the left side, and a dagger or asymmetrical knife on the right. The belt is visible on both sides; near the dagger, it is only suggested. The rear of the piece shows an attribute in the form of a rectangular-based motif again (reminiscent of a "stola" in the same manner as the menhir statue from Bouça). In addition to the other motifs, the front side also shows a stylised face, necklaces, possibly a third weapon hanging from the belt and an elongated symbol (erect phallus?).

Finally, the menhir statue from Faiões (Almeida & V. Oliveira Jorge 1979) was found in a fertile area in the county of Chaves; its exact archaeological context is again unknown. This sculpture, too, is clearly anthropomorphic and is shown on two opposed sides of a granite slab measuring 1.61 m in height (Ill. 10 C). At its discovery, the head no longer existed; presumably, however, it was only ever suggested. The arms are reduced to two stumps and the ribcage is schematically outlined, suggesting the presence of a belt. The lower part is worked rather sketchily. The front side shows only four small cup-marks, a row of necklaces or clothing accessories in a more or less concentric arrangement and a weapons belt shown at the right side like a border. In the lower middle area and on the two sides, linear motifs appear which are difficult to interpret, but which may have possessed some symbolic significance.

The rear is dominated by a vertical, rectangular-based motif whose significance is debated. As we have seen, similar also occur on the pieces from Bouça and Chaves – presumably representing an insignia of (or symbol for) authority.

Despite the sculptural heterogeneity of these pieces, the rear of all three show an attribute that may represent a symbol of political or religious power, comparable to the "anchor-like object" on the stelai of the Alentejo type. It is significant to note, moreover, that this motif survived into the Iron Age in northern Portugal. It appears on the late menhir statue of S. João de Ver (Feira) (V. and S. Oliveira Jorge 1983). Due to their schematic rendering, the weapons on the examples from Chaves and Faiões cannot be typologically categorised.

On the whole, despite a very general dating to the Late Bronze Age, this northern group of three menhir statues evinces clear formal differences to the contemporary stelai of the Estremadura type. They appear rather to correspond to artistic and perhaps ideological conceptions other than those observable in the southern regions of the Peninsula.

Conclusions

A final remark should be made concerning the ritual and symbolic context of the different groups of menhir statues discussed here. Despite the great gaps in our information with respect to the archaeological context of such important pieces as Longroiva, Chaves or Faiões, we still maintain that the pieces described here can be "accommodated" in a general way within two broad groups: those occurring in funerary context, such as the Alentejo stelai, and those that may have served as territorial markers, i.e. the Estremadura stelai and perhaps also the "northern" stelai and menhir statues.

In the first phase of the Bronze Age (Early and Middle Bronze Age), the display of power took place — in accord with Neolithic tradition – primarily in the context of burial places and shrines (rock-art sites and others). Regardless of the various sorts of cemeteries and shrines in the various regions of the Iberian Peninsula, power was everywhere manifested at the moment of burial of the charismatic leader. In the Middle Bronze Age in southern Portugal, the stelai of the Alentejo type demonstrate a similar assertion of power in the context of funerary ritual.

Beginning in the Late Bronze Age, on the other hand, the settings for the representation of power are withdrawn from the traditional sepulchral realm. These burial places now become archaeologically almost unrecognisable. The power extend to new ritual spaces, characterised by the practice of conspicuous consumption. In these new spaces, whose nature remains to be more clearly defined, rich gold jewellery and the entire range of specific bronze equipment of trans-regional typology have been discovered, goods whose complete interpretation ("gift", "hoard", "cache", etc.) is still largely unknown.

Within this new social structure, the Estremadura stelai and the northern menhir statues must now be viewed as detached from the previously dominant function of ruler glorification in context of the cult of the dead. The sculptural art of the Late Bronze Age succeeded in coming to terms with a new form of political and symbolic appropriation of space. In "transit corridors" and on the edges or boundaries of territories, representative monuments of heroised persons were set up as central "foci of attraction" for the different groups and communities.

Finally, we would also suggest that this shift of settings for the demonstration of power marking off the Early from the Late Bronze Age cannot be separated from an essentially parallel (though not entirely synchronic) phenomenon, namely the integration of the indigenous societies of the Peninsula into larger systems of European interaction (Sherratt 1993; Oliveira Jorge, S. 1995; 1996).

Bibliography: Almeida & Oliveira Jorge V. 1979; D'Anna 1998; Galán Domingo 1993; Gomes 1994, 1995; Gomes & Monteiro 1976–77; Oliveira Jorge S. 1995, 1996; Oliveira Jorge V. & S. 1993; Oliveira Jorge & Almeida 1981; Oliveira Jorge 1986; Sanches & Oliveira Jorge V. 1987; Sherratt 1993.

The Nuragic Bronze Statuettes

Fulvia Lo Schiavo

The nuragic bronze statuettes are votive offerings, which are mainly found in sanctuaries, well temples and sacred springs, together with weapons and ornaments – gifts to the gods. They were fixed in place by molten lead poured into natural cracks or into holes especially made in the stones.

They provide a fascinating insight, unusual in protohistory, into a society "photographed" in all its aspects: tribal chiefs, warriors with sword and shield or bow and quiver, nobles, women covered with elegant decorated cloaks or sitting on wooden stools with male figures reclining in their arms (e.g. the "Pietà" from Urzulei, Nuoro). Apparently lower down the social scale, shepherds and farmers offer flat bread, present jars, carry lambs on their shoulders, ride oxen, brandish crutches, whilst women carry baskets on their heads … and so on.

Many different animals are reproduced: both domestic, such as oxen, sheep, pigs, dogs, cocks, doves, and wild, such as foxes, boars, moufflon and deer. At times such decorate the high prows of the boats, at others they are hunting trophies. Human or animal imaginary figures are also represented: "heroes" – warriors with four eyes and four arms, or the "Centaur" of Nule (Lo Schiavo 1996).

The statuettes still astonish by their rich detail and expressive vigour. Many oriental influences are discernible, and the number and variety of the iconography is increasing, due to the new excavations and discoveries. Among recent examples the most remarkable are the Warrior-Chief of the tribe, bearing a spear and leading on a rope a ram (a totemic animal or the offering for the sacrifice) from the nuragic sanctuary of Serra Niedda, Sorso (Sassari) (Rovina 1986, 1990) and a composite figure consisting of a man with another under his feet, evidently an enemy, again in association with a ram (again possibly a totemic animal) from the nuraghic sanctuary of Nurdòle, Orani (Nuoro) (Fadda 1991).

Ritual and domestic objects are portrayed as well: stools, jars, wooden boxes, baskets, axes and "gamma-hilted" daggers. Even more impressive and certainly related to the symbolism of the nuraghe itself are the miniature reproductions of single- and four-tower nuraghi in bronze as well as in stone. Rams' and bulls' heads are often sculpted in stone as decoration for the ashlar masonry of the sanctuaries, as at S. Vittoria, Serri (Nuoro), Serra Niedda, Sorso (Sassari). Cuccuru Mudeju, Nughedu S. Nicolò (Sassari), Gremanu, Fonni (Nuoro) (Lo Schiavo, in print 2). Human figures, large stone statues of archers and boxers, probably the heroised protagonists of sacred games, have so far been encountered only at Monte Prama in the Sinis peninsula near Oristano (Tronchetti, Mallegni & Bartoli 1991; Lo Schiavo, in print 1).

More than a hundred votive bronze boats show clearly the interest in sailing and the skill in boat-building

1 Bronze statuette from the nuraghic sanctuary of "Serra Niedda" Sorso (Sassari), depicting a warrior-chief of the tribe, carrying a spear and leading a ram by rope (a totemic animal or a sacrificial offering?). Courtesy of the Soprintendenza Archeologica per le Province di Sassari e Nuoro.

2 Bronze statuette from the nuraghic sanctuary of "Nurdòle" (Nuoro); a composite figure of a man with another man, evidently an enemy, under his feet; upon whom also is a ram (again, possibly a totemic animal). Courtesy of the Soprintendenza Archeologica per le Province di Sassari e Nuoro

during the nuragic period: the accuracy achieved in portraying the proportions of the hull and for rendering technical details impresses (Lo Schiavo 1997).

The chronology of the bronze figurines is a problem that will be solved through the study of the datable contexts and through the analysis of the process of production, the "lost wax" technique. Evidence for an early inception in the Late Bronze Age is more and more frequently encountered and consistent; there is no doubt that Cypriot connections in metallurgical technology and trade, at least from LC III period, strongly influenced nuragic Late Bronze Age production (Lo Schiavo, Macnamara & Vagnetti 1985).

Nuragic votive swords found in association with actual flange-hilted, leaf-shaped swords in hoards and in sanctuaries and also shown in the hands of the modelled nuragic warriors date to the 11th–10th centuries BC the manufacture of the models (Lo Schiavo 1991; 1994). A bronze male figurine holding a spear is associated with amber beads of the Protovillanovan "Allumiere" type in a tomb of the same date at Antas, Villaperucciu (Cagliari) (Ugas & Lucia 1987); a fragmentary figure of a chief was found in an nuraghe, abandoned with its village, at the end of the Late Bronze Age at Sa Mandra 'e Sa Giua, Ossi (Sassari) (Ferrarese Ceruti 1985); and many votive offerings, including three bronze figurines, were deposited at the sacred spring of Su Tempiesu, Orune (Nuoro), destroyed by a landslide at the end of 10th century BC (Fadda & Lo Schiavo 1992).

At the beginning of the Early Iron Age, many bronze figurines (human figurines, miniature baskets and stools, "buttons", votive quivers, etc.) are traded or brought by way of gift or of marriage to Etruria and to the Vallo di Diano necropolis of Pontecagnano (Lo Schiavo 1996b). Certainly some of them, including the votive bronze boats, were long preserved as prestige and precious objects in the Villanovan and Orientalizing tombs and votive deposits, such as at the Hera Lacinia sanctuary at Capo Colonna (Crotone) (Spadea 1996) and the Gravisca sanctuary in Latium.

Bibliography: Fadda 1991; Fadda & Lo Schiavo 1992; Lo Schiavo 1991, 1994, 1996, 1996b, 1997 and forthcoming 1 and 2; Lo Schiavo, Macnamara & Vagnetti 1985; Rovina 1986, 1990; Spadea 1996; Tranchetti, Mallegni & Bartoli 1991; Ugas & Lucia 1987.

Wagon-Graves of the Late Bronze Age

Christopher F. E. Pare

At the beginning of the Late Bronze Age (13th century BC) Europe underwent a crucial process of social and economic change. Production and consumption of bronze increased massively; long-distance exchange intensified (for example between the Nordic zone, central Europe and the Mediterranean); technological advances were transmitted across much of Europe (e.g. sheet metal in the production of armour and drinking vessels, Aegean systems of metrology, a complex range of tools, weaponry and ornaments); a new symbolic language was adopted, indicating the spread of religious beliefs (e.g. water-birds, solar discs), and elite burials appeared in various regional cultural groups. All these innovations find expression in a series of wagon-graves found north of the Alps in Switzerland, southern Germany and Austria; seventeen examples can be assigned to the 13th and 12th centuries BC. Some of

1 Model of a chariot, Mycenae – Chamber Tomb
Late Bronze Age (Cat. No. 52)

the graves, such as Hart an der Alz and Poing (southern Bavaria), contain a characteristic "elite set" of grave furnishings, comprising a wagon, a sword and a service of feasting vessels, typical of the highest ranking burials both in the Late Bronze Age (Urnfield culture) and in the

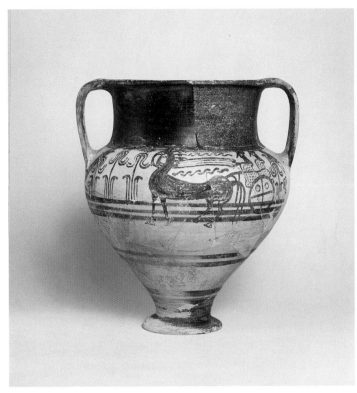

2 Amphoroid Krater, Nauplia – Chamber Tomb B
Late Bronze Age (Cat. No. 53)

Early Iron Age (Hallstatt culture). This continuity in the representation of high status is reflected in the wagons themselves: a recent study by C. Clausing (1997) has drawn attention to details of construction proving the existence of a continuous tradition of wagon production lasting up to 800 years, between the 13th and 6th centuries BC. Apart from graves, evidence for this tradition of wagon construction is also found in hoards (deposits of bronze objects).

Most of the wagons found in graves were severely damaged by the cremation pyre. Nevertheless, it is clear from detailed analysis of better preserved examples that some, at least, were definitely four-wheeled with spokes (Cat. Nos. 127, 128). There is more evidence about their

3 Amphora with wagon scene (detail), Slovakia
Middle Bronze Age (Cat. No. 124)

decoration: many surviving fragments show that the wagons were fitted with a mass of bronze decorative elements,
often including the water-bird symbol. To summarise the
available evidence, the wagons were elaborate and heavy
four-wheeled vehicles, drawn by a pair of horses; they
were not suited to use in battle, and are therefore best
understood as ceremonial conveyances.

Cemetery excavations in recent years, at Münchsmünster and Zuchering (Bavaria), have shed light on the
complexity of burial ritual. Some of the burnt remains of
the wagons were placed in "funerary deposits" separate
from the graves themselves. The body must have been
burnt on a cremation pyre with a wagon, but only a few
fragments of the wagon were selected to be among the
grave furnishings. For example, in grave E from Groß-
mugl (Lower Austria), under an urn containing a bronze
knife and an awl, excavations in 1938 uncovered a collection of about thirty fragmentary bronze rods (length
9.8–10.3 cm) and at least eleven nail-like rivets (length
18.7–19.7 cm) from a wagon box. As modern research
interprets many of the bronze hoards of the Late Bronze
Age as votive offerings which took place in the course of
cult activity, it seems that funerary ritual involved related
practices.

In the more advanced stages of the Late Bronze Age
these complex ritual practices become even more important. Only a few wagon-graves are known from the 11th,
10th and 9th centuries BC, and they contain but a handful
of wagon fittings. For example, a tumulus excavated in
1838 in the Lorscher Wald (Hessen) has part of a railing,
whilst Mühlheim-Lämmerspiel (Hessen) has a decorative
nail and Pfullingen (Württemberg) has four components
from the rear end of a wagon box. In view of the continuity we have mentioned in wagon construction and in status representation, we can be sure that ceremonial wagons were still used; but changes in religious beliefs and
the ideology of power meant that the dead were only very
rarely cremated and buried with a wagon.

After these centuries of simpler burial customs, in
which the dominant role of elites was negated in funeral
ritual, there was a resurgence of elaborate high status
burial at the end of the Late Bronze Age and at the transition to the Iron Age. Among these graves, often containing swords, horse-gear and bronze vessels, a few extremely rich graves were furnished with ceremonial wagons.
Examples include Lusehøj, a sword-grave in a huge
tumulus in south-west Funen (Denmark; see Thrane, pp.
127ff.) and tumulus 8 from Wehringen (near Augsburg,
Bavaria), with a four-wheeled wagon similar to Lusehøj,
a bronze sword, a gold cup and a richly decorated service
of pottery vessels. In the Early Iron Age (c. 725–475 BC)
elite wagon burial became much more common, with
about 250 examples known from Central Europe.

Bibliography: Clausing 1997; Pare 1987, 1992.

Princely Graves of the Late Bronze Age in the North

Henrik Thrane

A handful of graves round the Western Baltic stand out as exceptional by their contents and by the amount of energy spent on their construction. Sadly enough, most of them were excavated so early that little precise information is available.

Quite distinct from the others stands the monumental cairn – seventy-five m in diameter – of Kivik on the east coast of Scania from the 13th century BC. The maltreated carved slabs of the stone cist display a unique iconological program with a horse-drawn chariot of Mycenaean type as the easiest recognisable foreign element. The sparse remains of the grave goods indicate status objects like a bronze vessel. Trudshøj at Skallerup contained the famous wheeled cauldron with bird engravings but otherwise belongs to a wider group of male burials from the 12th century BC as does the grave-find of Peckatel (Mecklenburg) with the famous cauldron-wagon (Cat. No. 178).

To the 11th and 10th centuries BC belong the graves from Korshøj, Banie and Håga. Banie in Pomerania shows an interesting mixture of local bronzes with southern Urnfield and Nordic types (from Zealand) and the grave ritual reflects the same influences.

Korshøj at Vester Skjerninge on south Funen contained a Central European bronze bucket and a knife from the Banie region as well as several gold objects, including a sheet-plated sword, which are remarkably similar to the contents of "King Björn's mound" at Håga in Uppland. Excavated by Oscar Almgren in 1904, this last is one of the better documented graves. At the bottom of the mound was a charcoal deposit, five m in diameter, with the grave goods concentrated over 1.5 by 3.5 m, presumably fallen from the oak coffin. The cremated bones of a middle-aged individual of delicate build were placed on an oak bole with a gold-plated sword with a gold pommel and twenty-nine decorative gold nails, a gold-plated fibula and four double buttons plus two of bronze, two razors (one with gold wire), two bronze tweezers and pen-

dants from a pectoral(?). The grave was covered by a layer of oak boles and by a cairn of 3.2 by 45 m which was covered in turn by an earthen mound so that the complete mound measured eight by forty-five m. In the mound were found bones of at least three human individuals, two men and a female, as well as of several oxen and sheep, two pigs and some dogs (jawbones). As these bones had all been treated in the same way they are interpreted as remains from the funeral feast.

The bronzes and gold objects are clearly of South Scandinavian origin and the resemblance to the Korshøj assemblages is remarkable.

From the 9th and 8th centuries BC date a series of rich graves from southwest Funen, Holstein and Brandenburg. Little is known of the context of a collection of richly assorted bronzes from the mound "Kaiserberg" at Albersdorf in Dithmarschen on the west coast of Holstein but they are remarkably similar to those from the graves from Funen. At Voldtofte several mounds contained remarkable collections of gold and bronze objects, the most notable being those from the two graves from Lusehøj. One was excavated 1861 and is poorly documented. A stone cist contained an imported central European bronze bucket which had served as an urn. The bronze lid was smeared in birch pitch into which numerous small pieces of amber were stuck. In the urn were two razors, two bronze and two gold toggles, a gold armlet and a fine textile woven of nettles. Outside the urn were three bronze beakers; they had been wrapped with the urn in a woollen textile and an ox-hide. Also outside the urn was a decorated socketed axe. This grave has remained the richest Late Bronze Age grave north of the Baltic.

In 1973–75 Lusehøj was finally excavated and the context of the 1861 grave documented. It belonged to a turf built mound six by thirty-six m, as did another contemporary grave. This last was a simple cremation pit filled with unsorted remains from the funeral pyre. The pit had been covered by a straw mat and surrounded by an oval hurdle construction, three by 1.7 m. Over and around the hurdle had been built the mound, incorporating radially-set hurdles which presumably functioned as guide marks during the construction of the mound. The turves for the mound stripped more than seven hectares of grassland of its topsoil. With the bones of a thick-skulled adult and the charcoal in the cremation pit were the badly fire-damaged gold and bronze objects, largely reduced to molten lumps. A sword, a ceremonial chain and more than 400 tiny buckles for a leather belt, an iron finger ring as well as numerous nails, rings and cast fittings, presumably all belonging to a wagon box, have been identified. The variety of objects is second to none.

The settlement at Voldtofte, 1.6 km east of Lusehøj, is unique in so many ways that it has been interpreted as the settlement where the chiefs buried in Lusehøj lived and ruled over southwest Funen. The most striking expressions of the status of the Voldtofte settlement are the painted wall plaster from a cleared house and the evidence for the casting of the famous ritual horns of the Nordic Bronze Age, the "lurs" (Cat. Nos. 132, 133). This is the only case where it is possible to postulate the existence of a princely residence associated with princely burials. Twelve km southeast of Voldtofte another great mound, thirty-eight m in diameter (height unknown), has been excavated recently at Håstrup. Here a group of small mounds from the 7th century BC was covered by the big mound at the time when a stone cist was built, containing a large collection of minute bronze buckles for a leather belt (like Lusehøj), a razor, iron tweezers and pin, a southeast European glass bead and some textile of the Vače type also imported from the southeast. The cist stood on the funeral pyre which itself showed the same constructional details as at Lusehøj, namely a three-post setting. Other contemporary mounds from South Funen bear witness that the Final Bronze Age continued the traditions from the Lusehøj period.

The biggest monument, however, is "King Hinz' mound" at Seddin in north German West Prignitz with its remarkable oral tradition. The huge mound with central cairn measuring eleven by ninety m was excavated 1899. It was constructed over a two m wide stone chamber with a false vault. The walls were plastered with red-painted yellow clay. Little is preserved but there seems to have been curvilinear as well as meander-like decoration. In a huge clay pot was the bronze urn, an imported amphora with bronze lid and a bronze cup, a knife and a socketed-axe. The cremated bones belonged to a thirty to forty years old male and to marten and ermine (fur?). In the stone chamber were three or four urns, two containing

female individuals, as well as bronze and iron objects but their context is uncertain. A sword of local type presumably belonged to the "royal" burial.

Other contemporary mounds of size are known from the neighbouring tumulus cemeteries including Kemnitz I and Stralendorf. Unfortunately the more than three hundred graves from the Seddin area are poorly documented and published. The rich graves begin in the 10th and end in the 7th century but their apogee is the 9th–8th centuries BC. Most are but faint echoes of the Seddin mound itself.

Common to the princely graves are their monumentality and the richness of their equipment. The average cremation grave of the Late Bronze Age whether in south Scandinavia or in central Sweden contains no metal objects. This is true of some half of the adequately documented graves. A third to half of the graves contain one or two metal objects, mainly small and simple bronzes. Solid gold objects like those from the Lusehøj, Korshøj and King Björn's mound or even sheet-gold on buttons or sword hilts are conspicuously absent from the ordinary graves. Against this background the princely graves look even more distinct and distant from the normal; their status is correspondingly more obvious and remarkable.

The great mound with its rich armour from Čaka in Slovakia is roughly contemporary with Kivik and strongly reminiscent of the eloquently described Homeric grave ritual (*Iliad* XXIII.233 and XXIV.782). The echo of this Heroic Age practice at Kivik with its two-wheeled war chariot is strongly heard at Lusehøj where the bones were wrapped in textile. The wagon graves themselves may be another remote resonance of this tradition. How it survived for so many generations and how it was observed is well worth investigating.

Nearly all these burials are of adults characterised as male by a sword or an axe. They contain rare and exotic objects presumably denoting status, like the imported bronze vessels, gold and iron (in the late graves). It is also noteworthy that they are situated near the sea or navigable waters or, as at Seddin, in a favourable position by rivers which presumably were important for communication. The monumentality of the great mounds must express the desire of the ruling families to demonstrate their power in a lasting manner – in a situation where

1–2   Grave goods from the princely burial at "King Hinz'mound", West Prignitz, Germany, 9th–8th century BC

power was endangered? Apart from Seddin, southwest Funén and Albersdorf the brevity and lack of continuity at these sites is remarkable. The wealth expressed through the graves does not seen to have remained stable for more than one or two generations. Then the centre moved. The short distance between Voldtofte and Håstrup may demonstrate that the local circumstances favouring the acquisition of riches was access to communication lanes across the Baltic. The international network which supplied the Nordic area with the indispens-

able precious metals, gold and bronze presumably was the structure which spread the idea of the princely burials along with the status objects which feature so prominently in the graves, as well as other ideas of religious and political nature. When first the gold supply and later the bronze failed, the basis for the princely graves disappeared. It took four to five centuries before similar princely burials re-appeared – again employing wagons as an important element in the demonstration of rank.

Bibliography: Almgren 1905; Eggers 1936; Hänsel 1997; Kossack 1974; Menke 1972; Metzner-Nebelsick 1997; Randsborg 1993; Thrane 1966, 1984, 1994; 1995; Wüstemann 1974.

Chapter 4
The World of the Gods in the Bronze Age

Editor: Christiane Eluère

◁ The Chariot of the Sun from Trundholm, Zealand, Denmark
Early Bronze Age, 14th century BC (Cat. No. 175)

The World of the Gods in the Bronze Age

Christiane Eluère

We have no precise knowledge of the gods of the Bronze Age. Only a few names have come down to us from the Mycenaean world, prefiguring the Greek pantheon (Zeus, Hera, Poseidon, Athena, Dionysos, etc.) that would emerge several centuries later. While some scholars consider the mention of Greek gods in the Linear B tablets as proof of the age and continuity of their religion, some gods – such as Apollo, strangely enough – find no mention at all.

At the beginning of the epoch in question, i.e. at the beginning of the 4th millennium BC, the religious "instinct", understood in the broadest sense as the fear of or belief in higher powers and in life after death, was no innovation: as a trait inherent in *homo sapiens*, it had existed since the middle Palaeolithic age. This existential aspiration represents a universal constant, yet it appears under different aspects in different epochs and environments: "The archetypal conceptions produced by the unconscious should not be confused with the archetype itself. They are highly varied structures, all of which point back to a basic form which in itself is obscure. The archetype in itself is a psychoid factor, which belongs, as it were, to the invisible, ultraviolet part of the psychic spectrum.… One must always be aware that that which we call the 'archetype' is in itself obscure, but has effects that make possible visualisations, i.e. archetypal conceptions".[1]

Accordingly, an examination of the dominant expressions of spirituality in the Bronze Age may help us gain a better understanding of the epoch by revealing the issues of greatest concern to the people of that time as well as the intellectual remedies they devised to alleviate their fears. This period saw the growth of a far-flung network of trade routes, over which a great variety of valuable raw materials – such as amber from the Baltic, to name one example – could be transported throughout all of Europe by means of more or less hazardous expeditions. The beginnings of mining – perhaps under the stimulus of competition – date to this time, as do the exploitation of native sources of precious metals such as gold and the spread of metallurgical know-how (smelting and casting) for the working of copper and the production of tin-bronze. It is a period marked by the production of new kinds of weapons and tools, the emergence of new power structures with more precisely defined concepts of territorial defence, the formation of a hierarchy of social classes, the growth of specialised crafts and the beginnings of urbanisation. All of these innovations combined to revolutionise the traditional economic and social values that had characterised the essentially rural and static world of the Stone Age.

From the tattoos of the so-called "Ötzi" (see Leitner, pp. 24 ff.) to the stone monuments of the Atlantic coast to the frescoes of the Cretan palaces, archaeological evidence reveals the omnipresence of a divine world, a creation peculiar to the Bronze Age in which particular themes recur throughout all of Europe.

The Proliferation of Natural Sanctuaries

As well as the sacred grottoes, where the gods were worshipped and votive gifts were presented, vast sanctuaries grew up under the open sky, a development rooted in the human fascination with a nature that was gradually beginning to seem less hostile. The sanctification of particular tracts of land – sites that could be delimited, transformed (deforested, cultivated, irrigated, used as pasture) or traversed (whether on foot, on horseback, in a wagon, or even on skis) – extended even to places of difficult access such as mountains. The Alpine rock-sanctuaries of Monte Bego, Val Camonica and the Valtellina are the most spectacular examples of the physical exertion required to reach the sacred sites: "The difficult and dangerous path corresponds to the ritual reality of the mountain sanctuary".[2]

Open-air sanctuaries such as sacred springs are mentioned in the *Odyssey*. At Ithaca, for example, Athena shows Odysseus:

"…the pleasant, shadowy cave, sacred to the nymphs that are called Naiads. This … is the vaulted cave in which thou wast wont to offer to the nymphs many hecatombs that bring fulfilment …" (*Odyssey* XIII.347ff; trans. A.T. Murray, vol. 2 [London, 1919], 27).

Odysseus, in turn, greets the nymphs:

"Ye Naiad Nymphs, daughters of Zeus ... I hail you with loving prayers. Aye and gifts too will I give, as aforetime ..." (*Odyssey* XIII.356ff; trans. Murray, 27).

Water held great fascination for the non-Mediterranean peoples of Europe; we know of sacred springs such as those of St.-Moritz in Switzerland. In addition, numerous offerings of weapons have been found in rivers as well as abandoned votive hoards in the wetlands of northern and western Europe (cf. Cat. Nos. 119–121).

Minoan sanctuaries were early found on mountaintops or in caves, evidenced by votive statuettes and rituals involving fire. In the final phase of the Minoan civilisation, numerous field altars were also erected in connection with natural elements such as sacred trees. The first sanctuaries built of stone date to the 18th century BC. In the Mycenaean world, on the other hand, mountain shrines played a less significant role. Here rather the architectural sanctuaries differ little from houses: they are distinguished from the latter only by a number of votive figurines deposited on a bench in the megaron, the main hall of the Greek house, to which a large porch gave access. This arrangement can be observed in Tiryns, a cult centre as well as palace in the Mycenaean world, as well as at the shrine at Phylakopi on the island of Melos and the so-called "Shrine of the Double Axes" in Knossos. Special cult buildings are rare in western Europe; one example is the temple excavated at Bargeroosterveld (Drenthe), ornamented with horns carved from wood.

Rich and Varied Offerings

Food, grain, plants, dairy products, animals, personal gifts with a certain social or private status, such as the long braids of hair found in Denmark, and maybe even humans were all used as offerings and sacrifices. Our information in this regard comes in particular from the Mycenaean Linear B tablets: gifts of spices, wine, oil, honey, wheat, wool, vessels, gold jewellery (cf. the following section), and even persons – whether as human sacrifices or slaves bound to the service of a god, we do not know – were regularly recorded in the archives of the sanctuaries. The same sources also tell us of the organisation of festive ceremonies.

1   Female statue, Ayia Irini – Temple, Room 1, Kea, Cyclades, Greece, Late Bronze Age (Cat. No. 68)

So-called "Ritual" Objects or Motifs: Mute Reflections of an Early European Mythology

Explicit pictorial representations of the Bronze Age gods are extremely rare. While they appear to have existed in both male and female form, the former are less bound by the traditions of the previous era than the latter. Rather, the male gods appear to belong to a new era in which metal and the warrior played a dominant role. The attribution of terracotta figurines to the religious sphere as representations of gods or worshipers must rely on subtle nuances, whereas the religious character of monumental works such as the stelai and menhir statues particular-

2   Cult wagon with vessel, Orastie, Hunedoara, Rumania, Late Bronze Age (Cat. No. 176)

ly of southwest Europe (see Oliveira Jorge, pp. 114 ff.) and the entire Alpine region is beyond doubt.

Numerous objects are classified as "ritual" either on the basis of specific morphological or decorative characteristics, or because they were found in an environment resembling that of a sanctuary. Their iconography may suggest fragments of a mythology or evoke the ceremonies by which appeal was made to the gods. The new sense of mobility doubtless represents a constant, subliminal preoccupation manifesting itself in depictions of wheeled carts and migrating birds.

The numerous representations of vehicles include above all miniature chariots, frequently drawn by birds,

swans or ducks (Cat. Nos. 176–178). An important personage sometimes occupies these carts of terracotta or metal; the miniature terracotta chariot of Dupljaja (Serbia), for example, is drawn by three ducks or swans and bears a personage in the form of a bird-headed idol wearing a robe decorated with solar symbols. The famous bronze and gold-plated cult chariot of Trundholm (Cat. No. 175) shows a horse pulling a sun disk; it was probably meant to symbolise flight from the earth and rediscovery of the world beyond or the power of the sun. The horse, the most recent human conquest of the Bronze Age, made it possible to undertake long journeys; in addition, the sun is also associated with fire, essential for metalworking.

The motif of the sun is frequently found on dishes or round decorative disks of gold, generally adorned with engraved concentric circles. Another motif used to symbolise the cyclical journey is the barque of the sun. Occurring as miniature boats or petroglyphs, these schematic representations of ships contained figures such as warriors, wrestlers, musicians, or the solar star, a motif used to decorate razors and bronze vessels from Scandinavia to Italy and central Europe (Cat. No. 184).

In this way, technical innovations such as the wheel or the chariot, pulled first by oxen and then by horses, were progressively assimilated and integrated into the world of religion through rites and ceremonies (cf. Cat. Nos. 122–129).

Although their significance is largely lost to us, we know of many scenic representations of persons, animals and symbolic signs. In the Mycenaean world, for example, processions (persons bearing votive gifts, mourning women) appear on seal rings, frescoes and as painted decoration on sarcophagi like those at Tanagra (Greece). Similar themes are also found in the north, for example in the carved wall slabs of the stone chamber grave of Kivik (Sweden).

Ploughing scenes occur frequently as well, especially in the petroglyphs of Val Camonica and Monte Bego. These representations suggest definite rituals for which we also have archaeological evidence. At Snave on the island of Funen (Denmark), for example, the area under a long tumulus shows evidence of ploughing in preparation for the creation of a sacred area; in St. Martin-de-Corléans, ritual ploughing likewise appears to have played a role in the establishment of the sanctuary.

The daggers, axes, halberds, wheels and double-spiral pendants are metal objects with symbolic value: they are found in engraved form on monuments, as votive gifts (e.g. the votive hoard of double-spiral pendants from Stollhof, Austria), in pictorial representations on the stelai of Sion or Val Camonica, and on female terracotta statuettes from Rumania (Cat. No. 111). Sculpted daggers and axes have also been found at Stonehenge (England), votive hoards of golden daggers at Perşinări (Rumania, Cat. No. 99), double axes of gold at Arkalochori on Crete (Cat. No. 74), sculpted halberds on the stelai of Portugal, hoards of bronze halberds in central Germany – and so on.

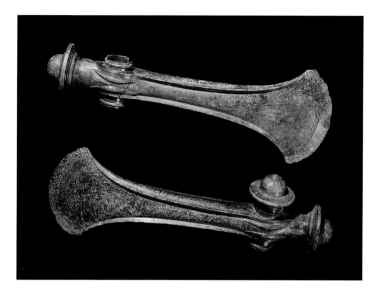

3 Cult axes, Viby, Zealand, Denmark
   Middle Bronze Age, 1400 BC (Cat. No. 182)

Particular animals played an important role among the powers of nature: in the petroglyphs of Monte Bego, cattle predominate, while in Val Camonica stags, ibexes and wild goats are more common. Particular "divine" animals are found on objects ranging from pendants and bronze roasting spits to the cult chariot wagon of Strettweg (Austria) or the golden bowl of Zurich from the beginning of the Iron Age. The motif of bull-taming or combat against wild animals is widespread in the Minoan-Mycenaean world (cf. Cat. No. 71), while that of the mythical hunt is common among a variety of peoples.

Other depictions appear in the rock art of northern Germany (Cat. No. 172), Zealand (Denmark, Cat. No. 77) and Bohuslän (Sweden): scenes of ritual mating, ithyphallic figures associated with the cult of the warrior (great god with lance, warriors swinging an axe, scenes of fighting heroes with horned helmets (cf. Cat. No. 190) that evoke the bull motif) and ploughing scenes associated with fertility rituals.

Human figures are often schematised or represented only in part: the idols of Los Millares (Spain) are reduced to engraved or painted pairs of eyes, while the anthropomorphic figures with outstretched arms found in the petroglyphs have a stick-like form. The menhir statues possess stereotyped, but clearly recognisable attributes (Cat. No. 171).

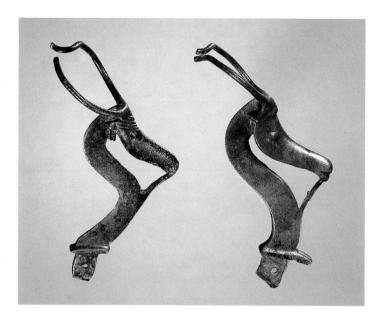

4   Figurines, Fårdal, Jutland, Denmark
Late Bronze Age, 9th–8th centuries BC (Cat. No. 183)

The Beginnings of Astronomy and the Mastery of the Heavens

Megalithic sanctuaries with a postulated astronomical orientation such as Stonehenge occur most frequently on the British Isles. Astral symbols appear in diverse contexts: we find the sun in the petroglyphs of Val Camonica and the Valtellina as well as on the engraved rocks of Scandinavia; both sun and moon appear on Mycenaean seal rings. Spirals – symbolic motifs of perpetual motion – were used throughout all of Europe to decorate objects such as sword blades.

The increasing appropriation of the celestial sphere is reflected in this symbolism, often in combination with concentric circles embossed on numerous objects reserved for cultic purposes, such as golden cups.

A Possible Belief in the Afterlife

At this point the problem of the interpretation of grave goods presents itself. Should the abundance of artefacts (axes, halberds, daggers, etc.) in certain graves such as that of Łęki Małe (Poland, Cat. No. 159) be interpreted as signs of the high rank of the deceased or as evidence of belief in an afterlife? The same question may be posed with regard to the "ship-graves" of northern Europe or the golden death masks of the Mycenaean kings. Another question relates to the religious role of secular lords: were they invested with some spiritual power as well?

The choice of burial place was likewise a matter of importance: in Brittany, sacred sites from the Neolithic period were frequently reused, with individual graves superseding the collective burials of the Megalithic monuments. An additional change in funerary custom, the shift from inhumation to cremation, probably reveals the emergence of new religious conceptions as well as the accompanying social changes: the small bronze vessels, mounted on wheels and adorned with the motif of a bird taking flight, resemble cult chariots.

Another phenomenon characteristic of the Late Bronze Age is the increasing prevalence of the votive hoard at the expense of ritual ostentation in funerary context.

In conclusion, it may be said that the peoples of the Bronze Age, regardless of region, shared similar beliefs in the existence of the "soul" and the omnipresence of gods and perhaps demons, whom they sought in the natural elements, as well as in the existence of privileged mediators – animals, places, substances, rites – necessary to gain access to the gods and communicate with them. The period seems to be marked as well by the emergence of a kind of mythology based on the four elements of fire, water, earth and air.

1 C.G. Jung, *Theoretische Überlegungen zum Wesen des Psychischen* (Olten and Freiburg im Breisgau, 1968), 239–40.

2 E. Neumann, *Zur psychologischen Bedeutung des Ritus. Kulturentwicklung und Religion* (Zurich, 1953).

Cabeço da Mina (Vila Flor, Portugal): A Late Prehistoric Sanctuary with "Stelai" of the Iberian Peninsula

Susana Oliveira Jorge

The Site of Cabeço da Mina

The river valley of the Vilariça, a tributary of the Sabor in the direct catchment area of the Douro, is one of the most striking landscapes in the Alto Douro region of Portugal. Between the Serra de Bornes, the plateaux of Carrazeda de Ansiães and the Serra de Cardanha, a wide, fertile *rega* with a distinctly Mediterranean climate opens up from north to south. Its climatic and phyto-geographical characteristics make it a privileged location in the north of the Iberian Peninsula.

At the north entrance to the Vilariça valley, but already fully within the *rega*, a small, relatively unimpressive hill rises amid the evenly undulating landscape. The local inhabitants call it "Cabeço da Mina" (Ill. 1). Recognised as an archaeological site since the 1980s, the Cabeço da Mina has received increased attention only in recent years through a preliminary investigation[1] and its elevation to the status of a national monument.[2]

How should the site of Cabeço da Mina be defined archaeologically?

Our knowledge is based on three types of information: (a) the analysis of numerous granite and schist "stelai" (both fragmentary and entire) discovered when the terrain of the hill was levelled; (b) the data obtained from preliminary excavations in the area surrounding the hill; and (c) the evaluation of aerial photographs of the Cabeço.[3]

The combination of these different types of information allows us to draw the following conclusions:

1. The Cabeço da Mina exhibits the greatest concentration of anthropomorphic "stelai"/menhirs of this type found on the Iberian Peninsula. This assertion might even be broadened to include southern France as well, where menhirs of comparable type have also been found.[4] At present, we know of a total of more than fifty examples, twenty-one with engravings and thirty without any sort of epigraphy.

2. The "stelai"/menhirs of Cabeço da Mina are found not in random locations, but are concentrated in particular areas of the hill.

3. The preliminary excavations and aerial photographs support a hypothesis that has been advanced for some time now, on the basis of information provided by two property owners who have cultivated the hill: namely, that the entire hill was surrounded by a ring of stones into

1 The site of Cabeço da Mina (light brown hill in the center) in the Vilariça river valley

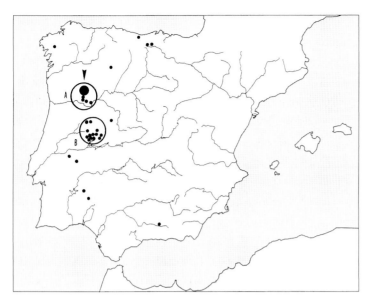

2   The location of the Cabeço da Mina (large black dot) on a map
showing the distribution of "stelai"/menhirs of the same type
throughout the Iberian Peninsula. The pieces are concentrated in
two regions: Trás-os-Montes and Alto Douro (A), and Salamanca
and Cáceres (B). (After Almagro-Gorbea 1993.)

which "stelai"/menhirs of various shapes and sizes were
integrated. The preliminary excavations revealed that a
part of this ring of stones may have been buried; it consists of granite monoliths, slabs of schist, and fragments
of quartz.[5]

4. If the hypothesis of a stone ring of this kind can
be confirmed, we may surmise the existence of a stone
enclosure surrounding the hill into which the "stelai"/
menhirs were incorporated. In other words, it appears as
if this were a sanctuary, well-integrated into the landscape and outside of any known settlements.[6]

5. In view of this obviously important discovery,
much remains to be done. Above all, it seems necessary to
develop a preliminary programme of geo-physical
prospection together with control-soundings. And thus to
rapidly move to the next step: the meticulous excavation
of what may prove to be the first sanctuary with "stelai"/menhirs of this type found on the Iberian Peninsula,
and perhaps even in all of western Europe.

The Decorated "Stelai"/Menhirs
A recent study of twenty-one decorated pieces from
Cabeço da Mina[7] permits us to briefly consider their
iconography, context and possible date.

1. The pieces constitute menhirs or "stelai" in the
sense defined by d'Anna;[8] they are small in scale with a
height of approximately twenty to eighty cm.

2. These slabs of granite or schist show representations of the human body, indicated not by unequivocally
anthropomorphic contours, but by engravings of anatomical motifs and/or complementary attributes on one or
more sides of the block. The (entirely conceivable) possibility that the pieces might have displayed painted "decoration", which could have supplemented or even replaced
the engravings, has not been considered; still, no traces of
pigment have been found on the examples studied up to
this point.

3. Among the pieces analysed, anatomical motifs
are few in number, consisting primarily of highly
schematic representations of the face (Ill. 3, I, three
examples; IIIA, one example; IIIC, one example). Only in
one case are an arm, legs and genitals shown in addition
to two eyes, a nose and a mouth (Ill. 3, IIIB). It should
also be noted that the representation of a mouth has thus
far been found only on the latter example. In this respect,
the finds from Cabeço da Mina differ from other pieces
occurring on the peninsula, where a mouth, head hair and
hands usually appear.[9]

4. Highly schematised, complementary attributes
predominate. Most common are "belts", appearing on the
great majority of the decorated pieces. These belts are
indicated by a single horizontal line, two parallel horizontal lines or two such lines delimited with "chevrons" (Ill. 3,
IIA1; IIB; IIIA; IIIB; IIC; IIF).

5. The complementary attributes include necklaces
with three, four, or seven rows (Ill. 3, IIA1; IIA2; IIIB;
IIIC), as well as a curvilinear ornament (?) encircling the
whole sculpture (Ill. 3, IIF; IIG; IIIA) and an X-shaped
ornament (?) bounded by parallel horizontal lines (Ill. 3,
IID; IIE). One piece (Ill. 3, 10) shows circular motifs that
are difficult to explain.

6. Weapons are not depicted.

7. As with the comparable "stelai"/menhirs of the
Iberian Peninsula[10] or southern France,[11] we may note
with d'Anna that "the anatomical characteristics" are
represented "with restraint" and that "there are no
explicit representations of sexual organs".[12] It thus proves
difficult to surmise the symbolic content of the pieces

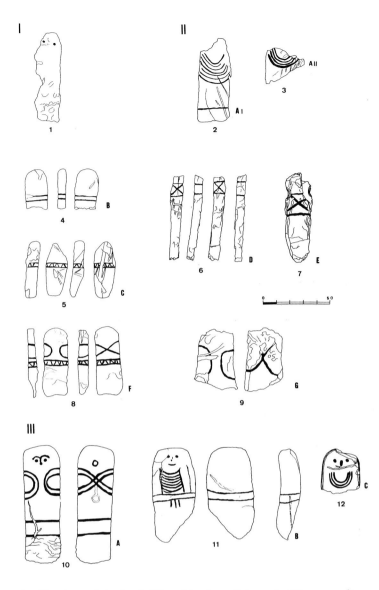

with respect to gender (male, female, other). Some scholars view the pieces with necklaces as female;[13] this, however, probably constitutes an ethnocentric prejudice, since in many known cultures this type of jewellery is worn by men under certain circumstances. In order to avoid controversial interpretations, it seems wiser at the present to advance no hypotheses in this regard, especially since schematic representations predominate at Cabeço da Mina.

8. Our attempt at a typology (Ill. 3) is based on the division of the pieces into three groups: (I) pieces whose anthropomorphic identification is based on the presence of eyes (i.e., the face is reduced to two anatomical elements); (II) pieces distinguished not by anatomical elements, but by belts, necklaces and curvilinear or X-shaped motifs (insignia?); (III) pieces whose anthropomorphic identification is based on the combination of faces with jewellery and/or articles of clothing.

Although a tendency toward increased complexity through the lavish use of attributes is discernible from the groups (I) to (III), and although, from a purely formal perspective, the group (III) consists of a combination of faces, jewellery, and articles of clothing, it nonetheless represents more than the mere sum of the attributes of the groups (I) and (II).

The categorisation suggested here is the necessary result of a particular method of selecting and ranking these attributes. Doubtless other typologies could be constructed as well, in which, for example, greater importance could be attributed to the face, necklaces, curvilinear motifs, belts or the X-motifs.

3   Typology of the "stelai"/menhirs from Cabeço da Mina according to the system developed by the author (drawings: Sousa 1996):

I. Human figure with schematic rendering of eyes;

II. Human figure with schematic rendering of jewellery:
A. Necklaces (A II), necklace and belt (A I), the latter indicated by a single horizontal line;
B. Belts, represented by two parallel horizontal lines;
C. Belts, represented by two parallel horizontal lines with "chevrons";
D. Two parallel horizontal lines delimiting X-shaped motifs on two of the four sides of the block;
E. The same motif as D, engraved on one side of the slab together with a loosely anthropomorphic outline (lateral sculpted notches);
F. Belt as in C, combined with a curvilinear motif tracing the form of a horizontal figure-of-eight ;
G. Simple curvilinear motif as in F.

III. Human figure with schematic rendering of face, jewellery, and other bodily attributes:
A. Face consisting of eyes, eyebrows, and nose combined with a double curvilinear motif and perhaps a belt; the reverse shows circular motifs;
B. Face consisting of eyes, nose, and mouth combined with necklaces, the possible outline of an arm, and a belt; below the latter appear elements that could be interpreted as either jewellery or the schematic representation of legs and genitals;
C. Face consisting of eyes and nose combined with necklaces; the lower half of the piece is destroyed.

139

4   Menhir statue from Cabeço da Mina (type IIIA): height: 85 cm.

The Chronology of the "Stelai"/Menhirs

The date of the Cabeço da Mina may be determined through the investigation of the archaeological context. First, however, in order to facilitate a solution to the problem, let us recall what we already know of the "stelai"/menhirs or similar phenomena encountered in megalithic and other prehistoric contexts on the Iberian Peninsula.

The following factors should be considered:

1. Some motifs appearing on finds from Cabeço da Mina also occur on other examples from megalithic contexts, particularly those of late date such as Chã do Brinco[14] or Boulhosa.[15]

2. On the other hand, the pieces from Cabeço da Mina show none of the engraved weapons that appear in numerous contexts since the beginning of the Bronze Age.[16] Not far from Cabeço da Mina, the well-known Early Bronze Age stele of Longroiva was found south of the Douro,[17] on which both weapons and a human figure are depicted.

3. Despite the specific characteristics of the pieces from Cabeço da Mina, they are formally related to other "stelai"/menhirs found above all in the western part of the peninsula, in particular those from the provinces of Cáceres and Salamanca (Ill. 2). Particularly important in this regard are the famous pieces from Hernan Pérez[18] or Ciudad Rodrigo[19] (Ill. 1), which along with others from Almagro-Gorbea's groups B2, B3, and B4[20] appear to belong to a "typological family" of Mediterranean background (Ill. 2 B).

For all these reasons, it seems plausible to date the initial phase of the occupation of the Cabeço da Mina to the period between the end of the Neolithic and the Chalcolithic age (4th–3rd millennia BC).

It is likely that the location was reused during a later period whose date is at present impossible to determine. Evidence of such reuse may be found in the engraving of an equine, apparently younger than the rest of the stelai on which it is found (Ill. 3, 6) and from which it differs stylistically as well as in other respects. Its very presence is, as far as we know, unusual among "stelai" of this type.

Of course we do not know how long this sanctuary was in use, whether its design represents the result of a single process of conception/execution, or whether it was subjected to architectural modification, etc. In any case, it represents a highly visible complex, strategically located within a fertile and presumably densely inhabited region. Thus we may assume that for a considerable length of time, it possessed symbolic meaning for the local population or for travellers passing through.

In conclusion, a remark and a hypothesis are offered: an gap in our information exists between the group of "stelai"/menhirs east of Trás-os-Montes and the Alto Douro (Ill. 5) and those from Salamanca/Cáceres (Ill. 2 and 5), the regions with the greatest concentration of these "stelai" in the Iberian Peninsula. In view of the proximity of the two regions and the existence of an ancient natural "corridor" extending along the west periphery of the plateaux,[21] it is conceivable that in the near future similar finds will be made in the region south of the Douro. This hypothesis has much to recommend it, especially when we consider that the particular qualities of the landscape of the Cabeço da Mina are also found, if on a smaller scale, in other valleys on either side of the Portuguese Alto Douro.[22]

1 O. Sousa, *Estatuária Antropomórfica Pré- e Proto-histórica do Norte de Portugal* (M.A. thesis, Universidade do Porto, Faculdade de Letras, 1996, photocopy); O. Sousa, 'A estação arqueológica do Cabeço da Mina, Vila Flor – notícia preliminar', *Revista de Estudo Transmontanos e Durienses* 7 (Vila Real, forthcoming).

2 Information courtesy of O. Sousa.

3 Sousa 1996, 41–52, 72–92.

4 A. D'Anna, *Les Statues-Menhirs et Stèles Anthropomorphes du Midi Méditerranéen* (Paris: CNRS, 1977); D'Anna et al., 'L'art mégalithique dans le Midi de la France: les stèles anthropomorphes et les statues-menhirs néolithiques', in *Art et Symboles du Mégalithisme Européen*, Revue Archéologique de l'Ouest, suppl. 8 (1997), 179–93; A. D'Anna, 'Les statues-menhirs du Sud de la France', in *L'Art des Mégalithes Peints et Gravés*, Dossiers d'Archéologie, 230 (1998), 48–55.

5 Sousa 1996, 80–83.

6 According to Sousa 1996, no materials pertaining to the domestic realm were found at Cabeço da Mina, although various prehistoric settlements, possibly contemporary with Cabeço da Mina, have been found in the surrounding area.

7 Sousa 1996, 41–52, stat. XLIII–LIX.

8 D'Anna 1998, 49.

9 M. Almagro-Gorbea, 'Les stéles anthropomorphes de la Péninsule Ibérique', in *Les Réprésentations Humaines de Néolithique à l'Âge du Fer* (Paris: Ed. C.T.H.S., 1993), 123–39, Fig. 5, B2, B3, and B4.

10 M. Almagro Basch, *Las Estelas Decoradas del Suroeste Peninsular* (Madrid: CSIC, 1966); M. Almagro-Gorbea, 'Los ídolos y la estela decorada de Hernan Perez (Cáceres) y el ídolo estela de Tabuyo del Monte (León)', *Trabajos de Prehistoria* 29 (1972), 83–124; P. Bueno Ramirez, 'Estatuas-menhir y estelas antropomorfas en Estremadura', *Revista de Estudios Extremeños* 60 (1984), 5–18; J. A. Barceló, 'Introducción al razonamiento estadístico aplicado a la arqueología: un análisis de las estelas antropomorfas de la Península Ibérica', *Trabajos de Prehistoria* 45 (1988), 51–85; Almagro-Gorbea 1993.

11 See n. 4 above.

12 D'Anna 1998, 50.

13 D'Anna 1998; Almagro-Gorbea 1993.

14 E. J. L. Silva, 'Réprésentations humaines sur deux monuments mégalithiques de la région nord du Portugal', in *Les Réprésentations Humaines du Néolithique à l'Âge du Fer* (Paris: Ed. C.T.H.S., 1993), 21–27.

15 V. Oliveira Jorge and S. Oliveira Jorge, 'Statues-menhirs et stèles du Nord du Portugal', in *Les Réprésentations Humaines du Néolithique à l'Âge du Fer* (Paris: Ed. C.T.H.S., 1993), 29–43.

16 While representations of weapons are found in the megalithic art of the Iberian Peninsula (cf. P. Bueno Ramirez and R. Balbín Behrmann, 'La Péninsule Ibérique', in *L'Art des Mégalithes Peintes et Gravés*, Dossiers d'Archéologie, 230 (1998), 76–83), they are rare and not very characteristic of this artistic "universe".

17 See n. 15 above.

18 Almagro-Gorbea 1972.

19 P. Bueno Ramirez, 'Estelas antropomorfas en la Península Ibérica: Ciudad Rodrigo II', in *VI Congreso de Estudios Extremeños* (1993), 11–14; Almagro-Gorbea 1993.

20 Almagro-Gorbea 1993, 132, Fig. 5.

21 S. Oliveira Jorge, 'Desenvolvimento da hierarquização social e da metalurgia', in *Nova historia de Portugal*, vol. I, coord. J. de Alarcão (Lisbon: Ed. Presença, 1993), 208.

22. Oliveira Jorge, 'O povoado de Castelo Velho (Freixo de Numão, Vila Nova de Foz Côa) no contexto da Pré-história Recente de Norte de Portugal', in *Actas do 1º Congreso de Arqueologia Peninsular*, vol. I, Trabalhos de Antropología e Etnología, XXXIII, 1–2 (1993), 196; Sousa 1996, 92.

Bibliography: D'Anna 1977, 1997, 1998; Almagro-Gorbea 1972, 1993; Barceló 1988; Almagro Basch 1966; Oliveira Jorge, S. 1993; Oliveira Jorge, V & S 1993; Ramirez 1984, 1993; Ramirez & Behrmann 1998; Silva 1993a, 1993b; Sousa 1996, forthcoming.

The Rock Sanctuaries of Europe

Emmanuel Anati

Examples of rock art on the walls of caves or under the open sky appear as early as the Upper Palaeolithic Age. Among the sanctuaries of this type, frequented throughout the millennia, two of the oldest are located at opposite ends of Europe: one in Gobustan in Azerbaijan on the Caspian Sea, the other in the valley of the river Côa in Portugal.

Two great centres of rock art from the Mesolithic period are found in Spain: one in the Levante, the eastern coastal area around Valencia, and the other in Galicia, characterised primarily by engravings. In the Alpine region, the first significant examples of rock art from the same epoch appear in the Val Camonica near Brescia and in the Totes Gebirge in Austria, not far from Salzburg. In northern and central Sweden and Norway, the first examples of rock art of the "Nordic" type appear at the same time; an analogous phenomenon is also encountered in Anatolia.

From the 6th millennium BC, Neolithic cult places which may be described as sanctuaries begin to prolifer-

1   Val Camonica (north Italy), Foppe di Nadro, rock art on block 30: two storehouse-like buildings (Late Bronze Age). (From *Scolpito nel Tempo*, 20, Fig. 30)

ate, displaying a remarkable typological diversity. Archaeological sites with thousands of votive statuettes from the Vinča and Tiszapolgár cultures have been excavated in the Balkans; in the same period, the first of the monuments that would later constitute the "megalith culture" were erected along the Atlantic coast in Portugal, Spain, France and Ireland. A few cultural centres manifest the beginnings of the oldest large-scale three-dimensional art in Europe: the groups of menhir-statues, stone monuments often decorated with anthropomorphic signs or symbols. The two oldest examples of this artistic form are found in southern Portugal and in the Danube Valley at the Iron Gate.

Rock sanctuaries showing a remarkable concentration of incised decorations – superimposed upon one another over the course of the millennia – flourished in Spanish Galicia, Swedish Bohuslän and other southern Scandinavian provinces, Val Camonica and the Valtellina in the central Italian Alps. In a later phase (toward the end of the Neolithic age) sacred caves decorated with rock paintings also appear in Porto Badisco, in the province of Lecce (Italy), and in Magura near Bielogradchik in Bulgaria. This complex situation with its wide range of sanctuary types, including rock sanctuaries, is already firmly established by the dawn of the age of metal.

In the Chalcolithic period and during the Bronze Age, i.e. in the 3rd and 2nd millennia BC, numerous regions of Europe place a high value on their rock sanctuaries and continue to develop them further. In certain well-defined areas (up to 100 km or more across), sites with tremendous concentrations of rock art are found in great number. The high-lying Val Camonica has over 350,000 drawings incised into the rocks, while the Valtellina, a valley extending outward from it, possesses 25,000. Close to 120,000 rock engravings have been found in Bohuslän and other southern Scandinavian regions with a high concentration of rock art. At Monte Bego, on the French side of the Ligurian Alps, 80,000 images carved into the rock are visible, while over 28,000 have been found at sites in Spanish Galicia. All these works bear witness to the tremendous energy and time expended in the creation of these products of the human intellect.

The remains of settlements are rarely found in these areas. It is probable that such cult places served as pilgrimage sites that were heavily visited, but not continuously inhabited. The major sites of rock art can be typologically divided internally into different sectors, suggesting that each sector was dominated by a clan or a community of priests. The hypothesis may be advanced that here, just as in the monasteries of India, China or Nepal, the more famous priests and monks were able to attract greater numbers of worshippers and more widely propagate their doctrine and teaching.

The archaeological evidence, particularly the rock art itself, enables us to identify some of the functions of these sanctuaries, which vary among themselves and from one period to the next according to the type of cult emphasised. In its themes, the rock art documents a development which may enable us, in a preliminary and tentative fashion, to identify a number of cults which persisted from the Neolithic period to the Iron Age, while others prevailed for only shorter periods of time.

Seasonal cults of growth and fertility were celebrated throughout the millennia; associated with the glorification of nature, they were probably performed at the solstices, though not exclusively then. The cult of the dead and the ancestors likewise persisted through the ages. In the rock art of Val Camonica in particular, but in other areas as well, a preference for cults oriented to the powers of nature, especially the sun, is visible from the Neolithic period to the beginning of the Bronze Age. In the Chalcolithic period, a cosmic vision emerges which might be characterised as pantheistic, a conception of the universe as a triad of heaven, earth and underworld. Together, these three form a cosmic unity, a cosmic body: the head is heaven and the torso earth, while the pubic zone is identified with the chthonic world.

In this phase, menhir statues were also created in the same regions as the rock art of Val Camonica and the Valtellina. A thematic change implies cultural influences coming from the Balkans and extending progressively to the Alpine regions, France and Spain. Other phenomena taking place in this context include the spread of copper metallurgy, with weapon prototypes originating in eastern Europe, and the introduction of the earliest wheeled vehicles, ox-drawn carts of similar origin. The Chalcolithic and Bronze Ages are marked by the emergence of the religious veneration of weapons and metal objects,

2 Val Camonica (north Italy), Capo di Ponte, Masso di Cemmo, no. 2, with rock art (detail): depictions of deer from the Late Bronze Age/Early Iron Age.

which are depicted with great frequency and possess special significance. After reaching a zenith in the Early Bronze Age, this cult of weapons declines in significance.

In the Bronze Age, one of the primary purposes of the rock sanctuaries was for instruction and initiation. Many of the rock faces decorated with figures and scenes resemble school blackboards; in addition, rituals related to coronation must have been performed there.

In the course of the Bronze Age, great importance also seems to have been attributed to the evocation of myths of origin. Mythical beings with recurrent characteristics are represented again and again. Combinations of pictograms and ideograms reveal aspects of a complex conceptual world, probably associated with "alchemical" activities (related to the transformation of materials in the smelting processes developing at that time) or to ideas about natural phenomena such as lightning, rain, weather changes or the cycle of the seasons.

In the rock sanctuaries of southern Scandinavia, numerous representations of ships appear to evoke a great mythical journey, undertaken from a hypothetical land of origin. In the region of Galicia in the northwest of the Iberian Peninsula, territorial markers probably refer to

143

3   Val Camonica (north Italy), Foppe di Nadro, rock art on block 6:
    sword fight between two warriors.

the stages of a journey, perhaps a great migratory movement. Topographical depictions showing hypothetical landscapes have been found at Val Camonica and Monte Bego, though it is not clear whether these are meant to represent territories from the world of the living or of the dead, of men or of spirits.

A number of sites show evidence of animal cults manifesting continuities from the Neolithic age. Animals appear repeatedly and in great number: classic examples are the stag in Val Camonica and the elk in Scandinavia, as well as the ox, symbolised on Monte Bego by the bucranium (ox skull). Another aspect of the cults most certainly practised in these rock sanctuaries is the art of divination, evidenced by pictorial representations of labyrinths, meanders and spirals. Remarkably, these forms resemble the ones still used today in the divination practices of certain Asian and African tribes.

Toward the end of the Bronze Age, two themes appear which were to reach a high point in the Iron Age. The first is a cult of monstrous anthropomorphic spirits – particularly evident in Val Camonica, where two categories of spirits can be discerned, both beneficent and malevolent. The existence of a cult of the spirits is also confirmed by the rock art of Galicia, southern Sweden, and various minor provinces such as the region of Derry-inablaha in Ireland. Early evidence of a cult of heroes has also been found, in which the latter were assimilated to demigods. This cult persisted in the proto-historical mythologies that have come down to us, such as the Greek and Germanic mythologies.

After the end of the Bronze Age, the rock sanctuary on Monte Bego began to experience decline, as did those of Galicia and the Spanish Levante. The artistic milieu of southern Scandinavia likewise shows visible signs of decay. In certain areas such as Val Camonica, the number of rock engravings increases, accompanied by a period of renewal in the Early Iron Age. In addition to a gradual decline and evidence of a certain degeneration in quality, the hero cult, as a commemorative cult exalting past deeds of fame, now comes to play a dominant role in both the Alpine areas and Scandinavia, which may likewise be viewed as manifesting a certain degree of degeneration.

The rock sanctuaries served an important function as stimulus and support for spiritual development. In their social function, they served as assembly places for alliances and confederations and as centres for great ceremonies and pilgrimages, the cult of the dead, initiation rites, and perhaps even weddings and other communal events. Like the present-day sanctuaries of Lourdes and Benares, they may also have represented significant markets and important centres of trade.

Instruments for the production of rock art have also come to light in these locations, including stone tools for the creation of drawings, pigments for painting them, scrapers for grinding and sticks for mixing and thinning the colours. Occasionally buildings, apparently of a religious nature, have also been found among the decorated rocks: these include a small temple discovered at Luine in Val Camonica, an alignment of orthostats not far from Masso di Cemmo in the same valley, the remains of architectural ornament in the Valtellina, or imposing alignments on Monte Bego. The interiors of the rock sanctuaries also show traces of ancient footpaths that often seem to lead nowhere, merely delineating a rock or a cliff. Along these paths, carefully cleared and lined with stones, heaps of rocks and other traces of human activity are found, whose motivations are often unknown to us. Such paths may have served to trace mythical journeys, the itineraries – whether real or imagined – of dancers or processions from one place to another.

The rock sanctuaries extending from the coasts of the Atlantic to the Caspian Sea thus serve to manifest the spiritual unity of the European continent in the Bronze Age.

Chalcolithic Stele-Statues of the Alpine Region

Raffaele C. de Marinis

Menhir-statues, stele-statues and anthropomorphic stelai are the first monumental stone sculptures of prehistoric Europe. Their appearance in the 4th and 3rd millennia BC over a broad geographical area extending from the Black Sea to the Iberian Peninsula and from Greece and Italy to Britain and Germany is characteristic of the Chalcolithic Age. Yet however widespread the custom of erecting stones of phallic or anthropomorphic appearance may have been in both space and time, and however clearly the phenomenon of the stele-statues may be rooted in local megalithic traditions in many regions of western Europe, the frequent and sometimes even surprising similarities within the different regional groups yet suggest the presence of a single, trans-cultural phenomenon manifesting itself in a wide variety of material and spiritual cultures at a particular moment in the Chalcolithic Age, beginning in the early 3rd millennium BC.

The late 4th and early 3rd millennium BC in Europe was a period of great change. Significant technical innovations including metallurgy, the plough, the wheel and the yoking of bovines, as well as new forms of husbandry such as pasturage and alpine dairy farming and the use of animals for secondary products such as milk and wool resulted in altered relationships within individual societies (the growth of a hierarchy and the concentration of power in the hands of chieftains) as well as between communities (competition for raw materials, war). Such changes could hardly fail to leave their mark in the realm of religion, ideology and cult practice, and it is within this context that the rapid spread of statue-stelai across Europe must be interpreted. The Alpine region of northern Italy, including a part of the Apennines (Garfagnana and Lunigiana), doubtless represents one of the better-documented examples of this phenomenon, in which interpretation of the evidence is possible not only on the basis of local conditions, but also within a broader semantic context. The most recent studies suggest a division of the northern Italian Chalcolithic into three periods: Chalcolithic I (c. 3400/3300–2900/2800 BC), Chalcolithic II (c. 2900/2800–2500/2400 BC), and Chalcolithic III (c. 2500/2400–2200 BC), the last corresponding to the Beaker period. Two cultural zones can be identified in the first two eras, developing over a period of almost 1000 years: the Remedello culture in the Po valley and the Tamins-Carasso-Isera 5 phase in the Alpine and lower Alpine region. Evidence of the latter culture is found near settlements like Castel Grande di Bellinzona, Breno in Val Camonica, Isera and Romagnano (Level Q) in Trentino. Its ceramics are characterised by flat-based cylindrical and blunt conical vessels decorated with bands, as well as vessels showing rows of depressions (designated *White Ware* by L.H. Barfield) and others decorated with a wavy edge and holes.

These groups also produced the numerous collective graves in small caves or rock shelters (so-called "*abris*"), known in the literature as "cultura di Civate". Outstanding examples of the latter include the *abri* of Val Tenesi at Sasso di Manerba near Lake Garda and that of Cavallino on Monte Covolo.

The Remedello culture, on the other hand – documented in particular through cemeteries and only secondarily through settlements – is characterised by individual burials in shallow graves. The majority of adult males were buried on their left side in the foetal position, accompanied by a collection of weapons including daggers, axes and arrowheads, while the women were buried on their backs, often facing eastward, with no grave goods or at most a ceramic vessel. Daggers with flint blades of laureate shape were produced – a weapon type exported to the northern Alpine region as well where it is found in settlements of the Cham culture. But otherwise, evidence of metallurgy exists already in the first phase of the Remedello necropoleis: metal artefacts include daggers of arsenical-copper with triangular blades and crescent-shaped pommels, characteristic of the developed Chalcolithic (Period II).

During this phase, the stable Alpine populations began to engage in regular mountain pasturage, as demonstrated on the one hand by the systematic reuse of rock shelters for metallurgical activities, animal husbandry and funerary rituals at the end of the 4th millennium, and on the other by the great number of artefacts

1   Stele from Arco VI, Trentino, 3rd millennium BC

recent discovery of two statue-stelai at Vestignè near Dora Baltea in Piemonte reveals the existence of an additional group as well.

Trentino-Alto Adige

The group from the Adige region consists of eighteen statue-stelai, six of which were found in Arco (Trentino) and four at Lagundo near Merano. The rest come from different places in the Isarco valley: Tötschling, Velturno, S. Verena and Aica di Fié, as well as from Revò in Val di Non, Termeno to the south of the Lake of Caldaro, and Laces in Val Venosta. There are also reports of an additional statue-stele, found some time ago in Corces near Val Silandro, but now lost.

The monuments may be divided into three categories with respect to iconography, form and size: male, female, and asexual. The backs of all of them are decorated with a vertical rectangular band or checkerboard motif, which may be interpreted as a mantle or cloak. The eleven examples of the male type are characterised by a height of one to two meters and a rectangular or slightly trapezoidal form; in a few cases, there are traces of an attempt to render the head and shoulders, as well as a T-shape suggesting eyebrows and nose. Above the belt, which consists of series of loops, combinations of axes, halberds and daggers appear in the chest area (Termeno, S. Verena, Arco I and II, Lagundo B and Laces); alternatively, a single, horizontal dagger may be shown positioned directly above the belt (Lagundo C and D).

The female type, which occurs in four examples, is smaller and shaped like a pointed arch, showing two breasts in relief. A broad band of curved lines above the chest may be interpreted as a necklace of many strands or a kind of mantle (Lagundo A, Arco III, IV, and perhaps V as well, though the front of the latter is strongly eroded).

The third type, which occurs in two examples in Arco VI and Revò, is defined as asexual since it possesses no gender-specific features. In addition, its facial features are slightly U-shaped.

With the exception of the fragment found at the excavations in Velturno, all the stelai were found in secondary positions, removed from their original context. Accordingly, they are dated primarily on the basis of the typological analysis of the objects represented on the

found at high altitudes. The Remedello populations of the plains, as well, must have been quite mobile, since pastural farming with seasonal changes of location is typical of this period. This fact serves to explain both the simplicity of the settlements and the importance of the necropoleis, which constituted a symbolic point of reference, safeguarding the traditions and ensuring the continuity of the community.

Such a function may also be attributed to a few cult places which, like Lunigiana, are located further to the south in the Alpine region and are characterised by statue-stelai and rock drawings. Here, several clearly-defined groups can be differentiated in specific areas: Trentino-Alto Adige, Val Camonica and Valtellina, Val d'Aosta and Vallese, Lunigiana and Garfagnana. The

statues themselves, particularly the Remedello dagger. Recent investigations based on the horizontal stratigraphy of the Remedello necropolis and the C-14 data deriving from it show that the Remedello dagger is characteristic of the second phase of the Chalcolithic Age, i.e. the period between 2900/2800 and 2500/2400 BC.

The monument of Velturno, unfortunately preserved only in fragments, shows a sheathed dagger typical not of the Remedello, but of the Beaker culture. The stele fragment was reused in a megalithic tomb structure on a triangular platform with a curved base, where beads from a necklace of limestone and steatite, arrowheads of flint, and calcined human bones were also found; in a second, smaller structure, fragments of a bell-beaker incised with decorative lozenges were discovered as well. Radiocarbon dating has confirmed the attribution to the Beaker culture. Two phases of decoration, however, are discernible on the stele fragment from Laces: the first recalls the composition of weapons and looped-belt characteristic of male stelai of Arco and Lagundo, while the second and later phase is related to the rock art of Val Camonica, with depictions of animals (including a cervine) and anthropomorphic figures, as well as two solar symbols.

Two small stelai found by chance at two sites on the Monti Lessini (Verona) may be distinguished from the types described above. They are c. thirty cm high and resemble the "asexual" form; one, however, shows the suggestion of a phallus and a T-scheme face (Spiazzo di Cerna), and the other a curvature in relief and two eye sockets (Sassina di Prun).

Many scholars maintain that the statue-stelai from Trentino-Alto Adige, like other, comparable European stele groups, served as commemorative representations of more or less mythical and heroised ancestors or an already established pantheon. Aside from the useful information they provide concerning ceremonial dress of the 3rd millennium BC, the detailed depictions of jewellery and weaponry may also be viewed as evidence of an already existing social stratification, with differences in status expressed through the type and number of weapons as well as elements of costume. The juxtaposition of men, women and asexual stelai observed in the Arco group has been viewed as evidence of distinctions in role and social status not only of individual persons, but also of entire

2   Stele from Arco II, Trentino, 3rd millennium BC

families. In any case, it is fruitful to consider the relation between the phenomenon of the statue-stelai and the seasonal movement of Chalcolithic herdsmen, as evidenced by the finds in the Isarco valley and in Val Venosta.

Val Camonica and Valtellina

The typology of the monuments from Val Camonica is irregular, consisting of rough-hewn boulders (Borno 1, 3, 4–6; Bagnolo 1, 2; Ossimo 1, 2, 5–8), slab-shaped stelai (Cemmo 3, 4; Ossimo 4, 9, 10, 12, 14), monumental compositions on large blocks (Cemmo 1, 2; Montecchio di Darfo; Foppe di Nadro), and vertical rock walls (Capitello dei Due Pini; Roccia del Sole di Paspardo). The finds are concentrated in two regions of Val Camonica: in the central valley near Capo di Ponte (Cemmo and Paspardo), and above all on the plateau of Ossimo-Borno. Here, along the eastern terraces that dominate the access to the plateau, more than thirty monuments have been found, as well as numerous fragments of other stelai set up in groups at intervals of a few hundred meters.

In Valtellina, a dozen stelai have been discovered at a few sites in the vicinity of Teglio (Caven, Valgella, Cornàl, Ligone, Castionetto), while only a single stele has been found in Tirano.

While most of these objects have been found in secondary positions, the excavations of F. Fedele in Ossimo-Anvoia have identified the original position of three stelai, all with their decorated side facing east, on the site of what must have been an open-air sanctuary. The fact that many of the monuments were found in the same place suggests that they originally constituted elements of this sanctuary, where additional groups of decorated boulders were also erected.

In this complex, anthropomorphic features are suggested only by the disposition of the images and occasionally by the sculptural treatment of the upper part of the stone, where the shoulders are emphasised in a very schematic fashion. In most cases, the representation is not of an individual person with attributes; rather, a group of such figures reflects a compositional program and a clear symbolic meaning, providing us with a basis for differentiating these stelai from the monuments of other Alpine groups. Another characteristic feature is the repetition involved over a period of time in the decorating process; motifs are often reproduced again and again on the same surface, creating palimpsests that are legible only with difficulty.

The stelai, decorated blocks and groups of stone monuments from Val Camonica represent a clearly defined phase of the Chalcolithic Age, the so-called Period III A of Val Camonica rock art. This phase can be divided into two main periods.

The first (III A 1) belongs to the Chalcolithic II (Remedello phase II, 2900/2800–2400 BC): it is characterised by depictions of weapons (the Remedello dagger occurs most frequently, but also seen are axes of copper or polished stone and daggers with laureate blades), animals and symbolic figures. Among these symbols, generally shown in the upper part of the composition, the solar motif also appears, consisting of a rectangle with side fringes comparable to the mantle with vertical bands from the statue-stelai of Trento. Finally, returning to the sphere of the sacred and the feminine, we find garlands with curved lines, possibly signifying necklaces or pectorals, pendants with double spirals and comb-shaped motifs. The symbols occur alone or in groups on the same surface, perhaps to convey the idea of one, two or three divinities.

The second phase (III A 2) brings us into the Beaker period with the emergence of a new dagger similar to the Ciempozuelos type and a halberd whose exact counterpart is found in Villafranca Veronese. The stylistic difference manifests itself in the disappearance of the symbols and the appearance of anthropomorphic figures

3   Stele from Arco I, Trentino, 3rd millennium BC

in their place. Among the latter, the most interesting shows a head crowned by a solar disk.

A few representations occur in both periods, though differing in a number of details. These are the ploughing scenes, normally represented in the lower part of the composition and associated with the religious sphere through the representation of solar symbols or anthropomorphic

148

figures with solar crowns. The ritual ploughing of St. Martin-de-Corléans in Aosta, associated with the delimitation and establishment of a sacred district, appears to confirm this interpretation.

The monuments of Val Camonica and Valtellina should not be interpreted as evidence of an ancestor cult,

4   Stele from Arco IV, Trentino, 3rd millennium BC

nor do they possess qualities indicating a funerary function. Instead, systematic analysis of these compositions reveals the presence of religious conceptions expressed in a symbolic language to which A. Leroi-Gourhan has given the name "mythogram". In this language, objects are not represented in a linear sequence of time and space, as is characteristic of pictograms or verbal discourse. The

stelai and boulders constitute the expression of a cult of images, originally through symbolic attributes and later through anthropomorphic references. The object of the cult appears to have been a divine couple or triad, in which a female goddess is always present, though the male sun god enjoys pre-eminence. The monuments from Val Camonica and Valtellina manifest a kind of syncretism; in addition, however, new elements like the sun and weapons, perhaps appearing as a result of Indo-European influence, already prefigure the ideological transformations of the Bronze Age. Still, the cult of a female divinity persists, a remnant of earlier Neolithic cultures.

The sun cult, generally derived from the seasonal cycles of a reawakening nature, symbolises the primacy of a male elite. The emergence of these new constellations of power parallels the development of new forms of pastural farming and new technologies such as the plough, wheel, cart and metallurgy, as well as the exchange of goods for the acquisition of ore.

Val d'Aosta and Vallese

Numerous statue-stelai have been found at St. Martin-de-Corléans (Aosta), where F. Mezzena excavated a large sacred district with evidence of different periods of use.

The first phase is represented by a row of post holes about thirty-five m long running northeast to southwest, some of which contained the skulls of rams and oxen. C-14 investigation of the carbonised infilling of the post holes revealed two phases of use, dating to the late Neolithic and early Chalcolithic periods. The excavation of ritual pits along an axis parallel to that of the postholes uncovered offerings of millstones and grain; in addition, a ploughed area of about 2500 m^2 was sown with human teeth in the furrows. Finally, two polygonal platforms of stone slabs and gravel and over forty anthropomorphic stelai were found on line with the row of postholes. The stelai were erected in three rows: one on the site of the sown teeth, extending twenty-five m to the southwest on the axis of the post-holes, a second c. ten m southeast of the post-holes, still on the same alignment, and a third at a right angle to the second row and extending as far as the post-hole line itself.

5   Stele from Arco I (detail), Trentino, 3rd millennium BC

and a large round chamber (7.5 m in diameter) with a central *"fossa"* tomb (t. IV) were erected, as well as a round platform (three m in diameter) with a central stone cist (t. V) and a dolmen of the *"allée couverte"* type. In a fourth phase, three new graves with rectangular cists were erected, likewise using whole or fragmentary stelai. Material from the large dolmen tomb and the other graves show that the site was used continuously until the beginning of the Early Bronze Age (Br A 1).

The stelai of Aosta, which are still largely unpublished, are generally two to three m high. They are approximately rectangular or trapezoidal and are widest at the top. Their anthropomorphic silhouette is produced by the sculptural treatment of the upper edge, which can show either a curved, head-like protuberance in the centre and rounded shoulders, or a sharp-angled point jutting upwards.

While a few of the stelai are undecorated anthropomorphic menhirs, the majority of around forty pieces possess decoration in low relief on the front. A first type shows long arms (with shorter bent fore-arms), a V-shaped necklace with a double-spiral pendant in the middle of the chest, a belt consisting of a horizontal band with fringe, and below it a horizontal dagger with a triangular blade, straight shoulders and a crescent pommel.

A second type seems to occur more frequently. It is characterised by a nearly rectangular body with a semi-circular protuberance for a head, which is clearly distinguished from the shoulders and a T-scheme face. The arms are bent at a right angle and the hands touch each other, thus dividing the decorated surface into two parts. On the male stelai, the area within the arms shows a shaftless axe on the left and a bow with a pair of arrows on the right. Above them appears a necklace with many strands or the collar band of a garment. The garment itself is meticulously decorated with a geometric checkerboard pattern, which continues for a short distance under the arms. A semi-circular, purse-shaped object, similarly decorated, hangs down from the lower edge of the fringed belt.

The female stelai, on the other hand, are characterised not only by the absence of weapons, but also by the depiction of a necklace with multiple strands covering the breast and a bodice decorated with curved bands of

F. Mezzena has described the arrangement of the post-holes, the ritual ploughing, the pits and the stelai as evidence of ritual practices related primarily to the seasonal rhythms of farming and herding, as well as to the cult of gods and heroes represented on the stelai. This religion was suppressed with the arrival of the Beaker folk, who transformed the site into a place of burial after destroying the earlier sanctuary.

Indeed, the third phase of use is marked by the demolition of the stelai, which were razed to the ground and partially reused for the erection of grave monuments. Evidence of this period is provided by a triangular platform fifteen m in length with its apex in the northwest, on which both a dolmen with side entrance and aisle (t. II)

6 Rock with petroglyphs of men overlaying pictures of bovides, deers and halberds. Capo di Ponte, Masso no. 3, Val Camonica, Italy

7 Stele with bovides and weapons from Tirano-Lovero, Valtellina, Italy

dotted triangles filling the entire area between the arms; below the arms is a long robe covered entirely with horizontal bands showing rhombus motifs, half-circles, dotted triangles and chevrons.

Many of these elements also appear on the stelai of Petit Chasseur in Sion. The latter were found in a cemetery characterised primarily by a dolmen with a lateral entrance erected over a triangular platform (M VI), dating from the time of the Saône-Rhône culture and constructed using an earlier anthropomorphic stele. The dolmen was desecrated by the Beaker folk, who in turn used the site for their own graves (in which bell beakers were found). Using other anthropomorphic stelai, they also

erected small dolmens with no platform (M I, V, XI) as well as cists (M II, III, VII–X) which may have been used until the beginning of the Early Bronze Age. The twenty-nine stelai that have been found there, all in secondary positions, predate the Beaker period, when they were destroyed and reused for construction material.

These stelai clearly divide into two types. Type A is large (over two m high) and more or less rectangular, with broad shoulders and a small protuberance for a head. It possesses short, bent fore-arms, while its attributes consist of a double-spiral pendant, a belt shown as a simple band and a Remedello dagger. Type B occurs in two versions. The first, reaching a height of 3.5 m, is trapezoidal with a broad, domed head and a T-scheme face. The arms are bent at the elbow to a right angle and the hands are joined. The surfaces between and under them are filled with a dense, geometric checkerboard pattern. In only one case (M I) is a bow shown as an attribute. The second version, wider with a height under two m, is rectangular or slightly trapezoidal with a domed head, T-scheme face and arms bent at a right angle. Stelai of this type show two kinds of decoration associated with different attributes. Bow and arrow, purse and dagger with laureate blade are combined with checkerboard patterns to represent male personages. Stelai showing no weapons, but rather necklaces with multiple strands, belts with clasps "ad occhielli", and rhomboid, triangular and zigzag decorations on them may be interpreted as female.

The attribution of Type A to the pre-Beaker period is suggested by the depiction of the Remedello dagger. A similar date is probable for Type B stelai as well, in view of their reuse in the dolmen with lateral entrance. According to A. Gallay, statue-stelai continued to be erected throughout the entire Beaker period until the beginning of the Early Bronze Age, though only the holes in which they were set up survive. The erection of stelai and their reuse in the construction of new tombs probably constituted an element of a complex rite, practised continuously from the time of the Saône-Rhône culture up to the beginning of the Early Bronze Age. The stelai appear to have represented the leaders of a society and to have been destroyed at their death to be used in the construction of monumental tombs. The cult of the ancestors – the founders of the clans constituting the upper strata of society – continued through many centuries of the Early Bronze Age, at which time cairns were erected in the area of the dolmens and offerings deposited in large vessels with decorative bands.

In their refinement, high quality of form, outstanding sense of composition and wealth and variety of images, the statue-stelai and anthropomorphic stelai of the Alpine region constitute a clearly defined group among the range of comparable monuments from many other regions of Europe. As recent studies have shown, particularly the excavations of F. Fedele in Ossimo, most of the stelai served no funerary purpose, nor were they erected in connection with graves. In this respect, Petit Chasseur in Sion is the sole exception, while in Aosta the stelai appear to be older than the construction of the tombs. Rather, the monuments were set up in rows, sometimes short and closely-spaced, in other cases longer and more widely separated, facing east toward the sunrise (Ossimo, but also Cemmo 1 and Lagundo). These stelai and their sites must have possessed extraordinary symbolic and topographical significance: particularly as sacred districts – often small levelled areas on the sides of terraces, flanked by higher ground – in connection with territorial organisation (tribal assembly places, sites for the exchange of goods, boundaries of pasture areas, springs, fords).

Bibliography: Casini 1995; Casini et al 1996; Fedele 1995; Gallay 1995; Ratti 1994; La Valle d'Aosta 1997.

The Rock Art of the North

Torsten Capelle

Among the most striking and enigmatic monuments of prehistoric northern Europe are the many thousands of images engraved or carved into rock (and occasionally painted as well), enduring witnesses of an otherwise unknown way of life. The spectrum of motifs is amazingly broad, including symbols, weapons, articles of clothing, people, animals, vehicles and many others – sometimes even combined into small scenes. Since comparable representations appear as engravings on small artefacts of bronze found in graves, most of the rock art can be dated with considerable certainty to the later Bronze Age.

Most of the images found in southern Scandinavia show motifs associated with settled populations engaging in agriculture and animal husbandry (ploughs, oxen, horses and wagons). Further north, however, the many depictions of stags, elks and fish point to hunting and fishing as the primary means of subsistence. Common to both regions are the countless images of ships with clearly distinguishable details of construction, expressions of a sea-faring people intent on long-distance communication. Depictions of ships are found with remarkable frequency in shallow channels carved into the rock by the ice and along which rain and melting snow flow – evoking a surprisingly lifelike scene.

The images are worked into the hard stone as silhouettes or in outline. Seldom do they exhibit hasty or awkward execution, as if they had been a matter of little importance to their creators. Rather, most of them are realistic and clearly legible, bearing witness to great care and effort. Despite an often stencil-like character, they even show individual stylisation; abbreviated and reduced to the essentials like a telegram message, they may thus be considered works of art. The considerable effort required to produce each of these images bears witness to their importance for their creators. Unfortunately we will probably never know the comparable depictions that may have existed in other, more perishable materials such as wood.

In northern Germany and Denmark (except for Bornholm), the images are found on loose blocks, surfaces that could be transported (albeit with difficulty) to

2   Dancing human figure, Järrestad, Scania, Sweden

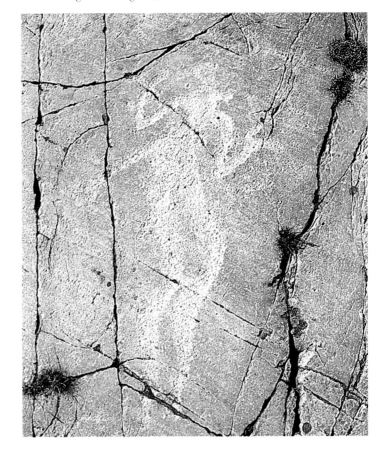

1   Procession with axes, Tanum, Bohuslän, Sweden

153

3 Rock surface near Hemsta, Uppland, Sweden, with ships worked
   on a naturally created drainage channel for water.

painting, carved into the rock? Were they religious documents, as is often surmised, or even both? In this respect, much room is left to the imagination.

In addition to purely illustrating antiquarian and everyday aspects of life, this fascinating world of images also shows ceremonial scenes of cult or religious character with solar symbols, representations of hunting magic, fertility scenes and processions. In an often cryptic manner, they reflect a worldview that was doubtless easily comprehensible to the viewer of the time (though only with difficulty for us today), an existence in which life and death were conceived as equally present.

The images on loose blocks placed in, on or over graves were doubtless intended only for the dead (cf. above all Kivik). The others, however, were meant to exert their (possibly magical) power in the sight of all. They were unhesitatingly left to posterity and were obviously intended to be visible as a constant, self-evident element of Late Bronze Age life – even if we in the digital age of information now receive their message only in part.

graves or other cult places. The rock art of Sweden and Norway, on the other hand, appears on flat outcroppings of rock cut away by glaciers, on horizontal or slightly inclined surfaces often found in groups in close proximity to each other and freely accessible in the open landscape.

The individual carved surfaces do not show compositions designed as a whole. Rather, collections of motifs appear to have grown up over time in irregular arrangements, even heedlessly superimposed on one another. The depictions show no perspective and display varying schemes of internal proportion, orientation and scale. Although they were created with no discernible practical purpose and in a virtually imperishable material, the images do convey the impression of pictures produced for short-term consumption – pictogram-like graffiti, comparable to later written examples and even modern-day comic strips.

The intended audience for this greatest body of pictorial material from prehistoric Europe is unfortunately unknown. Certainly the pictures were not made for their 154 own sake. Did these scenes serve as a kind of "history" in

4 Ship at Stora Viggeby, Uppland, Sweden

From the Megaron to Stonehenge

Chris Scarre

Bronze Age Europe was not a land of temples. In comparison with the lands of Asia lying just to the south and east, we can find few European monuments to rival the temples of pharaonic Egypt or the ziggurats of Mesopotamia. Yet this is not to say that religion and ritual did not play a crucial role in Bronze Age society in Europe, as indeed they did in all pre-modern societies. Certainly the scale of ritual architecture cannot be taken as a sure guide to the depth and significance of religious or mythological beliefs.

One problem of the term "temple" lies with our modern classification of the world, in which we divide ritual from the everyday, and build special purpose structures in which to house ritual and religious activity. This compartmentalisation of life, this separation of the ritual from the everyday, is not a feature of most traditional societies known to us through anthropology, and was probably not true of any part of Bronze Age Europe. In the *Odyssey* (VII, 136–138), for instance, Homer gives evidence of household rituals. When Odysseus entered the palace of Alcinous, "he found the captains and counsellors of the Phaeacians pouring libations from their cups to the keen-eyed Giant-slayer Hermes. It was their custom to pour the last cup to him before retiring to bed". Thus ritual, religion, ceremony and feasting merge into one in a context which is at once both domestic and religious.

That is not to say that there were no special-purpose religious buildings – temples – in Bronze Age Europe. Far from it. The world of Odysseus – in so far as it is a reflection of the Mycenaean world of the Aegean Late Bronze Age – was centred on towns and palaces, which had as their focus the megaron. This standard architectural form, which can be traced back into the very earliest Bronze Age of mainland Greece, consisted of a deep rectangular hall, fronted by a porch. The main room had a central circular hearth surrounded by four massive timber pillars supporting an upper storey. Libations and other household rituals may be envisaged as taking place in just such a setting. The regularity of the megaron plan in itself suggests ritual and ceremonial. But the megaron was not the primary location for Mycenaean cult; since the 1960s, a series of temples has been discovered on both the mainland and the islands. Modest in their size and architecture, these are identified as shrines largely on the basis of terracotta figurines which may depict worshippers, votive offerings (in the form of livestock) or even deities. The statuette known as the "Lady of Phylakopi" is one candidate for such a deity. Given the evidence for continuity in Greek religion from the Bronze Age to the Classical period, it is tempting to see these figures as the forerunners of well-known gods and goddesses. In terms of structure, however, the Bronze Age shrines have little in common with the grandiose temples of the Classical period.

A similar pattern – ritual within the household plus special-purpose "temples" of modest scale – can be seen also in the Balkan region, north of the Aegean. We have already remarked how the great central hearth – often richly decorated – is a key feature of the standardised megaron. At Wietenberg in Transylvania, a large circular hearth 1.5 m across stood at the very heart of the settlement. Around its edge was elaborate excised decoration in concentric bands, consisting of spirals and notches. The notches, according to some, may have been a form of calendar, in which case the ritual significance of the hearth is abundantly clear. A little further north, at Sălacea, remains of a rectangular building interpreted as a modest "temple" were found. This took the form of a rectangular room (or possibly two rooms) with raised clay altars against each of the side walls, fronted by an open porch. As in the Mycenaean examples, the identification of the Sălacea building as a shrine rests heavily on the material found within it: notably the nine pyramidal clay "idols" placed on each of the side altars.

Further to the west, from the Alpine zone northwards, evidence for shrines or temples is much rarer. True, the North Italian rock art from Val Camonica includes depictions of buildings, among them some which Anati, the leading authority on Val Camonica, identifies as special-purpose ritual buildings or shrines. Anati interprets a house carving at Coren del Valento as a ritual structure on the basis of the "bulls' horns" motifs shown on the long beam which marks the bottom of the roof

1   The Late Neolithic "temple" of Stonehenge, Wiltshire, England

space. There are a number of these "hut" carvings in the Val Camonica, and several of them have the same top-heavy structure with narrow base and oversailing upper storeys. It is perhaps logical to see the rectilinear and oblique lines as the timber frame of the house, and the forest of lines on top of the roof as either gable ornaments or an indication of roofing material. However, despite the occasional decorative elements (such as the bulls' horns in this example) there is little about these "huts" to convince us that they are special-purpose ritual structures. They also raise the important question as to whether the Val Camonica artists were depicting features from every-day life, or whether these are scenes from legend or mythology.

More solid evidence for Bronze Age ritual structures comes from Bargeroosterveld in the North Dutch province of Drenthe. Here was a small building in the midst of a marsh, 250 m from the nearest dry land. The limits of the site were marked by a circle of stones laid on the marsh surface, and within this ring two broad planks had been laid, parallel to each other through a little distance apart, with pegs fixing them in position and sockets for the insertion of uprights. Remains of curved oak terminals preserved by the waterlogged conditions suggested that this had been an elaborate structure with hornlike projec-

tions, providing a strong indication of its cultic (rather than practical) purpose.

The location of the Bargeroosterveld structure in a marsh is significant in itself. It is part of a growing preoccupation with watery contexts during the Late Bronze Age and Iron Age of northern Europe, for which the main evidence is the deposition of hoards which can include metalwork, ships and even human bodies. If these deposits were seen as offerings to the gods, then gods and water must have been associated and the Bargeroosterveld temple finds its setting in a special "ritual" location. Three hoards of metalwork were in fact discovered not far from the Bargeroosterveld site, confirming in some degree its special importance. Looking for the meaning which lies behind these activities, it is tempting to turn to what Roman writers – and especially Tacitus – tell us of religious belief and ritual practices among the Germanic peoples of the 1st/2nd century AD. In first place, he tells us that "their holy places are the woods and groves" (Germania VII); hence the archaeologist searching for timber temples might well expect to be disappointed. Later, when discussing the Langobardi, Tacitus refers to a particular sacred grove, on an island in the Ocean, where a sacred wagon was kept, to be brought out for processions on special festivals; at the end of each festival the wagon was washed in a sacred lake by men who were themselves subsequently drowned in the lake (Germania XL). Sacred groves figure prominently also in descriptions of the Celtic peoples of Gaul by Caesar, Strabo and Pliny. It is a situation which might well be projected back into the Bronze Age and be equally as valid for northern Europe in the 2nd millennium as in the 1st. It certainly underlines the notion that a society without temples is far from being a society without religious beliefs or practices.

If timber is the natural building material in much of central and northern Europe, yet in western Europe – along the Atlantic margins – we return to a land of stone. Here the greatest prehistoric ritual monuments – the megalithic tombs, and the circles and alignments of standing stones – belong to the period before the Bronze Age. Even the impressive stone structures of Stonehenge – until recently dated to the Early Bronze Age – have now been pushed back by new evidence into the Late Neolithic. But if the stones of Stonehenge were first dragged to the site and erected in the century or so following 2550 BC, it is abundantly clear that this in no way marked the end of the Stonehenge story. In the first place, minor adjustments to these stone settings continued to be made, and the final phase, the digging of the Y and Z holes (perhaps for a new stone setting which was never completed), did not occur until around 1600 BC. Thus we must not imagine that Stonehenge, like many prominent monuments of its type, was simply built and abandoned; it remained a centre of ritual importance long after the last of the sarsen monoliths was dragged all the way from the Marlborough Downs thirty km to the north. This much is shown not only the changes to Stonehenge itself but by the cluster of Bronze Age burial mounds which ring the horizon around the site; eloquent testimony, if such were needed, of the ongoing fascination exerted by this impressive prehistoric temple.

The journey from the megaron to Stonehenge spans a huge distance both in time, space and cultural variability. At the broadest scale, we may perhaps distinguish two principal categories of shrine or ritual focus in the European Bronze Age. In first place are the roofed buildings, not unlike ordinary houses, though usually incorporating special features. These are no doubt a simple development of domestic house and hearth-centred cults current from at least the Neolithic period onwards. They occur within settlements and are particularly represented, as we have seen, in eastern and southeastern Europe. The symbolic importance of the hearth as the focus of the house is thus one of the prime ingredients in later European ritual.

The second type of ritual focus groups together built structures such as Stonehenge and Bargeroosterveld with the sacred groves and lakes referred to by Classical writers: these are essentially open-air locations, away from ordinary settlements, where people were brought into contact with the natural elements such as wind and water, or (in the case of Stonehenge) with the heavens, the seasons, and the movements of the sun and the moon.

2   Reconstruction of the "temple" at Bargeroosterveld, Drenthe, Holland

The scarcity of clearly identified ritual or religious buildings in Bronze Age Europe can thus be explained in a number of ways. On the one hand, rituals may have taken place in ordinary houses, or in the open air in groves or by lakes or rivers. On the other is the difficulty of securely identifying ritual buildings, even where such buildings existed, given that ritual is a part of everyday life and the Bronze Age societies did not necessarily feel the need for self-standing shrines or temples. Yet of ritual activity and religious belief themselves there can be no doubt; of that the numerous cultic objects, the many precious items deposited in rivers and bogs, and the thousands of Bronze Age burial mounds furnish ample proof.

The Late Bronze Age Idols of the Danube

Henrietta Todorova

Clay sculpture represents a fascinating body of archaeological evidence from prehistoric Europe. It attained its widest dissemination in the Neolithic period, with clay idols rarely appearing after 4000 BC. Not until the 14th–13th centuries BC did clay sculpture once again come to play an important role in the cultures of southeast Europe. In the Danube region, the finds are concentrated in the area around the Iron Gate, in the region of the Late Bronze Age Žuto-Brdo-Kirna culture. This culture, the southeastern counterpart of the Urnfield culture, occupied northeast Serbia, southwest Rumania and northwest Bulgaria. The archaeological evidence comes primarily from cemeteries with cremation graves, equipped with elaborately decorated urns, dishes, bowls, cups and clay sculptures.

The idols represent stylised female figures, no taller than fifteen to twenty cm (Cat. No. 111). The long skirt is bell-shaped and hollow, while the upper body is rendered as a flat, rounded slab, probably intended to suggest arms crossed in front of the belly. The head and neck area is modelled schematically in a flat-topped, columnar form. The sculptures have a black, dark brown, or dark grey polished surface, largely covered with rich decorative patterns of white-inlaid grooves. This decoration suggests the female costume with a necklace, a fibula at the breast, a belt at the waist and a long braid at the back – and so on.

The varied decorative motifs of the skirt repeat the patterns found on the ceramics of the region, including volutes, spirals, angles, swastikas, circles, points, hatched rhomboids, stripes and triangles. The aesthetic power of the idols is due largely to their ornamentation, an effect clearly intended by their creators.

In the Danube region, male figures in the form of zoomorphic (eg. water-bird) and anthropo-zoomorphic sculptures also occur, although female representations predominate.

The ideas that produced the Danube sculptures seem to be closely related to those informing the contemporary small-scale sculpture of the Mycenaeans.

The function of these female idols is difficult to determine. The fact that they accompanied their owners to the grave excludes their identification as divinities (one does not bury gods with simple mortals). In a Mycenaean wall painting, a goddess, presumably Cybele, holds a similar sculpture in her hand – or more precisely on one finger – thus indicating the important magical function of these idols.

In this context, an Old Testament story more or less of a date with our find should be mentioned. Genesis 31 tells of the famous clay idols, the teraphim, which Rachel stole from her father Laban and on whose account Jacob was pursued by Laban. Their important protective role is expressly mentioned, and they constituted a part of Laban's personal belongings.

The range of possible interpretations for the clay sculptures of the Late Bronze Age will lie in much the same direction, since it is apparent that these too constituted personal property.

1   Clay idols from the Danube region
Middle Bronze Age. 14th–13th centuries BC. (After Müller-Karpe 1980)

Cycladic Marble Idols: The Silent Witnesses of an Island Society in the Early Bronze Age Aegean

Marina Marthari

Figurines of white marble are included in the arte-facts used by small communities scattered over the Cycladic islands at the centre of the Aegean, on which the so-called Cycladic culture evolved during the 3rd millennium BC (Early Bronze Age). The Early Cycladic world was one of the microcosms that flourished in the Aegean before the appearance of state formations with palaces and writing systems: that is, before the emergence of Minoan Crete and Mycenaean Greece during the following, 2nd millennium BC (Middle and Late Bronze Age).

The abundance of white marble in the Cyclades, especially on Paros and Naxos, supplied one of the stimuli to the creation of early sculpture. Other materials, such as lead, ivory, bone and seashells, were used only rarely to make figurines similar to those in marble. The other factors leading to the manufacture of the Cycladic figures are not known with certainty, since until recently very little was known of the social and economic organisation of the societies that created them.

Our ignorance of such matters complicates attempts to realise the meaning and use of these primitive sculptures. Approaches made so far to their interpretation may be divided into two basic categories: those that see the figurines as connected with religion and explain them as representations of deities, and those that associate them with everyday life. In the context of the first category of suggestions, the female figures – that is, the majority of the Cycladic figurines – have been considered to be images of the "fertility goddess" (Thimme 1977) or a goddess related to or identified with the sun (Goodison 1989). According to the views in the second category, the idols were, throughout a person's life, objects charged with magical properties, and accompanied their owner to the grave (Doumas 1983).

Cycladic idols in any event come mainly from cemeteries. Until recently the view was held that this might be purely fortuitous, since very few settlements dating from the early and mature periods of the Early Bronze Age had been excavated in the Cyclades, and even these were small and in a poor state of preservation. Recently excavated settlements, however, especially that at Skarkos on the island of Ios, have shown that the statu-ettes found in settlements are small, schematic ones, and not large anthropomorphic figurines. Skarkos is a well-preserved settlement with two-storied buildings, covering an area of c. 1.1 hectares and revealing a quite complex organisation, which flourished in the mature phase of the Early Bronze Age (Keros-Syros group period, Ill. 1). This lends support to the view that the main use of the large, naturalistic Cycladic figurines was to accompany the dead as grave goods.

The typology of Cycladic figurines advanced by C. Renfrew in 1969 (see also Renfrew 1991, Ill. 2) is still generally accepted, despite the fact that within the corpus of figurines there is greater variation than their classification into general types and varieties admits. The conventional names given to the types and varieties derive from the site at which representative examples have been found during excavations.

The general form of a Cycladic figurine is created by modelling, but many details are rendered by incision and paint (red and dark blue). On many idols, the eyes, mouth, hair, fingers, jewellery were rendered by paint, as

1   Buildings at the Early Cycladic II settlement of Skarkos on the island of Ios

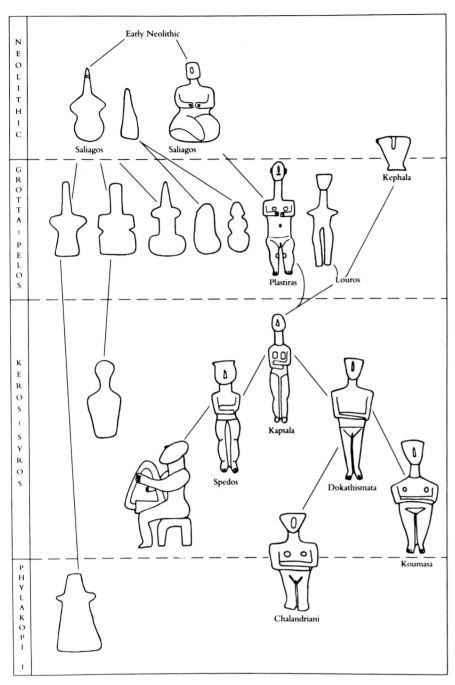

2   Development of the Early Cycladic figurines from their Neolithic prototypes, (after Renfrew 1991, 91, Fig. 5).

about 4800 BC: the naturalistic and the abstract. These two trends are found alongside each other throughout almost the entire Early Bronze Age, which is divided into three periods.

The earliest of these periods (Early Cycladic I, or Grotta-Pelos group period, c. 3100–2700 BC) saw the emergence of the characteristic features of Cycladic society, including cist-grave cemeteries and marble vases (Cat. No. 15) and figurines. There are two main types of figurine: the abstract, "violin" figurines that render the human figure in the shape of that instrument (Cat. No. 16), and the more naturalistic, though rather clumsy, Plastiras type. Plastiras-type statuettes stand on their feet, and their legs are separated for their entire length. Their arms are folded beneath the chest and above the waist, with their fingers touching. The ears, nose and more rarely the mouth are rendered in relief, while the eyes are in some cases inlaid. The navel, elbows and kneecaps are often depicted, as well as the ankles. Some wear a sort of hat on the head (Cat. No. 18). At the transition to the following period, about 2700 BC, the Louros type, which combines abstract and naturalistic characteristics, made its appearance. These are standing figures with the lower legs divided, with simple projections instead of arms, and a head in which neither the nose nor any other features are indicated. The three figurine types mentioned above are normally no higher than thirty cm and are found in the central and south Cyclades (Paros, Naxos, Thera and Amorgos).

During the mature period of the Early Bronze Age (Early Cycladic II or the Keros-Syros group period, c. 2700–2200 BC), the Cycladic world reached the peak of its development. Contacts with the rest of the Aegean are so extensive that Renfrew speaks of an "international spirit". At the end of this period, indeed, which coincides with the Kastri group phase, there was an intensification of the contacts between the Cyclades and the East Aegean. The predominant types during this period are the relatively naturalistic folded-arm figurine and the schematic Apeiranthos type. In the folded-arm figurines, the head is tilted backwards, the nose projects distinctly, and the mouth, eyes and ears are only rarely depicted in relief. The breasts are rendered plastically and the pubic triangle by incision. The legs are often completely joined together, separated only by a groove. The soles of the feet

well as facial and body colour decoration and tattoos (Ill. 4). The painted features are preserved only in very few cases, because of the fugitive nature of the paint, a circumstance that often gives a deceptive idea of the original appearance of the figures.

There seem to have been two trends in Cycladic sculpture that emerged as early as the Neolithic period, slope downwards with the toes to the ground. This feature has led some scholars to suggest that the figurines of this type are depicted in a reclining posture. Most render female figures on a small or medium scale. Some, however, are very impressive life-size female images, as high as 1.50 metres. These are works of true large-scale sculpture which, according to one interpretation, were used as divine representations in "sanctuaries" (Renfrew 1991, 95–105).

The folded-arm type occurs in many varieties. Figurines of the Kapsala variety have an oval head, distinctly bent knees, and legs separated just below the knees. Some stand on the ground with arched or flat soles, and others appear to be standing on their toes, like the figurines in the other varieties. The figure is not excessively slim in profile. Figurines of the Spedos variety are distinguished by their strong curves. The head is lyre-shaped. This type includes a large number of figures (Cat. No. 17). Idols of the Dokathismata variety are slender, flat, with angular outlines and a triangular head. Figurines of the Chalandriani variety which are rather clumsy in comparison with those of other varieties, have an almost rectangular sternum, triangular head, thick neck and long legs. In some of them the left forearm is placed beneath the right, whereas in figurines of the other varieties, the reverse is invariably the case. Figures of the Koumasa variety are broad at the shoulders, narrow at the feet, and are thin and flat in profile, with a long neck. They are found only in Crete and it has been suggested that they were made there as imitations of the Spedos variety, examples of which have been found imported into Crete.

Some special figures also belong to the folded-arm type, in that they have a similar anatomy and rendering of the head. They are images of both women and men sitting on simple stools or elaborate thrones. The male figurines are harp players (Ill. 5), or men bearing a drinking cup in their hand. These special figures also include standing musicians playing pipes, and two- or three-figure compositions. One particular group consists of hunter-warriors, who have the general features of the Chalandriani variety. These figures wear a baldric slung diagonally from one shoulder and hold a dagger.

Idols of the folded-arm type have been found on most of the Cycladic islands and Crete, where the

3   Violin-shaped figurine, Kimolos, Cyclades, Greece
Early Bronze Age (Cat. No. 16)

Koumasa variety was manufactured, and also in Mainland Greece, where they are possibly imports from the Cycladic archipelago. According to some scholars, Cycladic figurines probably travelled to various regions of the Aegean as prestige goods.

To the schematic Apeiranthos type may be assigned figures with a variety of such body shapes, while in some cases the head has a shape and backwards tilt similar to those of figurines of the folded-arm type.

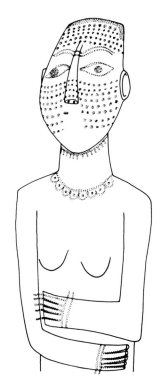

4   A folded-armed figurine of Kapsala variety with painted details,
(after Getz-Preziosi 1987a, 55, Fig. 29).

During the late Early Bronze Age period (Early Cycladic III, or Phylakopi I group period, c. 2200–2000 BC), significant changes may be observed in the Cycladic islands. Several of the earlier settlements were abandoned. New, large settlements emerged as the result of nucleation of smaller sites. The most characteristic features of the Early Cycladic world, the marble vases and anthropomorphic figurines, ceased to exist. Only one, entirely schematic type, continued to be made, the Phylakopi type, which is far removed from the earlier schematic Apeiranthos type, in which the head was relatively naturalistic.

The figurine types are assigned to periods in the 3rd millennium on the basis of the context of those examples discovered during the excavation of graves, since very few figurines have so far been found in stratified settlement contexts. The chronological assignment of the varieties of the folded-arm figurines to sub-periods has not been used, since this was based almost entirely on purely typological criteria.

Perceptions of modern art at the beginning of the 20th century AD led to the appreciation of simple, abstract,

162

"primitive" art. The Cycladic statuettes were then for the first time regarded as works of art, and came into great demand on the international art markets. Collectors and museums in both Europe and USA acquired figurines through the illicit antiquities trade in the Cyclades, and at the same time, forgeries began to be made. The treatment of the Cycladic figurines as works of "high" art by certain scholars in the 1960s and 1970s had its consequences on archaeological research itself, amongst other things, since it helped to create an exaggerated idea of the art of the Early Cycladic world, the social organisation of which was very little known.

Of critical importance in this were the views of Getz-Preziosi (1987a, 1987b), who attributed groups of works to specific "masters", as she calls them (Broodbank 1992, Cherry 1992, Gill and Chippindale 1993, Marangou 1990). It seems more probable, however, that these groups

5   Harp-player from a grave on the islet of Keros, National Archaeological Museum, Athens; height 22.5 cm.

reflect sculptural traditions that evolved within restricted chronological or local contexts (workshops), rather than specific artists. The structures of Cycladic island societies in the 3rd millennium BC, which are beginning to become better known thanks to recent excavations of settlements, do not warrant the positing of "master", like those active in Greece in historical times, though it is not impossible, of course, that some of the marble-carvers who worked on the islands in the 3rd millennium BC were more gifted and more famous than others.

In recent years, excavations of notable settlements both in the Cyclades themselves, like that at Skarkos on Ios, and on the islands and coasts of the Aegean sea more generally, as at Palamari on Skyros island, near Euboea, Poros on the north coast of Crete, and Liman Tepe (Klazomenai) on the bay of Smyrna in Asia Minor, are continually widening our knowledge of exchange systems and social organisation in the 3rd millennium BC Aegean. The future progress of these investigations is expected to shed light on the interpretation of the individual artefacts of Cycladic culture, including the figurines, the stone vases (Cat. No. 15), the clay "frying pans", some of which depict longboats (Cat. No. 14), the obsidian tools (Cat. No. 11), the slabs with figurative graffiti (Cat. No. 12) etc. Conversely, however, the conditions now permit us to examine Cycladic figurines from perspectives that may further illuminate the complexity of Aegean societies in the 3rd millennium BC, since it is now possible to understand the basic axes of their functions. The examination of the figurines not only from an artistic point of view, but also in relation to their subjects, taken together with recent excavation data, as far as the material permits, e.g. hunter-warriors, musicians, cupbearers, women in pregnant or post-parturition condition, provides these silent witnesses with their first chance finally to gain a voice and speak to us about the world that breathed life into them.

Bibliography: Broodbank 1992; Cherry 1992; Doumas 1983; Getz-Pretziosi 1987a, 1987b; Gill & Chippindale 1993; Marangou 1990; Renfrew 1969, 1991; Thimme 1977.

Ivory Sculpture of the Aegean

Jean Claude Poursat

The art of ivory working, in the form of small figurines, plated and inlaid decoration on wooden furniture and carved toilet articles, represents one of the most original achievements of the Aegean art of the Bronze Age. Along with seal engraving, it constitutes the most important manifestation of relief sculpture in a period when large-scale sculpture was virtually unknown here. It provides evidence of trade relations between the Aegean and the Near East, since ivory – the tusks of hippopotami or elephants – was imported from Syria or Egypt. The iconographic richness of the carved ivories, in which typically Aegean themes were combined with oriental influences, and their importance as prestige objects in the Aegean cultures of the 2nd millennium lend them particular significance.

The art of ivory working developed most in the Late Bronze Age, after 1600 BC. Previously, elephant ivory had been almost unknown in the Aegean; seals, often carved in the form of animals, as well as small figurines and inlaid work were all then fashioned either from hippopotamus ivory, which continued to be used throughout the entire Bronze Age, or simply from bone, employed in Crete from the pre-palace period toward the end of the 3rd millennium. Objects of ivory remained very rare even during the period of the First Palaces (2000–1700 BC). It was not until the height of the Second Palaces in Crete and the growth of Mycenaean power, as evidenced by the richly furnished tombs in the Grave Circles of Mycenae (Circles A and B, 1650–1500 BC), that ivory began to be imported in the context of new relations between the princes of Mycenae and Crete and their oriental counterparts: ivory was doubtless included among the prestige gifts exchanged by these rulers. Numerous elephant tusks were stored in the palace of Zakros on Crete at the time of its destruction around 1450 BC; the inventories of the palace of Pylos in Messenia, written in Mycenaean Greek (Linear B), record the presence of raw ivory there as well. The wreck of a ship from around 1300 BC, found at Ulu Burun off the south coast of Anatolia, contained elephant and hippopotamus ivory, clear evidence of the ivory trade between the Orient and the Aegean. In addition, we know of palace workshops of ivory artists in Knossos and Zakros on Crete and in Mycenae and Thebes on the Greek mainland.

Ivory figurines in the round, more or less related to the Cycladic type, were produced in Crete from the end of the 3rd millennium on. In the Second Palace period (1700–1450 BC), this tradition led to the creation of the figurines from the palace of Knossos representing acrobatic bull-leapers (Ill. 1). Another recently-discovered

1   Acrobat from the palace of Knossos, c. 1550 BC, Archaeological Museum of Herakleion; length 29.5 cm.

piece, the "kouros" of Palaikastro – a c. fifty cm high statuette of a standing man whose body is carved from hippopotamus ivory and decorated with precious stones and metal – doubtless represents the best example of this gold and ivory technique. Late Bronze Age works from the Greek mainland primarily include female figures shown in the traditional Minoan costume with flounced skirt. The ivory workers of Mycenae created masterpieces such as the ivory group found on the Acropolis, showing two crouching women holding a child on their knees (Ill. 2), or a splendid male head found in the "Citadel House", which must have belonged to a larger-scale statuette.

2 Two females and a child, from Mycenae; 1400–1200 BC,
National Archaeological Museum, Athens; height 7.8 cm.

3 Head of a warrior from Mycenae; 1400–1200 BC,
National Archaeological Museum, Athens; height 8.2 cm.

In the Aegean, ivory was used above all for decorative relief panels or carved inlays. Ivory relief sculpture is very rare in Mycenae before the period of the Grave Circles A and B. One of the oldest examples is the pommel of a sword from Circle A, adorned with four lions. The earliest toilet articles of ivory with carved decoration appear in the tholos graves of Mycenae and in Messenia. An influx of elephant ivory, apparently in the course of the 15th century BC, allowed the invention of new decorated forms that could not be created from hippopotamus tusks. These toilet articles included pyxides (cosmetic or ointment jars) fashioned from a single piece of hollowed-out tusk and supplied with a separate bottom and lid; large, rectangular combs, their backs/handles carved in two registers with a rosette in the centre of the upper; mirror handles in the form of a column or a palm, designed to hold the metal plate between two ivory panels; and small, shallow boxes with decorated sides and lids that probably served as jewellery cases.

The objects dating to the period up to the end of the 13th century BC were found for the most part in the great tholos or chamber graves of the Greek mainland and Crete, where the dead were buried along with furniture and toilet articles. Examples include a pyxis decorated with fighting griffins and stags from a grave in the Athenian Agora, and a comb showing a sphinx and crocodiles from a tholos tomb at Spata in east Attica. The same conventions appear in Crete as well: a pyxis from Katsamba, the port of Knossos, shows a most beautiful bull-catching scene, with relief figures reminiscent of the acrobats of Knossos. A comb from the same site, decorated with a sphinx with outspread wings, employs one of the most common ivory motifs.

None of the furniture decorated with ivory has survived; only the applied or inlaid ivory elements have been found, ornaments which must have contrasted with the darker colour of the wood. The Linear B clay tablets excavated in the palace of Pylos, however, provide an inventory of tables, thrones, and footstools decorated with carved ivory panels or ivory inlay, naming specific motifs as well, including lions, palms, shells and war helmets; other tablets from Pylos and Knossos also mention ivory

165

4 Panel from Archanes; 1400–1350 BC, Archaeological Museum of
   Herakleion; height 3.2 cm.

5 Mirror handle from Enkomi; c. 1200 BC, British Museum,
   London; height 20 cm.

ornaments for chariots. Two buildings in the vicinity of
the citadel of Mycenae, the "House of the Shields" and
the "House of the Sphinxes" were probably workshops
with storage depots where ivory ornaments were fitted to
the furniture for which they were intended. The buildings
receive their names from the numerous ivory shields
found in the one and the panels decorated with sphinxes
discovered in the other.

Within this specific decorative framework, particular themes and motifs were favoured by ivory artists.
Some of the representations are drawn from other major
arts of the epoch, frescoes and seals. The depiction of a
woman sitting on a rock, carved in high relief on an ivory
panel from Mycenae, copies a scheme found repeatedly in
Minoan and later in Mycenaean frescoes. This type finds
its exact parallel on a seal from the acropolis of Mycenae.
Other decorative motifs are even more closely associated
with the medium of ivory. The footrests of thrones, for

example, were decorated with large "figure-of-eight"
shields (Cat. No. 51) and the heads of warriors in boar's
tusk helmets (Ill. 3, Cat. No. 47); the sphinx and the
crocodile were among the most popular motifs for combs,
while mirror handles show a novel motif of women bend-
ing toward each other, sometimes even holding a mirror.
An original animal style appears in the representations of
lions, sphinxes, griffins, and fighting animals decorating
pyxides or parts of boxes; in all these works, the Mycenaean artists successfully conveyed an impression of volume and depth through subtle modelling in relief.

These characteristic Mycenaean ivories from the
end of the Late Bronze Age enable us to trace the progress
of Mycenaean expansion throughout the Aegean in the
14th and 13th centuries BC. After 1400 BC, many richly
furnished graves at Archanes near Knossos (Ill. 4) and in
the region of Chania and Rhethymnon in western Crete
contain remarkable ivory groups; ivory panels from

166

footrests or thrones, combs and boxes resembling those from the graves of the Greek mainland – finds which seem to indicate Mycenaean domination of the island during this period. A few isolated works of Mycenaean ivory found elsewhere provide evidence of contacts established with other parts of the Mediterranean world: a helmeted warrior's head of ivory was found on Sardinia, for example, and another in Cyprus.

Works of ivory in a Mycenaean style, inspired more or less directly by Mycenaean iconography but originating in the Cypriot workshops of Enkomi, Kition or Paphos, have been found not only in Cyprus itself, but also on Delos in the Aegean and even at Ugarit on the coast of Syria and Meggido in Palestine. A group of engraved ivories in which Aegean themes are combined with oriental chiselling techniques appears in Cyprus in the second half of the 13th century BC; in these works, mostly decorated with fighting animals, the figures show a characteristic stylisation which later appears in certain ivory carvings from the Greek mainland. The production of ivory reliefs in Cyprus during the same period doubtless manifests the increasing influence of Mycenaean art, which frequently utilised the technique of relief sculpture. The lid of a pyxis from Ras Shamra shows a "mistress of the animals" (Potnia Theron), reminiscent of certain depictions from Mycenae; a panel from Delos showing the image of a foot soldier with a lance against the background of a shield likewise reflects this Cypriot-Aegean art of the last third of the 13th century BC. A number of beautiful mirror handles of the oriental type, produced in Enkomi (Ill. 5) or Paphos and showing animal scenes or fights between a warrior and a lion or a griffin, date from the period immediately following, i.e. the beginning of the 12th century.

At the end of the Mycenaean period, these Cypriot ivories were to transmit certain elements of Aegean iconography to the Near East, aspects that would survive in Syria and Palestine into the Archaic period of the 9th and 8th centuries BC in works such as the ivories of Nimrud and Samaria. As a "palace art", the art of ivory in the Aegean world disappeared around 1200 BC, along with the Mycenaean palaces themselves.

The Golden Treasures of the European Bronze Age

Christiane Eluère

The goldsmith's art emerged at different times in different places in Europe. In the Balkan peninsula and the south of France, for example, it began as early as the Lower Palaeolithic Age; in most other regions, works in gold appear in the Chalcolithic Age (in central and most of western Europe), and sometimes even later (the Early Bronze Age in the British Isles and Scandinavia, the Middle Bronze Age on the Italian peninsula).

It is clear that from the beginning gold was used to demonstrate the power of particular persons, especially men. The best example of this function is the necropolis of Varna from the late 5th millennium BC, where an exceptional number of gold objects were buried with certain deceased men: not only jewellery (anthropomorphic pendants, beads, appliqués, ornaments for the ears and other parts of the face), but also pectorals, sceptres, diadems of gold and weapons such as bows. These finds clearly show the symbolic power already invested in this unmistakable and easily-worked material. The earliest hoards of golden weapons in central Europe (dagger blades and axes of gold) manifest similar conceptions of the metal's significance. In regions closer to the Atlantic, the first gold bands or small appliqués, perhaps used to decorate the clothing or armour of the deceased, are often associated with the warrior graves of the Beaker culture.

The Problem of Gold Vessels

The question arises as to whether objects of similar type were used in the same way throughout all of Europe. A category of objects like gold vessels reveals the wide range of archaeological contexts in which such artefacts have been found. In western Europe, for example, a few gold cups with handles, dating from the Early Bronze Age (Cat. No. 201), were found in chieftains' graves (e.g. the gold cup from Rillaton, Cornwall, or the silver cup from St.-Adrien, Côtes-du-Nord). The great majority of gold vessels from the Middle Bronze Age or the beginning of the Late Bronze Age, above all in central Europe, were apparently found in hoards and "normal" burials, often in pairs (Villeneuve-St.-Vistre, Haute-Marne; Axtroki in Basque country) or even with vessels of bronze (e.g. the hoard from Unterglauheim in Bavaria [Cat. No. 211]). Golden vessels also appear in great number in "votive hoards" or hoards of cult objects, together with other articles such as pieces of jewellery or rolled gold wire (e.g. the treasure hoards of Caldas de Reyes near La Coruña or Eberswalde near Berlin).

In the Aegean world, on the other hand, vessels of gold appear to have been deposited primarily in the "richest" graves (Cat. No. 44). They are also decorated in a different manner, for while the central European vessels are systematically embellished with abstract, stamped circular motifs, often interpreted as symbols of the sun or the cosmos, the corresponding vessels from the Minoan-Mycenaean world are decorated with figural representations in addition to symbols. The best-known example of the latter is the famous Vapheio cup. Other vessels show recurring motifs such as the birds on the handles of the "cup of Nestor" or the spiral and floral motifs found on other vases.

The Gold of the Tombs

The earliest finds of gold come from graves, where they were obviously intended to emphasise the social rank of the deceased. This holds true for the cases mentioned above, but also for the burial mounds of the Wessex culture of England (Cat. No. 160) and the "minor princes of Armorica", which contained gold-studded dagger hilts, vessels and jewellery pendants (Cat. No. 163), as well as the graves of the El Argar culture in Spain containing spirals and diadems of gold.

In the course of the Middle and Late Bronze Age, the use of golden artefacts as grave goods slowly diminished in non-Mycenaean Europe, dwindling to a few rings and some gold leaf. From this point on, it is the Middle and Late Bronze Age graves of Denmark and Sweden that show the finest examples of gold-plated swords.

Objects of solid gold seem to have been reserved for "ritual hoards". Gold for mortals appears to have been

1   Hoard of gold cups, Borgbjerg, Zealand, Denmark ▷
    Late Bronze Age, 11th–9th centuries BC (Cat. No. 209)

168

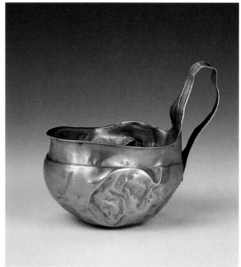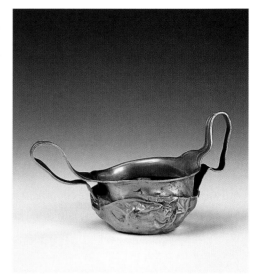

2–4   Hoard of gold cups, Radeni, Neamt, Rumania, 1800–1600 BC (Cat. No. 191)

less important than the gold reserved for the gods; at any rate, these hoards no longer served to represent the wealth of a community.

In the Mycenaean world, different conceptions seem to have prevailed; the greatest number of golden objects are found in the graves of the 2nd millennium BC, particularly those of rulers: suffice it to mention the death masks, the gilded arms, the great diadems, the armbands and the numerous appliqués that were probably sewn onto organic materials (fabric, leather clothing or burial shrouds). To be sure, most of these large objects were only gilded. Their weight in gold was thus relatively modest in comparison to the decorative rings of the western "hoards".

Golden Votive Necklaces in the West

In regions such as Ireland, the British Isles, the French Atlantic coast and the western Iberian Peninsula, an unusual number of gold hoards have come to light, representing a significant total weight in gold.

Beginning in the Early Bronze Age, objects typically encountered in Britain are pairs of disk-shaped appliqués and above all the so-called "lunulae", necklaces of beaten gold in crescent form. The latter were widespread on both sides of the Channel and above all in Ireland, frequently appearing in multiples (Cat. Nos. 193–195). These finely-worked pieces of jewellery are never found in graves; sometimes they are recovered in small wooden boxes, as at Killymoon in the Irish county of Tyrone.

With the lunulae, we are still dealing with objects of small weight. The Middle and Late Bronze Age, however, saw the production of another kind of jewellery – long twisted gold necklaces known as "torcs". The longest, found in Plouguin in Brittany, measures 1.5 m; these necklaces, of which the most famous are those from Tara (Ireland) and Cesson (Brittany), frequently possessed a weight of up to 400 grams.

Along the entire Atlantic region of western Europe, numerous votive armrings of solid gold have been found. They are smooth and either semi-cylindrical or lozenge-shaped in section. Often weighing as much as 200–300 grams, they are known to have existed since the Early Bronze Age in hoards such as that of Caldas de Reyes (La Coruña) and in numerous examples from Brittany, the Loire region and southwest France. In Ireland and the British Isles, hoards containing such armrings are not infrequent; a dozen pieces were found in Downpatrick (County Down). Typical of central Europe is the armband with spiral terminals, found in gold hoards such as that of Biia (Magyarebénye, Cat. No. 181) in Rumania. Hoards of spiral armbands frequently appear in the Danube and Carpathian regions, for example in Bodrogkeresztur (Hungary) or Bilje (near Osijek, Serbia).

The golden armring may have had particular significance in the Bronze Age. It is also found in extraordinary graves, such as the Early Bronze Age princes' tombs at Leubingen and Helmsdorf in central Germany. The custom of burying a golden armring with certain deceased males continued in northern Europe. The most remarkable pieces, however, are the small group of solid gold necklaces found in Brittany (the lost hoard of Vieux-Bourg-Quintin on the Côte-du-Nord, consisting of gold necklaces and armbands with a total weight of eight kg), Portugal (above all the Evora necklace with a weight in gold of 2.13 kg (Cat. No. 200) and the Sintra necklace), and Spain (the Berzocana necklace). All of these necklaces possess clasps, indicating that despite their weight, they were meant to be worn. But by whom – by humans or by statues? All are decorated with engraved geometric motifs, a characteristic mode of ornamentation in western Europe.

Gold – A Solar Symbol?

Gold is an imperishable metal, possessing a remarkable brilliance. Its yellow colour has contributed to its instinctive association with the sun. We know, or at least may surmise on the basis of certain indications, that the religious beliefs of Bronze Age peoples were closely bound to natural phenomena. The sun, associated with the seasons as well as with day and night, must have played an important role in the context of this "religion". Thus it comes as no surprise to find allusions to the sun in the form of disk-shaped appliqués decorated with points and lines, found equally in Ireland, the British Isles and northern Germany (disk from Glüsing). These disks can be quite large (ten to twenty cm in diameter), as is shown in particular by the "sun chariot" of Trundholm (Denmark, Cat. No. 175), which itself has come to symbolise the Bronze Age. In some ritual procession, a horse strides out, drawing on a chariot of bronze containing a large, gold-plated sun disk. The surviving portions of the gold plating show a concentric design of geometric motifs chiselled into the bronze surface.

The stamped circle motifs so often found on gold vessels in western Europe should also be mentioned in this context. The great "cones" or golden hats found at

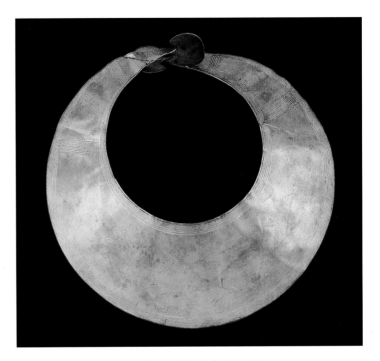

5   Lunula, Kerivoa, Bourbriac, Côtes-du-Nord, France
    Early Bronze Age, c. 1800 BC (Cat. No. 195)

Avanton (Vienne, Cat. No. 204), Ezelsdorf (Bavaria, Cat. No. 205), and Schifferstadt (Rhineland-Pfalz, Cat. No. 206), as well as the example in the Museum für Vor- und Frühgeschichte in Berlin, all show decorations of this type occurring in various forms (concentric circles, disks, etc.). The small gold cups that occur so frequently throughout northern Germany and central Europe, often found in pairs, are decorated in the same way, sometimes with a large star motif on their bottom as well (Cat. No. 167). Should we surmise that all these vessels were used for libations reserved for a cult of the sun? It should be noted that these circular motifs are not confined to western Europe; they also occur in great number in the Mycenaean world, on objects such as diadems.

In conclusion, it appears that the basic concepts associated with gold were shared by different population groups throughout all of Europe. The only substantial difference seems to lie in the fact that in the Mycenaean world, gold may have been reserved only for the leaders of their society, whereas in western Europe it played a role in the religious practices of the whole society.

The Berlin Gold Hat: A Ceremonial Head-dress of the Late Bronze Age

Wilfried Menghin

The items referred to as "gold cones" are among the most impressive evidence of the exercise of religion in the European Bronze Age. Since the discovery of the first example in the vicinity of Schifferstadt near Speyer,[1] scholars have puzzled over their function, whether as head-dress, vessel or a device put atop a pole. The poor state of preservation of the examples subsequently found at Avanton near Poitiers in 1844 and Ezelsdorf near Nuremberg in 1953 served to further confuse rather than to clarify the issue.[2] Most recently, S. Gerloff has explored the question, arguing convincingly for an interpretation of the gold cones as head-dresses.[3] This thesis is confirmed by a previously unknown sheet gold cone, acquired in December 1996 by the Staatliche Museen zu Berlin for the Museum für Vor- und Frühgeschichte (Cat. No. 207).[4]

The cult object, found in unusually good condition and above all preserved in its entirety, exhibits remarkable precision of ornamentation. It consists of a hollow, pointed cone 74.5 cm in height, fashioned of hammered gold with no seams. A separate cap and a horizontal brim of paper-thin sheet gold is adorned with twenty-one horizontal zones, consisting of repoussé bands with rows of stamped beading, enlivened by embossed ornament in concentric circles of varying number and size, none of which overlap (Ill. 1). The top of the cone is marked by a six-pointed star with attenuated arms, between which a regular stamped bead pattern appears. The fourth zone from the top shows a decorative band of horizontally-set half-moons with a central dot and a parallel pattern of ovoids with pointed ends (like eyes). The junction of the cone proper to the cap is marked by a band of parallel vertical grooves. The brim, 5.3 cm wide, is marked off from the ten cm high cap by a fold into which has been inset a circular strip of bronze; the brim is further reinforced by turning over its rim around a bronze ring (30.7 x 29.5 cm in dimension) of twisted metal. With a height of 74.5 cm and an average thickness of 0.06 mm, the cone, together with the stabilising bronze base and brim reinforcements, weighs some 490 grams. The Berlin example provides conclusive proof for the heretofore controversial thesis that the gold cones served as head-dresses.[5]

With respect to the function of the object, it is significant that the base of the cone has an oval diameter (20.3 x 17.5 cm) and that the decorative patterns on the underside of the brim are positive.

The high oval cap with the inset bronze ring at its base corresponds to the hat size of an average adult male, with allowance made for an inner lining of leather or felt, now lost. The positive decoration on the underside of the brim clearly indicates that the wearer of the tall conical hat appeared to his viewers from an elevated position.

The four known conical hats resemble each other in their form, symbolism, technique and above all the circumstances of their discovery. The examples from Schifferstadt (Cat. No. 206), Avanton (Cat. No. 204) and Ezelsdorf (Cat. No. 205) represent isolated, chance discoveries, unrelated to any broader archaeological context. They belong to the category of so-called hoards from the Bronze Age and may be viewed as "votive gifts" in the broadest sense. For reasons unknown to us, cult objects such as these mitre-like gold hats or ceremonial vessels of gold or bronze were withdrawn from ritual use and surrendered to subterranean powers in secret or sacred places.[6]

Although the place, date, and circumstances of the discovery of the Berlin gold hat are unknown – it is said to have belonged to an anonymous private collection in Switzerland, supposedly assembled in the 1950s or 60s, its excellent state of preservation and the minimal damage that it shows indicate a deposition history similar in character to that reported for the "Golden Hat" of Schifferstadt.[7] Our gold hat, which must have originally possessed an inner lining of organic material – now long since decayed, appears to have been buried upright in a soft,

1 "Conus" or Head-Dress, Schifferstadt, Speyer, Rheinland- ▷
Pfalz, Germany, Middle/Late Bronze Age (Cat. No. 206)

humus soil. Only two lateral dents on the cone and a crease on the cap are visible, as if the whole had only gradually been deformed by the pressure of the earth. This hypothesis is confirmed by the fact that the layers of corrosion are present only on the outer skin, while the interior of the hollow body shows an even gold patina.

All four ceremonial hats were hammered up whole from a single piece of gold, an achievement that presupposes extraordinary metallurgical skill and craftsmanship on the part of the Bronze Age smith. The analysis of production technique by M. Fecht has shown that the embossed ornaments were created by forcing the metal into a hollow mould, of bronze or some organic material, applied to the exterior – so that the patterns appear there in relief. The decorative zones and ornaments were laid out using a template to mark up the surface: on the gold cone from Ezelsdorf, for example, twenty different punches, six ornamental wheels and a decorative comb were used. Such detailed technical analyses have yet to be performed for the gold hat in Berlin.

The main ornamental motifs are disks and circles, which in the context of Bronze Age culture are generally interpreted as solar symbols (Ill. 2). Stars with multiple points crown the tops of the cones of Avanton, Ezelsdorf and Berlin, while the "eye" motif is found on the examples from Schifferstadt, Ezelsdorf and Berlin; on the last, the embossed "almond" shapes are positioned separately one from the another. The two decorative zones displaying miniature cones and the prominent frieze of eight-spoked wagon wheels are unique to the gold cone from Ezelsdorf, while the horizontally arranged half-moons with a central dot – probably strongly stylised sunbarque motifs – occur only on the example in Berlin.

It remains for future studies linking cultural traits, form and questions of mathematics and astronomy to explore the meaning of the individual ornaments and to address the question of whether the number or combination of patterns, decorative zones and bands represents a systematic scheme such as a cosmic pictography or calendar. It is certain, however, that the golden cone hats pos-

2 "Conus" or Head-Dress, probably from southwest Germany or Switzerland, Late Bronze Age (Cat. No. 207)

sessed extraordinary significance in a Bronze Age cult of the 14th–8th centuries BC, probably constituting the ceremonial head-dress of the priests or priest-kings of an archaic religion now known to us only obscurely. The period in which the Berlin gold hat was manufactured, how long it was used, and why and above all when it was ritually buried cannot be determined from the object itself.

The circumstances and location of the discovery are, as stated, unknown. The circumstances of the deposition, no matter how well excavated, are unlikely to lead to the recovery of associated material – such the flanged bronze axes found with the golden hat of Schifferstadt. Details of technique, however, such as the twisted bronze ring at the edge of the brim, the quality of the repoussé work and the precision of the ornamentation when taken together with the typological relation of its decorative motifs with others from more securely dated archaeological contexts, all suggest a probable date of manufacture in the Late Bronze Age, that is in the 8th–10th centuries BC.

1 L. Lindenschmit, *Althertümer unserer heidnischer Vorzeit* 1, 10 (1858), pl. 11; P. Schauer, *Die Goldblechkegel der Bronzezeit. Ein Beitrag zur Kulturverbindung zwischen Orient und Mitteleuropa* (Mainz 1986), 2 n. 16; 24 f.; 52 f.; pl. 1.
2 Schauer 1986, 2 ff.
3 S. Gerloff, 'Bronzezeitliche Goldblechkronen aus Westeuropa. Betrachtungen zur Funktion der Goldblechkegel vom Typ Schifferstadt und der atlantischen 'Goldschalen' der Form Devil's Bit und Atroxi', in *Festschrift für Hermann Müller-Karpe zum 70. Geburtstag* (1995), 153 ff.
4 W. Menghin, 'Der Berliner Goldhut. Ein Zeremonienhut der Späten Bronzezeit', *MuseumJournal* 11, 2 (1997), 76 ff.
5 Cf. Schauer 1986, 61 ff. and Menghin 1977, following Raschke (G. Raschke, 'Ein Goldfund der Bronzezeit von Etzelsdorf-Buch bei Nürnberg [Goldblechbekrönung]', *Germania* 32 [1954], 1 ff.) in W. Menghin & P. Schauer, *Magisches Gold. Kultgerät der späten Bronzezeit*, exh. cat. (Nuremberg 1997), 17, as well as the correction in Gerloff 1995, 175 ff.
6 B. Hänsel, 'Gaben an die Götter. Schätze der Bronzezeit Europas – eine Einführung', in *Gaben an die Götter. Schätze der Bronzezeit Europas*, Bestandskataloge des Museums für Vor- und Frühgeschichte Berlin, vol. 4 (1977), 15 ff.
7 Schauer 1986, 2 n. 16: the golden hat of Schifferstadt reportedly stood upright in the ground on a stone slab, its point extending to just beneath the topsoil. Three flanged bronze axes were found leaning against the conical hat.

Bibliography: Gerloff 1995; Hänsel 1977; Lindenschmit 1858; Menghin 1997; Menghin & Schauer 1997; Raschke 1954; Schauer 1986.

The Golden Cone of Ezelsdorf-Buch: A Masterpiece of the Goldsmith's Art from the Bronze Age

Tobias Springer

The Discovery

In the spring of 1953, tree stumps were being cleared on the south slope of the hill of Brentenberg on the boundary between the towns of Ezelsdorf (Mittelfranken) and of Buch (Oberpfalz, Bavaria). At one point, the work was hindered by a piece of sheet metal lying only eight cm beneath the surface of the earth, wedged between the roots of a tree. It was chopped to bits and heedlessly thrown aside. Only later, when the midday sun revealed the gleam of gold, were the paper-thin pieces of metal collected.

A test on the melting point of the material, performed by a dentist, established that the material was gold. Inquiring further, the finders approached Dr. Georg Raschke, then director of the prehistoric collection of the Germanisches Nationalmuseum in Nuremberg, who immediately recognised the characteristic circular ornamentation. Since the tip of the cone had survived relatively unscathed, the form of the object could also be guessed at (Ill. 1, Cat. No. 205). Parallel examples were already known in the "Golden Hat" of Schifferstadt (Rheinland-Pfalz) found in 1835, and in the cone from Avanton (Vienne, France), discovered in 1844.

The pieces of sheet gold, weighing 280 grams, were acquired by Raschke. Subsequent investigation of the find-spot uncovered additional fragments weighing thirty grams as well as pieces of both a broader and a narrower bronze ring. Other parts were found at a depth of eighty cm lower down.[1]

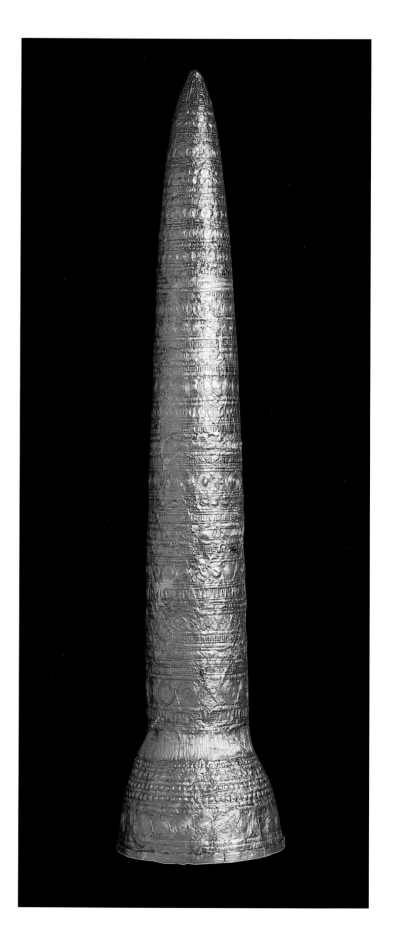

1 "Conus" or Head-Dress, Ezelsdorf-Buch, Bavaria, Germany, Late Bronze Age (Cat. No. 205)

Identification of Function

At its discovery, the Ezelsdorf-Buch cone was mutilated to such an extent that the individual fragments, deprived of the rigidity formerly given to them by zoned repoussé decorative scheme, seemed much to fragile to be viewed as elements of a head-dress. Thus an interpretation of the object as a cult device placed atop a pole was widely accepted.[2] Only recently has S. Gerloff presented convincing arguments in favour of an identification of the sheet gold cone as a head-dress.[3] Shortly after the publication of her study, her thesis found confirmation in the previously unknown gold hat acquired in December 1996 by the Staatliche Museen zu Berlin for the Museum für Vor- und Frühgeschichte (see Menghin, pp. 172ff., Cat. No. 207).[4]

Although its original archaeological context is unknown, the Berlin hat has contributed greatly to our understanding of this group of objects as a whole. It has become apparent, for example, that the brim reinforcement was characteristic not only of the Berlin cone, but that the "Golden Hat" of Schifferstadt, always identified as a head-dress, likewise had once possessed a ring of twisted metal inset at the edge of the brim, of which only the impression is preserved today.

In this light, the fragments of the second, slighter ring found by Raschke,[5] in part still edged with sheet gold, as well as a small bronze strip (32 mm in length, 2.8 mm wide, and 1.4 mm thick) uncovered in the subsequent investigation, may both be interpreted as the remains of a brim reinforcement for the Ezelsdorf cone (Ill. 2).[6] No pieces of the brim itself were discovered. It is likely that, rather than being removed before the burial of the piece, the brim was lost between the time of the original discovery and the subsequent investigation. In any case, the sheet gold at the base of the cone appears to have been roughly torn away rather than separated cleanly (Ill. 3).

With respect to the function of the gold cones, it is significant that the base of the Berlin gold hat is ovoid in form. With allowance made for an inner lining, the measurement (of 20.3 x 17.5 cm) corresponds to an adult head-size. The Ezelsdorf cone too was probably ovoid in shape (at some 21.0 cm across), although this fact was not initially recognised due to the identification of the

2 Fragments from the cap of the Ezelsdorf-Buch cone: showing pieces both of stabilising bronze ring from cone base and of a much narrower band partially edged with sheet gold, possibly belonging to the brim reinforcement (below centre).

3 Cap and main stabilising bronze ring of the Ezelsdorf-Buch cone. The sheet gold has been torn away from the ring.

piece as a cultic pole crown and to the deformation of the base ring, which was broken into a number of pieces (Ill. 2). The lower edge of the cap from the "Golden Hat" of Schifferstadt has a comparable diameter of 18.1 cm.

Description

The Ezelsdorf cone is in its present state 88.3 cm tall and weighs 310 grams. Adding the missing pieces (though still excluding the brim), an original weight of 331.4 grams may be assumed. The thin material, only

177

0.78 mm thick, was given a degree of stability by the horizontal decorative zones embossed onto it; these, however, were extensively distorted during the processes of recovery and reconstruction.

Originally, the cone was somewhat shorter (Ill. 1): according to the information provided by the finder (the cone's top lay eight cm below the surface) and according to the details of the subsequent investigation (when fragments were found as deep as eighty cm down), it must have measured at least c. 72 cm in height. The cone proper, 73 cm long now, is ten cm across at its junction with the cap. This last is fifteen cm high, and twenty-one broad.

Like the other known examples, the Ezelsdorf gold cone is fashioned out of a single piece of gold, originally about the size of a matchbox; it has been beaten up whole and lacks a seam along its entire length. Even under present-day conditions, this would represent an outstanding achievement of metallurgical craftsmanship and one that required great experience. According to M. Fecht's analysis of production technique, the ornamentation was added by working the metal into hollow punches/moulds of bronze or some organic material held on the outside – thereby producing the repoussé effect. The decorative zones and ornaments were laid out on the surface with a template. The craftsman employed twenty different decorative punches, six ornamental wheels and a decorative comb.

The most important decorative motifs are disks and circles, which may be interpreted as solar symbols (Ill. 1). A ten-pointed star crowns the top of the Ezelsdorf piece; below it, 154 additional horizontal decorative zones extend to its base. In addition to the alternating bands of circular motifs and ribbing, whose possible symbolic significance remains obscure to us, the cone shows three sets of special motifs: small horizontally-set pointed ovals (eyes), miniature cones and wheels. As in the Berlin example, the problematic region of where the shaft turns into cap is treated to a thirty mm wide band of vertical grooving, produced with the decorative comb.[7]

◁ 4   Gold cone from Ezelsdorf-Buch: detail with cone and wheel
       motifs

   5   "Conus" or Head-dress, Avanton, Vienne, France   ▷
       Middle Bronze Age (Cat. No. 204)

Dating

The variation in the combination and sequence of decorative zones on each of the cones is striking. The "Golden Hat" of Schifferstadt, for example, shows a very simple decorative scheme. The Avanton cone (Cat. No. 204) has a star at its tip as well as very finely-worked decorations; nonetheless, the overall impression is more austere and shows less variation than the example from Schifferstadt. The cone in Berlin is remarkable for its clear articulation and far greater range of motifs, whilst the Ezelsdorf cone exhibits an almost baroque-like elaboration in the wealth and variation of decorative elements. It seems likely that these typological differences indicate different periods of manufacture as well.

On the basis of stylistic comparisons with similarly decorated objects whose dates can be established through other artefacts discovered at the same site – for example the flanged axes found buried with the Golden Hat of Schifferstadt, these and similar finds can be dated to the 14th–8th centuries BC. The Ezelsdorf cone was probably created in the Late Bronze Age, between the 10th and the 8th centuries BC, perhaps the last of the gold ceremonial hats known up to now.

Interpretation of the Special Motifs

The 92nd decorative zone displays an ornament consisting of a horizontally placed ovoid with pointed ends, which may be interpreted as a stylised eye. The motif is found too on the Schifferstadt (Cat. No. 206) and Berlin (Cat. No. 207) cones. In this context the eye stands for the viewer; it is the most important organ of sense by which to perceive the sun. In the 120th zone, a frieze of twenty-one eight-spoked and naturalistically depicted wagon wheels encircles the cone (Ill. 4). This (sun-)wheel symbol suggests the movement of the sun. Both seven zones higher and fifteen zones lower than this, the decorative bands are filled with miniature cones placed base to base: this is a motif that unique to the gold cone of Ezelsdorf and probably served to amplify the (symbolic) power of the cone in accordance with some belief-system of magical imagery. Presumably, the cone was believed to transmit the power of the sun to the wearer and therewith to other worshippers as well. A corresponding influence on the sun by the magician should not be ruled out as an additional intention.

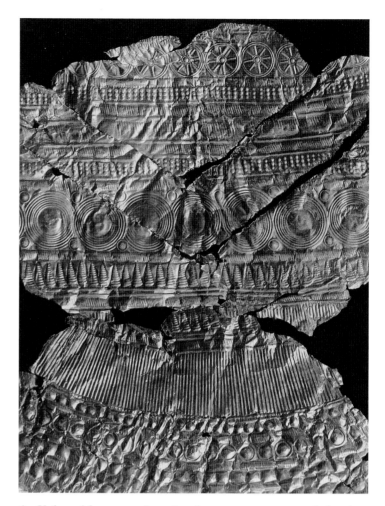

6 V-shaped fragments show that the cone was compressed already before its mutilation by the spade. The fold runs through the point of the "V."

The Burial

When, why and how the gold cones were consigned to the earth remains a mystery. The artefacts from this entire corpus, embracing not only the gold cones but also gold caps, gold vessels and gold disks – all with similar circular ornamentation, – were generally buried as individual objects. Seldom are they found with other items and even more rarely as grave goods.[8] The latter circumstance suggests that objects of this kind, used in religious rituals, were not considered the property of individuals. Generally, those hoards interpreted as votive gifts contained valuable objects of personal use. Since cult objects were not generally used as votive gifts, it is likely that their burial took place at the end of the period during which they were used, concurrent with the decline of associated religious beliefs. Other artefacts found together with them can indicate no more than a *terminus post quem*. Even if they too represented cult objects – as may well have been the case with the axes from Schifferstadt – a considerable span of time may still have elapsed between the manufacture of these objects and their burial.

The archaeological report on the finding of the Schifferstadt cone and the state of preservation of the Berlin cone, as well as the fact that additional fragments of the Ezelsdorf cone were found at a depth of eighty cm during the subsequent investigation of the site, together suggest that all of the cones were buried upright in the ground. With walls 0.1–0.25 cm thick, the Schifferstadt cone was able to withstand the pressure of the earth. The well-preserved Berlin cone shows two lateral dents opposite one another, the result of the pressure of the soil. The Ezelsdorf cone seems to have been compressed in the same way. Photographs of the ruined cone before its restoration show V-shaped fragments which could have resulted from the modern-day mutilation only if a special set of circumstances with regard to events were met with, which seems perhaps unlikely (Ill. 6).

As regrettable as the poor condition of the Ezelsdorf-Buch cone may be, the perfection of its craftsmanship reveals aspects of Bronze Age culture unparalleled by anything known from previous finds.

1 G. Raschke, 'Ein Goldfund der Bronzezeit von Etzelsdorf bei Nürnberg (Goldblechbekrönung)', *Germania* 32 (1954), 1ff. The spelling "Ezelsdorf" is correct.
2 P. Schauer, *Die Goldblechkegel der Bronzezeit. Ein Beitrag zur Kulturverbindung zwischen Orient und Mitteleuropa, mit einer handwerkstechnischen Untersuchung von Maiken Fecht*, RGZM Monographien, 8 (1986).
3 S. Gerloff, 'Bronzezeitliche Goldblechkronen aus Westeuropa. Betrachtungen zur Funktion der Goldblechkegel vom Typ Schifferstadt und der atlantischen 'Goldschalen' der Form Devil's Bit und Atroxi', in *Festschrift für Hermann Müller-Karpe zum 70. Geburtstag*, ed. A. Jockenhövel (1995), 153ff.
4 W. Menghin, 'Der Berliner Goldhut. Ein Zeremonienhut der Späten Bronzezeit', *MuseumJournal* 11, 2 (1997), 76ff.
5 Raschke 1954, 1, 3.
6 M. Fecht, 'Handwerkstechnische Untersuchungen', in Schauer 1986, 82ff.
7 Fecht 1986, 83, 101ff.
8 Schauer 1986, 51ff.

Bibliography: Fecht 1986; Gerloff 1995; Menghin 1997; Raschke 1954; Schauer 1986.

Chapter 5
The Birth of Europe

Editor: Katie Demakopoulou

◁ Fragment of a Krater, Argos, Argolid, Greece
Archaic Period, second quarter of the 7th century BC (Cat. No. 235)

The Birth of Europe

Katie Demakopoulou

The Aegean Bronze Age (c. 3300–1000 BC)[1] saw the evolution of great civilisations, whose fame and influence transcended their narrow geographical bounds. Major historical events occurred during the two millennia of the Bronze Age that brought changes to almost the entire Mediterranean. The 2nd millennium in particular is thought to have been very important in the formation of the great civilisations. Developments that had begun in the 3rd millennium led to the rise of Aegean palatial societies, whose legacy was the creation of the subsequent historical civilisations of Greece and of the Western World in general.

The earliest advanced civilisations in the Prehistoric Aegean were the Minoan, which developed on Crete, and the Mycenaean, which was born in Mainland Greece and was formed under the catalytic influence of Crete. Both these civilisations are described as "advanced" since they were the first on European soil to imitate the models of the politically stratified Eastern societies and to develop a complex economic and administrative authority. Their characteristic features are the palace and urban centres, their social and political organisation, the practice of monumental arts, the growth of technology and, above all, a knowledge of writing, which was created to serve the palace administration system and facilitate control of the production and redistribution of produce.

The acme of Minoan Civilisation began towards the end of the 3rd millennium BC, when the First Palaces were built in Crete. Mycenaean Civilisation, named after its most important centre, Mycenae, appeared in Greece at the beginning of the 16th century BC, when the Second Palaces had already been erected in Crete. Mycenaean Greece rapidly entered into relations with the lands of Central and Northwest Europe, mainly with a view to acquiring metals. Large numbers of Baltic amber necklaces, found in the major Mycenaean centres and particularly in the Peloponnese, were clearly imported from Europe and confirm these relations, through which Greece created a cultural model in its European environ-ment. The cultural and social directions then established brought about changes in virtually the whole of Europe. In the Mycenaean Civilisation, Europe first acquired its own particular personality and its common features.

The centres of both Minoan and Mycenaean society were the palaces, the seats of monarchs in whom the political, military and religious authority was concentrated. It was from the palaces that the economy was run, in the sense that the products of the cultivation of the land, of animal husbandry and of trade were assembled in them for recording and redistribution. Scripts were first used in the Prehistoric Aegean to secure this tight control of production.

Crete was the first of the European countries to acquire a writing system. Between the end of the 3rd and the end of the 2nd millennia BC, three scripts were devised and put into use on the island: the Hieroglyphic script, Linear A and Linear B. In addition to their other functions, the large palaces were also responsible for the economic administration and the distribution of produce from the fertile areas in which they were built: most notably at Knossos, Phaistos, Mallia and Chania. This created the need for an accounting system in Crete, which was based on the political system of the lands of the East and was later transmitted to Mycenaean Greece.

The earliest writing systems are the Hieroglyphic script and Linear A, which developed and existed alongside each other in the period of the First Palaces in Crete. They are syllabic scripts, use ideograms as a means of rapidly recording certain objects or living creatures, and had numerals based on the decimal system (Cat. Nos. 219–223). Linear A continued to be used during the period of the Second Palaces in Crete, and also spread to some of the Aegean islands. Neither the Hieroglyphic script nor Linear A has yet been deciphered.

After the destruction of the Minoan palaces in the middle of the 15th century BC, Linear A fell into disuse and a new script, Linear B, came into widespread use in the Aegean. This script is descended from Linear A, most of whose syllabograms and ideograms were retained, as well as the numeral system. It was deciphered in 1952 by Michael Ventris. The Mycenaeans seem to have adopted it to write their own language, which was an early form of Greek.

1   Relief cut-out ornament, Delphi – Sanctuary of Apollo, Phokis, Greece, Archaic Period, second half of the 6th century BC (Cat. No. 237)

In Crete, Linear B was used by the Mycenaeans, who acquired control of the island after the middle of the 15th century BC. The Mycenaean palatial centres of Mainland Greece imitated the Cretan model and used the same accounting system for monitoring the movement of goods through the palace storerooms. Clay tablets with lists in Linear B and large storage stirrup jars and sealings bearing inscriptions in the same script, have been found at Mycenae, Tiryns, Midea, Pylos, Thebes and Orchomenos (Cat. Nos. 224–229). The largest archive of Linear B tablets was found in the palace at Pylos. Thebes has also yielded a large number of tablets, as well as many clay sealings.

Seals and sealings, which first appear in the Early Bronze Age (Cat. Nos. 39, 217, 218, 230) are further evidence of the existence of a central authority which, through its officials, controlled the production and distri-bution of goods. The frequency of exchanges of goods between the Aegean societies, and also between these societies and other parts of the Mediterranean, is also attested by lead weights found at various sites, which indicate the existence of a system of measurements (Cat. No. 231).

During the 14th and 13th centuries BC, when the Mycenaeans were all-powerful and when major technical projects were executed at the heart of the Mycenaean World, the fame and influence of Mycenaean Civilisation spread throughout almost the entire Mediterranean – by means of an organised network of commercial and cultural contacts. The 13th century BC, during which the predominant pottery style was that of LH IIIB1–2, is distinguished by a remarkable cultural uniformity which has been considered, perhaps with some exaggeration, to be an early form of Mycenaean empire – the famous Myce-

2　Inscribed stirrup-jar, Thebes – Old Kadmeion, Boeotia, Greece
Late Bronze Age (Cat. No. 226)

naean *koine*. There were frequent contacts with the Near East and the coast of Asia Minor. Relations with Troy, for example, are attested from a very early date. The nature of such contacts has been a matter of wide concern to scholarship, particularly the question as to whether a joint Mycenaean campaign against Troy, as recorded in the Homeric poems, may be regarded as an actual historical event. What is certain is that the Mycenaeans evinced great interest in the region of Troy, presumably with a view to obtaining there some of the commodities in which they were interested.

Towards the end of the 13th century BC, after a series of destructions that afflicted the major Mycenaean centres, the fundamental structure of the Mycenaean Civilisation collapsed and the central power emanating from the palaces was weakened. The writing systems of Mainland Greece and Crete, which had been created to serve the palace authority and secure its control over men and land, naturally did not survive the destructions and the disappearance of the Mycenaean palace society.

About the middle of the 12th century BC, during the Postpalatial period, a final glimmering of Mycenaean Civilisation can be observed, though it was now approaching its end. Despite the lack of a central authority and the migration and contraction of the population, several settlements flourished and new pottery styles were created. There was a brief period of increased prosperity and contacts, though also of disturbance and military enterprises. One important source of evidence is formed by the pictorial-style vases of the period, such as the "Warrior Vase" from Mycenae; these vases show frequently armed men on foot or riding in chariots, clearly going to battle. Fragments of vases with pictorial scenes recently found in Phthiotis (Cat. No. 232) depict armed men fighting on board warships, and not simply marching to the battlefield. These scenes recall similar depictions on Attic vases of the Geometric period (Cat. No. 233), and are a connecting link in the period of transition from the Greek Bronze Age to the Iron Age. At the same time, they recall the heroes of Homer, who sailed the seas and struggled with a host of adverse circumstances on their return to their homelands. Scenes inspired by the Homeric poems are, moreover, common in the iconography of the Archaic period in Greece (Cat. Nos. 234–236).

The Mycenaean Civilisation disappeared about the end of the 2nd millennium BC. It was the successor in the Aegean to the great Minoan Civilisation, to which it owed its formation and ideological orientation. It was also the precursor of the "Greek miracle" of the Archaic and Classical periods and of the later European civilisations. From this point of view, the Minoan-Mycenaean Civilisation, which was a true cultural, religious and, in a manner of speaking, ethnic amalgam, rightly stands at the beginning of Greek history. It thus is also placed at the beginning of European history.

1　The Bronze Age in the Aegean lasted more than two millennia (c. 3300–1000 BC). In Mainland Greece it is called the Helladic period (EH = Early Helladic, MH = Middle Helladic, LH = Late Helladic). The Late Helladic Period is also known as the Mycenaean period from the most important site of this time, Mycenae. In the Cyclades the Bronze Age is called the Cycladic Period (EC = Early Cycladic, MC = Middle Cycladic, LC = Late Cycladic). In Crete it is called the Minoan Period from the legendary king Minos of Knossos (EM = Early Minoan, MM = Middle Minoan, LM = Late Minoan). All these periods have sub-divisions.

Bibliography: Chadwick 1967; Davaras 1988; Dickinson 1994; Mee 1984, 1998; Olivier 1986; Ventris & Chadwick 1973.

Writing and Technique:
The Role of Writing in the Origin of Thought and the State

Louis Godart

Writing, which enables human beings to convey an unequivocal message across space and through time, is also an effective weapon in the hands of those who exercise power. The city-states of Mesopotamia were the first to invent writing around 3300 BC; the Egyptian realm, in turn, employed it from the end of the 4th millennium BC on. The earliest polities in the west, originating on Greek soil, likewise recognised the importance of writing for the establishment of their authority over subject populations, though not until about a thousand years later.

Of all the lands of Europe, Crete was without doubt the first to possess a system of writing. On the isle of Minos, three different scripts were created and developed in the period between the second half of the 3rd millennium BC and the end of the 2nd. Their discoverer, Arthur Evans, referred to them as the Hieroglyphic script, Linear A and Linear B.

In Greece and on Crete, just as in Mesopotamia and Egypt, writing appears to have been associated with the integration of a large number of individuals into an economic and political system based on the presence and activity of sizeable palatial residences. It was in this context that the first administrative instruments emerged, of which recent discoveries have provided thousands of examples.

The Clay Sealings

The first great residences known to us on Greek soil appeared around 2600–2400 BC (Early Helladic II) in Lerna in the Argolid and toward the end of the 3rd millennium BC on Crete. Four different functions were united in them: economic, political, religious and administrative. These structures, also called palaces, are found in fertile landscapes like that of the Argolid or the plains nearby Knossos, Mallia, Phaistos and Chania, or in such as the Amari valley in Crete. The produce of the territories controlled by the palaces was collected by the rulers for redistribution to those who worked for the palace or to be exchanged for other goods.

Thus the need arose for a system of "book-keeping" to enable the palace overseers to keep track of the goods coming into and leaving the storage magazines. In response, these officials invented a system of record-keeping like that introduced by their predecessors in the Near East and Egypt many centuries before. In order to record the issue of goods from their storehouses, they affixed small, soft cakes of clay to the containers or goods entrusted to them, on which they impressed a certain number of seals corresponding to the quantity of food or other goods present in their storehouses – thereby creating a sealing.

Each time goods were removed, the sealing was taken from its place and brought to an archive. A new one was meanwhile produced and used to label the vessel or equivalent storage place until the next such occurrence. In order to keep track of the quantity of goods entering and leaving his storehouse, the overseer needed only to consult the sealings held in the archive; a look at the various markings on them likewise informed him as to the identity and rank of the persons who had visited his storehouse. When the seals were tallied, the result represented the total quantity of food rations that had been removed over the course of time.

While this system of record-keeping, invented by the administrators of the first great residences of Bronze Age Greece to assess the contents of the storage magazines, may have been effective, it was also complicated and incomplete. Each sealing could only represent a single procedure of exchange; it could not indicate either the type of goods distributed or the circumstances of the transaction. What was needed, therefore, was a more precise and unambiguous method of record-keeping for the administration of the domains. Writing thus represented a necessity in a world where the political system and the mode of regional administration recalled oriental models.

While the method developed by the overseers of the storehouses in Lerna was to have little future, Crete was to play an essential role in the development of writing and its dissemination in the Aegean.

The Script of Archanes

The oldest evidence of writing in Crete goes back to the so-called Pre-Palatial period, more precisely to the Middle Minoan era (MM I A). This evidence consists of a few seals found in the cemetery at Archanes and again in a grave near Rhethymnon at the site of Pangalochori. The text engraved on these seals consists of a series of five signs which has been designated the "Formula of Archanes". This series of signs appears again in a word occurring on one of the votive documents in Linear A from the Second Palace period (Late Minoan I A and B). Thus the question may legitimately be posed as to whether this earliest Aegean writing represents the distant predecessor of the Linear A script, found some five hundred years later in the rubble of the first palace of Phaistos and some two centuries after that in most of the resi-

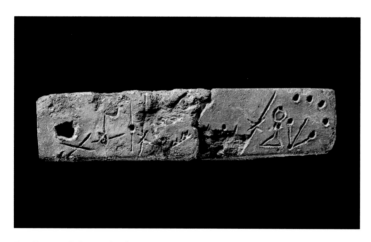

1   Bar with hieroglyphic script, Knossos, Crete, Greece
Middle Bronze Age (Cat. No. 219)

dences and shrines of the Second Palace period. Unfortunately, the samples of writing in the Archanes script are too few and brief to permit even the slightest conjecture as to their nature and content.

Linear A and Hieroglyphic Script

The First Palace period in Crete is marked by the development of two clearly defined graphic systems: Linear A, of which the oldest examples are the archival documents (primarily clay tablets) found in the destruction level of the First Palace of Phaistos, and the Cretan

Hieroglyphic script, evidence of which has heretofore been found primarily in Knossos and Mallia.

These two scripts possess a number of common features. Both are syllabic (like Japanese writing), use ordinal numbers in a decimal system and employ ideograms to designate objects, goods and living beings. Contrary to previous opinion and despite the similarity between the Cretan Hieroglyphic script and Linear A, it does not appear that the latter was derived from the former. Rather, the two writing systems existed side by side in the early palace period. Moreover, as the results of research in Mallia suggest it is possible that within one and the same palace some scribes wrote Linear A while others used the Cretan hieroglyphs. According to M. Tsipopoulou, tablets in Linear A and a hieroglyphic text were both found in the same destruction level at Petras in eastern Crete.

Whatever the reasons for the simultaneous use of Linear A and the Cretan hieroglyphs in the Early Palace period – today, the hypothesis that the two different scripts were used to write two separate languages must be seriously considered – Linear A appears to have prevailed on Crete and the Aegean islands during the Second Palace period (1600–1450 BC). It is clearly evidenced both in the archival documents found in palaces all across Crete and in the dedicatory inscriptions on votive objects discovered in cult locations.

Neither the Cretan Hieroglyphs nor Linear A have been deciphered. Most of the phonetic values indicated by the syllabic symbols are unknown, and the hypotheses advanced thus far for the deciphering of the two scripts have proven erroneous. There are a variety of reasons for this difficulty: the number of signs and sign groups available in the two scripts is very small; in addition, we have no bilingual evidence that would allow direct comparison between either of the scripts and a text composed in a written system already familiar to us. Furthermore, we do not know whether the Cretan Hieroglyphs and the Linear A script were used to write one and the same language, nor do we have any guarantee that the language of the hieroglyphs on the seals is the same as that of the hieroglyphs in the archival documents. Finally, it is uncertain whether the archival documents in Linear A from the Second Palace period were written in the same language as the contemporary texts found on votive inscriptions.

2 Linear A Tablet, Ayia Triada, Crete, Greece
Late Bronze Age (Cat. No. 222)

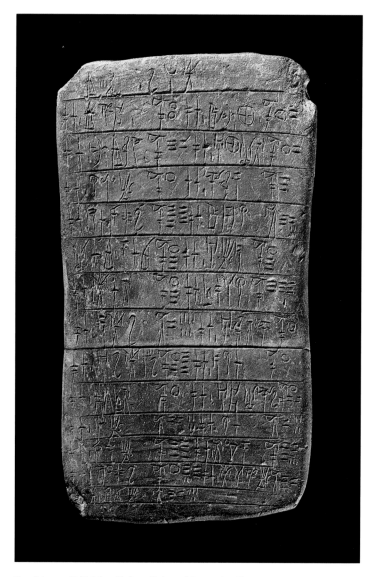

3 Linear B Tablet, Pylos, Palace Messenia, Greece
Late Bronze Age (Cat. No. 224)

The Linear B Script

After the destruction of the Minoan palaces in the Second Palace period (c. 1450 BC, i.e. Late Minoan IB), Linear A disappeared. A new script, Linear B, spread throughout the entire Aegean. This script, deciphered by M. Ventris in 1952, is clearly derived from Linear A, from which it adopted the ideograms and most of the syllabic signs. It was used by the Mycenaeans to write their own language, a pre-Doric dialect of Greek belonging to the Arcado-Cyprian family of languages.

But when was Linear B invented by the Mycenaean Greeks? The Greeks took possession of Hellas towards the end of the 3rd millennium BC. These Indo-European invaders did not hesitate to make contact with the Minoan Cretans, who, as their archival documents found in Samothrace show, had developed a trading network extending over the entire eastern Mediterranean since the First Palace days. The existence of such contacts suggests the exchange of goods, a situation the Greeks masterfully exploited. As the possessors of extraordinarily fertile territories such as the great plains of Boeotia or the Peloponnesus, the Greeks grew rich. As a result, the economic and other developmental conditions associated with the emergence of writing were established on the Greek mainland

189

4   Inscribed stirrup-jar, Armenoi – Chamber Tomb 146,
Rethymnon, Crete, Greece, Late Bronze Age (Cat. No. 228)

the Late Helladic IIIB. And in fact the Greek Archaeological Service did succeed in finding a flat stone with an
inscription in Linear B on one of the hills overlooking
Olympia, in a place where a sanctuary is known to have
existed. The inscription, which dates to Middle Helladic
III, contains the syllables *ka-ro-qo*, which corresponds to
the Greek proper names Χάρψ or Χάροπος: evidence
that the inhabitants of the Peloponnese already spoke
Greek in the 17th century BC. This unprecedented find
shows that the Mycenaean scribes, just as their Minoan
counterparts, wrote not only on clay but on a variety of
surfaces; that as with Linear A, Linear B was used in
sanctuaries; and above all and contrary to previous opinion, Linear B was in use not merely for two centuries, but
for as long as five. The study of the tablets and the painted vase inscriptions from halls, archives and storehouses
in Knossos, Chania, Pylos, Thebes, Mycenae, Tiryns and
Midea now permit us to discern at least the outlines of the
organisation of the Mycenaean states.

Mycenaean Greece was divided into kingdoms, each
of which was ruled by a king, the *wa-na-ka*, i.e. the ἄναξ
of the Homeric epics. The territory of each kingdom was
divided into administrative districts governed by local
officials who acted on behalf of the palace, i.e. of the king.
The religious sphere and in particular the sanctuaries
enjoyed a certain autonomy with respect to the central
power, although palace scribes were still involved in the
registration of goods belonging to the sanctuaries and the
priests.

Numerous Mycenaean gods are found again in the
Greek religion of the 1st millennium BC, e.g. Zeus, Hera,
Hermes, Artemis, Dionysos, Poseidon and even Mother
Earth (Demeter) and her daughter Kore, as demonstrated
by the new documents found between 1993 and 1996 in
Boeotian Thebes.

The economy of the Mycenaean kingdoms was
largely dependent on agriculture, i.e. the cultivation and
transformation of plant or animal products. Economic
relations between Mycenaean states were intensive,
although the tablets seldom mention foreign places or
persons within the areas controlled by the state. The fortunate exception in this regard is a series of references in
the texts of Pylos to places in the eastern Aegean such as
Lemnos, Knidos, Miletus and Halicarnassos, or the island

well before the end of the 13th century BC, the period to
which most of the documents from the Mycenaean palace
archives on the mainland are dated (eg. at Thebes, Mycenae, Tiryns, Pylos and Midea). Clear evidence of their
readiness is provided by such as the tholos graves of
Messenia (like those of Routsi or Koryphasion), the burial
caves west of Eleusis, and by the early Mycenaean habita-
tions of Peristeria or Nichoria in Messenia, Hagios
Stephanos in Laconia, the Menelaion in Sparta, Tsoun-
giza near Nemea, by the finds from Corinth and Kolonna
in Aegina, the discoveries of the settlements of Kiapha
Thiti in Attica and of Thebes in Boeotia, and above all the
graves of the Circles B and A at Mycenae.

Thus it would be expected that the Greek mainland
would produce documents in Linear B dating from before

Kythera southeast of Laconia, and even, as has recently been shown on the basis of a number of repetitions in the newly discovered tablets from Thebes, to a Lacedaemonian, his son, and an important personality from Miletus.

But although the tablets provide few references to commercial contacts between states, the painted vase inscriptions bear irrefutable witness to the existence of relations between different kingdoms in Mycenaean Greece. At Thebes and Tiryns, stirrup-jars have been discovered that were produced in the Mycenaean palace of Chania in western Crete. Recently, one such was discovered in Midea bearing a name consisting of three signs. It was painted by an artist known to have produced two other stirrup-jars of this kind, found in Knossos and Armenoi. The clay of which these vases were made comes from Crete. The discovery from Midea thus offers conclusive proof of relations between Crete and the Argolid at the end of the 13th century BC.

With the destruction of the Mycenaean palaces around 1200 BC, the Linear B script disappeared forever. Created to support the authority of the palaces and to strengthen their power over subject peoples and territories, the writing systems of Crete and Mycenae of the 3rd and 2nd millennia BC did not survive the great catastrophe that destroyed the Mycenaean palace system at the end of the 13th century BC.

Seals and Sealings in the Bronze Age Aegean

Alexandra Alexandri

Seals provide one of the most complete and complex records of Bronze Age Aegean art. They are widespread and appear in most regions of the Aegean. They have been found in palaces, graves and sanctuaries. Their sheer numbers are impressive: from just the Late Bronze Age we have thus far recovered close to 5000 different designs from sealstones, engraved finger-rings or sealings bearing impressions. They come in a variety of shapes and materials and their decoration ranges from simple geometric designs to complex figured scenes. Despite their small size – sealstones are usually about two cm in diameter and rings are only slightly larger – they are often products of great workmanship. The object of numerous studies, they have been used to illustrate religious beliefs, to reconstruct administrative practices or to support theories of social stratification.

Seals make their first appearance in the Aegean during the middle of the Early Bronze Age, at a time when administrative sealing practices were already firmly established in the Near East. They probably evolved from local Neolithic stamps which were used primarily for the decoration of various items and materials (for example, cloth or pottery). Seals, however, became more versatile and they were often used as ornaments, votive offerings, amulets or administrative tools. These aspects of seal use were not mutually exclusive and a seal used to mark the ownership of an object may be also worn by its owner as an ornament or as a protective charm. Sealstones can be set in rings but most are perforated and can be worn around the wrist or the neck using a string or a cord. Images on frescoes show both women and men wearing sealstones around their wrists. Material and colour must have been important factors in choosing a stone. This is true especially during the later part of the Bronze Age when semiprecious stones seem to be favoured, some of which are brightly coloured (like jasper) while others are translucent (like carnelian). Sealstones and rings were certainly valued possessions and some show signs of repair. A number of seals were used over a large period of time and may have been handed down to younger generations as heirlooms.

Early Bronze Age seals were made of soft stones (like steatite or serpentine) or soft materials like bone, ivory and clay. Some may have even been made from perishable materials like wood. Unfinished sealstones recovered from settlements like Myrtos in the south of Crete indicate that, in most cases, manufacture was local. Nevertheless, these artefacts did travel and imports from other areas have been identified at many sites. Seals come in a variety of shapes including conical, cylindrical, button-shaped and even zoomorphic (shaped like animals). The sealing surface was engraved using obsidian burins and, occasionally, a portable drill. These tools, while adequate for working with soft materials, could not be used for the engraving of fine details and the development of elaborate iconographic schemes. For the most part seal decoration seems to be distinctive. The most widespread type of decoration involves schematic motifs of geometric designs and linear patterns. Figures of animals or insects are more rare and rendered in outline, while representations of humans cannot been identified with any certainty. Although variation is not striking there seem to be some identifiable regional preferences in the choice of decoration. For example, balanced and symmetrical linear patterns are favoured on the mainland, while Cretan seals depict less static arrangements. The meaning of these designs remains elusive and it is quite possible that they were thought to be imbued with magical powers.

A great number of the seals were recovered from funerary contexts, deposited as grave goods with the dead. On Crete, where we have extensive cemeteries often containing structures with multiple burials, we find frequent and rich burial gifts. These grave goods, as well as the elaborate construction of some of the tombs, may be signs of changes in the expression of social differentiation and the establishment of a ranked society. In most cases, due to the reuse or communal use of tombs, it is difficult to assign grave goods to particular burials and, consequently, we cannot draw a correlation between the ownership of seals and various social categories like gender, age or occupation. Nevertheless, it is reasonable to assume that during this period seals could have acted as indicators of social status or even as emblems of clan membership. On the other hand, the administrative use of seals appears to have been a more rare and localised phenomenon. The small number of recovered sealings points towards local small-scale administration.

The clearest picture of an administrative use of Early Bronze Age seals comes from the mainland, particularly from the site of Lerna in the Argolid. A large collection of sealings was discovered in a small outer room of

imports, as well as local conical stamps bearing simple linear designs.

By contrast, seal production on Crete continues unabated from the Early to the Middle Bronze Age. The palatial system established during the Middle Minoan IB period brought significant changes in the production and use of seals. During this period we find the first evidence for elaborate sealing practices which firmly incorporate the use of seals into an administrative structure. Large

1   Seal, Lerna – Settlement IV, Phase B, Argolid, Greece
     Early Bronze Age (Cat. No. 218)

2   Seal, Lerna – Settlement III, Phase C, Argolid, Greece
     Early Bronze Age (Cat. No. 217)

the House of Tiles. The objects they had sealed were not found nor were the seals that had impressed them; indeed, the House of Tiles did not provide much else in terms of artefacts. It is likely that the seals had been made from perishable materials or that the sealings, which had been deliberately fired to preserve them, had been collected elsewhere. The designs on these sealings are among the finest of the Aegean Early Bronze Age and it seems that local workshops in the Argolid were the main centre of seal production on the mainland.

During the Middle Bronze Age seal production and use declines on the mainland. Middle Helladic society was based upon small-scale settlements which exhibited some degree of internal differentiation. Administrative needs no longer seemed to warrant the use of seals while social status was expressed in other ways. The scant evidence for seals during this period consists of some Cretan

sealing deposits are found in palatial sites like Phaistos or smaller complexes like Monastiraki. Administrative needs prompted extensive and constant sealing activity involving the direct sealing of objects. This practice suggests that there was a need for greater control of goods. Most of the sealings bear impressions of wooden pommels or of cylindrical pegs and they must have sealed boxes or doors, but there is also a good number which appear to have been pressed directly onto rush matting or jars. Alongside these sealing systems, presumably borrowed from the Near East, we also find the beginning of distinctive Minoan practices. The Hieroglyphic deposit at Mallia contains a series of crescent-shaped sealings which were hung by cords through a string hole in the centre. These hanging nodules give us no information as to the type of objects they sealed. In the slightly later Hieroglyphic deposit at Knossos we also find flat-based sealings which

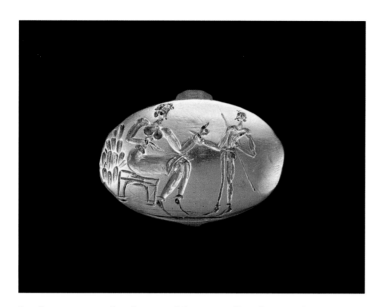

3   Signet-ring with cult scene, Mycenae – Chamber Tomb 66, Argolid, Greece, Late Bronze Age (Cat. No. 69)

had been apparently applied to documents. It seems reasonable to assume that the seals were owned by particular individuals forming an administrative elite but, equally, they may have been linked to specific functions. Some seals appear to have been used more often than others, while in other cases we have recovered only one impression of a particular seal. Similarly, some seals or rings appear to have been used only on some types of sealings: for example, only on hanging nodules or only on direct sealings. Alongside their administrative function seals were still used as personal ornaments and status indicators and they continue to turn up as offerings in graves or votive contexts. Their protective or magical powers may have very well continued despite (or even because of) their use in administration.

The increasingly central role played by seals in the administration prompted a significant increase in the number of these artefacts as well as changes in the materials and techniques used in their production. Whereas in the Early Bronze Age and the greater part of the Middle Bronze Age soft materials were predominant, requiring less effort in their carving, we notice the increasing introduction of hard, semiprecious stones such as jasper, carnelian or agate. Some of these materials were imported from outside the Aegean area, from the Near East or even more distant places, and were previously used for the pro-

duction of ornamental beads. The introduction of a new tool, the bow-lathe, played a decisive role in seal manufacture. This tool, still used today, enabled the drilling of hard stones and prompted the development of new shapes that provided better working surfaces. Alongside the earlier shapes we now find disks, cushions and lentoids, as well as Petschafts (elaborate forms of handled stamps).

Seals were produced in local workshops which seemed to be closely connected to palatial administration. Such workshops have been identified at various sites, like Mallia (the workshop closely associated with Quartier Mu) or Phaistos (Room 25). There are some stylistic and iconographic differences between the various workshops. On the other hand, there does not seem to be a special link between iconography and sealing activity. Older motifs, like geometric motifs (e.g. circles, crosses, panels), continue to be popular and account for the majority of the iconography. Nevertheless, they are now arranged in elaborate architectonic designs and a new class of patterned talismanic seals emerges. Towards the end of the period we find an increase in figured motifs, predominantly animals, sometimes rendered naturalistically. Humans are more rare. Although seal decoration is now more elaborate and varied we can derive no direct information on everyday practices and beliefs.

Towards the end of the Middle Bronze Age, following the destruction of the First Palaces, the rise of the Second Palaces (the Neopalatial period) signals the heyday of seal production. Large numbers of sealstones are now manufactured from both precious and common materials, while the production of metal finger-rings, usually made of gold, increases. During this period Minoan society undergoes a number of changes some of which appear to be the culmination of previous trends, while others emerge as new elements. The increased power of the palatial centres is coupled by a general increase in the number and size of the sites. The new palatial system is accompanied by changes in administrative practices. Document sealing and the use of hanging nodules, both aspects developed in the earlier period, predominate. These sealings provide evidence for increased interaction between the palatial centres and smaller sites such as villas. However, not all sites produce sealings (for example, there is a general absence of sealings from Mallia) and this seems to reflect differences in their administrative role within particular regions. We also have evidence that a number of "lookalike" sealstones and rings were produced and used. Sealings from these artefacts may appear at more than one site. These seals appear to be close replicas of an original design and suggest that authority may have been shared or delegated. The existence of some clay nodules which do not appear to have sealed anything may be another indication of a more diffused structure of authority.

A considerable number of the sealings preserve multiple impressions, often combinations of different seals but also multiple impressions of the same image. The sealings are sometimes countermarked with inscriptions but care is taken to keep these inscriptions and the seal impression on different faces of the day. It appears that the sealings did not simply ensure the integrity of the goods; they were also used to monitor the inflow of various materials. Large groups of sealings were usually found in single deposits located in one room (for example, at Aghia Triada or Zakros).

Ownership of most of these seals was probably determined by social status and position within the palatial structure. The thematic range of glyptic images as well as the new administrative patterns suggest that the palatial authorities maintained control over the production and dissemination of certain types of images. Some images may have been the privilege of selected individuals while others may have been used by a larger number of people. Recent studies have attempted to identify individual hands and "schools" of artists, and, by extension, to calculate the number of artists employed during each period and to reconstruct the patronage system in operation. Artists probably belonged to specialised workshops operating under the auspices of palatial authority. This suggestion is supported by the quantity of the artefacts, the quality of the raw material, the often highly skilled workmanship involved and the identification of workshop areas in or near the palaces. The archaeological evidence further suggests that artists worked in a number of media, rather than specialising only in the engraving of sealstones or the production of gold rings. The finds from the Lapidary's Workshop at Knossos indicate concurrent sealstone and stone-vase production.

It is clear that, by this stage, artists have acquired the artistic skill, the tools and the know-how to produce a limitless range of images; yet, we encounter instead the extensive elaboration of a relatively limited number of themes. These iconographic themes are widespread and more idiosyncratic renditions are not frequent. However, it is important to note that there is still great variation in the treatment of a theme. Often, in the same deposits we find examples of excellent engraving as well as more schematic or careless executions.

Over half of the seals depict animals in various poses. In some cases, they are hunted or killed by humans but most of the time they appear either on their own or with other animals. Lions, bulls and agrimia predomi-

4   Sealstone with metal fittings, Vapheio – Tholos Tomb, Laconia, Greece, Late Bronze Age (Cat. No. 46)

nate. They are often shown attacking one another but we also have more serene scenes sometimes involving animals with their young. A few seals depict geometric motifs or plants. Older seals continue to be used alongside the new ones, and Talismanic, Architectonic and Hieroglyphic motifs are still reproduced. Scenes with humans have increased but they are still few and account for about a sixth of the images. The full range of human activities is not represented and the more intricate scenes seem to depict some form of religious activity. Women and men appear in equal numbers but we cannot readily discern any age differentiation nor do we see many examples of striking status distinctions. Many of the figures may represent divinities but they may also be interpreted as priestesses and priests performing rituals or receiving homage by adorants. Agonistic scenes involving animal games (like bull leaping) or hunting and fighting are also popular and they too may have had a religious significance.

The widespread destructions during the end of the Late Minoan IB period, which resulted in the collapse of the Second Palaces, caused a sharp decline in the production and use of seals. Knossos survived as the primary centre of religious, political and administrative control. It is virtually the only site to have yielded substantial numbers of sealings during this period. The administrative practices seem to have changed yet again: containers are now sealed directly and document sealings essentially disappear. These new administrative needs have a direct impact in the quantity and quality of the seals produced. Based on stylistic criteria it is thought that quite a few of the sealstones and rings now in use were created during the previous period. No new iconographic schemes can be identified. Older themes can still be recognised but the overall range of images is restricted and there is greater emphasis on the representation of more standardised poses or heraldic constructions. The vast majority of scenes depicting human figures still appear on precious materials. Seal ownership was probably restricted to a small number of individuals and the value of these artefacts as prestige objects was emphasised. After the final destruction of Knossos, sometime during the third phase of the Late Bronze Age, seal production becomes sporadic and soft stones return.

Mycenaean Greece reveals a different picture of seal use and production. The first and most impressive indications of change occur at the end of the Middle Bronze Age during the transition from the Middle to the Late Helladic period when seals and finger-rings appear in the Shaft Graves at Mycenae. Although relatively little is known about the production and use of seals in the period before the Mycenae Grave Circles, there does not seem to be much evidence that the glyptic style and quality of workmanship we observe are indigenous. Minoan influence in the early design and production of these artefacts is evi-

5   Sealing, Mycenae – House of Shields, Argolid, Greece
     Late Bronze Age (Cat. No. 39)

dent and, in fact, most early examples are considered to be Cretan imports while it is also quite possible that some Minoan craftsmen may have moved to the mainland. The numbers of Mycenaean seals increase steadily, peaking during the Mycenaean palace period, after the final destruction of Knossos on Crete. However, even during this period their numbers, and one could argue their overall quality, do not reach the level of the Minoan output. The presence of these artefacts on the mainland is neither as pervasive nor as ubiquitous as in Crete. These differences in distribution and production rates appear to be directly related to the differences in the use of sealstones and rings.

Initially seals acted as prestige objects, only later acquiring an administrative use. During the early part of the Late Bronze Age the overwhelming majority of the sealstones and rings are made of precious materials. Large groups of seals were recovered from funerary contexts where they formed part of rich assemblages which were meant to impress. In the Vapheio Tholos tomb over forty seals were discovered, at least thirty-one of which were associated with one burial. Seals in these contexts were an advertisement of the worth or achievements of individual and families; a strategy aimed at the consolidation of a new social structure.

Evidence for the use of seals in palatial administration does not occur until the Late Helladic IIIB period when the destruction levels of the palaces finally yield sealings and nodules. Even then sealings do not seem to play as central a role as the one they were accorded in Minoan administration. Indeed, the Mycenaean archival and recording systems seem to be different from the kind of organisation we observe in Neopalatial Crete. Clay tablets inscribed in Linear B carried the bulk of the administrative weight and sealings were relegated to an ancillary position. There appear to be no large concentrations of sealings and nodules resembling the deposits in separate buildings and rooms seen on Crete. At Mycenae the finds are spread out, occurring both within the citadel (in the cult area) and outside the Acropolis, in building complexes that act as residential, administrative and storage areas. Similarly, at Pylos and Thebes small concentrations of sealings and nodules (no deposit exceeding fifty or sixty pieces) were found in archival, workshop and storage areas. Some of the clay nodules were countermarked but no care was taken to preserve the seal impressions and the Linear B inscriptions were placed directly over them. These inscriptions usually offer information on the type of goods that were being transported or stored. At Thebes, for example, we have numerous sealings inscribed with ideograms of domestic animals and they may have been related to shipments of hides or wool. In fact, it seems that during this period sealings acted primarily as labels indicating content or provenance and, perhaps, the persons responsible for the shipping or storing of the goods. However, there is no obvious connection between the inscriptions and the iconography of the sealings.

In the early part of the Late Bronze Age iconography is heavily influenced by Minoan prototypes, seals manufactured during this stage continue to be used over a long period of time. However, iconographic requirements do change and seal decoration becomes schematic and stylised. The thematic range decreases and becomes rather repetitive, animal representations still accounting for the majority of the motifs. Lentoids made of soft stones grow increasingly popular but the overwhelming majority of scenes with humans appear on gold rings or precious stones. Men seem to be more frequently represented than women and they usually appear in bull games and hunts, or in heraldic schemes between two animals. Women are also depicted with animals, often in heraldic poses, but they are frequently seen in religious scenes, near shrines or in processions.

Throughout the Mycenaean period seals acted primarily as prestige objects. The long use of many of the seals, the decline in their numbers, or finds like the group of forty-five Near Eastern cylinder seals discovered at Thebes, in all likelihood a gift to the local ruling elite, all suggest that seal ownership was restricted to a small number of individuals and was not necessarily dependent on their administrative role within the palaces. Burial evidence further supports the idea that individuals may have owned a number of seals and rings. The simultaneous use of seals and writing on the sealings may be an indication that some of these artefacts may have been allocated provisionally to individuals, perhaps scribes, working under the auspices of higher-ranking officials. By the end of the Late Bronze Age seal production declines dramatically. Having become inextricably linked to the fortunes of the ruling elite, Aegean seals finally disappear with the collapse of the palatial system.

Bibliography: Dickinson 1994; Palaima 1990; Younger 1991; CMS.

The Times of Ulysses

Kurt A. Raaflaub

The title of this essay reminds us of a famous book by the late Sir Moses Finley, *The World of Odysseus*, first published in 1956. At that time, many scholars believed that the Homeric epics, especially the *Iliad*, described not only events that took place in the Bronze Age but also the societies that once inhabited the great palaces of Mycenae and Pylos and the fortress of Troy, brought to light by the discoveries of Schliemann, Dörpfeld, Blegen and many others. To them, Homer was a guide to the Bronze Age. A minority used a commonsense approach and simply assumed that the poet would naturally model epic society after that of his own time. Finley, a great believer in comparative history, approached the problem not only from a historical but also from sociological and anthropological perspectives. His conclusions, though still debated, have transformed our understanding of the "World of Odysseus" or, as it is often called, "Homeric society", and laid new foundations for all subsequent research on the questions of its consistency, historicity and date.

Hesiod believed that the society of heroes described in Homeric and other epics existed in a somewhat distant past, between the Bronze and the contemporary Iron Ages (*Works and Days* 157–68). By the 8th century BC, at the latest, ancient tombs were venerated as those of heroes, and ancient sites and ruins attributed to them. Elite families traced their genealogies all the way back to individual heroes, and 5th century historians as well as Alexandrian scholars tried to date and interpret the events connected with them. In short, in antiquity the Trojan War and the dramatic events involving the Atreidae of Mycenae, Oedipus and his children in Thebes and the ruling families of many other cities were believed to be ancient but historical.

With the modern distinction between myth and history the question of the nature of epic society has become an important problem. By "Homeric society" we mean not the heroic figures and their deeds, but the social environment and background in and against which these heroes live, act, excel and suffer, including their customs and relationships, their ethics and values, their ambitions and weaknesses. (We are thus not directly concerned here with the "Trojan War Question", discussed elsewhere in this Catalogue (cf. Iakovidis, pp. 203 ff.), which concentrates on the origin of the Trojan War myth and the possibility that memories of a Trojan War in the Bronze Age might have formed the core of the story told by Homer.) Given the extant evidence, certainty is beyond our reach, but if we can establish a plausible case that Homeric society corresponds mostly not to poetic fiction but to historical reality and can be dated and located with sufficient probability, we gain a valuable literary source to illuminate a period in Greek history that precedes non-epic literary and epigraphic sources and for which we would otherwise have to rely mostly or entirely on archaeological evidence. Hence the stakes are high: we are dealing with much more than an academic pastime. (This essay uses "Homer" as a label for the poet or poets who composed the extant monumental epics roughly in the second half of the 8th or in the early 7th century, the *Iliad* about a generation before the *Odyssey*; they are thus close enough to one another to be examined as a unit.)

Just at the time when Finley's book went to press, Ventris and Chadwick published their discovery that the clay tablets found in several Bronze Age palaces were inscribed in a Greek dialect. The decipherment of these tablets confirmed what the ruins had already indicated: the "Mycenaean" palace-fortresses are a world apart from the houses of the Homeric leaders; the centralised, hierarchical economic and administrative system run by the palaces resembles contemporary (2nd millennium) Near Eastern civilisations and is incompatible with anything found in Homer or known from later Greek history. Comparing the evidence from the tablets and epics in the sphere of property and tenure, Finley concluded, "The Homeric world was altogether post-Mycenaean, and the so-called reminiscences and survivals are rare, isolated and garbled. Hence Homer is not only not a reliable guide to the Mycenaean tablets; he is no guide at all."

Finley insisted that the break brought about by the destruction of the Mycenaean civilisation around 1200 BC was deep, complete and permanent. Others emphasise that in many spheres of life continuity is visible through the so-called Dark Ages (1200–800 BC) into the Archaic

1   Squat jug, Aegina – Sanctuary at Kolonna, Saronic Gulf, Greece, Archaic Period (Cat. No. 236)

period (700–500 BC). As so often the truth in all probability lies somewhere in between. Much light has been shed on the Dark Ages by recent archaeological exploration; the immense significance of this period in shaping the culture of later centuries is increasingly recognised. But opinions still clash on the overall nature of the period as well as on partial questions. At this point, the destruction of the palaces, the nerve centers of Mycenaean economy and society, still appears as a traumatic event with irreversible consequences. The general impression of the "Submycenaean period" (c. 1125–1050 BC) still is one of a greatly reduced population living in small and scattered villages, in simple conditions and in relative isolation. The subsequent Protogeometric and Geometric periods show many new beginnings, and especially the 8th century witnessed rapid changes, a veritable "structural revolution" (Snodgrass), in which everything was open to challenge. Overall, the transformation of the Greek world in the four centuries of the Dark Ages was deep and comprehensive. The Archaic period was radically different from that of the Bronze Age. Not surprisingly, therefore, Bronze Age survivals in the Homeric picture are rare and

199

non-essential exceptions. More importantly, it is the Protogeometric and Geometric periods that increasingly show features resembling the Homeric picture.

An entirely different question is whether this picture is sufficiently coherent to be historical. From his comparative perspective, Finley answered this question positively:

"A model can be constructed, imperfect, incomplete, untidy, yet tying together the fundamentals of political and social structure with an appropriate value system in a way that stands up to comparative analysis, the only control available to us in the absence of external documentation... The critical point is ... that the model is so coherent, and this also rules out the common statement that what we find in the poems is either a fiction ... or a compositive drawn from different eras... [S]uch a composite would be blatantly artificial, unable to withstand careful social analysis."

Some scholars accept this only for part of the picture; they focus on real or perceived inconsistencies and consider the supposed "amalgamation" of heterogeneous elements, taken from many societies and times, if not from pure fiction, an insurmountable obstacle to the historicity of this society which they therefore see primarily as an artificial and artful product of poetic tradition and imagination. Others have carefully reanalysed particular aspects of Homeric society (including social values and norms, social and economic structures and relations, warfare, political institutions and interstate relations, and the customs of feasting) and confirmed a high degree of consistency which, overall, by far outweighs the sum total of undeniable and presumed inconsistencies and contradictions.

From these discussions a new understanding of Homeric society has emerged that can be summarised as follows. First, persons, events and a few other components may have formed an old, perhaps even historical core of epic traditions, perhaps reaching back into the Bronze Age. Even if so, in the course of long-term transmission and constant reinterpretation, such core stories are likely to have been transformed so profoundly that it is impossible to trace their beginnings.

Second, the picture includes some anachronisms, archaisms and perhaps some genuine memories of the Mycenaean and Submycenaean periods and the Dark Ages. The list of such items is small and under constant revision. It includes, on one level, objects such as bronze weapons, war chariots, and the famous boar's tusk helmet. Explanations for such items vary. Chariots, for example, may have been remembered from a distant past; they may have been found centuries later in Bronze Age tombs (as boar's tusk helmets probably were), or they may have been observed in Anatolia, where they were still used in the 8th century, and adapted by the Greeks for use in hunting and racing. On another level, the exclusion of "modern" phenomena that must have been known to the poet probably also represents deliberate archaisation: writing, attested only once, is a case in point, riding another, officials with limited appointments perhaps yet another. At any rate, archaisms had their proper place in such poetry, and their combined weight is negligible.

Third, exaggeration and fantasy form important elements in heroic poetry; in most cases, they can easily be identified. For example, the shields of Hector and Ajax are described as man-sized, reaching from neck to feet, round, thick, with several layers of ox-hide and an outer layer of bronze. Van Wees observes rightly that there is no historical parallel for such a shield, and there cannot be one, since a man-sized shield can be neither round – this would make it unnecessarily wide – nor made of bronze because it would be too heavy to carry. In all probability Homer is simply describing the fantastically big and heavy armour of fantastically big and strong heroes. We should think in the same way of the fabulous wealth attributed to epic figures or the vastly exaggerated numbers (of the army at Troy or the slaves and herds of various leaders). Such elements of fantasy combine with those of deliberate archaisation, mentioned before, to create a "heroic sphere" populated by figures who are larger than life and thus to establish what Redfield calls an "epic distance" which consciously separates the world of song from that of the audience.

Fourth, recent research shows that knowledge of Near Eastern events, traditions, objects and motifs has substantially influenced the epic narrative and picture. The exceptional importance attributed to the siege of cities or individual motifs such as the Trojan Horse may be due to such foreign influence. This phenomenon is part

200

of a much broader range of interactions, reaching a first climax precisely in Homer's time, between Anatolia, Mesopotamia, the Levant and Egypt on the one side and, on the other, the Aegean and the western Mediterranean.

Fifth, what remains is the large bulk of the material used to depict the social background to heroic action. In contrast to the main events, persons, and individual objects, this background is not emphasised. Its description is sufficiently consistent to allow us to recognise a society that, as Finley and many others have shown, makes sense from an anthropological perspective and can be fitted into a scheme of social evolution among early societies.

In all this, however, we should not forget that the poet is an artist, not a historian or sociologist: he does not intend to give a complete picture; hence the argument from silence is rarely valid. Rather, the poet selects and emphasises according to his own dramatic and interpretative purposes. This factor of "poetic selection" is often underestimated. For example, the Odyssey is concerned with a hero's homecoming and his efforts to regain control in his household (*oikos*). Although the community is deeply affected by these events, the poet's primary attention rests on Odysseus' *oikos*. This does not mean, however, as many scholars have concluded, that this particular community was unimportant, undeveloped or even hardly existing; nor does it mean, more generally, that the *oikos* was the only focus of identification for Homeric people.

This society must have existed in time and space outside of the epics. Given the traditions associated with Homer, the region most likely was Ionia, at least originally. Due to the epics' panhellenic aspirations, however, most local or even regional specificities must have receded early on and been replaced by a panhellenic outlook and, accordingly, a deliberate focus on issues, values, patterns of life and modes of behaviour that were familiar and important to Greeks in many parts of Hellas.

How should this society be dated? Research on oral tradition and oral poetry is helpful here. In preliterate societies, collective memories of the past are preserved beyond a period of roughly three generations only if they are important to the present; even so, they are constantly reinterpreted to fit the changing needs and expectations

2 Krater sherd with representation of a warship, Kynos, Phthiotis, Lamia, Greece, Late Bronze Age (Cat. No. 232)

of the present audience. Despite its formulaic nature, oral epic diction is highly flexible and adaptable. Oral poetry depends on the interaction between singer and audience; in each performance the singer, using traditional diction, elaborates traditional material into a new and unique full story. Its success depends on how meaningful it is to the audience. Entertainment value is essential, but so is the potential for identification. Hence oral song focuses on typical conflict situations and ethical dilemmas. Heroic epic, nourished by historical consciousness, embeds such stories in a "historical context", but this context is incidental and secondary – no matter whether it is based on vague but authentic memories or results from "historicising fiction" that is artificially connected with monuments of a distant past. Hence heroic epic is "historical" in appearance but contemporary in meaning. In order to facilitate identification, the heroically elevated actions of individuals are set in a social context that is familiar to the audience. Many scholars believe, therefore, that Homeric society should be dated not, as Finley thought, to the 10th or 9th centuries BC, but to the poet's own time.

This seems to be confirmed by three observations. First, a direct line of development leads from Homeric institutions (such as council and assembly, the role of 201

3   Pithos fragment, Tenos – Xobourgo, Cyclades, Greece
     Archaic Period (Cat. No. 234)

leaders, or the beginnings of mass fighting in tight formations) to those attested by other evidence in the late 7th and 6th centuries BC. Second, the epics show features that are typical of the late Dark Ages and early Archaic period: the heroes are situated in a world of early *poleis*, they participate in a panhellenic venture and they move around in a wide Mediterranean world that shows clear traces of early colonisation. Third, modern psychiatry is able to recognise in Achilles' and other heroes' behaviour specific patterns that are well known from syndromes inflicted on modern soldiers by their war experiences (especially in Vietnam); hence the poets and their audiences must have known exactly and from first-hand experience what was being described in epic song.

Yet in other respects this is not the late 8th or early 7th century society we know from other sources. Even taking into account some time-lag for adjustments which must have been normal in traditional poetry, the poet clearly did not want heroic society to appear blatantly contemporary. Hence his effort to preserve "epic distance" or to use an "alienation effect", to preserve traditional elements and to endow his social picture with a "patina". The social background of heroic poetry needed to be modern enough to be understandable but archaic enough to be believable. We should therefore consider Homeric society near-contemporary rather than contemporary with the poet and date it within the time-span that could be covered by the audience's collective memory – in the late 9th and 8th centuries BC.

Bibliography: Burkert 1992; Donlan 1989; Finley 1977; Latacz 1996; Morris & Powell 1997; Murray 1993; Nagy 1979, 1996; Patzek 1992; Raaflaub 1997a, 1997b, 1997c, 1998; Redfield 1975; Scully 1990; Shay 1995; van Wees 1992; West 1997.

Homer, Troy and the Trojan War

Spyros Iakovidis

The *Iliad*, one of the poetic masterpieces of all times and our main source for the Trojan adventure, was composed in the 8th century BC by a genius who, according to ancient belief, was named Homer. The *Iliad*, however, as also its sequel, the *Odyssey*, is not a literary invention. Its composition is the high point and, at the same time, the concluding stage of a long process which had lasted for centuries. Clearly, it originated with popular memory retaining a kernel of historical truth, being transformed with the passage of time by oral poetry into saga. This cycle of epic narrative provided the poet not only with his story but also with a repertoire of expressions, crystallised into ready-made verse and parts of verses and used extensively in both epics. They include antiquated forms of language, extinct place names, material objects and patterns of behaviour which had meanwhile become not only obsolete but also incomprehensible. Their very existence proves that the poet drew on a long oral tradition, some aspects of which may well go back to the original stages of epic composition, namely the Mycenaean past. Such are, for example, the handling of chariots in formation by Nestor in his youth, the boar's tusk helmet of Meriones, the long thrusting spears of Achilles and the Euboean Abantes, the big tower-like shields of Ajax and Periphetes and the greaves worn by the Achaeans, all of them typical Mycenaean arms, suggesting different tactics than those described in the epic. Many sites, moreover, some with specifically descriptive epithets (strong-built Aipy, windy Enispe) had been abandoned at the turn of the millennium and could not be located in historical times. Also, the Achaean chiefs are addressed invariably as *anaktes*, a title recurrent in Mycenaean tablets, but which had vanished along with the function at the time the epics were composed. All these elements and quite a few more, originating considerably earlier than the 8th century BC, show that the *Iliad* was based on some remote form of epic narrative, most probably evoking actual events.

Another strong indication that this is so is the fact that this final version includes part only of the epic cycle from which the *Iliad* and the *Odyssey* drew, which was eventually incorporated in epics like the *Cypria*, the *Ilias parva*, the *Iliupersis* and the *Nostoi*, echoes of which have come to us haphazardly by way of later literary sources and mainly through the Attic drama. Far from inventing anything, Homer used but a fraction of the material handed down by his predecessors.

The story is well known: Aphrodite encouraged Paris, son of Priam, king of Troy, to abduct fair Helen, wife of Menelaos, king of Sparta. Menelaos called at once upon Helen's former suitors to come to his aid and a host of 1186 ships and more than 100,000 men coming from twenty-two different states and principalities set out against Troy under the command of Menelaos' brother Agamemnon, king of Mycenae. The expeditionary force laid siege to Troy for ten long years, at the end of which the Trojan champion, Hector, was slain by Achilles. The poem ends there and does not mention the stratagem of the Trojan horse and the sack of Troy, after which the Achaeans set forth on their journeys home.

But legend and the saga remembered more: the Achaeans, sailing for Troy, disembarked by mistake on the coast of Mysia, where the ruler, Telephos, tried to repulse them and was wounded by Achilles. The next morning, the Achaeans discovered their mistake and realised that Telephos was not only their compatriot, but also a relative of the Heraclid rulers of the Dodecanese, who were among the attackers. So they hastened to be reconciled with him and to tend his wound. He gave them fresh provisions and showed them the route to Troy, though he himself remained neutral in their quarrel with Priam. Also, throughout the whole expedition the Achaean forces were supplied by sea, having captured the islands of Lesbos and Tenedos. Moreover, their leaders attempted personal expeditions in various directions, capturing and plundering other, smaller cities like Killa and Kolonai. Ajax crossed into the Thracian peninsula where he forced the king, Polymnestor, to abandon his alliance with Priam. Later he raided Phrygia, where he destroyed the kingdom of Teleutas and abducted his daughter, Tekmessa. Achilles made off with Aeneas' herds from Ida and destroyed twelve coastal towns with his fleet and another eleven in the hinterland, among which were Thebe, Pedasos and Lyrnessos. So, tradition seems to imply that the siege of Troy, which captured the imagination of the *rhapsodists* and became their favourite subject, was not the only objective of the Achaeans and that the expeditionary force undertook at times what amounts to a campaign against the northwestern seaboard of Asia Minor.

In the second book of the *Iliad* the order of battle of the Achaean army is given. It lists the cities and places from which every contingent came and gives the names of the leaders and the numbers of their ships. This Catalogue of Ships, as it is named, is a part of the saga believed to have originated in Mycenaean times and does indeed reflect the political organisation of Greece as we know it from excavation evidence. It is followed by the list of Priam's allies, the inhabitants of the Troad and the Hellespont region, the peoples of the northern shores of the Aegean, of the coasts of the Propontis and the Black Sea and, finally, those of western Asia Minor.

To the Greeks of historical times, who knew the traditional accounts and legends far more completely than we do, the Trojan expedition was an accepted fact and the participants were regarded as real people. We, however, are much better informed than they were about the times, the historical situation and the traceable remains which bear witness to what really happened. So, an attempt at examining the available evidence in order to reconstitute these happenings as fully as possible would not be unjustified.

The 14th and the 13th centuries BC are the period of Achaean expansion in the Eastern Mediterranean. The distribution of Mycenaean wares abroad indicates that there was a constant flow of goods and of more important but less obvious cultural notions radiating from the Aegean, which kept expanding steadily in volume as well as in range, and had a marked effect on their neighbours in the Levant.

This civilisation was basically Greek and its spiritual centre was the mainland. But it had assimilated various Cretan and Eastern elements and had become entirely dependent on the sea for expansion and enrichment. It covered the Aegean, was established in the Dodecanese, on Cyprus and the Anatolian coast, embracing many scattered communities of people of the same nation speaking the same language. It did not correspond to any single, all-powerful Achaean state. Its homeland was the Peloponnese and the Greek mainland east of the Pindos range, but it extended to Crete in the south and to Thessaly and the Pelion mountains to the north. To a lesser extent it had spread to Acarnania, Epiros and the Ionian islands to the west. It seems to have been divided into four or five larger and several smaller sovereign and independent states, possibly combined in various leagues or confederations. Politically, these states dominated the Aegean but very little beyond that. Achaean establishments at Miletus, Lassos and Halicarnassos as also in Enkomi, Kition and Kourion can hardly be called colonies. They were as a rule *emporia*, ports-of-call situated at strategic points along the Anatolian and Levantine coast. Achaeans posed no threat to and sought no quarrel with their neighbours. The influence they exercised abroad was cultural rather than political. But the general trend was definitely towards constant expansion.

This was the state of affairs in the late 13th century BC, the time at which the Trojan war is supposed to have taken place.

At the northern tip of the coast of Asia Minor, on the hill known now as Hissarlik, the city which Greeks of historical times knew as Troy was situated. It was first excavated in 1870 by Heinrich Schliemann, followed by Wilhelm Dörpfeld who worked there till 1894. Research was resumed in 1923–1938 by Carl W. Blegen and again in 1988 by Manfred Korfmann: this has all led to a much better understanding of the stratigraphy, the industries, the foreign contacts and the chronology of the place.

The excavations uncovered a large and very ancient city that had been continuously settled from 3000 BC down to historical times. It passed through seven main successive prehistoric phases, one built on top of the other, numbered Troy I–VII. The successive cities were from the beginning fortified by well-built strong ashlar walls which separated the citadel from the Lower Town. The biggest, most splendid, and longest-lived of all the cities, built c. 1800 BC, was Troy VI. Its civilisation had much in common, particularly in pottery, with the contemporary civilisation of Mainland Greece and it is thought that its founders were newcomers, a branch of the tribes who, apparently, came into Greece and the Troad during the course of the same general movement southwards. The

1 Pithos with relief decoration depicting the siege of Troy. From a tomb on Mykonos, Cyclades, Greece; first half of 7th century BC. (Archaeological Museum, Mykonos, Inv. no. 2240)

late levels contained much Mycenaean pottery, mostly locally made, which suggests that they were in regular contact with Greece. This rich and prosperous city was destroyed a little after 1300 BC by a devastating earthquake. The surviving inhabitants immediately patched up the walls and built the new city, Troy VIIa, on the ruins of the old. The finds show no cultural break between Troy VI and Troy VIIa. The defences were repaired and, indeed, strengthened: the South Gate was cleared of fallen debris and rebuilt on a somewhat higher level. To the wall which flanked the entrance of the East Gate from the outside, a further long wall was attached which transformed the approach to the gate into a long, narrow, well-defended ascent.

Manifestly, these defensive measures were taken none too soon. Excavations uncovered a densely settled city, in which all available space was taken up and more was created by unusual and seemingly desperate expedients. Houses are small. As a rule, they have storage bins and jars sunk into their floors, which would allow people to store considerable quantities of provisions without giving up any of their limited living space. An earlier well was cleaned, repaired and used. Troy VIIa presents the aspect of an overcrowded town the population of which, probably swollen by refugees from the Lower Town, underwent a long and hard siege.

The end, when it came, was very much in keeping with the poet's description of events. To quote Blegen: "The layer comprising the remains of Troy VIIa was everywhere marked by the ravages of fire ... scattered remnants of human bones discovered in the fire-scarred ruins ... surely indicate that its destruction was accompanied by violence. Little imagination is required to see reflected here the fate of an ancient town captured and sacked by implacable foes."

From the ruins of the city a certain amount of Mycenaean sherds were recovered. The bulk belongs to the period of transition from LH IIIB to IIIC. This would place them, and with them the end of Troy VIIa, near to 1200 BC.

Tradition has it that the mighty city of Priam was conquered by the Achaeans three generations before the downfall of Mycenae itself (Agamemnon – Orestes – Tisamenos), and archaeological research shows that Troy VIIa met a similar fate a century or so before the total disintegration of the Mycenaean world. Archaeologically speaking, if any layer at the mound of Hissarlik has a claim to being the city immortalised by the *epos*, this would be Troy VIIa.

Greek historians possessed no other information than what legend had handed down to them. Nowadays we have a few sources more or less contemporary with the events and therefore much more actual than centuries-old heroic poetry. They consist mainly of texts from the Hittite archives found at Bogazköy.

The west coast of Asia Minor was very much within the Hittite sphere of political influence and was kept steadily under control. The main concern of the kings of

2–3   Bowl, Eleusis – South Cemetery, grave 11, Attica, Greece
Geometric Period (Cat. No. 233)

Hatti was, and always had been, their southern and south-eastern borders, where they confronted Egypt and Babylon. After the battle of Qadesh and the ensuing peace these borders had been stabilised but in the meanwhile a new powerful enemy had appeared in the east, the Assyrians.

The Annals of the Hittite king Tudhaliyas IV (1250–1220 BC) reflect his effort to cope with the Assyrian threat and to put down repeated rebellions in the West, organised by the confederation of Assuwa. He defeated the rebels in two successive campaigns, but was then compelled to turn east. This seems to have been the last serious Hittite attempt to control Assuwa.

So, at the end of the 13th century BC the Hittites had withdrawn, leaving behind a political vacuum and an Assuwa which had been defeated but not annihilated. It must have been a sizeable and wealthy region. As it happens, the same Hittite annals enumerate the twenty-two lands and cities of the confederation. Two (Lukka and Karakisha) appear in Egyptian sources and Lukka is mentioned in the Armarna tablets. These cross-references have helped to establish the location of two or three of the place names given by Tudhaliyas and to determine that they are listed in a sequence beginning with Lukka (Lycia) in the south and continuing northwards. The two last and therefore northernmost places are spelled Wilushiya and Taruisha and have been tentatively identified with Filios (Ilios) and Troy. The equation of Taruisha with Troy cannot be rejected out of hand, but Wilushiya-Filios is more than doubtful. Be that as it may, the Assuwan confederation seems to correspond to the part of Asia Minor which lies between the Meander and the Hellespont and which had not been penetrated by the Achaeans to the same extent as the southwest coast. It also covers most of the lands of Priam's allies.

Thus the evidence of the excavations and the memories retained in epic and legend show that the capture and sack of Troy at the end of the 13th century BC may have been one of the incidents of an expedition mounted by the Achaeans against the northern part of the Anatolian seaboard, which must have been part of the confederation of Assuwa. It is very likely that the Achaeans, taking advantage of the political vacuum created by the Hittite withdrawal, tried to establish themselves on the part of the coast which had been, till then, out of their reach. They seem to have succeeded in capturing and pillaging some towns but to have failed in their major objective. Excavations have not turned up evidence for Late Mycenaean settlement in the area and the *epos* describes the return journeys of the expeditionary force. Thus the campaign was apparently unsuccessful, but the siege of Troy, over-shadowing the rest of the expedition, became the subject of the *Iliad* and of a gift forever to civilisation.

206

Catalogue

1 NECKLACE

Troy, Asia Minor (Turkey)

Gold

Early Bronze Age, Troy IIg, c. 2300 BC

Length 12 cm

National Archaeological Museum, Athens

Inv. No. 4331

The gold necklace consists of beads of an unusual form (with four convex sides) graded and assembled by their size. It comes from Treasure A or one of the other minor treasures discovered by Schliemann in the ruins of Troy IIg. This accumulation of wealth (gold, silver and bronze objects) reveals the prosperity of the city, one major contributing factor to which was metalworking. Troy, like Poliochni on Lemnos, is considered one of the early proto-urban centres in the Aegean.

The gold necklace was part of Heinrich Schliemann's private collection in Athens, which his Greek wife, Sophia, donated to the National Museum after his death in 1890.   L.P.-M.

Schliemann 1881, nos. 712, 714, 721, 724; Blegen et al. 1950, 367, pl. 357; Müller-Karpe 1980, no. 91; Demakopoulou 1990, 83–85, 152, no. 8

2 PAIR OF EARRINGS

Troy, Asia Minor (Turkey)

Gold

Early Bronze Age, Troy IIg, c. 2300 BC

Length 2.1 cm, Diameter 1.1 cm

National Archaeological Museum, Athens

Inv. No. 4333

Each earring consists of two parts, the body and the simple hook of gold wire for fastening it to the ear. The main body is formed out of six pieces of gold wire decorated by rows of five tiny granules on the outside. The earrings are exquisitely worked pieces of miniature art and bear witness to the artistic tradition of the city of Troy in the Early Bronze Age. They belong to Treasure A, found in the "burnt layer" of Troy IIg. The Treasures of Troy were donated by the excavator to Berlin and are now in the Pushkin Museum, Moscow.

This pair of earrings, as also the necklace (Cat. No. 1), the anthrophomorphic vase (Cat. No. 3) and the depas amphikypellon (Cat. No. 4), were part of Schliemann's private collection in Athens that went to the National Museum.   L.P.-M.

Schliemann 1874, pl. 196, nos. 3558, 3568; Demakopoulou 1990, 83–85, 149, no. 5

3 ANTHROPOMORPHIC VASE

Troy, Asia Minor (Turkey)

Clay

Early Bronze Age, Troy II–V, c. 2600–1800 BC

Height 12 cm, Diameter 10.2 cm

National Archaeological Museum, Athens

Inv. No. 4436

This anthropomorphic vase is characteristic of the Trojan Culture in the Early Bronze Age. It has a spherical body and a neck with an everted rim. On the brown, burnished surface the distinguishing features of a female figure are rendered plastically. On the neck of the pot, the eyes and the nose are supplied by added clay, while the eyebrows are indicated by a continuous relief line. On the body are the breasts and the navel, the latter denoted by a flat round disc. The two wing-shaped handles resemble raised forearms. The making of these strange vases must have served a special purpose, probably a religious function   L.P.-M.

Demakopoulou 1990, 154, No. 12; for the shape see Podzuweit 1979, 193–194, pl. 15.2

4 DEPAS AMPHIKYPELLON

Troy, Asia Minor (Turkey)

Clay

Early Bronze Age, Troy II–IV,

c. 2600–1900 BC

Height 17.5 cm, max. Diameter

(with handles) 14.5 cm

National Archaeological Museum, Athens

Inv. No. 4400

The name "depas amphikypellon" applies to a two-handled cup with a tall, narrow, funnel-shaped body, a flaring rim and a small flat base. A reddish or brown slip covers the surface. The term comes from Homer's *Iliad* and it was assigned by the excavator of Troy, Heinrich Schliemann. This cup actually comes from Schliemann's private collection that was donated to the Greek National Museum (cf. Cat. No. 1–3). This form of drinking vessel is typical of the Early Bronze Age and does not survive later. Besides Troy and other sites in Asia Minor, the type is also known in the Aegean islands, at Poliochni on Lemnos, Samos, Palamari on Skyros, Kastri on Syros and Keos in the Cyclades, and at Orchomenos in Boeotia and Pefkakia in Thessaly on the Greek Mainland.

L.P.-M.

Unpublished. For the type see Podzuweit 1979, 151–153, pl. 6.1; Demakopoulou 1990, 181–183, nos. 63, 65; Parlama 1994, 3

5 BRACELET

Leukas, Tumulus R, Greece

Silver

Early Bronze Age II, second half of the 3rd millennium BC

Diameter 6 cm, Thickness of wire 0.3 cm

National Archaeological Museum, Athens

Inv. No. 6285

Bracelet of thick silver wire, worked into eight coils. At both ends the wire gradually thickens to form two conical finials. Intact, very good state of preservation, it was found with a similar bracelet and other gold ornaments in a tomb. The bracelets were worn one on each of the dead woman's arms.

K.D.

Dörpfeld 1927, 290, pl. 50.7; Müller-Karpe 1974, no. 143, pl. 410.4 and 7; Branigan 1975, 37–49; Hood 1978, 192, fig. 189F

6 NECKLACE

Poliochni, Lemnos, Greece

Gold

Early Bronze Age II, Poliochni Yellow, middle of the 3rd millennium BC

Length 24 cm, Diameter of largest bead 0.6 cm

National Archaeological Museum, Athens

Inv. No. 7187

The necklace is composed of fifty-five intact, delicate gold beads, all roughly spherical in shape and with a tubular perforation. Their size varies, ranging from very small to miniature. They belong to a hoard of gold ornaments dated to the Yellow period of Poliochni, which was an important settlement of the Aegean in the Early Bronze Age. Similar beads are known from Treasure A and other smaller treasures from Troy.

K.D.

Brea 1976, 289, pl. 247c; Müller-Karpe 1974, no. 141

7 FLOWER-SHAPED PIN

Mochlos – Tomb XIX, Crete, Greece

Gold

Early Bronze Age, EM II–III, second half of the 3rd millennium BC

Length 8.5 cm, Diameter 2.8 cm

Archaeological Museum, Herakleion

Inv. No. 261

Gold hair-pin in the shape of a flower with eight petals. The flower was made from a single sheet of gold. It has been suggested that such pins were used independently or in combination with the diadems (threaded through perforations visible in the latter). Fine example of goldworking in the Early Minoan period.
E.B.

Seager 1912, 72, fig. 41. XIX.Ii.b; Müller-Karpe 1974, pl. 370.27, no. 179; Vassilakis 1996, 170, pl. 79b

8   PAIR OF EARRINGS

Poliochni, Lemnos, Greece
Gold
Early Bronze Age II, Poliochni Yellow, middle of the 3rd millennium BC
Height 7–8 cm
National Archaeological Museum, Athens
Inv. No. 7159

Basket-shaped earrings consisting of a main body, from which hang five chains adorned with leaf-shaped cutouts ending in figurine-pendants. From the hoop springs a plain wire that bends to end in a hook, with which to fasten the earring in the ear. The band-hoop and figurine-pendants have delicate granulated and repoussé decoration.
The earrings are intact and in a very good state of preservation. They come
from the hoard dated to the Yellow

period of Poliochni and are similar to gold earrings known from the Troy treasures. Outstanding examples of the jewellery of the northeast Aegean in the Early Bronze Age, they impress by virtue of the perfection of the metal-working and their combination of advanced decorative techniques, such as granulation, filigree and repoussé.
K.D.

Brea 1976, 286, pls. 241.a-b, 242.a-b; Müller-Karpe 1974, pl. 356.1.3 no. 141; Champion et al. 1984, 182

9   SINGLE AXE

Poliochni – Building XIII, Room 829, Lemnos, Greece
Bronze
Early Bronze Age, Poliochni Red, middle of the 3rd millennium BC
Length 16.3 cm, Width 4.5 cm, Diameter of hole 3.1 cm
National Archaeological Museum, Athens
Inv. No. 7205

Intact single-edged axe of bronze. It is in a good state of preservation, and consists of a rectangular blade ending in a curved cutting-edge and with a collared socket by which the tool was attached to the wooden handle. The axe was found along with other bronze tools and weapons, constituting a hoard, in a building at the important fourth settlement of Poliochni. This prehistoric city grew alongside and in continuous contact with Troy during the Early Bronze Age; it partook of the high culture achieved in the northeast Aegean, spe-

cialising in the production of high quality metal objects. This axe could have been used either peacefully – for hunting or other domestic needs, or in battle.
N.D.-V.

Brea 1964, 352, 661–662, pl. 173; Müller-Karpe 1974, no. 141, pl. 356.20–29; Mendoni 1997, 117, fig. 3

10   DIADEM

Mochlos – Tomb II, Crete, Greece
Gold
Early Bronze Age, EM II–III, last third of the 3rd millennium BC
Height 0.36 cm, Length 29.5 cm
Archaeological Museum, Herakleion
Inv. No. 268

Gold diadem found in tomb II at Mochlos. In the centre are set amygdaloid-shaped eyes and a dotted outline, in repoussé technique. At both ends are visible groups of perforations to assist in its fastening to the head. Signs of wear acquired during the lifetime of the owner are visible.
E.B.

Seager 1912, fig. 8.II.5; Müller Karpe 1974, pls. 368–370, no. 179; Vassilakis 1996, 98, pl. 22

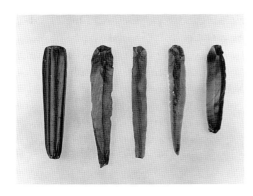

11 CORE AND FOUR BLADES

Naxos, Cyclades, Greece
Obsidian
Early Bronze Age, EC II, 2700–2300 BC
Core Height 8 cm, Width 1.9 cm;
Blades Length 6.5–9 cm
National Archaeological Museum, Athens
Inv. Nos. 6204.7, 9

The obsidian core (in the shape of a truncated cone) and the prismatic blades, ten in all, are the sole goods found in a rather poor grave of the Spedos cemetery. This hard volcanic glass was the basic raw material for the manufacture of chipped stone tools, usually blades for knives and razors, while the core could also serve as a pestle or a polisher. The source of the obsidian and centre of distribution in the Aegean was the island of Melos in the Cyclades. The use of obsidian dates from the Neolithic period but the material became common in the Early Bronze Age. It was also used, on a much reduced scale, in later times during the Bronze Age.   L.P.-M.

Papathanassopoulos 1961/2, 120, pl. 51a;
Renfrew-Wagstaff 1982, 183–221

12 SLAB WITH SCENE OF HUNTING

Naxos, Cyclades, Greece
Marble
Early Bronze Age, EC II–III, 2700–2200 BC
Length 28.5 cm, Width 15.5 cm,
Thickness 4.2 cm
Archaeological Museum, Apeiranthos, Naxos
Inv. No. 14

On the relatively smooth surface of this irregular, trapezoidal slab is depicted a deer with large antlers and elongated body, rendered in profile. A human figure is standing behind the animal, the head and feet shown in profile. A few facial features are denoted such as the nose and the eye. Movement is suggested by the two bent arms. The physical nature of the stone, a grey dolomitic limestone, creates a contrast between the worked, pitted areas and the natural surface. The scene is apparently a representation of hunting. This stone and nine other similar slabs, which may have originally formed a kind of frieze, were found in a small installation on the peak of a hill called Korphi t'Aroniou, on the southeast coast of the island of Naxos. Pastoral and hunting scenes, boats on the sea, even a dancing scene are depicted on the stones. The possibility that the stones were dedicated to a deity in a small shrine cannot be ruled out.
L.P.-M.

Doumas 1965, 52, 59–62, fig. 6, pl. 36c;
Hood 1978, 94, fig. 74b

13 EGYPTIAN STONE VASE

Mycenae – Chamber Tomb 55, Argolid,
Greece
Diorite
Predynastic-Early Dynastic,
3rd millennium BC
Height 15 cm, Diameter 13 cm
National Archaeological Museum, Athens
Inv. No. 2919

Piriform jar made of black diorite, speckled with white. It has two horizon-

tally pierced lugs on the shoulder and a hole in the centre of the base: this transforms it into a rhyton. One of the oldest stone imports into the Aegean, it was nevertheless found in a chamber tomb of much later date at Mycenae, from the 15th–14th centuries BC. It seems possible that the vase came from a plundered Egyptian tomb, whose contents were smuggled abroad as exotic and luxurious items. So the jar found its way, possibly via Crete, to a Mycenaean tomb.   L.P.-M.

Warren 1969, 114; Sakellarakis 1976, 178,
pl. IV.8; Müller-Karpe 1980, no. 126;
Sakellariou-Xenaki 1985, 175, pl. 73;
Cline 1994, 201.604

14 "FRYING-PAN"

Syros, Cyclades, Greece
Clay
Early Bronze Age, EC II, 2700–2300 BC
Diameter with the handle 30.7 cm
National Archaeological Museum, Athens
Inv. No. 4333
Ill. p. 18

"Frying pans" with a forked handle are characteristic vessels of the Early Cycladic culture. Burnished inside and out, they bear incised or stamped decoration, sometimes filled with white paste, on the outer main surface. The interior, bordered by a low rim, remains undecorated. This piece has incised decoration of running spirals, representing the sea waves. In the middle is a multi-oared Cycladic boat with a fish emblem, a banner at the high stern and a projection at the prow. The scene, bordered by a band of impressed triangles, bears witness to the competent seafarers of the Cycladic islands. On the handle incised lines below the main scene indicate the pubic triangle. The function of the "frying pans" is obscure. The decorated ones probably had a religious, ceremonial use but a more practical use is assumed for those that are undecorated.   L.P.-M.

Zervos 1957, 37, fig. 204; Müller-Karpe 1974, pl. 362.5, no. 158; Coleman 1985, 208, 18, pl. 32

15   STEMMED JAR

Paros, Cyclades, Greece
Marble
Early Bronze Age, EC I, 3200–2700 BC
Height 29 cm, Diameter 27 cm
National Archaeological Museum, Athens
Inv. No. 4763

This collared and footed jar of excellent workmanship, comes from a grave that also produced a violin-shaped figurine. The type was popular in EC I: manufactured pieces can be attributed to different sculptors, all working in the Cyclades. A vessel of this type is termed "kandila", after the rather similar hanging oil lamps used in the Greek Orthodox Church. They are exclusively found in graves; being heavy and perhaps rather impractical for everyday use, they probably played a role in the funerary rites.   L.P.-M.

Tsountas 1898, 155, pl. 10.16; Müller-Karpe 1974, pl. 358.25, no. 153; Getz-Gentle 1996, 5ff, 28–29, 35–39, pl. 4

16   VIOLIN-SHAPED FIGURINE

Kimolos, Cyclades, Greece
Marble
Early Bronze Age, EC I, 3200–2700 BC
Height 23 cm, Width 8.3 cm
National Archaeological Museum, Athens
Inv. No. 3937
Ill. p. 161

The body is violin-shaped and completely flat; shallow incisions denote the arms, the loins and the abdomen. The tall neck was broken and mended in antiquity. Two incisions at the base of the neck indicate a necklace. Traces of red paint are visible on the surface. A fine example of the early type of the stylised anthropomorphic figurines, marking the beginning of their evolution to the more common folded-arm type.   L.P.-M.

Zervos 1957, 81, pl. 56b; Müller-Karpe 1974, pl. 360.12, no. 153. For other examples see Doumas 1977, 16, fig. 4; for the use of paint see Getz-Preziosi 1987, 53–54

17   FEMALE FIGURINE

Naxos – Spedos, Tomb 10, Cyclades, Greece
Marble
Early Bronze Age, EC II, 2700–2300 BC
Height 43.5 cm, Width 9 cm
National Archaeological Museum, Athens
Inv. No. 6140.22
Ill. p. 54

This female figurine, with arms folded across the chest, belongs to the Spedos variety, named after the cemetery on Naxos, where this piece was actually found. The head is broad and the large nose is plastically rendered. The body is in a standing position with slightly bent knees and feet pointing down. The legs are divided by a deep groove. Faint incisions indicate the pubic triangle.

The folded-arm type is the most common and widely distributed type of the Cycladic figurines. It is usually of small size, but larger pieces, like this one, do occur and exceptionally it may reach a height of 1.5 m. The study of the details has lead to the recognition both of different styles and of the now anonymous "master"-sculptors that were at work in the Cycladic islands. These enigmatic figures, either idols of gods or images of mortals, are found in graves and settlements. They apparently played an important role in the religious beliefs and practices of the Cycladic islanders. Their abstract, simple forms have also intrigued the imagination of modern man and inspired contemporary artists.   L.P.-M.

Papathanassopoulos 1961/2, 115, pl. 46b; Müller-Karpe 1974, pls. 359–360, no. 150; Getz-Preziosi 1987, 14–18.

18   MALE FIGURINE

Amorgos, Cyclades, Greece
Marble
Early Bronze Age, EC I, 3200–2700 BC
Height 25 cm, Width 6 cm
National Archaeological Museum, Athens
Inv. No. 3911
Ill. p. 54

This male figurine is standing firmly on his feet. The elongated head wears a conical, ribbed hat. The short body has robust legs, narrow shoulders and atrophied arms. Primary sexual distinctions are clearly indicated. Male figurines are comparatively rare, the female type being predominant in Cycladic art. This piece belongs to the Plastiras group, named after a site on the island of Paros.

Male figurines represent a high percentage (about 20%) of the total number of figurines within this group. Naturalistic, in the manner of its Neolithic predecessors, the Plastiras group is yet roughly contemporary with the schematic violin-shaped figurines (Cat. No. 16). L.P.-M.

Zervos 1957, 73, pl. 43; Müller-Karpe 1974, pl. 360.26; Getz-Preziosi 1987, 20, fig. 11a

19 OX-HIDE INGOT

Kyme, Euboea, Greece
Copper
Late Bronze Age, 16th–15th centuries BC
Length 40 cm, Width 23 cm, Weight 13.2 kg
Numismatic Museum, Athens
Inv. No. 1906–7
Ill. p. 37

The ingot was cast in a mould; the irregularities on the surface were produced as the material cooled. Rectangular in shape with concave sides, it has been thought, because of its shape in combination with the surface texture, to resemble an oxhide (or double axes). In this manner copper was transported to the Mediterranean ports, arguably becoming a standard means of commercial exchange.

Bronze is an alloy of copper and tin, the latter in a small percentage, admirably suited to the manufacture of vessels, tools and weapons.

A group of nineteen copper ingots was found in 1906 off the Kyme harbour. They belong to the standard type, known both from painted representations in Egyptian tombs and from actual finds, which last are widely distributed in the Mediterranean from Sardinia and Sicily to Mainland Greece (Mycenae), Crete (Aghia Triada, Zakros), Cyprus and Asia Minor. A large number of copper ingots was also recovered from the Gelidonya and the Ulu Burun shipwrecks off the coast of Asia Minor. The island of Cyprus has long been considered a prime source for raw copper and

it is the home of the miniature votive ingots, incised with signs of the linear Cypro-Minoan script (cf. Cat. No. 20).
L.P-M.

Svoronos 1906, 168–171; Buchholz 1974, 325ff; Sapouna-Sakellaraki 1984, 157, fig. 2b; Gale and Stos-Gale 1986, 81ff

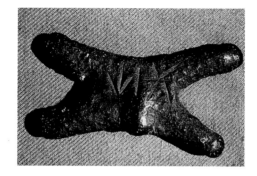

20 MINIATURE INGOT

Enkomi?, Cyprus
Copper
Late Bronze Age III, LC III, 13th–12th centuries BC
Height 5 cm, Length 9 cm
Cyprus Museum, Nicosia
Inv. No. 1936/VI-19/1

The miniature copper ingot (*talent*) has been stamped with two Cypriot-Minoan symbols that are separated by a vertical bar. P.Ph.

Demakopoulou 1988, 169, no. 130

Only in Athens

21 MAN AND BULL GROUP

Cyprus
Bronze
Late Bronze Age
Height 10 cm
Musée de Louvre, DAO, Paris
Inv. No. MNB 336

The group is set on a frame (apparently broken in antiquity), which in turn was supported on top of two rings that allowed the axle with its small wheels to pass through. A naked man leans against

the left flank of a bull, his right arm around the neck of the animal, while he holds the horns with his left. A small dog is seen at the right side of the bull.
J.-P.M.

Art Antique de Chypre, Louvre, 1992

Only in Copenhagen, Bonn and Paris

22 RHYTON WITH BULL'S HEAD

Cyprus
Clay
Late Bronze Age, LC II, 1400–1230 BC
Height 29.5 cm; Diameter at rim 8 cm
Musée de Louvre, DAO, Paris
Inv. No. AO 14913

Ceramic, brown fabric, fugitive coating brown; incised and relief decoration. Elongated piriform shape – perhaps deriving from the combination of Aegean conical and peg–topped rhyta, but Cypriot in type (in Base-Ring I-II series?). Vertical relief ridges give fluted effect to body, slightly bulbous tip. Vertical loop handle just below shoulder is placed opposite a small, three-dimensional bull's head added on. Contexts confirm cult nature of these pieces.

C. E.

Art Antique de Chypre, Louvre, 1992; Caubet et al. 1981, 30.CKY.50, pl.11

23   ROD TRIPOD

Episkopi, Cyprus
Bronze
Late Bronze Age III, LC III, 12ᵗʰ century BC
Height 39.5 cm, Diameter 26.5 cm
Cyprus Museum, Nicosia
Inv. No. T 40/299

The legs finish in the form of cows' hooves; their upper ends in spiral-volutes, where they are attached to the circular rim. Half-way up the outside of each leg is set a cast cow's head, from which point on the interior various supporting struts depart; from the upper ones depend two pendants below the rim.

P.Ph.

Demakopoulou 1988, 169, no. 132

24   OFFERING STAND

Kouklia, Cyprus
Bronze
Late Bronze Age III, LC III, 13ᵗʰ century BC
Height 15.6 cm
Cyprus Museum, Nicosia
Inv. No. RRKM 9

The bowl to take the offering is missing, though the large rivets on the upper end of the stem are still intact. Just below the rivets is a collar made of bronze wire wound round the stem, itself fashioned to give a spiral-twist to it. Another similar collar marks the point where the stand's legs branch out. These are made from two simple, round-sectioned rods whose ends each turn up into a volute-spiral; the ring base of the stand is affixed to these.

P.Ph.

Demakopoulou 1988, 169, no. 131

25   PLOUGH SHARE

Cyprus
Bronze
Length 24.5 cm
Cyprus Museum, Nicosia
Inv. No. 1983/X-10/11

Ploughshare from the Bronze Age: such a blade was attached lengthways to the rear part of the wooden plough. Ploughs begin to appear towards the end of the Neolithic period. As a rule they

are pulled by oxen and guided by men. The plough made it possible to create furrows in the field and thus to channel rainfall onto the seeds (and later the plants). Depictions of ploughing are found in the rock art of Mont Bego in France, of the Val Camonica in Italy and of Scandinavia.

J.-P.M.

26   STIRRUP-JAR

Perati – Chamber Tomb 15, Attica, Greece
Clay
Late Bronze Age, LH IIIC, 12ᵗʰ century BC
Height 21.5 cm, Diameter 18.6 cm
National Archaeological Museum, Athens
Inv. No. 9151

The stirrup jar has a globular body shape, a cylindrical spout with nearby a "false mouth" or stem, that ends in a pointed disc, set between the two handles. The quality of the clay and of the lustrous paint is excellent. The vase is richly decorated – combining elements of the two styles that are prevalent in fine Mycenaean pottery of the LH IIIC period: the Octopus Style and the Close Style.
The body has two symmetrically placed octopuses, while the remaining space is taken up with four fish and two birds, one of which appears to be flying. Rosettes are depicted on the shoulder along with a number of supplementary motifs, consisting of scales, hatching, joining semi-circles and festoons.

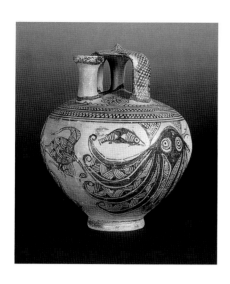

The Octopus Style, possibly ultimately derived from the Marine Style of the 15th century BC on Crete, is found mainly in the islands of the Dodecanese and the Cyclades, particularly Naxos and in important coastal sites such as Perati in Attica. The Close Style is characterised by the excessive use of decorative, mostly abstract, motifs, while birds and rosettes are also present. It is a purely Argolid creation that was disseminated and imitated in the Aegean.   L.P.-M.

Iakovidis 1969–70 A, 251; B, 149, 184, fig. 23; C, pl. 73.21; Schachermeyr 1980, 128 ff, fig. 18b; Vermeule & Karageorghis 1982, 148, 226, XI 145; Demakopoulou 1988, 126, no. 67

27   PIRIFORM JAR

Prosymna – Chamber Tomb II, Argolid, Greece
Clay
Late Bronze Age, LH IIA–B, middle of the 15th century BC
Height 51 cm, Diameter belly 36 cm, Diameter rim 20 cm
National Archaeological Museum, Athens
Inv. No. 6725
Ill. p. 55

Large, three-handled jar with tall piriform body, a wide and rather tall neck, broad flat rim, three strap handles on the shoulder and a torus-moulded base.

The neck, handles and base are monochrome painted, whilst a vivid, naturalistic scene covers the body – three octopuses (painted upright) with their long, spreading tentacles seem to be swimming in the sea; rock work, sea-weed and trefoils fill the spaces between the tentacles. This vase belongs to the Palatial Class of Mycenaean pottery of this period (LH IIA), with shapes and decoration of Minoan inspiration. The Prosymna jar is a characteristic Palace Style (Marine) vase manufactured on the Mainland by skilled Mycenaean craftsmen.   N.D.-V.

Blegen 1937, 178, 417, no. 177, fig. 437, pl. 7; Demakopoulou 1988, 89, no. 21; Mountjoy 1993, 41, 44–45, 48–50

28   OSTRICH EGG-SHAPED RHYTON

Knossos, Crete, Greece
Clay
Late Bronze Age, LM IB, 15th century BC
Height 13 cm
Archaeological Museum, Herakleion
Inv. No. 5832

Ostrich egg-shaped rhyton decorated with an octopus and other motifs in the so-called Marine Style of the special Palatial tradition. Marine elements appear in various forms of Minoan art (pottery, wall-paintings, clay reliefs,

faience production) as a general style at the highest point of the palatial artistic production. Rhyta were used for pouring libations in religious ceremonies.   E.B.

Evans 1928–35; Pendlebury 1939; Raison 1969; Koehl 1981, 179 ff; Betancourt 1985, 132, fig. 100

29   MOULD

Mycenae – Acropolis, Argolid, Greece
Steatite
Late Bronze Age, LH IIIA–B, 14th–13th centuries BC
Length 10 cm, Width 7 cm
National Archaeological Museum, Athens
Inv. No. 1018

Almost rectangular block of reddish-brown steatite, chipped at the edges and broken at one corner. On both surfaces there are matrices for casting mainly glass and faience beads and pendants in various shapes, destined for necklaces and bracelets. These are in the shape of a papyrus (twice), a coil, a chain, an argonaut, an octopus and a rectangle with double crossed bands on one side, and a papyrus-lily, a half-rosette and a bracket/tassel – cf. the necklace Cat.

No. 34 – on the other side. The same moulds were also used for making gold and silver beads.

Similar stone moulds, usually of steatite, have been found in several Mycenaean centres and are connected with the centralised jewellery production in the well-organised palatial workshops.

N.D.-V.

Schliemann 1878, 108, fig. 162; Higgins 1961, 16–17, 43; Demakopoulou 1990, 321, no. 280; Evely 1992, 29–31

30   DECORATIVE INLAY

Deiras – Chamber Tomb VI, Argos, Argolid, Greece

Ivory

Late Bronze Age, LH IIIA, 14th century BC

Height 2.7–4.4 cm, Width 1.7-2.5 cm

National Archaeological Museum, Athens

Inv. No. 5577

A decorative cut-out plaque in the form of a palm-tree. The upper surface bears incised decoration, while the rear surface is left plain. The palm-tree has its trunk set in the centre and three branches hanging symmetrically on either side. The fruit is visible at the top between the branches. Similar plaques, at different sizes, must have been used as inlays to decorate wooden objects or furniture. They were probably mass-produced items, as is evident from their rather

careless workmanship and manner of incised decoration. N.D.-V.

Vollgraff 1904, 364ff; Poursat 1977b, 113, pl. 38; Demakopoulou 1988, 219, no. 205

31   DECORATIVE INLAY

Deiras – Chamber Tomb VI, Argos, Argolid, Greece

Ivory

Late Bronze Age, LH IIIA, 14th century BC

Height 2.4-2.6 cm, Width 1.9-3 cm

National Archaeological Museum, Athens

Inv. No. 5576

A decorative cut-out plaque in the form of an argonaut. The portrayal is achieved by incised decoration on the upper surface of the plaque. The argonaut has a central spiral to its shell, surrounded by wavy lines depicting its vaguely heart-shaped body and three tentacles. Similar plaques must have been used as inlays to decorate wooden objects or furniture. N.D.-V.

Vollgraff 1904, 364ff; Poursat 1977b, 113ff, pl. 38; Demakopoulou 1988, 219, no. 205

32   KAMARES STYLE JUG

Phaistos, Crete, Greece

Clay

Middle Bronze Age, MM II, 18th century BC

Height 27 cm

Archaeological Museum, Herakleion

Inv. No. 10073

Beaked jug in the polychrome style of mature Kamares Ware. The light-on-dark decoration with prominent spiral designs is perfectly in balance with the shape of the vase, creating a pleasing effect. One of the best examples of the ceramic production of the Old Palace Period. E.B.

Guarducci 1939–40, 233, fig. 3; Zervos 1956, 247, 342; Betancourt 1986

33 NECKLACE

Pylos – Tholos Tomb IV, Messenia, Greece
Amethyst
Late Bronze Age, LH II, 15th century BC
Diameter of beads 0.9-1.4 cm
National Archaeological Museum, Athens
Inv. No. 7893

The necklace is made up from spherical
beads of light and dark-coloured
amethyst, in different sizes. Amethyst, a
semi-precious stone, was used in Mycenaean jewellery-making mostly during
the early Mycenaean period. It was
imported from the East.   N.D.-V.

Blegen et al. 1973, 124–125, fig. 194.36;
Müller-Karpe 1980, no. 133; Demakopoulou
1996, 114, no. 54

34 NECKLACE

Mycenae – Chamber Tomb 93, Argolid,
Greece
Glass
Late Bronze Age, LH IIIA–B,
14th–13th centuries BC
Length 5.5–6.6 cm, Width 1.2–2 cm
National Archaeological Museum, Athens
Inv. No. 4550

Seven glass ornaments in the shape of a
stylised tassel (bracket), with design on
the front surface, while the rear is flat.
On the narrow side of the ornament is a
circular cavity, with two holes for fasten-

ing. Glass ornaments and beads were
mass-produced during this period, being
cast in steatite moulds, similar to that
from Mycenae, see Cat. No. 29.

N.D.-V.

Müller-Karpe 1980, no. 126, pl. 229; Sakellariou-Xenaki 1985, 265, pl. 132.4550 (12);
Demakopoulou 1988, 218–219, no. 204
(for the ornament)

35–36 PLAQUES, "TOWN MOSAIC"

Knossos, Crete, Greece
Faience
Middle Bronze Age, MM II–III,
18th–17th centuries BC
Height 4.1 cm, Width 2.8 cm; Height 4.7 cm,
Width 3.2 cm respectively
Archaeological Museum, Herakleion
Inv. Nos. 9 and 18
Ill. p. 67

Two representations of houses in polychrome faience (one reconstructed with
plaster), which belong to the so-called
"Town Mosaic" from the Palace of Knossos. They represent facades of houses
with multiple storeys, flat roofs, timber-
framed windows and doors. According to
the excavator of Knossos, Sir Arthur
Evans, the "Town Mosaic" formed part
of a larger composition, as he inferred
from other plaques from the same
deposit that show animals, water plants,
warriors and negroid types.   E.B.

Evans 1921, 301–314; Foster 1979,
107–110, figs. 50–81, pl. 27

37 NECKLACE

Dendra –Tholos Tomb, Argolid, Greece
Gold
Late Bronze Age, LH IIB, second half of the
15th century BC
Diameter beads 1.9 and 2.45 cm
National Archaeological Museum, Athens
Inv. No. 7342

The necklace is made up of thirty-six
relief beads in the shape of eight-
petalled rosettes, in two sizes and in an
excellent state of preservation. The dou-
bly-outlined petals spread from a central
relief circle. Each bead is provided with
two string-holes in parallel. Such gold
relief-beads are characteristic ornaments
of Mycenaean jewellery production in
the 15th and 14th centuries BC. Their
upper surface was fashioned by forcing
metal foil into moulds; the forms of the
various stylised and marine motifs are
well known in the Minoan and Mycenaean repertoires.   N.D.-V.

Persson 1931, 40, pl. XVIII.1; Higgins 1980;
Demakopoulou 1996, 106, no. 40

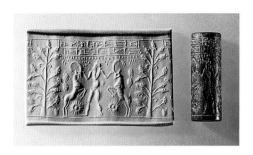

38 NEAR–EASTERN CYLINDER SEAL

Thebes – New Kadmeion, Boeotia, Greece
Lapis Lazuli
Late Bronze Age, 13th century BC
Height 4.3 cm, Diameter 1.5 cm
Archaeological Museum, Thebes
Inv. No. 199

On the cylinder is engraved the Master of the Animals, a male divinity here. He holds by their horns two goats, rearing on their hind legs. Two sacred trees frame the scene and above the heads are signs in the cuneiform script. A group of forty-five cylinder seals of Near Eastern origin were found in the Mycenaean Palace at Thebes, which give evidence of official and commercial contacts between the two regions. The cylinder seals have scenes of gods and heroes of the Near Eastern tradition and they have been interpreted as gifts to the kings of Thebes. L.P.-M.

Platon 1964, 861, fig. 10; Platon 1981, 58; Porada 1981–1982, 49–50, pl. 3.26; Demakopoulou 1988, 252, no. 274

39 SEALING

Mycenae – House of Shields, Argolid, Greece
Clay
Late Bronze Age, LH IIIB, 13th century BC
Height 4 cm, Width 2.3 cm
National Archaeological Museum, Athens
Inv. No. 7630
Ill. p. 196

An irregular piece of baked, blackened clay with a perforation running along its longitudinal axis. On one side is a seal impression depicting a bearded man armed with a dagger fightin≠g a lion, with a dog running between his legs towards the animal. On the reverse side there is an impression of a piece of rope. The seal used in the sealing of the clay nodule belongs stylistically earlier – to the so-called style B or Mycenaean style (15th century BC); and such seals and sealings of the 13th century BC bear witness to a renaissance of seal-engraving during this period. The heroic subject of the man fighting a lion is well known in the iconography from the early Mycenaean period onwards. The clay nodule with the seal impression was probably used for sealing and preserving particular products or objects by the official responsible, who arguably was also the owner of the seal.
Clay sealings or nodules were usually inscribed with Linear B inscriptions or ideograms and make up the main evidence, together with the Linear B tablets, for the well-organised bureaucratic administration of the Mycenaean palace centres. N.D.-V.

Bennett 1958, 13, figs. 76–77; Sakellariou 1964, no. 165; Demakopoulou 1988, 210–211, no. 190

40 MODEL OF A GROUP OF DANCERS

Palaikastro – Block D, Room 44, Crete, Greece
Clay
Late Bronze Age, LM III, 14th century BC
Height 13 cm
Archaeological Museum, Herakleion
Inv. No. 3903
Ill. p. 57

Group of four female figurines in long skirts, of which three are dancing in a linked circle with the fourth in the middle playing a musical instrument (a lyre or cithara). The model comes from a context at Palaikastro which according to the excavators furnished ritual objects connected with the Minoan cult of the Snake Goddess, ie. figurines of doves, kernoi etc. The dance possibly illustrates the classical Cretan dance called *hyporchema* or *Kernophoron orchema*. E.B.

Dawkins 1903-04, 217, fig. 6; Zervos 1956, 479, pl. 794; Lowler 1940, 166–167; Müller-Karpe 1974, pl. 391C.1, no. 171

41 PYXIS

Kalami – Chamber Tomb 1, Apokoronou, Crete, Greece
Clay
Late Bronze Age, LM IIIB, 13th century BC
Height 13.6 cm, Diameter 16.7 cm
Archaeological Museum, Chania
Inv. No. 2308

The vase has a cylindrical body and four strap handles; its lid is missing. The decorated surface is divided into panels. The main scene is a male musician, wearing a sleeveless chiton. He is holding a branch in one hand and with the other is touching a large seven-stringed musical instrument, a lyre or cithara. Two flying birds complete the scene. Religious symbols such as horns of consecration and double axes are depicted beneath the handle. Flying birds with

42 HYDRIA

Mycenae – Grave Circle A, Shaft Grave IV,
Argolid, Greece
Bronze
Late Bronze Age, LH I, second half of the
16th century BC
Height 54 cm, Diameter 41 cm
National Archaeological Museum, Athens
Inv. No. 603

43 CONICAL RHYTON

Akrotiri, Thera, Cyclades, Greece
Clay
Late Bronze Age, LM IA, 16th century BC
Height with the handle 33.4 cm,
Diameter 10.9 cm
National Archaeological Museum, Athens
Inv. No. 1493

spread wings in a large panel, and narrow panels with linear patterns occupy
the rest of the surface of the vase.
The vase is a fine example of the Kydo-
nia (Chania) pottery workshop that
flourished in Mycenaean Crete. Pottery
from this west Cretan workshop has
been discovered all over the island and
in mainland Greece. The musical scene
on the pyxis seems to have a religious or
funerary character and the performance
takes place in a sacred area. A reconstructed ivory lyre found in the tholos
tomb at Menidi in Attica, the Aghia Triada sarcophagus on Crete, the wall-
painting in the palace of Pylos, and a
few pieces of pictorial pottery (such as
the krater fragment from Nauplia in the
Argolid) give evidence of the presence of
musicians in Late Bronze Age Greece,
antecedents of Apollo *citharodos*, familiar from Greek mythology.   L.P.-M.

Tzedakis 1969, 365–368, fig. 2; Tzedakis
1970, 111–112, fig. 1.2; Dragona-Latsoudi
1977, 89ff, 95, pl. 22a; Vlasaki in:
Demakopoulou 1988, 149, no. 105

The bronze hydria is made up of three
hammered bronze sheets that are fastened together with rows of tiny rivets.
The two handles, a vertical strap handle
and a horizontal handle (which is cast),
are also fastened with rivets to the neck
and shoulder, and the lower body
respectively. The body has a piriform
shape and a torus-moulded base. The
short neck is slightly waisted, forming a
rudimentary spout to assist in pouring
the liquid contents. Repair work at the
base of the vertical handle gives evidence
for the actual use of the hydria, prior to
its deposition into the grave.
This type of bronze vessel is considered
of Cretan origin; it is also found in the
settlement of Akrotiri on the island of
Thera. It has a limited distribution in the
Greek mainland and, as a prestige and
valuable item, is found mainly in rich
graves.   L.P.-M.

Karo 1930-33, 118, no. 603; Matthäus 1980,
166, pl. 27.222

The rhyton has a tall, conical body with
a raised strap handle. It is pierced at the
pointed tip. The rich decoration, in
black-brown and white paint, is
achieved by two decorative techniques
(light-on-dark and dark-on-light). It follows a spiral-based pattern, arranged in
horizontal registers. Mainly this consists
of rows of rosettes in circles, connected
by tangents and framed by undulating
lines. In the middle register the running
spiral is executed in light-on-dark. The
rhyton is considered a ritual vase, used
for libations, but it could also have a
practical function.
The rhyton from Thera is a fine product
of the east Cretan workshops and it was
imported into the island. A similar piece
was found at the settlement at Gournia
in east Crete. The Akrotiri settlement
maintained relations with the Minoans
on Crete and the Mycenaeans on the
mainland; but it was the Minoans who
exercised the more profound influence
on Thera, before the volcanic destruction.   L.P.-M.   219

Marinatos 1972, 31, pl. 63; Niemeier 1980, 63–65, figs. 34–35; Marthari 1987, 362ff, 373ff; Demakopoulou 1988, 152, no. 108

44 GOLD CUP

Mycenae – Grave Circle A, Shaft Grave V, Argolid, Greece
Gold
Late Bronze Age, LH I, second half of the 16th century BC
Height 10.5 cm, Diameter rim. 15.5 cm, Weight 254 g
National Archaeological Museum, Athens
Inv. No. 629
Ill. p. 99

The cup, made of heavy gold sheet, belongs to the Vapheio type – basically conical, widening towards the rim and a with high strap handle; a wide embossed zone divides the body into two unequal parts. Both parts are here decorated with thickly interlaced running spirals in the repoussé technique. The shape and the decoration alike are common among the rich finds of the Shaft Graves at Mycenae. This exquisite piece, fit for the table of a king, is considered the work of a local Mycenaean craftsman.

The accumulation of wealth in the royal graves is indicative of the high social status of the men, women and children buried in them. In the same Shaft Grave, gold burial masks, other vases of gold, silver and bronze, inlaid metal daggers and a great number of bronze weapons give a clear picture of the warrior aristocracy that now emerges and marks the beginning of the Mycenaean age.

L.P.-M.

Karo 1930–33, 122, pl. 125; Davis 1977, 141–142, fig. 122; Matthaeus 1980, 242, pl. 75.7; Demakopoulou 1990, 306, no. 257; Graziadio 1991, 411–412, 434–436

220

45 FIGURINE OF AN ARMED MAN

Petsofas, Crete, Greece
Clay
Middle Bronze Age, MM I–II, 19th–18th centuries BC
Height 17.5 cm
Archaeological Museum, Herakleion
Inv. No. 3405

Votive male figurine with arms in front of the chest, loin-cloth type of kilt and with a very large dagger at his waist; from the peak sanctuary of Petsofas, one of the many open-air shrines in early Minoan times.

E.B.

Zervos 1956, 23, 192.232; Hood 1978, 103, fig. 85; Rutkowski 1991, pl. B.1

46 SEALSTONE WITH METAL FITTINGS

Vapheio – Tholos Tomb, Laconia, Greece
Jasper and gold
Late Bronze Age, LH IIA, first half of the 15th century BC
Diameter 1.75–1.95 cm
National Archaeological Museum, Athens
Inv. No. 1775
Ill. p. 195

The sealstone is lentoid in shape and has gold fittings set around the two ends of the stringhole. On the front surface is engraved a hunting scene. Two men

strive to bind together with a cord the front and rear legs of a dead lion. The lifeless head of the animal falls back, as it is hoisted into the air.

The lion symbolises power in the monumental relief on the Lion Gate at Mycenae and a lion hunt is also depicted on the well-known inlaid dagger from Shaft Grave IV at Mycenae.

L.P.-M.

CMS I, 224; for the lion hunt, see Buchholz, Jöhrens & Maull Archaeologia Homerica II, J.9-27

47 HEAD OF WARRIOR

Spata – Chamber Tomb, Attica, Greece
Ivory
Late Bronze Age, LH IIIB, 13th century BC
Height 7.4 cm
National Archaeological Museum, Athens
Inv. No. 2055
Ill. p. 52

The strongly-modelled piece is portrayed with its head in left profile: a warrior wearing a boar's tusk helmet. The tusks are set in four rows on the conical cap, with another five rows on the cheekpiece, which extends down to the jawline. The back of the neck is protected by three sets of obliquely angled tusks. The knob on top of the helmet is decorated with incised lines.

The ear is rendered in low relief; the nose and mouth are carved in higher. The almond-shaped eye is indicated by a relief line and the eyebrow by a groove. The rear of the inlay is completely flat. A hole/mortise served to attach the head to a (?)wooden surface.

An impressive piece of work, this is one of the finest examples of the Mycenaean ivory carving, as well as an interesting portrayal of a Mycenaean warrior wearing the helmet typical of the period. Such helmets are found at many sites of the Aegean from as early as the Middle Bronze Age and are also depicted on ivory plaques, in frescoes and seal-carving and on pottery. The Spata head was found in a rich chamber tomb which contained many other ivory objects of the finest craftmanship.   K.D.

Borchhardt 1972, pl. 2.3 (5.II); Poursat 1977, 161, no. 466, pl. L

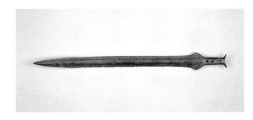

48   SWORD

Mycenae – Acropolis, Argolid, Greece
Bronze
Late Bronze Age, LH IIIC, 12th century BC
Length 60 cm
National Archaeological Museum, Athens
Inv. No. 1017

The sword is preserved in excellent condition. The handgrip and the handguard are both flanged; eight rivets were used to secure in place the hilt plates of some organic, now perished material. The stout blade tapers towards the point and has a broad, low midrib. The weapon was cast in a two-piece mould, while the rivet holes were opened later. It was found in the House of the Warriors Vase on the Acropolis of Mycenae. This is a fine example of the so-called Naue II sword (after the name of the first archaeologist who classified them). It belongs to Catling's group I, which has no pommel spur. This class of swords, ultimately of west European origin, was introduced into the Aegean by way of the Adriatic in the second half of the 13th century BC. During the course of the 12th century Naue II swords, now of local manufacture, were widely distributed in the Greek Mainland, especially in Achaea in the Peloponnese, and were also found in the islands, such as Naxos in the Cyclades, Kos in the Dodecanese, Crete and Cyprus.   L.P.-M.

Catling 1956, 109.1; and 1961, 119; Schauer 1971, 105ff; Harding 1984, 162–165; Bouzek 1985, 122; Demakopoulou 1990, 323, no. 283; Kilian-Dirlmeier 1993, 94ff; Drews 1993; Papazoglou-Manioudaki 1994, 177–179

49   BOAR'S TUSK HELMET

Spata – Chamber Tomb, Attica, Greece
Boar's tusks
Late Bronze Age, LH IIIB, 13th century BC
Height (incl. restored parts) 19.2 cm,
Diameter 19 cm
National Archaeological Museum, Athens
Inv. Nos. 2097–2098
Ill. p. 88

The helmet is reconstructed from forty-two boar's tusks found in the rich chamber tomb at Spata. The tusks are placed in three rows graded according to their height, which varies from five cm in the upper row, to seven and eight cm respectively in the other two. The reconstruction of the helmet is based on depictions of such pieces in Mycenaean vase-painting and ivory-carving (see Cat. No. 47). The boar's tusk helmet is considered to be a Mycenaean invention and was a characteristic part of Mycenaean defensive armour until the 13th century BC. Recent excavations at Thebes, at Argos and on Aigina have shown that the type was already in use on the Mainland during the Middle Helladic period. Representations of boar's tusk helmets were used as decorative motifs in ivory-carving, seal-engraving and painted pottery. They symbolised the courage of the warrior-officers who owned them, required in the dangerous hunting that was necessary to obtain the tusks.
                              N.D.-V.

Haussoulier 1878, 185ff; Borchhardt 1972; Borchhardt 1977, 57ff; Demakopoulou 1988, 237, no. 239

50   FRESCO FRAGMENT

Mycenae – Cult Centre, Argolid, Greece
Plaster
Late Bronze Age, LH IIIB, 13th century BC
Height 10 cm, Length 9 cm
National Archaeological Museum, Athens
Inv. No. 11652

A female torso is preserved on the fragment, holding a griffin in a "flying gallop" stance. The female figure and the creature are painted white against a blue ground; the details are rendered in black paint; the griffin's wing is painted yellow.

The presence of the griffin in the arms of the figure suggests her divine nature, because in Minoan-Mycenaean iconography this mythical creature usually accompanies deities. The typical Mycenaean boar's tusk helmet that the goddess is wearing probably indicates that she is connected with war. Perhaps she was worshipped in the cult centre of Mycenae as a divinity of war with properties similar to those of the goddess Athena, as later crystallised in the Classical Olympian Pantheon.   N.D.-V.

Hampe & Simon 1980, 49, fig. 70; Kritselli-Providi 1982; Mylonas 1983; Demakopoulou 1988, 182, no. 149

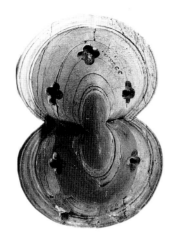

51 "FIGURE-OF-EIGHT" SHIELD

Mycenae – Acropolis, Argolid, Greece
Ivory
Late Bronze Age, LH IIIA2–B, 14th–13th centuries BC
Height 14.3 cm, Width 9.5 cm
National Archaeological Museum, Athens
Inv. No. 1027

Large ivory model of a "figure-of-eight" shield, with a broad rim. The body has five quatrefoil openings for inlays in a different material. The back has four rectangular mortises to enable the shield to be attached as decoration to a piece of furniture. Ivory was imported as raw material from Syria and then worked with great success at Mycenae in special workshops attached to the palace. The "figure-of-eight" shield was a Mycenaean cultural symbol. It was also a popular decorative motif in their miniature art, especially in ivory-carving, and others are known also in gold and of semi-precious stone.   L.P.-M.

Poursat 1977a, 98–100, and 1977b, 81ff, pl. XXII; Demakopoulou 1988, 86, no. 16

52 MODEL OF A CHARIOT

Mycenae – Chamber Tomb, Argolid, Greece
Clay
Late Bronze Age, LH IIIA–B,
14th–13th centuries BC
Height 10 cm, Length 12 cm
National Archaeological Museum, Athens
Inv. No. 2262
Ill. p. 125

A stylised model of a two-horse chariot with two occupants. The horses, with elongated bodies and each pair of legs fused together into a conical pin, are harnessed to a crude horizontal yoke placed across their necks. A pair of thin round-sectioned strips, joined together, run from the middle of the yoke to the charioteer's chest: they represent both the reins and also the pole connecting the yoke to the semicircular box of the chariot body. The two human figures, with their bodies conjoined and leaving only two separate birdlike heads, rise directly from the chariot's rail. Between them there was once a parasol, of which the end of the handle survives. The chariot and the horses' bodies are decorated with fine wavy and zigzag lines in reddish-brown paint.

The widespread use of the chariot in Mycenaean Greece is attested by its frequent appearance in the iconography of the period in frescoes, on rings and seals, stone funerary stelae and Linear B clay tablets, and in the decoration of the Pictorial Style pottery. Numerous terracotta models of chariots have also been found at various important Mycenaean sites.

K.D.

Xenaki-Sakellariou 1985, 162, pl. 63; Crouwel 1981, 145, 147, T23

53 AMPHOROID KRATER

Nauplia – Chamber Tomb B, Argolid, Greece
Clay
Late Bronze Age, LH III A–B,
14th–13th centuries BC
Height 45 cm, Diameter belly 34 cm,
Diameter rim 27 cm
Archaeological Museum, Nauplion
Inv. No. 15180
Ill. p. 125

This krater is a characteristic work of the Mycenaean Pictorial Style. It has a piriform body, a wide and tall neck, two large vertical strap handles from rim to shoulder and a short torus-moulded base. On each side of the upper part of the body is depicted a chariot drawn by two horses and carrying two men, set between stylised palm-trees. The horses have their bodies painted monochrome, long curved nuzzles and spreading manes. The charioteer and his companion wear dotted garments; their heads and necks are solid painted, with their profiles marked by strongly protruding noses. A chain of quirks borders the reins.

Amphoroid kraters with pictorial scenes constitute the main body of the Mycenaean Pictorial vases. Their shape ultimately derives from the Minoan Palace Style Jar and their pictorial decoration usually comprises birds, fish and quadrupeds in various compositions. Chariot scenes which depict a peaceful ceremonial parade, rather than a warlike event, were very popular on kraters. Pictorial decoration occurs also on the other types of kraters (stemmed and ring-based), on jugs, on stirrup-jars but less often on other closed and open shapes. The Mycenaean Pictorial Style, which existed within the Aegean artistic tradition, was developed in the Argolid, especially at Berbati, and at other Mycenaean centres. Through commercial exchange such vases spread to the east Mediterranean and especially to Cyprus, where many pictorial kraters, most probably imported from the Argolid,

222

have been found as funeral gifts in tombs. Some of them can, moreover, be attributed to the same workshops and painters as similar vases recovered from the Greek mainland.   N.D.-V.

Deilaki 1973, Chron. 90ff, pl. 90; Åkerström 1987, 111ff, 117ff, fig. 80; Demakopoulou 1988, 239, no. 242.

54 HORSE BIT

Mycenae – Acropolis, Argolid, Greece
Bronze
Late Bronze Age, LH IIIB, 13th century BC
Length of rod 24 cm, Length of cheek pieces 13 cm
National Archaeological Museum, Athens
Inv. No. 2553

This well-preserved part of a horse's bridle consists of a bit of two rods, formed of heavy twisted wire, and two spiked cheek-pieces. The bit was placed in the horse's mouth; the cheek-pieces will have lain against the outer side of its jaw. The leather reins passed through the loops at the end of the bit. This object provides factual evidence for the horse-drawn chariots, used by Mycenaean aristocrats for transportation, hunting or military purposes. It comes from a hoard of bronze objects, which was deposited on the Acropolis at Mycenae, probably at the end of the 13th century, just before the great destruction that put an end to the Mycenaean palatial system. A similar complete example was found in the Kadmeia, the Mycenaean acropolis at Thebes, a centre to rival Mycenae. Two more such, apparently forming a pair,

are known from a Mycenaean chamber tomb at Miletus in Asia Minor.   L.P.-M.

Spyropoulos 1972, 43–44, 140–143, fig. 77, pl. 14; Donder 1980, 21, pl. I.3; Crouwell 1981, 101ff, 104–107, 158, pls. 3–4

55 SEALSTONE

Voudeni – Chamber Tomb 4, Patras, Achaea, Greece
Lapis Lacedaemonius
Late Bronze Age, LH II/IIIA, 15th–14th centuries BC
Diameter 2.05–2.13 cm
Archaeological Museum, Patras
Inv. No. AE 125

The sealstone, found among the grave furnishings of a rich chamber tomb, is lentoid in shape. On the surface is engraved a scene of a daemon carrying on its shoulder an apparently dead man. The daemon, shown in profile, stands in the middle of the scene while the body of the man, wearing a belt and a loin cloth, falls lifelessly to either side. The man's head is facing upwards; a necklace adorns him. The scene is perfectly adapted to the round surface of the sealstone. The subject is treated with exceptional skill.
The daemon figure is a Minoan adaptation of the Egyptian hippopotamus goddess Ta-urt. These imaginary creatures (genii) are usually lion-headed, while their back is covered with a kind of loose hide attached by a belt at the waist. They are often depicted in miniature art carrying libation jugs and participating

in rituals as ministers or servants of the deity. In a few cases they carry animals on the shoulder or tied on poles, the latter possibly suggesting a hunting scene. The scene of a daemon carrying a dead male figure on the sealstone from Voudeni remains unique and reveals the association of the apotropaic figure with the world of the dead.   L.P.-M.

Kolonas 1989, B1 Chron., 168–170, fig. 16; CMS V Suppl. IB, 161–163, no. 153, co.pl. 1d; see Baurain & Darcque 1983, 3ff, 40–48; Sambin 1989, 77ff, 85

56 SWORD

Mycenae – Grave Circle A, Shaft Grave V, Argolid, Greece
Bronze
Late Bronze Age, LH I, second half of the 16th century BC
Length 43.2 cm, Width shoulder 8 cm, Thickness of blade 0.8 cm
National Archaeological Museum, Athens
Inv. No. 747

The sword has a rectangular-sectioned, small hilt-plate; the shoulders of the blade near this are rounded and point slightly upward. The blade tapers off toward the tip, which is worked to a sharp point. The impressions left by the handle (of organic material) are still visible; it was fastened by large bronze rivets, four of which have survived, their heads covered with thin silver foil. The blade is ornamented on both sides with incised decorations in the form of griffins at a "flying-gallop". This pose echoes a typical Minoan style of representation: the front and back legs of the creatures so engaged stretch out beyond its body in a near straight line, which gives the impression that they are mov-

ing at great speed, as if flying.
The sword belongs to Sandars' Type B. These broad and short swords, which are very robust, are thought to be a Mycenaean development. The narrow, long swords of Type A, on the other hand, are thought to be Cretan in origin. Both of the sword types that dominated in the early Mycenaean period were intended more for thrusting than for slashing. Both of the Grave Circles at Mycenae had several such swords, often with decorated blades and handles with gold or ivory inlay. Along with other weapons, they were placed there as grave goods for the Mycenaean princes. 　　　K.D.

Karo 1930–33, 135, figs. 49–60, pls. 91–92; Sandars 1961, 22; Hood 1978, 178, fig. 176b; Müller-Karpe 1980, pl. 228.6; Demakopoulou 1988, 85, no. 15

57　DIADEM

Mycenae – Grave Circle A, Shaft Grave IV, Argolid, Greece
Gold
Late Bronze Age, LH I, second half
of the 16th century BC
Length 45.7 cm, Width 7.2 cm
National Archaeological Museum, Athens
Inv. No. 286

The diadem is made of fine gold sheet. It has a long, elliptical shape, tapering towards the ends. Here it is drawn out into wires that form an eyelet used for fastening the diadem round the head. It has embossed decoration of dotted concentric circles. At the ends the circles are given tangential lines and thereby form running-spirals.

Gold diadems are among the commoner grave furnishings in the Shaft Graves at Mycenae. These and other gold sheet jewellery decorated in the repoussé technique are all similar in style and are considered the work of local Mycenaean craftsmen. They were actually worn in life prior to their deposition in the grave after the ceremonial funeral. 　　L.P.-M.

Karo 1930–33, 80, pl. 38; Dickinson 1977, 74–75; Hood 1978, 198; Demakopoulou 1988, 78, no.7

58　DAGGER

Mycenae – Grave Circle A, Shaft Grave V, Greece
Bronze and gold
Late Bronze Age, LH I,
second half of the 16th century BC
Length 24.3 cm, Width 4.1 cm
National Archaeological Museum, Athens
Inv. No. 744

This dagger has a broad, triangular blade with a large-headed rivet capped in gold near the hand grip, by which the handle would have been held in place. Both sides of the blade are inlaid with a gold strip, which tapers towards the point. The strip is worked with intertwining spirals with rosette centres and the decoration is emphasised by the use of "niello". Once the incised/traced decoration had been achieved, the "niello" compound was positioned in the channels (?by rubbing) – thereby picking out the design more emphatically.
This dagger is one of the group of the famous bronze daggers known from Mycenae and elsewhere in Mycenaean Greece; their inlaid decoration in gold, silver and "niello", with a variety of fig-

ured scenes, well deserves to be known as "painting in metal". 　　　K.D.

Karo 1930–33, 135, pls. 91–92, figs. 49–50; Hood 1978, 178 ff; Müller-Karpe 1980, pl. 228.6; Demakopoulou 1988, 84, no. 14; Drews 1993, 198

59　LARNAX

Tanagra – Chamber Tomb 6, Boeotia, Greece
Clay
Late Bronze Age, LH IIIB, 13th century BC
Length 105 cm, Width 39 cm, Height 75 cm
Archaeological Museum, Thebes
Inv. No. 7
Ill. p. 101

The larnax is a rectangular coffin set on four feet, all made of a piece. This one is made of coarse clay, covered with a dilute white wash, now faded. The lid, either gabled or flat, is missing. The body of the deceased was laid on the floor of the larnax.
The scene on both the long sides is a procession of mourning women. The women, moving right, are depicted in profile with their hands on their heads, a typical gesture of mourning. They are elegantly clothed and wear head-dresses. Their garments are a bodice and a full skirt with a small waist and fringes. Decoration on these is indicated by linear motifs on the bodices, and for the skirts oblique lines on the illustrated side and rows of semicircles on the other. A female figure stands alone, in the same posture, on the ends.
Burial in painted larnakes, of the bathtub or the rectangular type, is common in Minoan and Mycenaean Crete but is rarely found in the mainland. The exception is the chamber tomb cemetery of Tanagra, which has produced the largest and finest corpus of clay larnakes known to date on the Greek mainland. The existing evidence of wooden coffins in Mycenaean chamber tombs argues that the rectangular type of larnax originated in Mycenaean Greece. 　　L.P.-M.

Spyropoulos 1969, 12–13; and 1967, 8,
fig. 4; Demakopoulou & Konsola 1981, 80,
pl. 43a; Demakopoulou 1987, 73–75; and
1988, 74, no. 5

60   STELE OF MENHIR TYPE

Soufli Magoula, Larissa, Greece
Greyish schist
Probably Early Bronze Age, 3rd millennium BC
Height 2.15 m
Archaeological Museum, Larissa
Inv. No. 824

This object is given an anthropomorphic
treatment. The triangular head, which is
distinguished from the main body and
on which no facial features are shown, is
encircled by a zone carrying a series of
shallow round depressions, representing
a diadem, head-dress or even a helmet.
The stylised torso has anatomical details
rendered in low relief, as well as elements of dress and ornament. The arms
are folded across the stomach.
The figure wears a short under-garment;
at shoulder height has a five-row necklace, beneath which are two small pro-
trusions, probably representing breasts.
The feet are shown beneath what is
probably the hem of a long, inner garment. The back is covered with a garment from the shoulders to the waist,
while both sides have in relief a vertical,
coiling element that probably represents
a snake. The bottom of the stele acted as
its base.

Typologically the stele is a menhir-type
of object, of a kind found in south
Europe. It belongs to the eastern sub-
group found from Russia to the Balkans
(3rd millennium BC). The figure is probably female, in view of the necklace and
the distinct breasts, though most of the
east European group depict males, some
of them carrying weapons – and frequently with a suggestion of breasts too!
As with the European parallels, it is not
clear whether the stele was a gravestone
or depicted a chthonic deity(?). Together
with part of a stele from Thasos (see
Cat. No. 61) it is the earliest near life-
sized depiction in Greece of the human
figure.   S.K.

Biesantz 1957 and 1959; Theocharis 1958;
Landau 1977, 2833, 51–53, pl. 14.5; Hood
1978, 102, fig. 84; Gallis 1992; Koukouli-
Chrysanthaki 1987, 389–398; 1988,
421–425; 1989, 507–513

61   STELE

Thasos, Greece
Thasian Marble
Early Bronze Age, 3rd millennium BC
Preserved Height 39 cm, Width 28 cm,
Thickness 16 cm, Height of head 27 cm
Archaeological Museum, Thasos
Inv. No. Λ 4348

Head of an anthropomorphic stele, with
part of the neck. The face is highly

stylised in its treatment, with the basic
features cut in. At the rear is but the
stylised outline of the head, neck and the
beginning of the shoulders and back
below.
Along with other fragments of similar
stelai, including one in schist of a warrior, this fragment of an anthropomorphic stele was found built into the
fortifications and buildings of the Early
Bronze Age settlement at Skala Sotiros
on Thasos. A C-14 date of 2500–2150
BC has been assigned to the settlement.
                                    Ch.K.-C.

Koukouli-Chrysanthaki 1987, 391–406;
1988, 412–431; 1989, 507–520; 1990,
531–543

62   FIGURINE OF A MALE
   WORSHIPPER

Skoteino Cave, Crete, Greece
Bronze
Late Bronze Age, LM I, 16th century BC
Height 9 cm
Archaeological Museum, Herakleion
Inv. No. 2573

A cast bronze statuette of a votary from
the Skoteino cave, assumed by Sir Arthur
Evans to be the sacred cave of Knossos.
The right hand is placed to the forehead,
while the left arm is held by the side; a
bulky loin cloth is wrapped around the
waist.

The bronze figurines in this gesture of adoration are seen as ex votos representing the adorant themselves and thereby perpetuating their presence in the sanctuaries under divine protection.

E.B.

Evans 1932, 460; Davaras 1969, 620–650; Verlinden 1984, pl. 12.27

properties of the Mother-Goddess. Many such female terracotta figurines of various forms (see Cat. Nos. 64, 65) have been found in tombs and settlements in Mycenaean Greece, as grave goods and as votive offerings with both divine and protective qualities.

N.D.-V.

Sakellariou-Xenaki 1985, 223, pl. 105; French 1971, 143

grave goods and in shrines and houses as votive offerings. They represent a familiar female divinity with protective qualities; they have also been interpreted as childrens' toys.

N.D.-V.

Blegen 1937, 356, fig. 220; French 1971, 107ff; Demakopoulou 1988, 224, no. 211

63 FEMALE FIGURINE

Mycenae – Chamber Tomb 80, Argolid, Greece
Clay
Late Bronze Age, LH IIIA, 14th century BC
Height 13 cm
National Archaeological Museum Athens
Inv. No. 3221

Female figurine of the proto-"phi" type, with a disc-like upper body set on a cylindrical stem for the lower, and with a narrow bird-shaped head. Her modelled arms hold an infant horizontally to her breasts. The child is barely distinguishable from the main body of the figurine, apart from the head, which faces downwards. A painted decoration of oblique wavy bands on the upper body and vertical bands on the lower denote the long garment the figurine wears. On the back a long plait is visible.
This type of female figurine is also called *"kourotrophos"*, after the Greek term for a nursing-mother; she stands as a symbol for this aspect of the archetypal

64 FEMALE FIGURINE

Prosymna – Chamber Tomb 27, Argolid, Greece
Clay
Late Bronze Age, LH IIIA, 14th century BC
Height 11.4 cm
National Archaeological Museum, Athens
Inv. No. 11146

Female figurine of the "phi" type with a disc torso supported on a cylindrical stem with a conical base. The breasts and the long plait down the back are modelled. On the small, bird-like face the eyes are denoted by a painted dot. Wavy painted bands on the upper body and vertical ones on the lower suggest a long dress.
This type of small Mycenaean female figurine was mass-produced in great quantities in the 14th and 13th centuries BC and constitutes, together with the "psi" type figurines, the main expression of the Mycenaean terracotta industry. They are usually found in tombs as

65 FEMALE FIGURINE

Prosymna – Chamber Tomb 38, Argolid, Greece
Clay
Late Bronze Age, LH IIIB, 13th century BC
Height 12.3 cm
National Archaeological Museum, Athens
Inv. No. 11163

A female figurine of the "psi" type with a disc-like torso and arms upraised; two low cones denote the breasts and the lower body is formed as a cylindrical stem with conical base. The figurine is wearing a *polos* and has a long plait hanging down her back. The features of the bird-like face are painted on; the body is painted with oblique wavy and vertical bands, representing a long dress. This type of female figurine, together with the "phi" and "tau" types, constitutes the main output of Mycenaean figurine workshops, and is directly associated with the burial customs and religious expressions of the period.

N.D.-V.

Blegen 1937, 359, fig. 308, 612; French 1971, 107 ff; Demakopoulou 1988, 224, no. 212

66 FEMALE FIGURE

Tiryns – Lower Acropolis, Argolid, Greece
Clay
Late Bronze Age, LH IIIC, 12th century BC
Height 35 cm
Archaeological Museum, Nauplion
Inv. No. 26171

Large wheel-made female figure of the "psi" type related to the "goddess with upraised hands" of Minoan and Mycenaean religion. The face and body details are rendered in relief and further emphasised with decoration in brown paint. The head is almost triangular and set on a long neck. The unusual-looking face has particularly striking round eyes, pronounced eyebrows, a protruding nose and a mouth with half-open lips. On the

head is a diadem and two long applied plaits hang down the back to the hips. The raised hands are reduced to mere upcurving stumps, the breasts are low relief cones with painted nipples, the lower body is a plain tube. The necklaces and the pendant in the form of a papyrus are also painted on, as well as the decoration of the long dress.
The slight turn of the head and the restrained smile on the face of the figure imbue it with life and graciousness. It

may represent a female divinity that was worshipped, together with other similar figures, in the little shrine at Tiryns where it was found. Such large wheel-made and mainly female figures have also been found at Mycenae and Midea in the Argolid and at Phylakopi on Melos. N.D.-V.

French 1971; Kilian 1978, 463, fig. 2; Kilian 1981, 49 ff; Demakopoulou 1988, 95, no. 25

67 FIGURE OF A GODDESS WITH UPRAISED ARMS

Gazi, Crete, Greece
Clay
Late Bronze Age, LM IIIB–IIIC, 13th–12th centuries BC
Height 52 cm
Archaeological Museum, Herakleion
Inv. No. 9306
Ill. p. 10

This large female figure made of buff gritty clay, with her upraised arms and palms to the front, is well-modelled, and set on a wheel-made base. Her rounded face carries clear facial features such as eyes, eyebrows and lips; her locks of hair at the back are neatly enough rendered. The torso in comparison is relatively lifeless: the skirt is a mere cylinder rendered in that extremely stylised manner of the post-palatial period. Around the rim of her conical hat are set sacred or fertility symbols, such as the dove and the horns of consecration. Fugitive red paint suggests the torso and skirt were solid painted.
The gesture, which perhaps suggests a blessing, a greeting or an attitude of prayer, was an fixed attitude in Minoan art, possibly under the influence of Mesopotamian religious iconography. The idol was found along with four more in a rural shrine at Gazi. E.B.

Marinatos 1937, 287–291, pl. 8; Alexiou 1958, 179–299; Rethemiotakis 1990, 97, fig. 63; French 1971

68 FEMALE STATUE

Ayia Irini – Temple, Room 1, Kea, Cyclades, Greece
Clay
Late Bronze Age, "LM" I, 16th–15th centuries BC
Preserved Height 55 cm, Height head 19 cm
Archaeological Museum, Kea
Inv. No. L 3613
Ill. p. 133

The head and the upper half of the body of this almost life-size (estimated height 1.20 m) terracotta figure are preserved. An imposing female figure in a standing posture, with a solemn face and naked breasts that hang low and have plastically rendered nipples. She is wearing a garland around the neck. The two circlets on the head are interpreted as a peculiar, formal hair arrangement: the upper develops into a single twisted tress at the back that hangs down to the waist.
The figure was found in Room 1 of the Temple at Aghia Irini, along with a group of other similar female figures, all wearing long flaring skirts: they are of Minoan inspiration. Made of coarse clay, they were built from the bottom up – by adding successive strips of clay and using wooden internal supports. The statues are thought to represent goddesses or perhaps their priestesses and worshippers awaiting an epiphany of the deity. It is interesting to note that the site of the Late Bronze Age Temple at Aghia Irini had become dedicated to the god Dionysos by around 700 BC: one of the female heads, apparently found accidentally in the debris, was made into a cult image of the Geometric sanctuary. L.P.-M.

Vermeule 1964, 217, pl. XL.A; Caskey 1964, 326–331, pls. 57–58; Hood 1978, 106–108, fig. 90; Caskey 1986, 4 ff. 32–43, 46–48, pls. 8–10

69 SIGNET-RING WITH CULT SCENE

Mycenae – Chamber Tomb 66, Argolid, Greece
Gold
Late Bronze Age, LH II, 15ᵗʰ century BC
Diameter bezel 1.75–2.75 cm, Diameter hoop 1.4–1.7 cm, Weight 9.18 g
National Archaeological Museum, Athens
Inv. No. 2971
Ill. p. 194

The ring has an oval bezel, set on a hoop of trapezoidal section; it was found among the grave furnishings of chamber tomb 66 at Mycenae. The scene engraved has aroused much discussion: a bare-breasted woman is seated on a stool and points with her right hand to a standing man, who holds a stick or a spear. The man, depicted on a smaller scale, is also pointing with his left hand to the woman, as if the two of them were engaged in animated conversation. The scene has been interpreted as "sacra conversazione" between the great Goddess and a male god, her consort, the prominent figures of the Minoan-Mycenaean pantheon. That the scene might be of secular character seems less probable. Most of the gold signet-rings, which are considered masterpieces of miniature art, have scenes of a religious character.

L.P.-M.

CMS I, 101; Mylonas 1966, 158, fig. 123.18; Sakellariou-Xenaki 1985, 191, pl. 92; and 1989, 135

70 BULL FIGURE

Phylakopi, Melos, Cyclades, Greece
Clay
Late Bronze Age, LH IIIB, 13ᵗʰ century BC
Height 32.5 cm, Length 36 cm, Width 8.1 cm
Archaeological Museum, Melos
Inv. No. 653

The animal has a cylindrical, wheelmade body and muzzle, slightly tapering legs, long horns and a tail. The eyes are

applied pellets, the nostrils two punched holes and the mouth is incised. The painted decoration, of parallel sets of oblique or wavy lines, covers the body from head to tail. There is a hole pierced at the rear end.

This impressively large bovine figure comes from the niche in Room A of the West Shrine at Phylakopi on Melos. Three more bovine figures were found in the niche in the same room and there were nine bovine figures in all in both the West and the East Shrines at Phylakopi. It seems that they played an important role in the religious ritual that took place in the Sanctuary of the Mycenaean settlement at Phylakopi.

Bovine figures of a later, LH IIIC date (12ᵗʰ century BC) are also a main feature of the shrine at Amyklaion in Laconia.

L.P.-M.

French 1985, 236–240, 248, fig. 6.18–20, pls. 41a,b and 42a,b; Renfrew 1985, 425–427; Demakopoulou 1982, 57–63, pls. 27–39

71 BULL-SHAPED RHYTON WITH BULL-LEAPERS

Koumasa, Crete, Greece
Clay
Early-Middle Bronze Age, EM II–MM I, late 3ʳᵈ – early 2ⁿᵈ millennium BC
Height (with handle) 15 cm, Length 20.5 cm
Archaeological Museum, Herakleion
Inv. No. 4126

A libation vessel (rhyton) made in the shape of a bull with three tiny human figures clinging to its horns. It comes from the Early Minoan tholos tomb of Koumasa and is one of the earliest representations of bull-leaping games in Minoan art. Bull-games *(taurokathapsia)* were performed, perhaps to music, by youths and maidens; they may have been connected with fertility rites practised on days of religious festivals.

E.B.

Xanthoudides 1924, pl. II; Zervos 1956, 220.279–280; Davaras 1976, 32, fig. 20

Only in Paris

72 BULL RHYTON

Cyprus
Clay
Late Bronze Age, LC III, 1200–1050 BC
Length 13.6 cm, Height 10.2 cm
Musée du Louvre
Inv. No. DAO MNB.105

Terracotta vessel in the form of a bull: an opening on the neck allows the entry

of a liquid, a smaller one in the nozzle its exit. The horns and legs are reduced to pegs, the ears to a pinch, and the eyes are added pellets. A loop handle exists low on the neck.

Many such examples of this sort of hand-modelled rhyton exist in the Late Bronze Age. C.E.

Caubet at al. 1981, 84, pl. 12

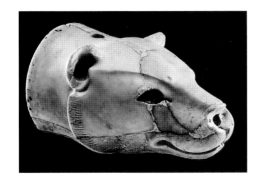

73 RHYTON IN THE SHAPE OF A LIONESS' HEAD

Knossos, Crete, Greece
Alabaster
Late Bronze Age, LM I, 16th century BC
Diameter 16 cm, Length c. 30 cm
Archaeological Museum, Herakleion
Inv. No. 44

Rhyton in the shape of a lioness' head, repaired from several pieces, fallen from a storage area for cult objects on the upper floor of the west wing of the Palace. The nozzle and eyes were inlaid with red jasper and rock crystal respectively. An excellent work of stone carving, probably inspired by metalwork.

Minoan iconography suggests a connection between the Mother Goddess (Rhea?) and her lion guardian. E.B.

Evans 1928, 826ff; Marinatos & Hirmer 1973, 99, 143

74 VOTIVE DOUBLE AXE

Arkalochori Cave, Crete, Greece
Gold
Height 4.8 cm, Width 4.0 cm
Late Bronze Age, LM I, 15th century BC
Archaeological Museum, Herakleion
Inv. No. 596
Ill. p. 12

Small gold votive axe decorated with traced lines. It was found in the cave of Arkalochori with an impressive quantity of bronze item (mainly swords, tools and other implements) and gold double axes. Although the excavator, Marinatos, considered these finds as evidence for the worship of a war-like deity, revaluation of the material tends to interpret the content of the cave as the remains of the workshop of a metal-worker, hidden away in a time of upheaval. E.B.

Marinatos 1962, 87–94; Müller-Karpe 1980, pl. 196b, no. 145

75 CUT-OUT RELIEF IN THE SHAPE OF A TRIPARTITE SHRINE

Mycenae – Grave Circle A, Shaft Grave III,
Argolid, Greece
Gold
Late Bronze Age, LH I, second half of 16th century BC
Height 7.5 cm, Width 6.9 cm
National Archaeological Museum, Athens
Inv. No. 26:1
Ill. p. 1

Of the three sections, the central is elevated and crowned by a complex set of "horns of consecration"; the two flanking wings are also topped by simpler ones. The birds with open wings, that

---

rest on the horns, indicate most probably the "epiphany" (presence) of the deity. Additional sacral elements displayed are the altar with incurved sides in the central section and the columns in the three niches near the base. Coursed masonry is depicted below them. The piece is perforated with six holes, possibly for stitching onto a costly, ceremonial garment. The image represents the Minoan tripartite shrine, known also from wall-paintings. L.P.-M.

Karo 1930–1933, 48, pl. 27.26; Hood 1978, 203, fig. 203h; Demakopoulou 1990, 281, No. 221

76 JUG WITH DOUBLE AXES

Aghia Triada, Crete, Greece
Clay
Late Bronze Age, LM I, 15th century BC
Height 28 cm
Archaeological Museum, Herakleion
Inv. No. 3936

Beaked jug, decorated in dark-on-light with double axes combined with the sacral knot motif, and with adder-mark, foliate band and stars. A fine specimen of the so-called Alternating Style in the special Palatial Tradition, possibly used for ritual purposes. E.B.

Marinatos & Hirmer 1973, 141, fig. 82 left; Betancourt 1985, 146

77 ROCK CARVING OF SHIP

Engelstrup (Grevinge, Holbæk), Denmark

Granite

Late Bronze Age, Periods IV–V,

11th–8th centuries BC

58 x 65 x 40 cm

National Museum, Copenhagen

Inv. No. B 6988

The Engelstrup stone was found in a stone wall in 1875. The stone is of granite and has a flat side on which are worked two ships, four people, an animal and a circle. The human figures and the animal are grouped around the large ship, which is manned by seventeen men indicated by vertical strokes. The other figures are characterised by circles for heads and stick-bodies and limbs. Two people are standing, one at the stern and one above the large ship. Below it are two others, one each side of the circle. One is a woman with long hair which streams out from the back of her head, and between her legs there is a cup-mark. The other figure has no particular distinguishing features but is probably a man. He is standing with a hand raised towards the circle, while the woman looks as if she is in rapid motion with widespread legs and both arms up in the air. The theme is evidently a dance around a picture of the sun or some other cult-object.   J.J.

Brondsted 1962, 129; Glob 1969, no. 36; Jensen 1988, 283; Kjærum & Olsen 1990, no. 16

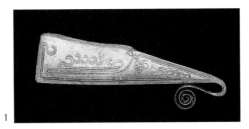

1

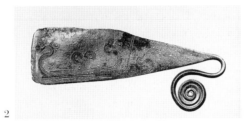

2

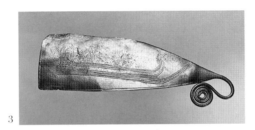

3

4

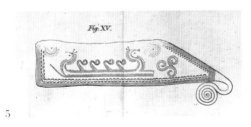

Fig. XV.

5

78 RAZORS DISPLAYING SHIPS

Denmark

Bronze

Late Bronze Age, Periods IV–V,

11th–8th centuries BC

National Museum, Copenhagen

Inv. Nos. UI/365, UI/366, MCCCXCVI, B 10127, B 9057

Razors from different findspots in Denmark, decorated with ships of a mythological nature. The motif of the ship had an overwhelming importance in Bronze Age art of this north European region: Denmark, along with south Sweden and northwest Germany, provides many such instances on a variety of bronze objects, primarily razors. Although the ship motif of the Bronze Age is evidently loaded with symbolism, such ships were probably based on actual ones. Valuable information concerning beliefs and rituals in which the ship evidently played a substantial role can be obtained from these objects.

1. Two ships set one above the other; the lowermost is a "folded" ship. Both ships have spiral-curls.
2. A large ship with both row and stern ending in a horse's head, set over a "folded" ship. The large ship is carrying a spiral-volute pattern.
3. One large ship with imposing horse-headed prow.
4. Five ships are portrayed on this broad blade.
5. One large ship with imposing horse-headed prow and sternpost. Note the manes and the elegantly curved muzzles.

F.K.

Kaul 1998

79 MODEL OF A BOAT

Caergwrle, Clwyd, Wales, Great Britain

Schist, tin and gold

Late Bronze Age or Early Iron age,

c. 1000–500 BC

Length 18.2 cm, Width 11.1 cm,

Height 7.6 cm

National Museums & Galleries of Wales, Cardiff

Inv. No. 12.128

This model of a boat was found in a bog – probably one of those objects that were deliberately disposed of. It is a bowl-shaped artefact whose surface is decorated with gold leaf. It arguably represents a model of a plank boat, or *curragh*. The lower half of the boat is covered with rows of zigzag lines that are probably meant to suggest water. These lines

end at the bow of the ship in two stylised depictions of eyes. Beneath the rim is a gold band on which is seen a series of concentric circles that could be read as sun ornaments.

The significance of the bowl is much debated. Some scholars go so far as to connect it with the ships of legendary Tartessos in southwest Spain. Both the nature of the object and the manner of its deposition suggest some form of cult or religious use. A.J./F.V.

Göttlicher 1978, no. 587; Giardino 1995, 265; Avant les Celtes 1988, 66–67, no. 8.05.05

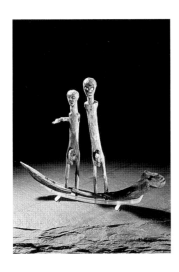

80   MODEL OF A BOAT

Roos Carr, Holderness, Yorkshire, Great Britain
Wood
7th– 6th centuries BC
Length 51 cm, Weight 600 g
Hull and East Riding Museum, Hull
Inv. No. KINCM 1997.134

In 1836 some labourers, employed in cleaning a dyke or ditch, discovered at about six feet below the surface in a bed of blue clay a group of figures, rudely carved in wood. The base or foundation of the group is a canoe or boat; the prow is given "eyes" of small pieces of quartz. The figures are set close together, and are nearly identical, the only difference being in their height. Each represents a warrior – apparently entirely naked, originally armed with a club and carrying round shields. The eyes of each warrior are formed from small pieces of quartz. J.J.

Lindqvist 1942, 235–242; Göttlicher 1978, no. 587

81   AMBER, NATURAL PIECE

Fanø, Jutland, Denmark
Amber
Weight 3 kg, Size 25 x 18 x 13 cm
National Museum, Copenhagen
Inv. No. A 34654

Unworked piece of amber from the island of Fanø, off the west coast of Jutland. The main sources of amber are in the area around the Baltic Sea: here, after storms, large quantities are washed up on the shores from submarine deposits.

In prehistory amber was used extensively for the manufacture of beads and other ornaments. In the Stone Age it was only used in areas close to the Baltic sources, but at the end of the 3rd millennium its distribution expanded over much of Europe. This expansion was clearly related to the rise of social hierarchies and their need for symbolic differentiation. In that respect, amber played the same role as other exotic and highly valued materials like gold, tin, copper, jet, jade etc. The amber had to be obtained by long-distance exchange, and during the Bronze Age it is found in the greatest quantities in areas which are also rich in other materials. J.J.

Beck et al. 1964; Beck 1974; Jensen 1982; Shennan 1982; Fraquet 1987; Schulz 1993; Grimaldi 1996

82   HOARD OF UNWORKED AMBER

Understed, Hjørring, Jutland, Denmark
Amber, bronze
Middle Bronze Age, Period II, c. 1400 BC
Weight amber 3.3 kg
National Museum, Copenhagen
Inv. No. B 573-574

Amber was collected in great quantities along the Danish coasts in the Bronze Age. The unworked amber in the hoard of Understed was found in a clay pot, together with two bronze collars dating to Period II, c. 1400 BC. Such deposits are sometimes found buried in the houses of Danish Bronze Age settlements, especially along the west coast of Jutland. In Danish Bronze Age graves, however, amber is relatively rare.　J.J.

Brøndsted 1958; Jensen 1982, 72ff

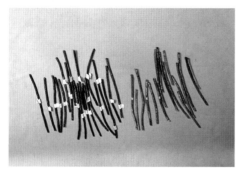

83 HOARD OF BEADS

Cioclovina, Bosorod, Hunedoara, Rumania
Amber, faience, glass, antler, bronze and tin
Middle Bronze Age, c. 1300 BC
Museul National de Istorie a Romaniei,
Bucarest
Inv. Nos. IV 638–75; 679–87; 701–850;
310001-32710

Sacrificial deposit or hoard consisting of, among other things, more than 1500 large and small "buttons", 80 lunate pendants, fourteen spiral discs of wire, 250 twisted wire elements, seventeen small staples and some 3000 beads, of which about 1000 are amber, 500 of faience and 1500 of blue glass, both simple and double in form.
The first group of these objects was discovered in 1953, and the second part in the years following. The site of the find was the water-filled cave of Cioclovina,

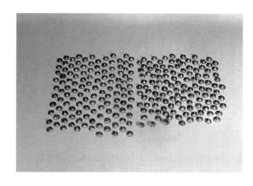

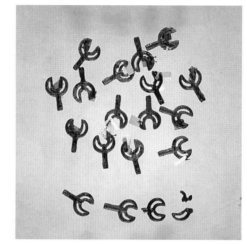

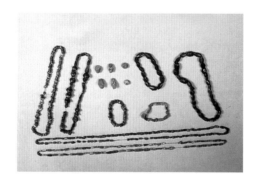

from which the Luncanilor stream flows. The region is very rich in karst formations.
The majority of the pieces were found in a higher gallery from which a precipitous drop leads to the main gallery. The pieces were deposited in several piles – two of which were substantial – but individual pieces were also scattered among the blocks of rocks in the middle of the gallery or in cracks. The hoard may have deposited in a deliberately dispersed way, because at least five groups of it were found several metres apart from each other. All of the pieces were found

directly on the ground, probably with a votive purpose, perhaps as a cenotaph. Discovered in the central Mures basin, an area rich in salt, this material may have resulted from intensive trading with areas that had tin, such as Bohemia or Saxony, or with the northern Baltic region, where amber was available (although amber was available closer to hand – in the region of middle Carpathia, near Buzau). The southern Aegean is another place from which glass beads might have been obtained.　G.T.

Comşa 1966, 169–174; Petrescu-Dîmboviţa
1977, 89–90, fig. 132; and 1978, 117–118,
no. 129; Emödi 1978, 481ff

84 NECKLACE

Mycenae – Chamber Tomb 518, Argolid,
Greece
Amber
Late Bronze Age, LH I–II,
16th–15th centuries BC
Diameter 1–4.5, Thickness beads 0.5–1.5 cm
National Archaeological Museum, Athens
Inv. No. 6433

The necklace consists of ninety-eight (biconical, spherical, depressed spherical and discoid) beads of amber in a range of sizes and in a rather good state of preservation. Amber was a precious material imported in the form of ready-made jewellery from north and north-west Europe. Its presence proves the existence of trade connections between

232

Mycenaean Greece and Continental Europe during the early Mycenaean period. N.D.-V.

Wace 1932, 86, fig. 34; Hughes-Brock 1985, 257–267; Demakopoulou 1988, 257, no. 281

85 CUP

Hove, Sussex, England
Amber
Wessex Culture, 18th –17th centuries BC
Diameter 9 cm
Royal Pavilion, Libraries & Museums, Brighton
Inv. No. R 5643/1 (230608)
Ill. p. 40

Amber cup, highly polished, of hemispherical form: slightly everted rim over broad groove set off by a band of five incised lines. The vertical ribbon handle is strongly curved and splays out at top and bottom where it joins the cup; two incised lines are worked across the top of handle and two sets of five more flank its outer edges.

It was found in a barrow excavated in 1821. The grave consisted of a tree-trunk coffin with decayed bones; the grave-goods were found in centre of the coffin, as if they had been resting on the breast of the corpse. The amber cup was found together with a bronze dagger, a whetstone-pendant and a stone battle-axe. J.J.

Gerloff 1975, no. 183; Müller-Karpe 1980, pl. 475H, no. 1027; Jensen 1982, 97; Clarke et al. 1985, 117; Grimaldi 1996, 147

86 NECKLACE

Blindmill, Rothie, Aberdeenshire, Scotland
Jet
Early Bronze Age, c. 2400–1700 BC
Royal Museum of Scotland, Edinburgh
Inv. No. E.Q. 85
Ill. p. 41

The necklace consists of a triangular fastener, a pair of triangular terminal plates, two sets of three spacer plates and fourteen extant beads; the others in the necklace are reconstructions. The necklace has only three strands throughout; most others of this class have multiple strands at the front, up to seven or eight. Notwithstanding these unusual features, the necklace is a fine example of the "spacer-plate" type, and its formal similarities with lunulae and amber "spacer-plate" necklaces are obvious. Jet occurs only rarely in Britain, in narrow strata amidst the fine-grained Cannel coals that are exposed in cliff falls and exposures along the eastern coast of North Yorkshire. Other jet-related substances may have been used, such as cannel coal and lignite, from Brora in Sutherland or shale from Kimmeridge in Dorset. Another source may have been the black lignitic shales commonly found as glacial erratics in the boulder clays of northern and eastern England. J.J.

Shepherd 1981; Clarke et al. 1985, 204; Davis & Sheridan 1993, 455–456

87 SAMPLES OF MINERALS

Geowissenschaftliche Sammlungen der Bergakademie Freiberg, Germany

3

4

5

6

1

2

7

233

The most important copper ore is chalcopyrite. Other well-known copper ores include cuprite, malachite and azurite. The most important, easily accessible deposits of copper ore are found along the coastal regions of the Atlantic Ocean, in the Alps, the Bohemian Erzgebirge, in the southern Balkans and Caucasia. Tin deposits are much rarer. During the Bronze Age, the deposits along the Atlantic coast, in the Bohemian Erzgebirge and in northwest Italy were being mined. J.J.

Various copper ores:
1: Chalcopyrite
2: Azurite
3: Malachite, chalcopyrite
4: Chalcopyrite from Victoria Mine, Müsen, North Rhine-Westphalia, Germany
5: Native copper from the Lizard, Cornwall, Great Britain
6: Azurite from Rudobanya, Hungary
7: Malachite from Gumesharsk, Urals, Russia

Only Copenhagen, Bonn and Athens
88   AXES

Le Pecq, Yvelines, France
Jadeite
3rd millennium BC
Length 15–18 cm
Musée des Antiquités Nationales, St. Germain-en-Laye
Inv. No. 86552

Jadeite axes are longer, on average, than axes of other materials, and very flat in section. This makes them substantially less robust, so that they are unlikely to have been intended for practical use but probably served rather as status symbols.

Their high value derived in part from the workmanship but especially from the material used in their production. This greenish stone is found in only a few places, so that it often had to be traded across great distances. It is thought that at this time the jadeite deposits in the West Alps were being exploited.
A.J./F.V.

Unpublished

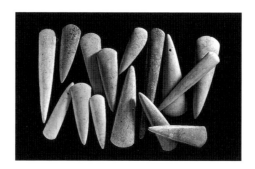

Only in Paris
89   POLISHED STONE AXES

Arzon, Morbihan, France
Stone
Neolithic
Length 14.5–30 cm
Musée des Antiquités Nationales, St. Germain-en-Laye
Inv. Nos. 34171–34181

90   HOARD OF DAGGERS

Hårbølle, Fanefjord, Præstø, Denmark
Flint
Late Neolithic, c. 2000 BC
Length 20–26 cm
National Museum, Copenhagen
Inv. Nos. A 38854–64

At the transition from the Neolithic to the Bronze Age, daggers were prized weapons and symbols of power throughout Europe. In Denmark the flint dagger played an exceptionally prominent role because the country lacked metal-bearing ore deposits and so the good local flint was utilised instead. These pressure-flaked daggers are made with eminent skill: some of the later ones are clearly imitations of metal daggers – even of swords. Their quality no doubt explains why the daggers were exported to many parts of Europe. They are found, for example, in the Baltic countries, in England and in central Europe. The daggers had to be made from large pieces of high quality flint and the best was mined from underground chalk deposits in two parts of Denmark: in the Møn-Stevns area (Zealand) and by the Limfjorden (Jutland). Deposits of daggers in mint condition have been found in both areas. J.J.

Lomborg 1973; Glob 1980, no 2

234

91 SCIMITAR/CURVED-TIP SWORD

Faurskov, Kerte, Funen, Denmark

Flint

Early Bronze Age, Period I, c. 1500 BC

Length 35.5 cm

National Museum, Copenhagen

Inv. No. 9192

In Northern Europe bronze was a rare and highly-valued material. Therefore, flint was sometimes used to copy metal products. This pressure-flaked flint sword, copied from a bronze equivalent (see Cat. No. 92), was found as a stray find.   J.J.

Rønne 1986; Lomborg 1973, 62–63; Glob 1952, no. 519

92 SCIMITAR/CURVED-TIP SWORD

Rørby, Holbæk, Zealand, Denmark

Bronze

Early Bronze Age, Period I, c. 1500 BC

Length 60.7 cm

National Museum, Copenhagen

Inv. No. B 14174

A scimitar of bronze was found in 1952 during drainage work in a bog; in 1957 a second was found at the same place. The two swords undoubtedly formed but a single deposit, presumably of a votive nature. Most probably they have been locally made in imitation of swords from the Carpathian Basin. A similar sword is known from south Sweden.   J.J.

Mathiassen 1952, 229 ff; and 1957, 38 ff

93 RING-INGOTS

Aschering, Starnberg, Bavaria, Germany

Copper

Early Bronze Age, c. 2000–1600 BC

Prähistorische Staatssammlung, München

Inv. No. 1921.8

The hoard contains sixty-five ring-ingots. Ingot hoards, which often contain more than a hundred, are found from south Germany through Austria and the Czech Republic into the Carpathians. Two groups of ingot hoards can be distinguished. One group, to which the hoard at Aschering belongs, consists entirely of ingots; the other group contains objects of other kinds.

The ring-ingots, which are usually pure copper, served as "pre-monetary" trade or exchange standards. They can be subdivided into a number of distinct classes by weight: progressing from ingots the size of finger-rings upwards to those the size of bracelets and necklaces. Indeed, the ring form was probably chosen in the first place because it reflected the basic blank of the popular necklace form.

A.J./F.V.

Lenerz-de Wilde 1995, 229 ff (F 2); Innerhofer 1997, 53 ff

94 BATTLE AXE

Someseni, Cluj, Rumania

Bronze

Middle Bronze Age, Wietenberg culture, 15th–14th centuries BC

Length 21.7 cm, Diameter 8 cm

Museul National de Istorie a Romaniei, Bucarest

Inv. No. 15.911

Collared axe with tubular shaft. The collar acts as a brace for the hafted handle. The cross-arm expands towards the offset blade.

Axes of this type are found in several variant forms; they were used over a long period of time; and over a wide area – originating in the Carpathian basin (northeast Hungary and Transylvania), by exchange they spread throughout large regions of central and north Europe.

The entire surface is decorated: on the disc there is a spiral with four hooks; on the surface of the blade is a chain pattern of spiral hooks between hatched triangles with uniform dots and horizontal garlands. On the narrower side there are bands of parallel lines, hatched triangles with uniform dots, concentric semicircles, etc.   G.T.

Schönbäck & Sofka 1970, no 18; Dumitrescu 1974, 367, fig. 408

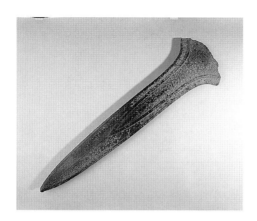

95   CEREMONIAL SWORD

Plougrescant, Côtes-du-Nord, France
Bronze
Middle Bronze Age, c. 1200 BC
Length 66.5 cm, Weight 2180 g
Musée des Antiquités Nationales,
St. Germain-en-Laye
Inv. No. 7600

Very large sword blade found in Brittany
in 1845. It was presumably produced for
cult purposes: the blade reveals no traces
for fixing a hilt; the shoulders have no
rivet holes; the edges are not sharp. The
type is named after a hoard found near
Ommerschans in Holland; all such stab-
bing swords were probably produced by
one and the same bronze founder. They
are good indicators of the great geographic distances over which certain
bronze objects could travel: Ommer-
schans-Plougrescant swords are found in
two places in Holland, two in France
and one in England (Norfolk).   J.J.

Butler & Bakker 1961; Briard 1965, fig.
28.2; Butler & Sarfatij 1971; Clarke et al.
1985, 102.318–319

Only in Copenhagen, Bonn and Athens

96   AXE

Kersoufflet, Le Faouët, Morbihan, Brittany,
France
Copper
Late Neolithic to Early Bronze Age
Height sleeve 54.5 cm, Length axe 24.4 cm,
Weight 2.7 kg
Musée des Antiquités Nationales,
St. Germain-en-Laye
Inv. No. 73764

The copper axe from Kersoufflet, Brittany, was found in 1882. It is said to
have been found in a mound lacking all
traces of a grave. A second example was
found at Trévé (Côte-d'Armor). It is difficult to date these isolated objects which
are only known in Brittany, but probably
they are from the end of the 3rd millennium BC.   C.E.

Briard 1965, fig. 11, no. 2; Jacob-Friesen
1970, 53, fig. 12

Only in Paris

97   AXE

Trévé or Loudéac, Côtes-du-Nord, Brittany,
France
Copper
Late Neolithic to Early Bronze Age
Height 29 cm, Width axe 17 cm
Musée des Antiquités Nationales,
St. Germain-en-Laye
Inv. No. 17048

This axe is often mentioned in connection with the preceding axe from Kersoufflet. They pose the same problems of
chronology and cultural significance. It
is difficult to date these isolated objects
which are only known in Brittany, but
probably they are from the end of the
3rd millennium BC.   C.E.

Briard 1965, fig. 11, no. 11; Jacob-Friesen
1970, 53, fig. 11

98   AXE

Bebra, Hersfeld-Rotenburg, Hesse, Germany
Copper
Late Neolithic to later Early Bronze Age
Length of shaft 40 cm, Length axehead
28.7 cm
Hessisches Landesmuseum für Vor- und
Frühgeschichte, Kassel
Inv. No. 1253

The axe was discovered as an isolated
find in 1905: a hammer-axe of the
Eschollbrücken type, cast entirely of
copper in a single process. A distinctive
feature of this type is a blade whose cut-

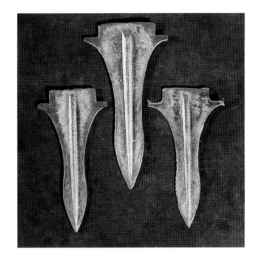

ting edge is expanded and set off; they may have a circular shaft-hole or, as in the present instance, the metal equivalent of a wooden handle. For most axes the line of the head is slightly arched. Several, like this axe from Bebra, have a prominent collar at the shaft-hole area. On one side of its blade there are traces of an angled linear pattern.

Found largely in the west part of central Europe, axes of the Eschollbrücken type are made of nearly pure copper: they almost never contain arsenic or tin and their blades are seldom very sharp. Consequently, they should be seen as primarily intended as ornamental status symbols. It is possible that the models for the form of these copper axes can be found in certain stone ones, as they resemble those produced by the Corded Ware culture.   A.J./F.V.

Jacob-Friesen 1970, 28ff; Müller-Karpe 1974, pl. 505.B5; Kibbert 1980

99   DAGGERS

Perșinari, Dâmbovița, Rumania
Gold
Middle Bronze Age, 17th (–16th?) century BC
Length 18.8–19.2–22.5 cm
Muzeul National de Istorie a Romaniei,
Bucarest
Inv. Nos. P23234, P23240, P23242

Gold daggers from a hoard consisting of a gold sword, several silver axes and twelve gold daggers: chance discoveries made between 1954–1976. The sword and the daggers imitated Mycenaean types, thus illustrating connections between the culture existing in north Thrace and that of the Aegean.
The hoard was recovered from the area of the Tei culture, generally dated to the 17th century BC (the Middle Bronze Age), though recently an earlier date, about 2200–2100 BC, has been proposed.   D.L.

Gimbutas 1965, 55ff; Zaharia 1968, 125ff, pl. 5.h; Vulpe 1978, 106; Müller-Karpe 1980, pl. 281A, no. 279; Leahu 1988, 232ff; Bader 1990, 185; Petrescu-Dîmbovița et al. 1995, 122ff; Vulpe 1995

100   PECTORAL AND DAGGER

Villafranca-Veronese, Italy
Silver and copper
Early Bronze Age, Remedello culture,
c. 2000 BC
Pectoral Diameter 20 cm, Weight 100 g;
Dagger Length 36.2 cm
Museo Civico di Storia Naturale, Verona
Inv. Nos. 2230–31

These objects were found in a grave that must have been, to judge from the goods found in it, that of a "tribal prince" from the Villafranca-Veronese region. The dagger, which originally had an offset handle, belongs to the Villafranca-Tivoli group. Of the four known examples of this type, three are from north Italy and the other is from the centre. They were probably intended less as weapons than as status symbols. The lunate pectoral is made of silver and decorated with embossed dots. Several stone arrowheads were also found in the grave.   A.J./F.V.

Peroni 1978; and 1994, no. 35, pl. 4.35

Only in Copenhagen, Bonn and Athens
101   INGOTS AND TOOLS

Larnaud, Jura, France
Bronze
Late Bronze Age
Total weight 66 kg
Musée des Antiquités Nationales,
St.Germain-en-Laye
Inv. Nos. 21571, 21614, 21628, 21630,
21635, 21638–21641, 21645, 21648–49,
21651, 21669, 21670A+B, 21677, 21684,
21707, 21712, 21751

This hoard was discovered in 1865. It consists of nearly 1500 objects with a total weight of 66 kilos: most show some signs of damage; some are only fragmentary.

This hoard contains objects covering a wide spectrum of functions. The *tools* include sickles, winged and socketed axes and various types of chisels. The *weapons* are primarily swords, spears and arrowheads; the *utensils* include many knives. The *jewellery* comprises many arm-rings, pins, belthooks and pendants, a variety of highly decorated and appliquéd metal sheets, decorative discs, tin rattles and ornaments. There are also fragments of *toilet items*, like razor blades; as well as *practical objects* such as bridle-gear for horses. Several of the pieces of metal sheet may also have originally intended for horse-trappings. Hoards of this sort are usually taken to be deposits left by traders or craftsmen. As the material value of this one would have been significant, it is possible that it belonged to a community of such; but the possibility that the objects were deposited for cult reasons cannot be completely excluded either.　　　A.J./F.V.

Coutil 1913, 451ff; Millotte 1963, 307

102　METAL-WORKING TOOLS

Génelard, Saône-et-Loire, France
Bronze
Late Bronze Age, c. 1000 BC
Lengths 2.2 to 25 cm
Musée Archéologique, Chalon-sur-Saône
Inv. Nos. 85.2.1. – 85.2.50
Ill. p. 32

This hoard came to light in 1975 during the digging of the foundations for a house. It basically consists of a remarkably complete set of tools for a metalworker, who was probably also a founder. The tools include raising hammers – one of which has a rectangular socket, the other round; both are decorated with anthropomorphic attributes (stumps of

arms and two breasts on each side), as well as a finishing hammer with a round socket. They go together with two anvils (one cruciform, the other rectangular) of solid proportions, with a large base and hole to secure each by. A conical stake with a fixing tang, a grooved block, a set of punches with which to impress concentric-circle patterns, others to achieve other effects, an embossing tool and a tracing compass – all are evidence of work with sheet metal. A T-shaped instrument with a cross-piece and prominently projecting sides defies comprehension still – as do some conical tubes. Part of a ring-shaped mould in bronze; a bronze bowl-shaped funnel, a modelling knife and two tanged knives with identical patterns of rivet-holes together suggest that the owner was also active in casting bronze. Other objects such as bar-ingots, a knife blade, a spearhead and a broken knife handle could argue for either work in progress or scrap. The hoard seems from its cruciform anvil very akin to others recovered in the Burgundy area, like those of Gray and Alise-Sainte-Reine. It also has similarities with material from the hoard of Larnaud (Jura).　　　C.E.

Cat. Archéologie de la France 1989, 208, no. 114; Darteville 1986

103　HOARD OF WEAPONS

Kozí Hrbety, Horomerice, Prag-zábad, Bohemia, Czech Republic
Bronze
Early Bronze Age, Únětice Culture, 18th–17th centuries BC
Narodni muzeum, Prague
Inv. Nos. 37493–37501
Ill. p. 103

Hoard of weapons of the Únětice culture, found in 1928 in the vicinity of Prague, then in Czechoslovakia. The hoard contained seven bronze daggers (and the blade of another), some with solid and some with socketed handles. One of the

handles is decorated with gold-capped rivets and amber. These elegant weapons were probably votive offerings.

Several hoards with valuable weapons are known from the Únětice culture, in particular in the region around Halle, in central Germany. One of the largest hoards from this region, that of Dieskau, contained 293 axes, as well as daggers and rings. The prized bronze weapons and tools travelled from the Únětice region to north Germany and south Scandinavia. Such rich hoards are evidence that the Únětice region had plentiful deposits of copper ore, salt and other raw materials.　　　J.J.

Böhm 1928–30, 1ff; Müller-Karpe 1980, pl. 299F, no. 433

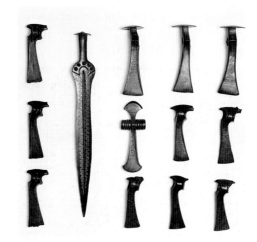

104　HOARD OF WEAPONS

Hajdúsámson, Hajdú-Bihar, Hungary
Bronze
Middle Bronze Age, 16th–15th centuries BC
Length sword 53 cm, axes 16–28 cm
Déri Múzeum, Debrezen
Inv. Nos. DMD 1907/1204–1214; 1907/1216; 95.6.
Ill. p. 89

Hoard of bronze weapons, discovered in 1907 near Hajdúsámson in northeast Hungary. This hoard is one of the richest of the Middle Bronze Age in the Carpathian basin. The weapons were

238

probably placed originally in some then flowing part of the river Szamos. The hoard consists of a short sword with a solid hilt and a blade with spiral decoration, one decorated and two undecorated battle axes, and eight more with spiral decoration. Both the form and decoration of the weapons reveal influences from the Aegean region, as well as from places to east and north. The composition of the hoard indicates the central position enjoyed by the Carpathian basin in the period around 1500 BC: from Hungary and Rumania valuable bronze objects travelled far into the north – even into south Scandinavia, where numerous swords parallel to those in the Hajdúsámson hoard have been found.

J.J.

Childe 1929; Mozsolics 1967; Vulpe 1970, pl. 69A; Müller-Karpe 1980, no. 349, pl. 289A

105   GRAVE ASSEMBLAGE

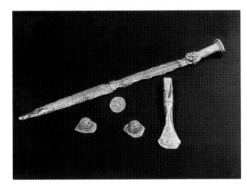

Aabygaard, Nyker, Bornholm, Denmark.
Bronze and gold
Early Bronze Age, Period II, 14th century BC
National Museum, Copenhagen
Inv. Nos. MDCXIX, MDCXXI–XXIV

In the period around 1400 BC the dead of south Scandinavia and north Germany were often buried in mounds. The grave itself would be either an oak coffin or a stone cist. This grave of a wealthy man was supplied with a bronze hilted sword and a highly decorated battle axe that probably had originally been fitted with a angled wooden shaft. The attire

of the dead man included two small bronze "buttons", their bosses treated to circle based patterns with zones of dots and zigzags about them: the gaps between these elements were filled with some resinous substance. His possessions also included a pommel with spiral decorations and set with amber. On his wrist the dead man wore a gold bracelet with ends split and made into spiral finials.

J.J.

Broholm 1943, 58, no. 376; Aner & Kersten 3, no. 1503; Randsborg 1968

106   GRAVE ASSEMBLAGE

Hverrehus, Viborg, Jutland, Denmark
Bronze
Early Bronze Age, Period II, 14th century BC
National Museum, Copenhagen
Inv. Nos. B 13259–67

In most of the graves from the Bronze Age all of the organic material has decomposed over the course of the centuries: as here with this rich grave where only the jewellery of the dead woman has survived. The deceased wore a neck-collar, a large disc on her belt, a dagger and a comb. Her wrists were adorned with bronze bracelets, and fourteen small "buttons" in all were attached to her clothing. The grave also contained a substantial quantity of small bronze tubes of sheet metal, in which were found the remains of threads that had

survived as a result of contact with the metal. The dead woman was therefore probably wearing a cord-dress, of the type that is familiar from several well-preserved graves with oak coffins – for example, that from the grave near Egtved. At the lower hemline the small bronze tubes were attached and would have tinkled like bells with the woman's every movement.

J.J.

Thomsen 1929; Broholm 1940, 117 ff; and 1943, no. 728

107   GRAVE ASSEMBLAGE

Gollern, Uelzen, Lower Saxony, Germany
Bronze and stone
Early Bronze Age, 14th century BC
Length sword 62.2 cm, flanged-axe 14.8 cm, spear 21.2 cm, pin 12.9 cm
Hamburger Museum für Archäologie und die Geschichte Harburgs
Inv. Nos. 1902:77–101

The body of the dead man of the Lüneburg culture was oriented east-west. The grave was piled about by stones and then covered with earth. A flange-hilted sword, a north German flanged-axe and a Lüneburg thrusting spear (with fragments of wood left in the socket) were deposited in the grave: along with a pin with a large biconical head and a decorated shaft, as well as a rectangular whetstone.

The grave is that of a comparatively wealthy warrior from a cultural region much given to displays of weaponry.

A.J./F.V.

Laux 1971. no. 478. pl. 45.1–5

108   GRAVE ASSEMBLAGE

Wardböhmen, Bergen, Celle, Germany

Bronze

Early Bronze Age, 14th century BC

Length disc-pin 24 cm, belthook 8.6 cm,

Diameter necklace A 13 cm, spiked discs

6.5 cm, arm-spirals 6.5 cm, leg ornament

9 cm, anklet 8.5 cm

Niedersächsisches Landesmuseum, Hannover

Inv. Nos. 1156–61:76, 1168–70:76,

1172–74:76

The skeleton of a lady of the Lüneberg culture lay in a tree-trunk coffin, under a mound. The grave goods were made up solely of dress accessories, such as a pin, which based on its position near the head must have served to control the hair or to decorate the same, and two necklaces of which one is made from large spiral-wound beads and a large bronze disc with a central boss decorated with running spirals. The second necklace is made from alternating spiral-wound beads and six discs with spiked central devices. Other accessories include a Lüneburg disc-pin decorated with bosses, lines and dots, an ornamented willowleaf-shaped belt-hook, a finger

240

ring, a leg-ring (made of round-sectioned rod) and a anklet with a milled decoration around the edges.   A.J./F.V.

Wegner 1996, 103, 289ff

Only in Copenhagen and Bonn

109   BOAR'S TUSK

Karlsruhe-Neureuth, Rheinbett, Germany

Boar's tusk and bronze

Middle Bronze Age, 15th–12th centuries BC

Length 21 cm

Badisches Landesmuseum, Karlsruhe

Inv. No. 88/0-24

Ill. p. 85

The tusk was found in early 1988. Although the circumstances of the find can no longer be understood in detail, it probably belongs to a group of objects that were deliberately deposited in running or standing water, and consequently should be thought of as a votive offering. In the present case, it cannot be decided with certainty whether the deposition was made in a flowing stream or in an old branch of the Rhine.

The larger end of the tusk is encased in a sleeve made of a sheet bronze and its entire length is incorporated in a braided framework of strong bronze wire. No direct parallel for this treatment of the tusk has been found, though a few close examples (see Cat. No. 110) are known from graves in northeast France.   J.J.

Behrends 1993

Only in Copenhagen and Bonn

110   BOAR'S TUSK MOUNTED IN A FRAME OF WIRE

La Colombine – tomb 101, Yonne, France

Boar's tusk and bronze

Late Bronze Age

Length 25 cm

Musée des Antiquités Nationales,

St. Germain-en-Laye

Inv. No. 82 952

Ill. p. 80

This piece of jewellery was found in a woman's inhumation grave during excavations at the cemetery of La Colombine that were carried out between 1920 and 1939. Other ornaments – bracelets, leggings, a pin, appliqué items – and a vase complete the grave goods. This is the earliest recorded example of this sort of ornament involving a boar's tusk, though it is not clear how such functioned (part of a diadem or a pectoral?). Similar jewellery has been found in a series of graves to the east of the Paris basin.   C.E.

Lacroix 1957, 167; Mordant & Mohen 1996, 466–471

111   FEMALE FIGURINE

Cîrna-Dunareni, Dolj, Rumania

Clay

Middle Bronze Age, 16th century BC

Height 15.6 cm, Diameter 6.8 cm

Museul National de Istorie a Romaniei,

Bucarest

Inv. No. 13.461

Discovered in a cremation tomb, this piece shows a woman in a bell-shaped dress. The head is reduced to a narrow peg-like projection; the disc-like upper torso has its schematic and three-fingered arms portrayed in low relief and resting on its stomach. The waist is slender, the dress cylindrical.

The entire surface is decorated by incised lines picked out by a white filling. On the breast there is a lunate pendant with a central device terminating in a butterfly or an arrow. The waist is encircled by a belt that is depicted by several rows of dashes. The dress is decorated with spirals of various sorts, zigzags, a complicated cruciform design, and with small impressed circles fringed by dots.

On the back, four braids hang down from the head. A curved line, bordered below by sixteen small holes (beads, medallions, pendants?), further decorates the rear of the upper torso. G.T.

Dumitrescu 1961, 149, 251, pl. 154; Müller-Karpe 1980, pl. 326, no. 253

112   KNIFE WITH HILT IN FORM OF FEMALE FIGURE

Beringstedt, Itzehoe, Schleswig-Holstein, Germany

Bronze

Late Bronze Age, Period V,

9th–8th centuries BC

Length 11 cm

National Museum, Copenhagen

Inv. No. OA. VIIe 86

Ill. p. 58

This knife comes from a stone cist near Beringstedt, north of Itzehoe. The broken blade is decorated with an image of a ship; the handle is in the form of a small female figure dressed in a woollen skirt of the type found in Bronze Age oak coffin graves of the North. She is wearing two neck rings, a bag at the back of her belt and an earring in her oversized ear. J.J.

Coles & Harding 1979, pl. 23b; Jockenhövel & Kubach 1994, 79

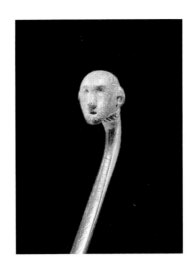

113   PIN WITH HUMAN HEAD

Horne, Svendborg, Funen, Denmark.

Bronze

Late Bronze Age, Period IV,

11th–9th centuries BC

Length 8.5 cm

National Museum, Copenhagen

Inv. No. B 217

The dress-pin with a small female head at its thickened top was found in an urn. The facial characterisation is rather ill-defined, though the arrangement of the hair is reproduced in fine detail.

The head follows the norms which generally govern Bronze Age representations of faces: namely, low forehead, strongly pronounced eyes and brows, long nose, pointed chin and ears reduced to circles to hold the heavy, high-status jewellery. The hairstyle is cut quite short at the sides, while a long lock falls from the crown down over the neck. J.J.

Broholm 1953, no. 65; Munksgaard 1974, 82 ff, fig. 57b; Jensen 1979, 40; Kjærum & Olsen 1990

114   PLATE DECORATED WITH FOIL

Cortaillod, Switzerland

Clay and tin

Late Bronze Age, 9th–8th centuries BC

Diameter 35 cm

Museum Schwab, Bienne

Inv. No. Cd 6220

The plate, along with two other fragments of vessels decorated with tin, comes from the lakeside settlement of Cortaillod. The outer surface is blackened with graphite so that the lighter tin-leaf stands out clearly against the background. The interior of the plate is divided into four bands of decoration that are organised concentrically. The two inner zones are filled with rectangles, followed by a meander pattern and finally a fir-tree pattern at the rim. Such patterns are created by embedding strips of tin in the clay or, as here, by working tin-leaf into grooves already made in the clay. Vessels decorated with tin-leaf are found from north Italy to south Germany.

In general, the use of tin seems to represent a certain desire for luxury among the upper class. Tin was transported over great distances, whereas the vessels were probably produced locally. A.J./F.V.

Stjernquist 1958, 17, fig. 11; Fischer 1993, 17–24

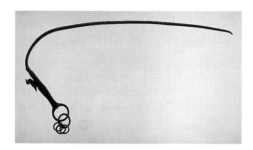

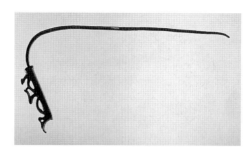

115 HOOKED "KEY"

Zürich-Alpenquai, Lake Zürich, Switzerland
Bronze
Late Bronze Age, c. 1000 BC
Length 42 cm, Weight 262.3 g
Schweizerisches Landesmuseum, Zürich
Inv. No. A-25748

The so-called key has a grip, somewhat thicker than the rest, decorated with representations of birds; from this the long shank curves sharply down and back. Some scholars have interpreted this object as a roasting spit, which presumes that the shank originally projected straight out from the grip. The connection in this item with representations of birds, which play an important role in the symbolism of the Urnfield period, suggests that the function was removed from the merely profane. If it is in fact a key, this identification would shed light on the practices of collecting and protecting wealth among the upper classes of the Urnfield period.
A.J./F.V.

Mottier 1971, 155; Speck 1981, 230 ff

116 HOOKED "KEY"

Zürich-Grosser Hafner, Switzerland
Bronze
Late Bronze Age, c. 1000 BC
Length 36 cm, Weight 182 g
Schweizerisches Landesmuseum, Zürich.
Inv. No. A-45241

This so-called key was found by a diver near the island settlement of Grosser Hafner. It is similar in form to the example from Zürich-Alpenquai (Cat.

242

No. 115). The upper surface of the grip has stylised representations of three birds; the ring at the end of the grip was broken in antiquity.
A.J./F.V.

Mottier 1971, 155; Speck 1981, 230 ff

Only in Copenhagen, Bonn and Athens

117 ROASTING SPIT

Forêt de Compiègne, Oise, France
Bronze
Late Bronze Age, 9th–8th centuries BC
Length 59.7 cm
Musée des Antiquités Nationales,
St. Germain-en-Laye
Inv. No. 13684

This roasting spit is of the so-called Atlantic type. In contrast to the spits of Etruria and Greece that are made of a piece, this type has a two-part handle. One part of the handle is trimmed by a ring-shaped sleeve that is usually ribbed. Above this a curved fork with two tines is attached to the handle. Occasionally the sleeve has stylised representations of birds, which links them to symbolic goods of the Urnfield period. The spit has a cross-section that is roughly

square, narrowing towards the tip. Spits of this type are found on the Mediterranean islands of Sardinia and Cyprus as well as along the Atlantic seaboard between the Iberian Peninsula and southern England. The oldest example is from Cyprus and dates from the early 9th century.
A.J./F.V.

Mohen 1977, fig. 2; Giardino 1995, 238, fig. 117

Only in Paris

118 ROASTING SPIT

Challans, Vendée, France
Bronze
Late Bronze Age, 9th–8th centuries BC
Length 12 cm
Musée des Antiqitiés Nationales,
St. Germain-en-Laye
Inv. No. 81348

Part of a spit of the same type as the other (Cat. No. 117), decorated with a red deer's head. The object comes from a rich hoard of various bronze pieces, especially weapons and jewellery.
J.-P.M.

Mohen 1977

119 HOARD WITH WEAPONS AND ORNAMENTS

Midskov, Mesinge, Funen, Denmark
Bronze
Late Bronze Age, Period IV,
11th–10th centuries BC
National Museum, Copenhagen
Inv. Nos. 3778–85

In the extensive lowlands region in north Germany, Poland and south Scandinavia many votive hoards of valuable bronze objects were deposited during the Bronze Age. Most of the hoards were submerged in wetlands, or in rivers and lakes: hence the thinking that these were probably sacrificial or votive offerings. The hoards contained objects from both male and female worlds.

This hoard from Midskov, discovered in 1836, contains, amongst other items, a fibula and two hanging vessels, which may have belonged to women. The objects belonging to men include seven spearheads, a socketed chisel, two armlets, four socketed axes, and three fragments of a sword. The long spearhead with a set-off socket and linear mouldings reveals influences from north Germany.   J.J.

Broholm 1946, 189, M.38; Jacob-Friesen 1967; Thrane 1965 and 1975, 55ff

120 HOARD

Villingerød, Esbønderup, Frederiksborg, Zealand, Denmark
Bronze
Late Bronze Age, Period V, 9th–8th centuries BC
Hanging vessel Diameter 21 cm. Belt buckle Diameter 16 cm
National Museum, Copenhagen
Inv. Nos. B 13681–86

Many of the rich hoards from north European regions included one or more complete sets of female jewellery. This hoard from a bog near Villingerød contains a hanging vessel and a belt buckle, four sickles, a neck-ring made from bronze sheet and a pair of spiral bracelets. These pieces are probably from a set of jewellery that was worn by one woman. The four sickles and the bracelets lay inside the hanging vessel, over which lay the belt buckle like a cover.   J.J.

Broholm 1946, M.101a

121 HOARD

Wierzchowo, Szczecinek, Koszalin, Poland
Bronze
Late Bronze Age, Period IV,
11th–10th centuries BC
Length cow horn 23 cm, spearhead 16.6 cm, sword hilt 11.1 cm, plate-fibulae 17.5 cm, 17.7 cm, 19.5 cm, fibula with spirals 31.1 cm; Diameter collars 13.7 cm, 24 cm, 24.8 cm; neck-rings 15.9 cm, 19.1 cm, decorative discs 10.3 cm, 10.4 cm
Museum für Vor- und Frühgeschichte, Berlin
Inv. Nos. Ic 3401, 3457–3466, 3469–3482, 3485–3488
Ill. p. 81

The hoard was found in 1901 during peat cutting north of Lake Bialla "in a pocket of sand"; it is largely intact except for a few objects that have since disappeared. It includes the hilt of a sword of the Mörigen type and an undecorated spearhead. The bulk of the hoard, however, is made up of objects of female attire, including three plate-fibulae, two slightly domed decorative discs, an arm-ring of ribbon, two neck-rings, four neck-collars, two fibulae with spiral finials, two spiral fibulae and two double spirals. In addition, the hoard contained two fragments of wire, four partially wound wires and a cow horn. The hoard seems to have been a votive offering in a bog. Several of the objects were heavily damaged prior to being deposited. Many, like the neck-collars, were made in the same workshop. The bronze objects represent the belongings of a warrior and several women.
                         A.J./F.V.

Sprockhoff 1934, 50, pl. 8; Hundt 1955; Sprockhoff 1956, 69ff, pls. 15.6; 21.1; 32.1.–3; 24.2; 26.2; 53.3; 54.2.5–6; 75.8; von Brunn 1980, no. 246, pls. 62, 63; Hänsel & Hänsel 1997, 223ff

122 WAGON MODEL

Budakalász, Luppa-csárda, Pest, Hungary
Clay
Baden Culture, 2400–2200 BC
Length 8.9 cm, Hight 8.1 cm
Ferencz Károly Museum, Szentendre
Inv. No. 61.2.35.5

More than 330 graves are known in a field near Budakalász; not all are yet excavated. The wagon model comes from an empty grave (?cenotaph): no skeletal remains were found.
The tops of the sides of the wagon rise up at their corners; the upper part of the longer sides and the front are decorated with a simple zigzag line cut into the clay, while the other end is completely covered by three zigzag bands separated by horizontal lines. The lower portions of the longer sides have four groups of two lines incised. The interior and exterior of the wagon alike are painted red. The wagon has four disc wheels that are fixed to the body of the wagon. The centre of each carries a small projection, suggesting an axle hub. The pole-shaft is attached to the lower edge of the front of the wagon and curves upwards, its end has not survived.   A.J./F.V.

Müller-Karpe 1974, pl. 479.A20; Banner 1956, 111–128

123 CHEEK-PIECES FOR A HORSE BRIDLE

Zbince, Michalovce, Slovakia
Bronze
Late Bronze Age, c. 1000 BC
Length 10.3 cm, Height 7.0 cm
Zemplínske múzeum, Michalovce
Inv. No. A 0076

The objects are from a bronze hoard discovered in 1955. In addition to the cheekpieces, the hoard consisted of bracelets, socketed axes, fragments of a sickle and a situla. The cheek-pieces are curved, turning almost through a right angle. A transverse circular hole is situated close to the angle, another is close by. One end widens to a round and lightly domed surface. The other tapered end is marked off and equipped with an opposed pair of small protuberances.

                    V.F.

Novotná 1970, 126–127; Furmánek 1979, 65, no. 43; Hüttel 1981

124 AMPHORA WITH WAGON SCENE

Veľké Raškovce, Trebišov, Slovakia
Clay
Middle Bronze Age, c. 1300 BC
Height 26.5 cm
Zemplínske múzeum, Michalovce
Inv. No. A 0440
Ill. p. 126 (detail)

Amphora from a cremation grave of the Suciul de Sus culture at Velké Raškovce. The amphora has an S-shaped profile.

broad base and a tapering neck (whose mouth acts like a funnel); the two handles are attached vertically on opposite sides at mid-neck. The incised ornamentation consists of a band of vertical strokes under the rim, below which are four symmetrically arranged and roughly-sketched wagons. Each has a pair of wheels with four spokes and is pulled by two horses. Behind the wagon stands a human figure presumably holding a sword, also very crudely sketched. At the angle where the neck of the vase meets the body run four lines from which the ornamentation of the body depends, consisting of three spiral motifs (each composed of three lines). In the spaces between the spirals are regularly distributed symbolic motifs, representing a standing human figure and two horse heads. This interpretation is confirmed by comparing them with those motifs on the amphora's neck. The incised ornamentation is filled with a white material that stands out against the outer surface which is dark grey.   V.F.

Vizdal 1972, 223–231; Furmánek, Ruttkay & Siska 1991, 45, no. 47

location from the Carpathian region into south Germany, from settlements that are usually fortified. They are important evidence of the then widespread use of horses to draw two-wheeled chariots.

V.F./A.J./F.V.

Müller-Karpe 1980, pl. 294.D, no. 461; Točík 1981, 69; 87–88, pl. 137.16, 143.14

construction, with four spokes and a rim made from eight sections that are placed over a wood core. The U-sectioned exterior of the rim is designed to take a wooden tyre or tread, of which, however, no trace has survived.

The wheels reveal close parallels to depictions of wheels in Late Mycenaean culture. Since two wheels were found deposited at both Árokalháról and Obišovce, it can be assumed that two-wheel vehicles were in use in the Middle Bronze Age in central Europe, as they were in the Aegean.

Thus, it is probable that these wheels reflect contacts with the Mycenaean region. It is not possible to say, however, whether the wheels are imports from the Aegean or native imitations.　A.J./F.V.

Hampel 1886, pl. LIX. 2; Pare 1992, 19

125　TWO CHEEK-PIECES

Surany-Nitriansky Hrádok, Nové Zámky, Slovakia

Antler

Mad'arovce culture, 16th century BC

Length 5.1 and 11.3 cm

Archaeological Institute, Nitra

Inv. Nos. H/20 Gr. 218 and CH/8 Sch

These parts of a horse harness were found in an excavation of the settlement of Nitriansky Hrádok. The smaller was found in a pit together with ceramics of the Mad'arovce culture.

This smaller item was made from antler; its cross-section ranges from round to oval. At its centre is a long, oval perforation, flanked by a round one near each end. Its highly polished surface has a set of grooves at either side of the central hole (one with a notched band).

The cross-bit is also made of antler and is slightly curved. It too has an oval hole in the center and rounder ones at the ends: all are inter-connected by another drilled right through the core of the antler. The polished surface is here ornamented with sets of incised grooves (some notched) that delineate zones of curvilinear ornament.

Material of this sort extends in date from the end of the Early Bronze Age into the early part of the Middle period, and in

126　WHEELS, A PAIR OF

Árokalháról (Àrokalja), Transylvania, Hungary

Bronze

Early Urnfield Culture, 12th century BC

Diameter 80 cm and 81 cm

Hungarian National Museum, Budapest

Inv. No. 25.1867

The two wheels were deposited without any other objects. They are of simple

127　WHEELS, A PAIR OF

Stade, Lower Saxony, Germany

Bronze

Late Bronze Age, Period V, 9th century BC

Diameter 58 cm, Weight 11.7 kg each

Schwedenspeicher Museum, Stade

Inv. Nos. 1038, 1039 GUHV, Stade

The wheels were found in 1919 standing vertically and in close proximity in the sandy-soil of a heath. They consist of a hub, four spokes and a U-sectioned rim. In this last, traces of oakwood could be seen, originally attached with studs. This formed a wooden tread that was apparently reinforced with bronze nails.

The wheels were manufactured in a single cast, but only one was successfully achieved; the others had to be reworked afterwards.

In contrast to earlier Bronze Age habits, four-wheel wagons now begin to appear. In view of the poor load-bearing tolerance of the wheels, it is unlikely that they were for secular use, but rather for cult-religious ones, as was the case for comparable wagons from La Côte-Saint-André (Isère, France). The wheels are found from the Pyrenees to the mouth of the Elbe, with groups named after important finds from Fa / Coulon / Hassloch / Stade (cf Cat. No. 128).   A.J./F.V.

Pare 1987; Hässler 1991, pl. 9; Jockenhövel
& Kubach 1994, 92

128   WHEEL

Champ de Maréchal, Coulon,
Deux-Sèvres, France
Bronze
Late Bronze Age, 8th century BC
Diameter 52 cm
Musée Bernard d'Agesci, Niort
Inv. No. 985.6.1

The wheel was found approximately a meter beneath the surface, together with some pottery and a stone palette and rubber. The bronze used to produce it has a tin content of 13%. The wheel consists of a fixed axle hub, with five spokes connected to a wide rim that has a hollow external groove, designed to hold a wooden tread. As holes drilled along the edge of the rim show, the tread was attached by means of studs.

Where the spokes connect to it, the rim has been engraved with three-cornered sun symbols that have been accented by an encrustation of red copper. Thus, this wheel belongs to a group of objects, some very costly, that were used in the widespread sun cult of the Bronze Age. Comparable spoked wheels, known by their site names of Fa / Coulon / Hassloch / Stade, have been found from the foot of the Pyrenees, through France and southwest German northwards. They served with ceremonial or cult wagons with four wheels.   A.J./F.V.

Avant les Celtes 1988, 13.09.04;
Cat. Archéologie de la France 1989, 214

129   HOARD WITH HORSE GEAR

Ückeritz, island of Usedom, Mecklenburg-
Vorpommern, Germany
Bronze
Late Bronze Age, Period V, 9th–8th centuries
BC
Weight 6.203 kg
Landesmuseum Mecklenburg-Vorpommern,
Schwerin
Inv. No. 75/241

This hoard was discovered in 1975. It lay no more than fifty cm beneath the ground-surface over a restricted area (40 x 30 x 30 cm), which suggests the presence once of a container of organic material (perhaps a wooden box). The hoard consisted of 110 bronze objects, which probably all belonged to horse harnesses – as well as four cheek-pieces made of deer antler, several pieces of leather and fragments of wood. The 110 bronze objects can be divided into fifty-three phalerae, or fragments thereof, thirteen rattles, sixteen ribbed bronze tubes, two semi-circular bronze tubes, seven more cheek-pieces, two decorated toggles, three ring toggles , three caps, two shell-like cylindrical rings, six small rings and two bronze pins.
The hoard is one of a series of similarly composed examples from the south bor-

der area of north Europe. Interestingly, particular objects reveal far-reaching connections with the Urnfield culture to the south and east. It is possible that the deposit represents the complete set of harness from two draw-horses and was offered intact in the course of some cult ceremony.   A.J./F.V.

Lampe 1982; Jockenhövel & Kubach 1994, 90

130   CULT OBJECT

Balkåkra, Scania, Sweden
Bronze
Early Bronze Age, Period I, c. 1500 BC
Height 27.5 cm, Diameter 42 cm
The State Historical Museum, Stockholm
Inv. No. SHM 1461
Ill. p. 56

The Balkåkra object was found in the autumn of 1847, during peat cutting in a bog. A cult object of uncertain use, it has been interpreted as a drum. In many respects, it is the twin of the object from Hasfalva (see Cat. No. 131). Both are certainly produced by the same crafts-man in their basic form, but the orna-ments and final adjustments to the pieces appear to have been made by others. The patterns of the two are in particular dif-ferent, though the weight and other measurements are very close.   A.J./F.V.

Knape & Nordström 1994

131   CULT OBJECT

Hasfalva, Hungary
Bronze
Middle Bronze Age, c. 1500 BC
Height 27.5 cm, Diameter 41 cm
Soproni Múzeum, Sopron
Inv. No. 64.83.1

In 1913 the "twin object" of the Balkå-kra find (see Cat. No. 130) was discov-ered in Hasfalva: like it this one has also been interpreted as a drum. It was found lying in a two-metre-deep sand pit with the wheels at the top. The round plate lay inside its bronze ring. In the excava-tion that followed the discovery, remains of prehistoric pottery, animal bones and particles of coal – all of which may have come from a destroyed grave – were found close by. Unfortunately, it could not be established whether there was any connection between these finds and the "drum".   A.J./F.V.

Knape & Nordström 1994

132   LUR

Brudevælte, Lynge, Frederiksborg, Zealand, Denmark
Bronze
Late Bronze Age, Period V,
9th–8th centuries BC
Diameter decorated plate 28.5 cm
National Museum, Copenhagen
Inv. No. 8117
Ill. p. 59

A well-preserved right-twist lur, number 5 from the set found (together with Cat. No. 133 and four other lurs) in 1797 in a small bog.

The tube is strongly curved and divided into three sections by ridged jointing-rings. The decoration on the bell-disc consists of eight large bosses set within a ridge; each of these is surrounded by a ring of concentric circle motifs (twenty-four in all – some shared); at the centre, around the mouth of the lur is a zone of concentric ridges of varying sizes. The disc is held in place by being slid over the lur's body, the end of which was hammered so as to secure the disc. A series of five "rattles" (trapezoidal plates) are fixed by the mouthpiece. About eighty lurs are known from the Late Bronze Age in Denmark, Sweden, Norway and north Germany. The instru-ment is a long, curved horn of relatively thin-walled bronze. The upper decorated disc does not serve any acoustic purpose. Attempts to play them have established that it is capable of producing eight or nine notes in a so-called natural tone series. The sound is pure and deeply res-onant. The lur, however, cannot be called a musical instrument in the mod-ern sense. It can probably be best com-pared to a signal trumpet, which can be used to play more or less well-formed signals but not real melodies.   J.J.

Broholm 1946, 165ff; and 1949, pl. 6; Lund 1986, 12ff, 151ff; Jensen 1992, 280ff

133   LUR

Brudevælte, Lynge, Frederiksborg, Zealand, Denmark
Bronze
Late Bronze Age, Period V,
9th–8th centuries BC
Diameter decorated plate 28.5 cm
The State Hermitage Museum,
St. Petersburg, Russia
Ill. p. 59

This lur (object 6 from the bog at Brude-vælte, see Cat. No. 132) is a well-pre-served, left-twist piece of exactly the same size, structure and decorations as the previous. Lurs are often found in pairs: a complete set of instruments con-sisting of a balanced pair of lurs – one of which is wound to the left, the other to the right. A single lur weighs about 3 kg; cast using the *cire perdue* (lost wax) technique, the result is an instrument of heavier weight than if made from sheet. This lur was presented in 1845 to the Russian Tsar Nicholai I by the Danish King Christian VIII.   J.J.

Jensen 1992, 280ff; and 1998a; Broholm 1949

134   HORN

Drunkendult, Antrim County, Ireland
Bronze
Late Bronze Age, 8th–6th centuries BC
Length 58.5 cm, Diameter mouth 6.5 cm
National Museum of Ireland, Dublin
Inv. No. N.M.I. 1930:107

This piece was found in a bog together with a fragment of another horn. It was produced in a two-part clay mould whose sides were not properly aligned during the casting process. For that rea-son, the ornamentation on the closed end is irregular; and on the upper surface traces of the metal flashings can be seen. The horn consists of a bronze tube that widens gradually, splaying out a little at the narrower end as well. Curved at its centre, the two ends lie approximately at

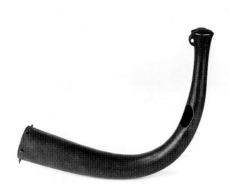

right angles to each other. The mouth opening, on the inner side of the horn, is oval. The closed, smaller end of the instrument is fashioned in the form of a domed disc; immediately behind which is a small loop on the inside. The open end is enlivened by six equally spaced prongs.

Bronze horns are found in widespread regions throughout North and West Europe, though the sideblown version is limited to Ireland. 120 such horns are known in Ireland, almost all of which came from hoards. These have been divided into two groups by Coles: form I is concentrated in northeast Ireland; form II in the southwest. E.P.K./A.J./F.V.

White 1945, 99; Coles 1963, 326ff; Kelly 1983

135 HORN

Moyarta, Clare County, Ireland
Bronze
Late Bronze Age, Dowris phase,
8th–6th centuries BC
Length 60.5 cm
National Museum of Ireland, Dublin
Inv. No. N.M.I. 1907:103

The hoard, seven to eight feet deep in a bog, comprised three horns, as well as a mouthpiece that has been bent slightly, though it is not clear whether it belongs to one of the three surviving horns. All belong to Coles' form II. A.J./F.V.

White 1945, 100, pl. XIV.1–3; Coles 1963, 326ff; Kelly 1983

136 ACROBAT-FIGURINE

Grevensvænge, Rønnebæk, Præsto, Zealand, Denmark
Bronze
Late Bronze Age, Period IV,
11th–10th centuries BC
Height 5 cm
National Museum, Copenhagen
Inv. No. 5311
Ill. p. 58

In the 18th century AD this figurine was found at Grevensvænge, together with several other figures. Of these only this one and a kneeling man with a horned helmet have been preserved (see Cat. No. 92). The standing female figure is portrayed arching herself backwards in an energetic movement. Perhaps it is a dance, or perhaps it is a acrobatic display she is engaged in. She wears a cord-skirt similar to the piece of clothing found in the oak coffin-grave from Egtved. The figure has a peg for attachment to a base. The figure no doubt represents some cult ceremony which was part of the Bronze-Age peoples' religious practices. J.J.

Broholm 1953, no. 318; Broholm & Djupedal 1952, 5ff; Kjærum & Olsen 1990, no. 20

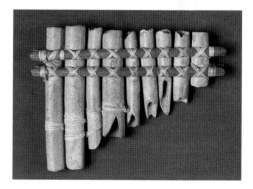

137 PANPIPES, AND RECONSTRUCTION

Przeczyce, Zawiercie, Silesia, Poland
Bone
Late Bronze Age, 9th–8th centuries BC
Height 12 cm, Width 9 cm
Muzeum Górnoslaskie, Bytom
Inv. No. B 4/322:62

The panpipe was found in the grave of a man approximately sixty years old, lying near his chest. It consists of nine bone pipes of different lengths that were originally joined together. In addition to the panpipes, the grave also contained various articles of dress, a boar's tusk and a disc of cow bone that probably served as amulets, and three vessels.

The oldest representations of panpipes are found in wall paintings from the 6th millennium at Catal Hüyük. The remains of the oldest surviving panpipes are probably those from the gravesite of Kitoy (Siberia), dating from the 4th to the 3rd millennia BC, while the present example is probably the oldest from central Europe. A.J./F.V.

Szydlowska 1965, 131ff; and 1968, 72; Coles & Harding 1979, 369

138 SISTRUM

Hochborn, Alzey-Worms, Germany
Bronze
Late Bronze Age, 9th–8th centuries BC
Height 33.5 cm, handle only 21, Width 11.5
Landesmuseum, Mainz
Inv. No. V 2229

The sistrum was found in the 1850s along with other objects in the cemetery of the Hochborn parish (formerly Blödesheim). The objects were probably not deposited together. Of the total height, most is taken up by the slightly bent handle. The U-shaped upper part, its open ends curving slightly inwards, is supplied with a removable cross-bar. Originally this could be locked in place at the side. On the opposite arm is a loop, which is partially broken off. Loops set at the external angle of handle and upper part hold three "paddle"-shaped pendants, partly restrained by a ring. There were probably two more such pendants attached on the now-damaged loop mentioned above.

A.J./F.V.

Schaaff 1984; Müller-Karpe 1980, pl. 439

Only in Copenhagen, Bonn and Athens

139 TINTINNABULUM

Wallerfangen, Saar, Germany
Bronze
Late Bronze Age, HaB3, 9th–8th centuries BC
Height 33.8 cm, Width 28.5 cm
Musée des Antiquités Nationales,
St. Germain-en-Laye
Inv. No. 8100

The tintinnabulum was found in a deposit together with five razor-pendants, fourteen hollow-sectioned arm-rings, a sword, three winged axes and one socketed, two phalerae, two snaffles, four curved cheek-pieces, four tubes with vase head terminals, two spiral-discs and other ornamental pieces; and a two-piece mould for winged axes. The circular ring of the tintinnabulum (made of sheet metal) has an integral attachment device in the form of a rod and, opposite this, a circle removed at its outer edge. The surface is decorated with three concentric zones of close-packed grooves. The attachment device terminates in an outer ring that is set off by a threefold series of constrictions. At its interior end, also with a ring, an open link connects to a pair of miniature versions of the main disc. These thus hang free and will have acted as clappers. Tintinnabula of this type are found exclusively in hoards. They are found from the southern Wetterau along the lower course of the Main River and in the Saar region into northern France. They may be cult objects, but it is also possible that they were used as decoration on horse-harness.

A.J./F.V.

Inventaria Archaeologica France 4, 1975; Millotte; Catalogue MANM, 9; Kolling 1968, 197, No. 125; Wels-Weyrauch 1978, 123ff, No. 729

140 BIRD-SHAPED RATTLE

Zürich-Alpenquai, Switzerland
Clay
Late Bronze Age, HaA/B. c. 1000 BC
Length 15.3 cm, Height 11 cm, Width 6.7 cm
Schweizerisches Landesmuseum, Zürich
Inv. No. A-27032

A hollow clay container in the shape of a bird, this was probably used as a rattle; its incised decorations are filled with a white paste; holes punched in it probably served to attach decorations such as ribbons. Along with "bird-barques", one of the most popular motifs of the Late Bronze Age, bird's heads appear in combination with cow's or ram's horns, a peculiar sort of symbiosis that is not at all uncommon.

W.F.

Kossack 1990, 89ff, fig. 5

141 BIRD-SHAPED RATTLES

Several find places, Poland
Clay
Late Bronze Age
Height 4–8 cm, Width 8–13 cm

Poznan Archaeological Museum
Inv. Nos. 1939.544; 1984.366; 1984.367;
1984.368
Ill. p. 58

Small zoomorphic sculptures, especially
in the form of birds, are widespread in
the regions of the Lausitz culture and its
successors. Isolated examples have been
found up to the Rhine, in south Germany and north Switzerland.
Models of birds exist as free-standing
figurines, as rattles and on clay vessels.
Representations of birds belong to the
symbolic vocabulary of the central European Urnfield culture. Because these
small bird sculptures appear to be created primarily during a dry climatic
period, it is possible that they are so
widespread during this period because of
magical ideas and practices attaching to
them.   A.J./F.V.

Gediga 1970; Buck 1979, 104ff

142 HOARD OF SWORDS AND SPEAR

Kehmstedt, Nordhausen, Thuringia,
Germany
Bronze
Late Bronze Age, 9th–8th centuries BC
Length biggest sword 76 cm
Landesmuseum für Vorgeschichte, Halle
Inv. No. 9388-9395

Road construction south of Kehmstedt in
Thuringia uncovered seven swords and a
spearhead, buried deep in the ground.
They had all been laid out so that their
points were close together. The swords
are elegant pieces of weaponry: several
of them have antennae, even spirals, at
the top of the handles; most of them
have a sold bronze hilt, though one has
only the tang left, the organic material
having perished.
Throughout the entire Bronze Age
weapons were offered as votive offerings;
frequently, they were submerged in bodies of water or bog. In central Europe,
this practice ended in the 8th century BC,

250

though it continued for another two centuries or so in north Germany and south
Scandinavia. The valuable weapons
from Kehmstedt were probably sacrificed near the end of the Bronze Age, i.e.
in 9th–8th centuries BC.   J.J.

Jockenhövel & Kubach 1994, 71

143 SPEARHEAD

Store Karleby, Hyllinge, Copenhagen,
Denmark
Bronze
Late Bronze Age, Period V,
9th–8th centuries BC
Length 27.8 cm
National Museum, Copenhagen
Inv. No. B6691

Spear of the so-called "West Baltic" type
– a copy of those used at the period in
central Europe. Most of the examples
from south Scandinavia are between ten
and fifty cm in length, in several cases
even longer. Their forms and decoration
are very uniform, normally the edges of
the sockets are decorated with groups of
linear motifs. In the south Scandinavian
region this type is widespread, but many
too have turned up in north Germany
and Poland. Most of the hoards are in
the nature of submerged votive offerings;
only rarely do such spears come from
graves.   J.J.

Jacob-Friesen 1967; Thrane 1975, 59ff

144 SPEARHEAD

Vejlegårds Mark, Vejle, Svendborg, Denmark
Bronze
Late Bronze Age, Period V,
9th–8th centuries BC
Length 39 cm
National Museum, Copenhagen
Inv. No. 25992

Spear of the so-called "West Baltic"
type, see Cat. No. 143.

Jacob-Friesen 1967; Thrane 1975, 59ff

145   SPEARHEAD

Unknown findspot, Denmark

Bronze

Late Bronze Age, Period V,

9th–8th centuries BC

Length 35.3 cm

National Museum, Copenhagen

Inv. No. UI/1377

Spear of the so-called "West Baltic" type, see Cat. Nos. 143–144.   J.J

Jacob-Friesen 1967; Thrane 1975, 59 ff

Only in Copenhagen, Bonn and Athens

146   ARMOUR

St. Germain du Plain, Saône-et-Loire, France

Bronze

Late Bronze Age, 9th–8th centuries BC

Height 50 cm

Musée des Antiquités Nationales,

St. Germain-en-Laye

Inv. No. 2757

This bronze body-armour, or cuirass, was found in the river Saône. It consists of a front and a back that are riveted together on the left side; the whole decorated with a star pattern. Such chest armour may originally have been lined with leather. Europe's oldest known examples were used in Greece in the 15th century BC, whilst the oldest from the region north of the Alps dates from the beginnings of the Urnfield culture, i.e.

from the 13th century BC. The armour from St. Germain du Plain probably ranks among the oldest such from north of the Alps, produced in the region of the Eastern Alps and the Carpathians.   J.J.

Deonna 1934, 118ff; Paulik 1968, 56ff; von Merhart 1969, 9,162, fig. 3,4; Müller-Karpe 1980, pl. 471.D, No. 980; Goetze 1984, 25ff

147   HOARD OF BRONZE ARMOUR

Petit Marais, Marmesse, Haute-Marne, France

Bronze

Late Bronze Age, 9th–8th centuries BC

Height 50 cm

Musée des Antiquités Nationales,

St. Germain-en-Laye

Inv. Nos. M.A.N. 83753, 83756, 83757

Ill. p. 91

Between 1974 and 1986 in the vicinity of a spring near Marmesse, a total of nine pieces of armour were turned up; the armour had been submerged in groups of three, probably as votive offerings. All of the items from Marmesse are to do with the front and back plates of a cuirass. The decorations, achieved by repoussé bosses of varying sizes, reflect the lines of the warrior's anatomy. The same decorative technique was also employed on helmets from Italy, Hungary and Denmark from the 11th to the 8th centuries BC. Body armour was a prestige item that was sometimes combined with helmets and greaves.

The armour from Marmesse belongs to the West Alpine group and dates from the 9th to the 8th centuries BC.   J.J.

Goetze 1984, 25ff; Mohen 1987; Cat. Archéologie de la France 1989, 192

148   BRONZE ARMOUR

Fillinges, Haute-Savoie, France

Bronze

Late Bronze Age, 9th–8th centuries BC

Height 50 cm, weight 2 kg each

Musée d'Art et d'Histoire, Génève

Inv. Nos. 14057-58

At the end of the 19th century AD three pieces of chest armour and at least four pieces of back armour were found near Fillinges, in east France. They do not seem to belong together, and thus must have come from the equipment of at least seven warriors. The armour had been collected for a colossal funeral pyre – a ceremony that is reminiscent of Homer's description of the pyre for the hero Patrokles (*Iliad* XXIII.173ff). The armour was decorated with rows of bosses, punched dots and lines in the same way leather was ornamented. Depictions of birds, suns and ships are symbols that were taken from Early Urnfield cultural motifs; the bird designs appear all over the region of the Urnfield culture, but no single place of origin can

251

National Museum, Copenhagen

Inv. No. B 10988b

Ill. p. 97

Found in 1920 together with another shield in a bog on the island of Lolland in south Denmark. The decoration of the Sørup shield consists of repoussé ridges and bosses of various sizes that form concentric circles as well as a cross- or wheel-shaped motif. Each of the spokes of the wheel is made up of nine to eleven lines of large or small bosses. The rim of the shield is fitted with metal, fastened with four small loops.

The decorative scheme of the Sørup shield is found on no other west or north European shield, and so the place of production cannot be determined with certainty. The shield was very probably first cast and then finished by hammer-work.

Bronze shields could hardly have been used in battle, being heavy; they were more likely prestige or parade weapons. In the Aegean region, shields are known since the 15th century BC, though north of the Alps they appear first only in the 13th century in central Europe, north Germany, south Scandinavia, England and Ireland. In France and Spain, shields were also used, but they are only known from depictions on stelae and rock carvings.   J.J.

Broholm 1946, 184, M.24; Coles 1962, 156ff; Patay 1968, 241ff; Thrane 1975; Schauer 1980; Goetze 1984, 25ff

U-shaped motif in its decoration, belongs to the so-called Pilsen type. In contrast to most other types, Pilsen shields are heavy, of thick metal and with simple ornamentation. Their dating is uncertain; they may be older than the Herzsprung shields (see Cat. No. 151). Bronze shields in south Scandinavia receive the same sort of treatment as do the helmets: a shared occurrence on rock carvings and as votives made in bogs – practices held in common with England, Denmark and Germany. The majority of the North Alpine shields have been found in wetlands, lakes or rivers where they were probably deposited as votive gifts.   J.J.

Broholm 1946, 184, M.24; Coles 1962, 156ff; Patay 1968, 241ff; Thrane 1975; Schauer 1980; Goetze 1984, 25ff

be located. Armour of thin bronze sheet (0.7–1.1 mm thick) was worn over leather or heavy cloth linings. Repairs made indicate that thin though it was, such defensive armour was used in battle. The Fillinges armour belongs to the group of Western Alpine bell-cuirasses that was probably produced in the 9th to the 8th centuries BC under Mediter-ranean influence.   J.J.

Deonna 1934; von Merhart 1969; Schauer 1978, 92ff; Goetze 1984, 25ff

149   SHIELD

Sørup, Eskilstrup, Maribo, Denmark

Bronze

Late Bronze Age, Period IV,

11th–10th centuries BC

Diameter 61.5 cm

150   SHIELD

Unknown findspot, Denmark

Bronze

Late Bronze Age, 12th–10th centuries BC

Diameter 62 cm

National Museum, Copenhagen

Inv. No. 8111

This heavy bronze shield, which was previously kept in the Royal Art Gallery in Copenhagen, is probably from Denmark. The shield, with the obvious

151   SHIELD OF HERZSPRUNG TYPE

Nackhälla, Spånarps, Halland, Sweden

Bronze

Late Bronze Age, Period V,

9th–8th centuries BC

Diameter 70.5 cm

Statens historiska Museum, Stockholm

Inv. No. SHM 3420

Ill. p. 15

Bronze shield from a votive offering in a bog. The shield is decorated with repoussé, concentric circles of bosses and ridges that are interrupted by a U-shaped device, also in repoussé. A frieze of birds is depicted along the edge. Shields with decorations of this sort are called Herzsprung shields, after a north German hoard. The U-shaped figure is found only on shields from central and north Europe, whereas shields from the Mediterranean region are decorated with V-shaped figures. The largest hoard of Nackhälla-type shields was found near Fröslunda, in Västergötland, Sweden, where sixteen virtually identical shields were submerged as a votive offering in a bog. Shield-bearing men are also seen on Scandinavian rock carvings, where the men swing an axe in one hand and hold a shield in the other. Though the Nackhälla shields show influences from the Bohemian-Hungarian/southeast Alpine region, yet the shields may have been produced in north or central Germany.

J.J.

Hencken 1959, 295ff; Coles 1962;
Stenberger 1964, 220ff; Gräslund 1967;
Thrane 1975, 71ff; Needham 1979, 111ff;
Burnehult 1983; Goetze 1984, 25ff

152 SHIELD

River Shannon, Barrybeg, County
Roscommon, Ireland
Bronze
Late Bronze Age, 12th–10th centuries BC
Diameter 66.3 cm
National Museum of Ireland, Dublin
Inv. No. 1987.174

In Great Britain and Ireland more than thirty Bronze Age shields have been found. The majority are large shields, ranging from forty-five to seventy centimetres in diameter and decorated with concentric rows of bosses and ridges. The numbers of these rows vary considerably, generally from eleven to thirty rows of bosses with their corresponding ridges. The source of this type of shield should be sought in southeast England,

with the style spreading north and westwards: a typological progression such as may have occurred with other Late Bronze Age objects, for example socketed-sickles. The decoration of the River Shannon shield shows relations with the bronze work of the Continental Late Urnfield culture.

J.J.

Coles 1962, 156ff

Only in Copenhagen, Bonn and Athens

153 CRESTED-HELMET

Blainville-la-Grande, Meurthe-et-Moselle,
France
Bronze
Late Bronze Age, 12th–9th centuries BC
Height 32.5 cm
Musée des Antiquités Nationales,
St. Germain-en-Laye
Inv. No. 86196
Ill. p. 95

Crested-helmet, manufactured in halves and joined at the line of the crest. The helmet was found in 1921 in sand, not far from the river Meurthe. The cap of the helmet is conical, with a slight vertical ridge, centrally placed and running down from the top of the cap. Originally, there was a repoussé boss placed on each side of the helmet; today, only one survives. The bosses symbolise a pair of eyes, like those on the helmets from Viksø (see Cat. No. 190).

In the north Alpine region, helmets are recovered not infrequently. They are divided into two groups – east or west of a line from Hamburg by way of Salzburg to the Adriatic Sea. East of this line, only the so-called bell-helmets (see Cat. No. 154) are found; to the west, one finds crest-helmets of the same type as the helmet from Blainville-la-Grande or of a related type.

J.J.

von Merhart 1941, 4–42; and 1969, 111ff;
Hencken 1971; Müller-Karpe 1980, pl. 471;
Goetze 1984, 25ff

Only in Paris and Athens

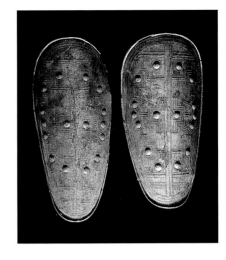

154 BELL-HELMET

Sehlsdorf, Parchim/Lübz, Mecklenburg,
Germany
Bronze
Late Bronze Age, 12th–9th centuries BC
Height 25.5 cm
Landesmuseum Mecklenburg-Vorpommern,
Schwerin
Inv. No. BR 315

Found while cutting peat in 1836, this
bell-shaped helmet, hammered up from
a single sheet, has a small cap. Such helmets were probably developed in the 12th
century BC in the Carpathian region and
in the Balkans, with helmets from the
Aegean region serving as their source of
inspiration.   J.J.

von Merhart 1969, 111f; Hencken 1971;
Goetze 1984, 25f; Schauer 1986

155 BELT AND HELMET

Le Theil, Billy, Cher, France
Bronze
Late Bronze Age
Length 39 cm
Musée des Antiquités Nationales,
St. Germain-en-Laye
Inv. No. 25039

This jointed dress accessory is made up
of three rows of flat, rectangular links
that terminate at either end in wire spirals. Attached to the lowest row are oval
pendants that have been hammered up
out of sheet metal flat and are ornamented by repoussé dots. It is one of the
westernmost examples of this type of
item, which is usually found in the
Alpine region. The piece was found with
other objects, including a helmet, around
1875.   C.E.

Cordier 1996, 77, fig. 48

156 GREAVES

Pergina, Trento, Italy
Bronze
Late Bronze Age, 9th–8th centuries BC
Height c. 30 cm
Museo Provincale, Trento

During work on the highway through
the Valsugana in May 1940, near
the small church by Pergina four bronze
greaves were happened upon in alluvial
earth. This defensive leg-armour consists
of a thin, oval of sheet bronze and
all have been decorated with embossed
designs. Based on the decoration,
the four pieces can be grouped in two
pairs.   J.J.

Fogolari 1943; Schauer 1982, 10

157 GREAVE

Schäfstall, Donauwörth, Swabia, Germany
Bronze
Late Bronze Age, HaB, 10th–8th centuries BC
Height c. 30 cm
Archäologisches Museum, Donauwörth
Inv. No. D 027

This greave from Schäfstall consists of a
thin, curved and oval bronze sheet with
repoussé decoration. Greaves are only
known from central Europe, most coming from the central and upper Danube
regions: none has been found in England, Scandinavia, north or central Ger-

many. In the Aegean greaves have been found, dating from the 15th century BC onwards; in central Europe only after 1300 BC. These finds are proof of close relationships between the Aegean, Italy and the Danube regions.   J.J.

Dehn 1980; Krahe 1981; Schauer 1982

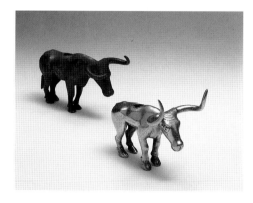

158   GRAVE ASSEMBLAGE

Maïkop, Russia
Copper, silver and gold
3rd millennium BC
Dimensions: three silver vases Height 20 cm, Weight 200 g each; one gold vase Height 13 cm, Weight 300 g; one silver bull statuette 8 cm, Weight 199 g; nineteen gold appliqués 5–6 cm across, Weight 200 g in total; one bronze bucket Diameter 17.5 cm, Weight 500 g
The Hermitage, St. Petersburg
Inv. No. 34–19ff

Near Maïkop in the Koban region a large mound or kurgan was excavated; it was ten m high with the wood-lined grave chamber measuring four by five m. In this grave-pit, a chieftain was buried together with two women. The dead man was richly decorated with gold jewellery, e.g. his clothing was trimmed with numerous appliqués of animals. His grave goods consisted of a large amount of gold jewellery, precious stones like turquoise and carnelian. In addition, the grave contained six long items made of gold and silver with sculpted animal figures – probably the remains of a canopy that was used in the burial.

Several vessels of silver and gold were found in the grave. One of the silver vessels is decorated with engraved depictions of mountains, trees and animals. Two rivers can be seen flowing into a lake; two rows of animals stand around the lake: cattle, horses, lions, antelopes, panthers, wild boars and birds.
The rich grave goods are clear evidence of connections between south Europe and the Middle East. Several of the objects were apparently imported from Anatolia and Syria; others came from Iran and India. Parallels with material from Troy II can be suggested. The great opulence of the Maïkop grave is based on access to the rich deposits of gold, copper and silver in the northwest Caucasus.   J.J.

Müller-Karpe 1974, pls. 686–87

159   GRAVE ASSEMBLAGE

Łęki Małe, Koscian, Poland
Bronze
Únětice culture, 20th–19th centuries BC
Halberd Length 72 cm, Width 18 cm
Muzeum Archeologiczne, Poznan
Inv. Nos. 1953:440, 444, 452b–c

Rich grave assemblage from the northern region of the Únětice culture. In the vicinity of a fortified settlement (Bruszczewo) on the river Warta, a series of eleven mounds were identified in all. One of the smaller – 24 m across, 4.5

high – was excavated in 1953. The original grave of stone and wood contained two sets of remains: a male burial and a female. The dead man was fitted with a halberd and a triangular dagger, an axe, a knot-headed pin and gold spiral. The woman wore two bronze rings on her ankles. The grave also contained clay vessels and remains of wooden objects. Until recently, it has been assumed that the rich graves of the Únětice culture were from the same period as the Shaft Graves at Mycenae. However, analysis of the annual growth-rings on the wooden objects found in the grave chambers of the Únětice graves of Helmsdorf and Leubingen have shown that these graves date from 1850 BC, i.e. about two centuries earlier than the graves at Mycenae.   J.J.

Kowianska-Piaszykowa 1953, 1956, 1968; Müller-Karpe 1980, no. 876, pl. 308B; Champion et al. 1984, 212

160   GRAVE ASSEMBLAGE

Clandon Barrow, Winterborne St. Martin, Dorset, Great Britain
Gold, bronze and amber
Wessex culture, Wessex I, 18th century BC
Length dagger 17.5 cm, gold plate 15.5 cm, mace-head 7.7 cm, Height amber cup 9.9 cm
Dorset County Museum, Dorchester
Inv. Nos. 1884.9.26, 36–37, 39–40
Ill. p. 102

Richly outfitted grave from one of the many barrows in the Wessex region. In addition to the dead man, the small cairn of stones originally contained many grave goods, including a bronze dagger with the remains of its wooden sheath. The dagger has a strongly defined midrib bordered by two or three lateral grooves. In addition, there was a lozenge-shaped gold plate with traced or engraved ornamentation. This gold jewellery could have been produced by the same goldsmith who made the gold jewellery of Bush Barrow. The grave also contained a shale macehead with decorative gold caps mounted over shale insets, as well as a small conical cup that was made from a single piece of amber. Many of the graves of Wessex contained amber: surely thanks to the large amounts available on the coasts of East Anglia, where it is still cast up by the waves on the Norfolk shores in big lumps. There is, however, some doubt whether the amber used in the Early Bronze Age in Britain came from harvesting it on the east coast or from "trade" with the Baltic area.   J.J.

Gerloff 1975, 74, no. 127; Müller-Karpe 1980, pl. 475.A, no. 1054; Taylor 1980, 45–49, pls. 24–26; Clarke et al. 1985, 211, 274–75

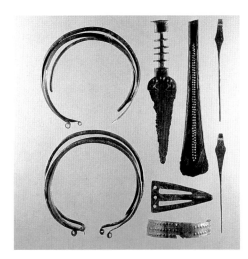

161   GRAVE ASSEMBLAGE

Thun "Renzenbühl", Bern, Switzerland
Bronze, copper and gold
Early Bronze Age, Br A2, c. 1600 BC
Length axe 24.1 cm
Bernisches Historisches Museum
Inv. Nos. BHM 10327–28, 10331–33, 10336, 10339, 10343, 10346–7, 10351, 10353

During the removal of a low moraine in 1820, a grave lined with slabs of stone was found. The grave contained a skeleton and an impressive quantity of grave goods, including a bronze axe or hatchet of a long, narrow shape. Each face is set with a band of copper, itself inlaid with

256

a number of smaller gold pieces. Six bronze neck-rings with outturned ends, a bronze dagger with hilt, two bronze pins with swollen, lozenge-shaped heads, an armband of bronze sheet and a bronze belthook.

The manner of the decoration of the axe (gold lozenges let into a copper strip along the centre of the blade) has been compared with that found on the far more elaborate daggers from the Shaft Graves at Mycenae.   J.J.

Strahm 1966; and 1972; Schauer 1984b; Barfield 1991

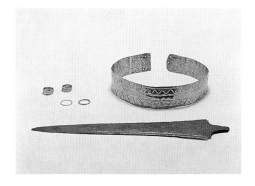

162   GRAVE ASSEMBLAGE

Quinta da Agua Branca, Vila Nova de Cerveira, Viana do Castelo, Portugal
Gold and copper
Early Bronze Age
Length dagger 35 cm, diadem 60.2 cm
Museu Nacional da Arqueologia, Lisbon
Inv. Nos. 85–89, 11017

In 1906 this grave was found in a cist near Quinta da Agua Branca. The corpse, probably a man, was laid out on its back. On the skull lay a gold diadem that was decorated along the edges with straight lines and zigzags in the centre. To the left of the corpse lay a large copper dagger. The grave also contained two small gold rings and two small gold spirals with pointed ends.   J.J.

Fortes 1905–08, 241ff; Pingel 1992, 303, No. 313

Only in Copenhagen, Bonn and Athens

163   GRAVE ASSEMBLAGE

La Motta, Lannion, Côtes-du-Nord, France
Bronze, flint, gold
Armorican Tumulus culture, 1800–1700 BC
Length sword 48.4 cm, daggers 10.8–24.8 cm, arrows 3.7–4.7 cm, axes 11.3–15 cm; pendant 6.8 mm
Musée des Antiquités Nationales, St. Germain-en-Laye
Inv. Nos. 86.175-86.180

"La Motta" is one of the richest tumulus graves from the Early Bronze Age in Brittany. The large mound lies on the north coast of Brittany. During the excavations in 1939, the ground surface below the mound was found to have a cist made from flat stones set in the natural rock. Within were valuable grave goods: a bronze sword, two bronze axes, six bronze daggers, a slate whetstone and a number of flint arrowheads. Under the stone floor of the cist, gold jewellery of unknown function was found: it could be a pendant or a symbolic wrist-guard. It is not clear whether the jewellery had originally been placed in the stone chest with the other grave goods. The dead man's grave goods point to close relations between the Bronze Age population of Brittany and the Early Bronze Age people of Wessex, on the opposite side of the English Channel.   J.J.

Butler & Waterbolk 1974, 107–167; Müller-Karpe 1980, no. 958, pl. 459B; Eluère 1982, fig. 34.1; Avant les Celtes 1988, 145

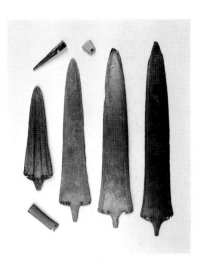

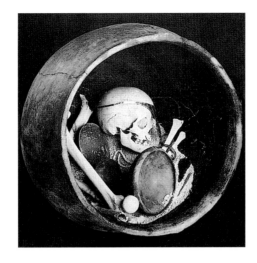

Only in Paris
164   GRAVE ASSEMBLAGE

Forêt de Carnoët, Quimperlé, Finistère,
France
Copper, bronze and stone
Early Bronze Age
Length dagger 28 cm, sword 48–52 cm,
wrist-guard 9 cm, pendant 3 cm, arrowheads
3–4 cm
Musée des Antiquités Nationales,
St. Germain-en-Laye
Inv. Nos. 30490, 30490 bis and ter,
30491, 30492, 30492 bis, 30493

In a tumulus were discovered in a stone
cist in 1842 a series of grave goods typical of a "rich" burial in Armorica. For
the most part they were weapons of
bronze and copper: four swords and
daggers, seven arrowheads, an archer's
wrist-guard; but also present were items
of jewellery. Gold bangles and rings,
some linked together to appear like a
chain; that of silver has corroded away.
These items demonstrate a close connection between Brittany and the Iberian
Peninsula.   C.E.

Briard & Mohen 1974, 46–60, Briard 1984,
266-267

165   GRAVE ASSEMBLAGE,
RECONSTRUCTED

Different localities in Murcia and Granada,
Spain
Copper and other materials
El Argar culture, 18th–16th centuries BC
Museo Arqueologico Nacional, Madrid
Inv. Nos. 1983/162/6; 83/57/158-9;
82/99/62; 25.546; 83/62/2; 17.131;
84/149/4; 1964/28/1

The earliest Bronze Age culture on the
Iberian peninsula is called the El Argar
culture. It is found in the southeast part
of the peninsula, between Granada and
Murcia. The eponymous cemetery of El
Argar held some thousand graves, many
of them pithos burials. The male graves
often contained a dagger or a flat copper
axe as well as various pieces of jewellery.
The female graves frequently had silver
diadems. This grave was reconstructed
from objects of a number of different
localities. In addition to the remains of a
skeleton, the grave has a pithos, two
copper spiral rings, one copper awl,
three clay pots, a necklace of sea-shells
and a copper dagger.   J.J.

Schubart 1973, 41–59; Müller-Karpe 1974,
pl. 453E; Coles & Harding 1979, 214ff; Lull
1983; Siret 1887; Avant les Celtes 1988, 147,
No. 15

166   GRAVE ASSEMBLAGE

Store Kongehøj, Vester Vamdrup, Jutland,
Denmark
Bronze and wood
Early Bronze Age, Period II, 14th century BC
Length sword 78 cm
National Museum Copenhagen
Inv. Nos. 25714-718

Burials in oak coffins sometimes created
unusual conditions that were suitable for
the preservation of organic materials. In
the mound of Store Kongehøj in south
Jutland, an oak coffin was excavated in
1862 in which a fully dressed body was
found under a large woollen blanket.
The dead man wore a round woollen
cap; a bronze sword in a carved wooden
sheath was placed with him; his belt was
held together by a bronze hook. At his
feet stood two wooden bowls, the smaller
of which was decorated by hammering
in a pattern of tin pins.
The fine state of preservation of the
organic material is due to the circumstance that a layer of iron oxide formed
around the coffin, which hampered the
penetration of moisture into the hill
grave and thereby the decomposition of
the organic material.   J.J.

Broholm 1943, no. 1000; Capelle 1976; Aner
& Kersten 1973, No. 3832; Jensen 1986

167 GRAVE ASSEMBLAGE

Gönnebek, Segeberg, Schleswig-Holstein,
Germany
Gold, bronze, tin and other materials
Middle Bronze Age, Periods II/III,
14th–13th centuries BC
Length sword 67 cm, Diameter gold cup
13.5 cm and Height 7 cm; Weight cup 134 g
Archäologisches Landesmuseum, Schloss
Gottorf
Inv. Nos. KS 5954 a–n

Excavations at the grave mound
"Schwarzer Berg" in 1884 uncovered in
one half of it, underneath a large stone
cover, a grave chamber (2 m x 0.7 m,
1 m high) with cremated remains. On
and beside the ashes of the deceased
were grave goods such as a gold bowl, a
gold armband, a length of gold wire
wound in a spiral, a tin disc wrapped in
gold wire, five gold spirals finger-rings

258

and six small gold spirals (?beads), as
well as a bronze sword, two bronze
knives, a pair of bronze tweezers, a
bronze chisel and a bronze awl, a bronze
pin, the remains of two dress-pins of
bronze, a bronze trepanning chisel, a
piece of haematite and clay sherds from
a handled vessel.   J.J.

Menghin & Schauer 1977, 64ff, no.8; and
1983, 74ff, no. 8

168 GRAVE OF A CHIEFTAIN

Hagenau, Regensburg, Oberpfalz, Germany
Bronze
Middle Bronze Age, Br C 2, 14th century BC
Museen der Stadt Regensburg – Historisches
Museum
Inv. No. 1975/131
Ill. p. 106

The grave was found in a tumulus. The
dead man was probably placed in a
stone cist (2.50 m x 1.60 m), of which
only traces remain. Above the head were
found a long and a short flange-hilted
sword with a medium-sized flanged axe.
The dead man's other handweapons
included a dagger that was found next to
his left hip. Four socketed arrowheads,
which were found at his left shoulder,
served as his long-distance weapons,
while the forty-three larger and smaller
nails suggest that a wooden shield decorated with them had been included as a
defensive weapon. A belthook next to the
left breast of the dead man probably
belonged to a baldrick.
The dead man's jewellery included a
long, ribbed pin that had a round disc
ornamented with projections, two gold
spirals that were found one above his
right shoulder and the other next to his
right wrist. Beside the body, along with a
razor, were two bracelets and two armlets. The other grave goods included
three objects next to his left elbow that
are probably tattoo needles, a clay vessel
in the right-hand corner of the grave and
a chert ?whetstone.

The accessories in the grave not only
point to the wealth of the upper classes
at this time but also demonstrate their
wide-ranging contacts that stretched
from east Germany to Bohemia and
Lower Austria.   A.J./F.V.

Stary 1980; Schauer 1984a

Only in Bonn, Paris and Athens

169 STELE

St.-Martin-de-Corléans, Aosta valley, Italy
Stone
Copper Age, 3rd millennium BC
Height c. 3 m
Museo archeologico di Aosta, Italy
Inv. No. 03–949

This anthropomorphic stele from St.-
Martin-de-Corléans shows a male warrior: at top left is an axe with a angled
shaft; a bow is depicted on the right, and
attached to the belt around the middle of
the figure are two daggers and a
pouch(?). Near St.-Martin-de-Corléans,
a large area was excavated that had been
used as a cult site for a long time during
the 3rd millennium BC. Numerous stelae
were found there: more than forty, along
with two polygonal paving stones.
At one time the stelae had formed three
long rows. The site had a cult function in
which the gods and heroes depicted on
the stelae were honoured. However, at
the end of the 3rd millennium BC, the

shrine was destroyed; the stelae were smashed and their fragments used to construct a burial site. J.J.

Zidda 1997

Only in Bonn, Paris and Athens

170 STELE

St.-Martin-de-Corléans, Aosta valley, Italy
Stone
Copper Age, 3rd millennium BC
Height 1.92 cm, Width 0.92/0.75 cm
Museo archeologico di Aosta, Italy
Inv. No. 03–950

Female stele in grey stone, with collar and adornments. See also Cat. No. 169.

Zidda 1997

171 STELE

St. Sernin, Aveyron, France
Stone
3rd millennium BC
Height 1.08 m, Width 70 cm, Depth 20 cm
Musée Fenaille, Rodez
Inv. No. 891.1.1

Of the 115 known menhir statues of the red-coloured group, this one from Saint Sernin is without a doubt the most famous. It was presented to the scientific world in 1893. It is a red-brown slab of Permian sandstone that is distinguished by the particular quality of its sculpting and its iconographic opulence. The following anatomical motifs appear on the front: the face, consisting of a nose and eyes (but no mouth), the upper limbs and the legs spread out, the hands placed somewhat below the breasts. For the back, however, the depiction is limited to a representation of the shoulder blades, the arms and, down the middle, the long hair. The dress and other attributes cover the entire front: tattoos either side of the nose, a piece of neck jewellery made up of six strings of beads surrounds the lower face, a Y-shaped pendant and a belt represented by two parallel ridges. At the back, in addition to the belt, a number of perpendicular relief lines can be seen, which can be interpreted as depicting folds in the clothing. Since the discovery of the "Ice-Man", however, these could also suggest

strips of cloth or of fur in various colours sewn together.

The breasts and jewellery suggest that this menhir-statue should be considered that of a female. C.S.

Hermet 1893, 1–22, pl. XIV; d'Anna 1977, 289, fig. 55.

172 STELE

Anderlingen, Rotenburg/Wümme, Lower Saxony, Germany
Stone
Early Bronze Age, Period II, 14th century BC
Height c. 120 cm, Width 70 cm,
Weight c. 200 kg
Niedersächsisches Landesmuseum, Hannover
Inv. No. 16961
Ill. p. 105

During the excavation of a mound near Anderlingen, a rectangular stone cist was found with the remains of a burial in it. The stone at the southwest side had a picture carved on the interior: three human figures that seem to be wearing animal masks. The figure on the left stands with raised hands and outstretched fingers; the middle figure raises into the air an axe with a broad blade; the figure at the right has an unidentifiable object in his hands (perhaps a sacrificial offering?). The figure is flanked by so-called bowl symbols. The whole scene probably depicts rituals 259 connected with the sun cult. The dead man may have played an important role in this cult.   J.J.

Asmus 1990/91; Wegner 1997, 16.3; Jocken-hövel & Kubach 1994, 76; Randsborg 1993, 78ff; Jacob-Friesen 1963

173   STELE

El Viso I, Córdoba, Spain
Stone
Late Bronze Age/Iron Age, 9th century BC
Height 1.25 m, Width 0.4 m
Museo Arqueológico Nacional, Madrid
Inv. No. 1976/103/1

Grave stele with various depictions: a human figure with horned helmet, two swords, a shield, a spear, a bow and arrow and a wagon, as well as other objects that are difficult to identify. Grave stelae like this one are found primarily in portuguese Estremadura and in west Andalucia in Spain. The function of these stelae is much debated; they may have served to mark territory. The decoration is put on by cutting lines into the surface. Weapons such as swords, shields and spears may often be combined with human figures and, for example, wagons with two yoked horses. Also shown are weapons such as the bow and arrow, as well as various pieces of jewellery.   J.J.

Almagro Gorbea 1978; Galán Domingo 1993, 107, no. 58

174   STELE

Santa Vitória, Beja, Portugal
Stone
Middle Bronze Age, c. 1500 BC
Height 95 cm, Width 55 cm, Thickness 6 cm
Museu "Rainha Diameter Leonor", Beja
Inv. No. MRB.1.2
Ill. p. 118

The Santa Vitória stele is engraved on one face only. The motifs consist of a sword, an axe and an anchor-shaped object, i.e. symbols which are probably linked to the power of a local leader. On this type of stelae human figures are never represented.
Stelae of the Santa Vitória type appear near small tombs (cists) belonging to the region's Middle Bronze Age culture.   J.J.

Gomes & Monteiro 1977, 281–344

175   THE CHARIOT OF THE SUN

Trundholm, Højby, Holbæk, Zealand, Denmark
Bronze and gold
Early Bronze Age, Period II, 14th century BC
Length 59.6 cm, Diameter sun 24.4,
Weight 3 kg
National Museum, Copenhagen
Inv. No. B7703
Ill. p. 130

The "Chariot of the Sun" from Trundholm is the largest and most beautiful piece of metal sculpture from the North European Bronze Age. It was found in 1902 when a drained bog was being ploughed near Trundholm. The wagon had been placed on the surface of a then relatively stable bog.
The sculpture consists of a horse on a four-wheel supporting frame and a disc carried on a two-wheel chariot. The disc consists of three parts: two separate, slightly convex discs are held together by a cast ring (some 3 mm wide). The two discs differ in but a single respect: only one of them has had gold foil applied, on which the patterns underneath can be seen. The thin-walled horse was cast over a clay core. Various features suggest that the horse was trained and in harness: holes by its mouth, and hooks in its neck and on the disc are all likely to have been designed to accommodate reins.
The Chariot of the Sun dates to Period II of the Nordic Bronze Age, that is, in the 14th century BC. From the condition of the find, it is clear that it was a sacred object that was intentionally destroyed and sacrificed.
The interpretation of the disc as the Sun, which is pulled on a chariot through the sky, is thought to be certain. The gold foil covered side of the disc probably represents the day, the bronze side the night. A disc glittering with gold on a chariot drawn by a horse suggests a parallel to the four-horse chariot of the Greek Sun-God Helios, in which he crossed the heavens during the day.   J.J.

Müller 1903; Drescher 1962, 19; Brøndsted 1962, 87; Gelling & Davidson 1969, 16ff; Aner & Kersten, 1976, no. 867, pls. 138–140

176   CULT WAGON WITH VESSEL

Orastie, Hunedoara, Rumania
Bronze and iron
Late Bronze Age, BrD-HaA,
13th–12th centuries BC
Length 17 cm, Height 10 cm, Weight 3 kg
Naturhistorisches Museum, Vienna
Inv. No. 51.254
Ill. p. 134

This small cult wagon was made of bronze, with iron axles. Only one of the four-spoke wheels has survived intact. The whole is decorated with twelve similarly-shaped bird protomes. A pair on both the front and the back are so arranged as to form a sort of enclosed space, in the middle of which a cauldron is mounted. This last has two further pairs of bird protomes, one set above the other;

the cover is treated in the same way. Cauldron-wagons of this sort appear especially in the Urnfield period, but they are found later still. As far as can be determined, all of the comparable pieces to the wagon of Orastie come from male graves. Their function is still uncertain, but the depictions of birds of the sort associated with symbolic goods in the Late Bronze Age point to some kind of ritual function. A.J./F.V.

Hampel 1887, pl. LVIII. 2a,b; Piggott 1983, 120ff; Pare 1992

177 CULT WAGON WITH VESSEL

Bujoru, Teleorman, Rumania
Bronze
Late Bronze Age, 8th century BC
Length 15.3 cm, Width 13.2, Height 5.3 cm
Musul National de Istorie a Romaniei, Bucarest
Inv. No. 135.281

This small, cauldron-wagon of bronze comes from a grave near Bujoru. The four wheels have each four spokes and well-defined hubs; the axles are of iron and the wheel-rims are lined with the same. The wagon has no body to it, so the wheels are attached directly to the cauldron; the latter is oval and has a cover.

On each of the cauldron's narrower sides are two large protomes of aquatic birds and two more appear on the cover in the same alignment. Each of these birds has a curved beak that expands greatly at the tip; their necks are decorated with symmetrically placed, incised lines, and at the breast of the birds attached to the cauldron is set a semicircular handle. The cover is crowned with a ring-shaped handle that is in turn topped by a further pair of opposed bird's heads. Finally, a seated bird has been mounted on each hub.

The cauldron-wagon from Bujoru belongs to a group of comparable examples – all characterised by a bronze cauldron with large, bird protomes arranged in a balancing pattern. The group is closely related to certain pendants that are widespread in Macedonia and Thessaly. G.T.

Beda 1976; Moscalu & Beda 1988, 23–47; Pare 1992, 184

178 CULT WAGON WITH VESSEL

Peckatel, Schwerin, Mecklenburg, Germany
Height 37.7 cm, Diameter cauldron 38 cm
Middle Bronze Age, Period III,
13th–12th centuries BC
Landesmuseum Mecklenburg-Vorpommern, Schwerin
Inv. Nos. BR 1146–1148
Ill. p. 6

A four-wheeled wagon with curved axles on which rests a small cylindrical support for the cauldron. The cauldron itself is shallow, urn-like and has a very broad and rounded profile, with two pairs of twisted handles; like the stand, it is decorated with repoussé dots; the stand has abstract symbols of birds. It was found together with a sword, knives, a golden bracelet, a socketed axe and bronze arrowheads.

Its findspot was the "Königsberg" mound, some 30 m across and 1.5 high; this was surrounded by a circle of stones and contained the remains of several humans underneath stone cairns. J.J.

Belz 1910, 193, 203; Schubart 1972; Müller-Karpe 1980, no. 842, pl. 514; Pare 1992, 179

Only in Copenhagen, Bonn and Paris

179 MINATURE CULT WAGON

Cyprus
Late Bronze Age III
Length 9.4 cm
Musée de Louvre, DAO
Inv. No. AM 1707

Cult wagon on wheels: it comprises a person with outstretched arms behind two oxen that are not obviously in harness but rather standing side by side. All were made of bronze using the "lost-wax" technique (*cire perdue*). The group were placed on a kind of platform, equipped with wheels, of which only two (with four spokes) have survived. J.-P.M.

Art de Chypre, Louvre, 1992

180 DOUBLE-AXE SHAPED OBJECTS

Lundsbakke, Værlose, Copenhagen, Zealand, Denmark
Bronze
Early Bronze Age, Period II, 14th century BC
Length 3.6 and 3 cm
National Museum, Copenhagen
Inv. Nos. B 14452 and B 14453
Ill. p. 13

The Aegean influence in Europe is much debated: it seems, however, that the double-axe symbol of that region is detectable in south Scandinavia. Among the finds in a man's grave in a tumulus were two small double-axe shaped objects. With their flat form they seem suitable for affixing to some object or other.   J.J.

Randsborg 1967, 1–28; Aner & Kersten I, 1973, 123, No. 364, pl. 75.150

181   DOUBLE-AXE

Friedelsheim, Bad Dürkheim, Germany
Copper
Early Bronze Age
Length 40.1 cm, Width 9.7–9.3 cm,
Weight 1447 g
Landesmuseum, Mainz
Inv. No. V 2976

The double-axe (Zabitz type, Flonheim variety) was found on the Feuerberg in a large "urn" in 1884. The characteristics of this variety consist of: medium weight, an extended and rectangular middle section with an expanded cutting edge, a small circular shaft-hole and decoration composed of short dashes. Double-axes were particularly widespread in central Germany and in the central Rhine Valley; other scattered examples have been found as far as east France. It is improbable that they were used as "money", that is, as means of economic exchange: if that were the case, one would expect greater standardisation in terms of weight. It cannot be ruled out that the ingots were used as "valuables" for a specific reason – perhaps as a votive offering. Given the small number known (thirty-two speci-

mens), the most plausible interpretation is that they were symbols of rank or cult objects.   J.J.

Buchholz 1960, 39ff; Müller-Karpe 1974, pl. 534H; Kibbert 1980, 43; Lenerz-de Wilde 1995, 234ff

182   CULT AXES

Viby, Zealand, Denmark
Bronze
Middle Bronze Age, Period III,
13th–12th centuries BC
Length 46 cm, Weight 5 kg
National Museum, Copenhagen
Inv. Nos. B 17019–20
Ill. p. 135

The two axes were found at Viby, where they had been deposited as votive offerings in the Middle Bronze Age. Rock carvings in Scandinavia sometimes depict men carrying enormous votive axes. That the rock carvings have not only symbolic value, but also reflect historical reality is evident: twenty-four such votive axes are known from Denmark, Sweden and Norway. These very heavy objects were most likely symbols of the political and ritual power which rested in the hands of rich chieftains and their families. The axes can be dated to approximately the same period as the famous oak coffin-burials, such as those from Egtved and Skrydstrup – at a time when bronze was scarce and a prized material. Even so the people of the Bronze Age still allowed large quantities of the valued metal to go out of circulation – by leaving it in desolate and inaccessible surroundings.   J.J.

Jensen 1978, 17ff; Jensen 1988, 239

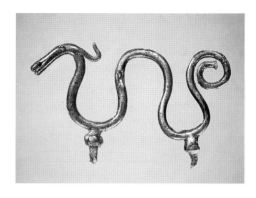

183   FIGURINES

Fårdal, Viskum, Viborg, Jutland, Denmark
Bronze
Late Bronze Age, Period V,
9th–8th centuries BC
Height woman 5 cm
National Museum, Copenhagen
Inv. Nos. B 11661–65
Ill. p. 136

Some small animal figurines, together with a kneeling woman were retrieved, along with female jewellery in a votive deposit at Fårdal: they were buried in a mound composed of gravel. The collection of figures consists of a kneeling woman, a wriggling snake (apparently harnessed with a "bit" and a loop for reins), four, horned animal-heads in pairs (one set with a duck). The species of the horned beasts is uncertain: they might be goats, bulls, horses with horns or imaginary creatures. All were equipped with pegs for attachment to a base and undoubtedly belonged together in a group composition.   J.J.

Kjær 1927, 235ff; Forssander 1942, 177, fig. 1, 189, fig. 9; Brøndsted 1958, 206, fig. 225; Broholm 1946, 236–37, M.199; Hagen 1954, 105, fig. 4; Drescher 1958, pl. 17; Ingstad 1961, 38, fig. 6; Sprockhoff & Höckmann 1974, 120–121; Broholm 1953, nos. 313–317; Kjærum & Olsen 1990, 74, No. 23

184 RAZORS

1. Unknown findspot in Denmark.

2. Neder Hvolris, Jutland, Denmark

3. Vandling, Jutland, Denmark

4. Skivum, Jutland, Denmark

5. Veddinge, Zealand, Denmark

6. South Jutland, Denmark

Bronze

Late Bronze Age, Periods IV–V, 11th–8th
centuries BC

National Museum, Copenhagen

Inv. Nos. B 17739, B 13141, B 6597, B 8343,
B 17610

Moesgaard Museum, Aarhus

Inv. No. 4066 A

1

2

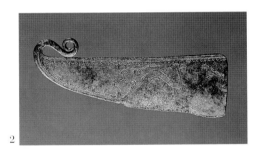

3

5

6

1. Razor with two ships, one set over the other: the lower is sailing to the left, the upper right. A fish pulls the sun upwards on the right. What is here depicted must be sunrise, an important moment in the daily cosmological cycle: the fish helps the sun from the lower ship of the night/underworld into the ship bearing the sun during the day.

2. Razor with a "folded" ship. In front of the horse-headed handle is seen a sun-horse drawing along the sun (with its halo) by a line. Probably we are witnessing the moment when the sun-horse has just brought the sun from the ship.

3. Razor with a ship onto which the sun-horse seems to be landing with the sun (at the left). Between the horse and the sun is seen a mushroom-shaped symbol, comparable in form to some cult axes (perhaps a heavenly-symbol).

4. Razor with a magnificent horse-headed ship. Over the ship is seen a stylised sun-horse which repeat itself in its spiral curls also being the sun.

5. Razor with a "folded" ship. Over the largest part of the ship (and set upside-down) is a magnificent snake, its body meandering in typical per. V-spiral-curls.

6. Razor with two human figures rowing a ship. Note that the heads are shown in the same manner as is the sun, even down to the halo. Perhaps the sun is being depicted as an anthropomorphised twin deity, a Dioscuri-like sun-god.   F.K.

Kaul 1998, nos. 378, 243, 339, 217, 61

185   ORNAMENTAL RIBBON-BAND

Roga, Neubrandenburg, Germany

Bronze

Late Bronze Age, Period V,
9th–8th centuries BC

Length 55 cm

Landesmuseum Mecklenburg-Vorpommern,
Schwerin

Inv. No. BR 844

A piece of jewellery from Roga, ornamented with purely figurative designs, was found in a belt, whose size is so small, however, that it would only have fitted the most delicate of hips. Given the known parallels on hanging vessels and razors, it can hardly be doubted that the designs represent horses. This is particularly obvious with the second, more simply-drawn animal: with its four legs, mane and the tail with a bird's head (?)attached, (unless the last detail meant to somehow to suggest a second horse). Even if the details of the scene cannot be explained exactly, it is nevertheless clear enough that it has something to do with cult rituals in which the sun played an important role. Such ceremonies included dances as well, and a dance is visible on the reverse side of this item.

J.J.

Sprockhoff 1955

186　FIBULA

Krivoklát, Ilava, Slovakia

Bronze

Late Bronze Age, 1100–1000 BC

Length 37 cm

Etnografické Múzeum, Martin

Inv. No. D 335

This fibula was a single find in the vicinity of Krivoklát. It belongs to the group of so-called "Posamenterie" fibulae: it has two spiral-discs on each side; the catch for the pin also terminates in the same manner. The middle section has fixed to it a row of loop-ended strips, which on one side end in stylised depictions of birds and from the other have leaf-shaped pendants fixed by a link or two of chain.

This highly-decorated fibula is one of finest products of Late Urnfield period costume accessories. Much wire, some of them over a meter in length, was used to produce it. Such splendid fibulae were certainly not simply ornaments, but also had a symbolic and/or religious significance. They are primarily found in Moravia, Slovakia and the central Danube region.　　　　A.J./F.V.

Budaváry 1940, 55–58; Furmánek 1979, 98, no. 69

187　HEADREST WITH ANIMAL DECORATION

Høstad, Byneset, Norway

Birchwood

Late Bronze Age, Periods V–VI,

9th–6th centuries BC

Length 30.5 cm, Width 29.5 cm,

Height 6.2 cm

Museum of Natural History and Archaeology,

Trondheim

Inv. No. 5898

Wooden headrest found with wooden bowls in a bog in 1899 at the Høstad farm. The body is carved from a single piece of birchwood, without any kind of jointing. It consists of a rest slightly concave in profile along its length; the ends are cut straight; the sides bowed; four stumpy legs support this.

On the upper surface are carved in low relief a mirror pair of motifs: an Ω-like arrangement of a ribbon-body with two animal heads, one set on each end. Enclosed by these at the centre is a "four-spoked wheel" motif, rendered in multiple lines.　　　　J.J.

Marstrander 1979, 61–88; Capelle 1980

188　CULT MASK

Silica, Majda-Hrašková cave, Rožňava,

Slovakia

Bone

Late Bronze Age, c. 1000 BC

Height 10.4 cm

Slovenské múzeum ochrany prírody a

jaskyniarstva in Liptovsky Mikulás

Inv. No. 223

Cult mask made from the facial part of a skull of a grown man: from the Kyjatice culture site in the Majda-Hrašková cave. This and another similar mask that was only half-finished were found in excavation in the cave in 1953. That the Majda-Hrašková cave served a cult function in the Late Bronze Age is demonstrated by other human remains, ceramics of the Kyjatice culture and part of a deer's skull and antlers.　　　　V.F.

Bárta 1958; Furmánek, Ruttkay & Siška 1991, 70, no. 76

189　FIGURINE

Grevensvænge, Rønnebæk, Præstø, Zealand,

Denmark

Bronze

Late Bronze Age, Period IV,

10th–9th centuries BC

Height 10.2 cm

The National Museum, Copenhagen

Inv. No. DCCCXL

Ill. p. 94

The kneeling man is almost all that is left of a figured group found at Grevensvænge in the 18th century AD. An old drawing, made about 1780, shows that originally there were two men who belonged together, twins in all likelihood. They each wore a horned-helmet and held in one hand a large ceremonial axe. With them were several other figures including three female acrobats/dancers. Only one of these has been preserved too. All were intended to be fastened to a base as is evident from the small pegs underneath the figures.

J.J.

Djupedal & Broholm 1952; Broholm 1953, no. 105; Coles & Harding 1979, pl. 23a; Glob 1990, 66, no. 19

190   HORNED HELMET

Vikso, Frederiksborg, Zealand, Denmark
Bronze
Late Bronze Age, Period IV,
11th–10th centuries BC
Height 39.7 cm
National Museum, Copenhagen
Inv. No. B13552
Ill. p. 86

Two identical horned helmets were found together during peat-cutting in a bog in 1942, where they had been deposited as a votive offering. The helmets belong to the class of crested helmets with a hemispherical form, but they differ widely from others of this group. The front of the helmet is ornamented with a grotesque face: eyes, eyebrows and a curved beak. The hollow horns are riveted into cast bronze mountings which are in turn riveted to the helmets. The ornamental designs are composed from repoussé bosses of various sizes. At the front and back of the rim of each helmet, is an opposed pair of bird's heads, linked laterally by a line of small bosses (so forming representations of boats with a bird's head on the prow and another on the stern).
The Vikso helmets are the only horned helmets recovered from north Europe, but horned figurines occur in Denmark (see Cat. No. 189); and some of the figurines of warriors from Sardinia too wear horned helmets.
The Vikso helmets are probably made in a workshop which was strongly influenced by East Alpine bronze technology, located in all probability in Bohemia-Silesia or in central/north Germany.   J.J.

Norling-Christensen 1943; Broholm 1946, M.105; Hencken 1971; Thrane 1975, 62 ff; Levy 1982, 130, no. 96

191   HOARD

Radeni, Neamt, Rumania
Gold
1800–1600 BC (?)
5548: Height 13.2 cm, Width 13.0 cm,
Weight 458.6 g
5549: Height 9.2 cm, Width 10.4 cm,
Weight 243.3 g
5550: Height 12.7 cm, Width 11.0 cm,
Weight 203.5 g
Musée d'Histoire de Piatra Neamt
Inv. Nos. 5548–50
Ill. p. 170

The circumstances of the find are unclear. Reports from a local inhabitant indicate that the hoard was found in 1965–66 in working a field, at a depth that can no longer be determined. It contained several metal vessels with flecks of rust and verdigris. Later examination revealed that the objects were eight in number: seven "smaller" ones which were attached by wire (probably gold) to a "large" vessel with two handles. The cups were deliberately damaged before being deposited, having been crushed and beaten: this is especially clear in the case of the three specimens that had not been subjected to any significant damage after deposition. Most of the cups are flat-based; they have decorative, high-flung handles.   A.J./F.V.

Vulpe 1985, 47 ff; Petrescu-Dîmbovița 1995, 123

192   CUP

Biia, Alba, Rumania
Gold
Late Bronze Age, 13th–12th centuries BC
Height 5.8 cm. Diameter 9.8 cm.
Weight 144 g
National History Museum of Rumania,
Bucarest
Inv. No. 47584

Some time before 1880, there was found by chance at Biia a hoard of gold objects. It consisted of a two-handled vessel, with rich embossed decoration; a bracelet or arm-ring with elaborate crescent finials, richly engraved and embossed with geometric motifs; and seven single-twist hair-rings. This pot, which is raised from a gold sheet, has a depressed-globular body and a everted rim. From the rim, two opposed and free-standing handles end in double spirals. High on the shoulder, a zigzag-based pattern in dots runs around the vessel. On the upper body are two rows of larger bosses; on the lower another such, interrupted by four groups of concentric ridges based around a boss. A similar ornament is found at the centre of the base, with further linear arrangements of bosses about it.

D.L./A.J./F.V.

Popescu 1956, 232–234, fig. 144; Dumitrescu 1974, 398–401; Müller-Karpe 1980, no. 246, pl. 287.B; Florescu, Daicoviciu & Rosu 1980, 59

trade or whether the craftsman himself travelled overseas and produced the lunulae on site. A.J./F.V.

Müller-Karpe 1980, pl. 460a; Eluère 1982, fig. 144; Archéologie 1989, 196; Eogan 1994

193 LUNULA

"Mr. Trench's Estate", Galway County, Ireland
Gold
Early Bronze Age, c. 1800 BC
Weight 35.7 g
National Museum of Ireland, Dublin
Inv. No. W 10

Very delicate lunula of hammered gold-work. Like most of the pieces from the British Isles and especially from Ireland, this is one of those particularly finely designed pieces of neck jewellery that are assumed not to have been used in daily life but instead were purely for votive purposes. C.E.

Wilde 1862, 18–19; Taylor 1980, 105, CoGw 10

194 LUNULA

Mayo County, Ireland
Gold
Early Bronze Age, c. 1800 BC
Weight 46.3 g
National Museum of Ireland, Dublin
Inv. No. 1909:4

Found in a bog; such locations were the preferred sacrificial sites in northwest Europe during the Bronze Age. The nature of the site is in keeping with the religious character of the lunula. It should be recalled that these pieces were never found in graves, but rather individually or in hoards with other objects of this sort. The only example that was found in connection with a tool is the lunula of Harlyn Bay in Cornwall: there an axe was also found. This association acts as a confirmation of the date assigned to the lunula. C.E.

Armstrong 1920, 56–57, VII.39; Taylor 1980, 108, CoMa 2

Only in Copenhagen, Bonn and Athens

195 HOARD WITH LUNULAE

Kerivoa, Bourbriac, Côtes-du-Nord, France
Gold
Early Bronze Age, c. 1800 BC
Diameters external 20–25 cm,
Weight 217.8 g, 92.6 g, 98.1 g
Musée des Antiquités Nationales,
St. Germain-en-Laye
Inv. Nos. 76.492 a–e
Ill. p. 171

A hoard of gold objects: three lunulae, a neck-ring/torc with paddle-shaped finials and a piece of sheet gold (from diadem?). The lunulae of Kerivoa belong to three different types, though all appear to have been of local production. One of these lunulae is identical with that from Harlyn Bay (Cornwall); thus providing evidence for contacts across the English Channel. It remains uncertain whether this was the result of

Only in Paris

196 LUNULA

Saint-Potan, Côtes-du-Nord, France
Gold
Early Bronze Age, c. 1800 BC
Diameter 21 cm, Weight 194.5 g
Musée des Antiquités Nationales,
St. Germain-en-Laye
Inv. No. 72 399

This gold lunula was found under a rock in 1890. It has a simple pattern of deeply traced lines. Lunulae of this sort, like that of Kerivoa (see Cat. No. 195), are characterised by the relatively thick sheet gold from which they worked. This distinguishes them from the thinner, more delicate examples from Ireland, which is sufficient evidence that they were produced locally in France. They do appear, however, to have been based on Irish models, corroborating the argument concerning the existence of cross-Channel trade and contacts. A.J./F.V.

Beda 1976; Moscalu & Beda 1988, 23–47; Pare 1992, 184

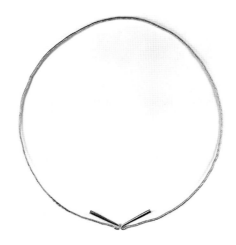

197 TORC

Naas, Tipper South (aka Kingsfurze),
Kildare County, Ireland
Gold
c. 1200 BC
Diameter 32, Thick 0.8, Weight 567 g
National Museum of Ireland, Dublin
Inv. No. 1946:391

A bar-twisted torc (four-flanged) with
recurved terminals, this was found with
a pennanular bracelet and a neck-ring.
This piece of neck jewellery is a typical
example of those often large and heavy,
bar-twisted pieces that appear on the
British Isles and in West France at the
beginning of the Bronze Age. As a rule,
these generally isolated finds (perhaps
votive offerings?) are goldsmiths work of
high quality. The artisans had to give a
exact and crisp cross-section to the bar,
and then twist it to give regular form to
the torc.   C.E.

PRIA III 1845, 98–9; Taylor 1980, 106.
CoKd 15; Eogan 1994

198 TORC

Near Mullingar, Westmeath County, Ireland
Gold
c. 1200 BC
Diameter c. 25 cm, Weight 336.9 g
National Museum of Ireland, Dublin
Inv. No. 1884:6

This bar torc (four-flanged) is an example of a large class of jewellery designed
for the neck, arms and probably also the
waist: all are produced by twisting a
metal bar. Bronze torcs made from
twisted bars developed in central Europe
under Eastern influence and are found
as far away as Britain and Ireland
around 1200 BC.   C.E.

Proceedings of the Society of Antiquaries of
London XXIV, 1912, 47; Taylor 1980, 114.
CoWm 10; Eogan 1994

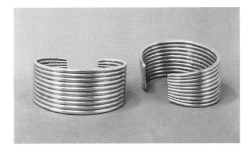

199 HOARD

Alamo, Sobral da Adica, Moura, Beja,
Portugal
Gold
Late Bronze Age
Total Weight 1.483 g
Museu Nacional da Arqueologia, Lisbon
Inv. Nos. 188-192

This gold hoard was found in 1930
while moving earth. It consisted of three
neck-rings and two bracelets. Unfortunately, there is no further information
about the circumstances of the find.
The two bracelets have an elliptical form
that narrows to open finials that taper
off in a straight line. They each consist
of ten smooth rings, which may have
been brazen together.
One neck ring is composed of three hollow rings that are joined by a strip of

metalength It is closed by means of a
separate latch with a "plug connector".
The body of the ring is ornamented with
a delicate pattern of geometrical
engraved lines. The second neck ring has
a body that becomes slightly thicker, and
it is closed in the same way as the first.

The third neck ring, by contrast, has a band-shaped body with thin finials that end in hooks, to which is attached a latch that is also band-shaped. The outside of both pieces is decorated with geometric lines and patterns of circular eyes.

The unusually rich hoard contains outstanding works at least some of which are from the same workshop. The material came from a number of sets of female jewellery and was probably deposited for ritual reasons.   C.E.

Ethnos 1 1935, 245ff; Pingel 1992, no. 207, pl. 99

200   TORC

Evora, Alentejo, Portugal
Gold
Late Bronze Age
Diameter 15.5 cm, Weight 2.1 kg
Musée de Antiquités Nationales,
St. Germain-en-Laye
Inv. No. 67071bis

This torc with its detachable clasp is decorated with traced geometric motifs. It is one of the heaviest objects of the Atlantic group.   C.E.

Pingel 1992, pl. 53

201   CUP

Wachtberg-Fritzdorf, Rhein-Sieg-Kreis,
Nordrhein-Westfalen, Germany
Gold
Early Bronze Age, 18th–16th centuries BC
Height 12.1 cm, Diameter 12.2 cm,
Weight 221g
Rheinisches Landesmuseum, Bonn
Inv. No. 55.9
Ill. p. 39

One-handled cup, with everted rim decorated by two rows of dots punched from the outside; concave neck giving onto carinated shoulder, hemispherical lower body and base with omphalos. Strap handle attached to rim and above carinated shoulder (in both cases with four rivets, each of which has a lozenge-shaped washer). The handle is decorated with three grooves on each side.

The form of the cup has its closest parallels in the early Mycenaean Shaft Graves of Greece. Outside the Aegean, the very few comparable pieces range from Cornwall and Brittany to Switzerland. Detailed correspondences (for example, the lozenge reinforcing plates with the rivets) prove that this cup is unlikely to stand independent of the other, widespread pieces, but rather has an origin in common. This is evidence that even in the earliest Mycenaean period the elites in Greece, Germany and England had contacts and that they probably exchanged valuable gifts.   J.J.

Uslar 1955, 31ff; Müller-Karpe 1980,
pl. 312A; Clarke et al. 1985, 117, no. 173;
Demakopoulou 1988, 261, no. 287

Only in Copenhagen, Bonn and Athens

202   HOARD

Rongères, Allier, France
Gold
Middle Bronze Age, 14th century BC
Diameter bowl 9.3 cm, Height 6 cm;
Diameter bracelet with spirals 6.4 cm;
Diameter wire-spirals 2–2.3 cm; ring 2.3 cm;
Weights respectively 63.3 g, 77.1 g, 21.5 g,
ring 8.8 g
Musée du Louvre, Dept. des Antiquités
grecques, etrusques et romaines, Paris,
depot St. Germain-en-Laye
Inv. Nos. BJ 1886–MND 958, BJ 970–MND
959, BJ 1161–MND 962, BJ 1180–MND 961,
BJ 1179–MND 960

This hoard of gold objects is composed of an elaborately traced bracelet with spiral finials, wire-spirals and a ring, all deposited in a vase. The last is decorated with horizontal zones of vertical lines, bosses and grooves on the upper body, and below with further bosses and concentric circles: motifs typical of and produced in the same way as on the comparable vases that have be found throughout the east and north parts of central Europe.   C.E.

Müller-Karpe 1980, pl. 461.D, no. 976a;
Eluère 1982, 157

Only in Paris

203   HOARD

Villeneuve-St-Vistre – Champ des Grès,
Marne, France
Gold
Middle Bronze Age, 14th century BC
Height goblets 11.8–12 cm, Diameter
bracelets 6.1–6.4 cm, Diameter rings
2–2.7 cm;
Weights respectively c. 49 g, 37 g, 2.7, 3.1 g,
71.1 g of wire
Musée des Antiquités Nationales,
St.Germain-en-Laye
Inv. Nos. 81 707 – 81 712

Hoard discovered in 1910, buried under
an enormous sandstone block. It consists
notably of two tall matching goblets,
decorated in relief in zones of concentric
circles, bosses, grooves and vertical
ridges, with triangles on the neck (some
filled with dots). The bracelets are plain,
the rings of various sorts – doubled-wire,
sheet decorated by dots and lines. The
loosely wound-up wires look to have had
some of their ends subjected to heat:
perhaps they were intended as ornaments of doubled wire, still being
worked on – a sort typical of central and
north Europe.   C.E.

Eluère 1982, 269, fig. 158

204   "CONUS" OR HEAD-DRESS

Avanton, Vienne, France
Gold
Middle Bronze Age, 14th century BC
Height 53 cm (fragmentary), Weight 321 g
Musée du Louvre, Dept. des Antiquités
grecques, étrusques et romaines, Paris
Inv. No. BJ 2151
Ill. p. 179

Tall upper part of "conus" or ritual
head-dress: the lower part (cap, brim) is
missing, the tip is heavily damaged;
raised from a single piece. The surviving
part is ornamented with horizontal zones
of embossed work: thirteen bands of circular motifs (lines around a central boss)
are each separated by a repeating
sequence of three/four ridges and three/
four rows of dots. The tip originally had
a many-pointed star left reserved against
a background filled with lines of dots. At
the lower end of the surviving fragment
are traces of a zone of vertical embossed
ridges that mark the zone of transition to
the missing cap/brim section. The
"conus" was found in 1844 in Avanton
near Poitiers. The circumstances of the
find are not known.   J.J.

Müller-Karpe 1980, pl. 472.11; Eluère 1982,
fig. 128; Menghin & Schauer 1983, 66,
fig. 30, 30b; Schauer 1986

205   "CONUS" OR HEAD-DRESS

Ezelsdorf-Buch, Bavaria, Germany
Gold
Late Bronze Age, 10th–8th centuries BC
Height 88.3 cm, Thickness wall 0.078 cm,
Weight 310 g
Germanisches Nationalmuseum, Nürnberg
Inv. No. Vb. 8007
Ill. p. 176

In 1953 a worker removing a tree-root
struck a gold "conus" that was buried
upright and by itself just below the surface (up to a depth of eighty cm). The
"conus" has a tall, slender shaft, with a
broader and off-set basal element, acting

as a cap. The entire piece is worked up
from a single piece. The embossed ornaments were put on with at least twenty-
five different stamps in the paper-thin
gold foil: they feature – in bands – multiple and single circles, bosses, hatched
triangles, vertical and oblique lines,
grooves, spoked wheels and "eyes" (the
last two but once). A plain star marks
the top. Where the shaft joins the base, a
broad zone of ornament, vertically
ribbed and grooved, is visible. A band of
bronze sheet (1.8 cm wide) serves to
strengthen the very base, the gold foil
rim being turned up at its edge and
round it to hold it in place.   J.J.

Müller-Karpe 1980, pl. 412A; Menghin &
Schauer 1983; Schauer 1986; Raschke 1954,
1ff

206   "CONUS" OR HEAD-DRESS

Schifferstadt, Speyer, Rheinland-Pfalz,
Germany
Gold
Middle/Late Bronze Age, Reinecke BrC-D,
14th–13th centuries BC
Height 29.6 cm, Diameter cap 18.1,
Thickness 0.1–0.25, Weight 350.5 g
Historisches Museum der Pfalz, Speyer
Inv. No. 1934/20
Ill. p. 173

The so-called "Golden Hat" was found
in 1835 while the soil of a field was
being turned over. This gold "conus",
shorter than the preceding, has preserved its cap and brim; all worked up from
a single piece. Where the cap base turns
out to become the brim, several pairs of
holes are punched on opposite sides. The
rounded tip of the "conus" is plain and
set off from the shaft by zones of multiple horizontal grooves flanking a row
of simple bosses. The shaft is decorated
by horizontal bands of five grooves alternating with small dots, larger bosses in
circular ridges and "eyes". The cap and
the brim continue much the same pat-
terning.

The brim, which was bent when found, was supposed to have been turned up alongside the shaft. Alongside and leaning on it were three bronze axes. J.J.

Müller-Karpe 1980, pl. 439; Menghin & Schauer 1983; Schauer 1986

207 "CONUS" OR HEAD-DRESS

From southwest Germany/Switzerland; unknown provenance
Gold
Late Bronze Age, 10th–8th centuries BC
Height 74.5 cm, Thickness 0.06 mm,
Weight 490 g
Staatliche Museen zu Berlin – Preußischer Kulturbesitz, Museum für Vor- und Frühgeschichte
Inv. No. IIc 6088
Ill. p. 174

This gold "conus" was bought on the art market, so that it is no longer possible to determine the original site or circumstances of its find. It belongs to a group of only four known examples that, as far as can be determined, all come from southwest Germany or east France.
Their precise function is still debated, but it was surely something to do with cult or religious activities (for further details and bibliography, see Menghin, pp. 172ff.). A.J./F.V.

208 CUP

Dohnsen, Celle, Germany
Bronze
LH I-II, 16th–15th centuries BC
Height 5.7 cm, Diameter 12.6 cm
Niedersächsisches Landesmuseum, Hannover
Inv. No. 22:61

Bronze cup of hemispherical shape; its bottom is rounded and without any defined base. The cup was held by a vertical strap handle, whose broader upper end is provided with small extensions to assist its riveting to the outside of the wall just below the rim; the rounded lower end of the handle, which is approximately in the middle of the vessel, is held by a rivet. It has a narrow spout at the rim, at a right-angle to the handle. Below three grooves at the rim is a foliate band traced or cast on.
It is probably a genuine Minoan-Mycenaean product. Its closest relative is found in the settlement of Akrotiri, Thera, which was destroyed in a natural volcanic catastrophe in the late 17th–16th centuries BC. J.J.

Matthäus 1978, 59ff; Demakopoulou 1988, 260, no. 286

209 HOARD WITH CUPS

Borgbjerg, Boeslunde, Sorø, Zealand, Denmark
Late Bronze Age, Period IV,
11th–9th centuries BC
Ladle Height 10.3 cm, Diameter 11.5 cm;
Beaker Height 10.2 cm, Diameter 10 cm;
Bowl Height 9.4 cm, Diameter 17.5 cm.
Total weight 1260 g
National Museum, Copenhagen
Inv. Nos. Ladles B 1066, Beakers B 1067,
Bowls 7046
Ill. p. 169

The six gold vessels were found on a terraced hill-side at two separate places in 1842 and 1874. Two identical *ladles* are of chased/embossed gold plate: the basic form is a round-bottomed bowl with a carinated shoulder leading to a straight-sided neck and everted rim. The lower body has two registers of concentric circles separated by bands of cording (small vertical/oblique ridges); in the upper part bands of small dots alternate with several of cording; the neck is plain, the rim corded. To this is riveted a fairly large bronze handle terminating in a stylised horse's head with a "horn" on the forehead. The handle has a narrow gold ribbon wound round it.
The two identical *cups* have cylindrical feet, opening rapidly into the lower body, a carination marking off the upper part with its everted rim. The upper part is treated to bands of cording; the lower an unusual vertical zoning by dashes; the foot is a mix of plain and corded bands.
The two identical *bowls* have a depressed hemispherical body, with a plain neck and slightly everted rim with cording and dots. The upper body has various bands of circle/boss ornament with some linear components; the lower has similar elements in now a more vertical arrangement. The base has an omphalos. J.J.

Broholm 1946, 271; Jensen 1981, 48ff

210 DRINKING SERVICE

Dresden-Dobritz, Saxony, Germany
Bronze
Late Bronze Age
Height 60–20 cm. Weight, combined 10 kg
Landesamt für Archäologie Sachsen mit
Landesamt für Vorgeschichte, Japanisches
Palais, Dresden
Inv. Nos. S:2314–2331/52 (D 258–275/83);
D 848/89.
Ill. p. 45

This tableware was found in 1948 in the
vicinity of a large settlement; it includes
a large bucket, a sieve, two ladles and
fourteen handled bowls. At the time it
was the richest find of bronze tableware
recorded in central Europe. Most of the
vessels are highly decorated with a range
of repoussé bands, bosses/dots and various linear designs, with a pattern on the
base reminiscent of a star (or spider's-
web) set about an omphalos. The bronze
vessels are representative of the utensils
of a princely household. The number of
cups may correspond to the number of
guests at this meal.   J.J.

Hänsel & Hänsel 1997; Jockenhövel &
Kubach 1994, 81–82

211 DRINKING SERVICE

Unterglauheim, Dillingen, Bavaria, Germany
Bronze and gold
Late Bronze Age, 10th–9th centuries BC
Bowls Height 7 and 8.5 cm. Weight 51 and
41 g. Cauldrons Height 12.5, Diameter 27.
Bucket Height 33.5, Diameter 31.3
Römisches Museum, Augsburg
Inv. Nos. VF 1,1–2, 4–6

Two conical gold bowls, with a pair of a
bronze cauldrons of different sizes, a
bronze handled bucket and some gold
wire – all were found in 1834 during
fieldwork at the village of "Hinterfeld".
The gold bowls had apparently been
stacked in each other, wrapped with the
gold wire and placed in a bronze cauldron that was filed with bones and
ashes, above which a second cauldron of
a similar type was upturned. All were
then were deposited in the bronze bucket
with its lid.
The gold bowls were treated to a good
decoration, based on the usual circular
and linear motifs; the bronze ones had
bands of dots below the rim. The
bucket's shoulder boasts more elaborate
work – grooves and dots below the rim,
lower down come circles/bosses and
duck devices.   J.J.

Menghin & Schauer 1983, 88–89; Jockenhövel & Kubach 1994, 81–82; Jacob 1995

212 HORN MOUNTING

Wismar, Mecklenburg-Vorpommern,
Germany
Bronze
Middle Bronze Age, Period III,
13th–12th centuries BC
Height 14 cm
Landesmuseum Mecklenburg-Vorpommern,
Schwerin
Inv. No. 80 a.b.c.

The so-called Wismar horn, or more
accurately the three bronze mounts from
one such (mouthpiece, terminal and suspension loop) were found in 1836 deep

in a peat-bog. This find differs from
other bronzes of the Late Bronze Age in
being richly decorated not only with the
more usual geometrical and curvilinear
forms of ornament – running spirals,
chevrons, zones of lines/dots, and
zigzags, but also with images which are
reminiscent of rock carvings – boats,
warriors with spears and spoked wheels,
for example. The depictions here are
divided into bands and can be "read"
consecutively, just as the individual
zones can be assessed in relation to each
other.   J.J.

Schmidt 1915, 142ff; Sprockhoff 1956,
249ff; Randsborg 1993, 98ff

213 VESSEL

Siem, Ålborg, Jutland, Denmark
Bronze
Late Bronze Age, Period IV,
11th–10th centuries BC
Height 28 cm
National Museum, Copenhagen
Inv. Nos. 20419

A bucket of the Hajdu Böszörmény type.
Two near-identical buckets were found
in 1862 during peat-cutting in a bog.
The buckets are made from three sheets,
held together by rivets that have been
hammered flat so that their heads cannot be seen on the outside. The buckets
are ornamented with embossed dots,

bosses and ridges; those directly under the shoulder are in the form of vertical rows of bosses between dots, in places in conjunction with the so-called bird/sun-barque motif. Both buckets have been repaired in different manners. Indeed, though very similar, a number of differences do exist between them: e.g. one has the tips of the handle rivets hammered flat, one not. All of the other differences are in the details of the ornamentation.

These Hajdu Böszörmény buckets are likely to have been made outside the Hungarian area. The circumstances of the find indicate that bronze vessels were imported for the use of the upper levels of society, maybe in connection with religious practices rather than with everyday use. They do not seem to have had any significant impact on the local production of bronzes or of pottery. J.J.

Broholm 1946, M.73; Thrane 1965a, figs. 16–19; and 1975, 142

Only in Copenhagen and Bonn

214 AMPHORA

Gevelinghausen, Olsberg, Westphalia, Germany
Bronze
Late Bronze Age, Period V,
9th–8th centuries BC
Height c. 56 cm, Diameter 37.4 cm
Westfälisches Museum für Archäologie, Münster
Inv. No. 1961:22

This amphora was found during excavation work in 1961, just one meter below the surface. It stood inverted, its mouth facing downwards and served as a grave vessel, as is apparent from the cremated remains of the corpse, which were wrapped in a textile. The amphora contained two rectangles of bone with circular "dot-and-circle" patterns on the top. Thus far, no other burial sites have been found near this one.

In addition to a handle that broke off long ago, and is now missing, the conoid foot must have been once some three cm longer.

The amphora, which holds about fourteen litres, consists of eight joined parts (upper and lower body, base, conical foot, strengthening ring at rim, handle(s) and the rings hanging in them – all held together by two different types of rivets). It is richly decorated in a variety of ways. The corded rim is slightly everted from the short, cylindrical neck around which runs a band of large bosses surrounded each by a ridge, and flanked by a line of smaller ones. The shoulder is emboldened by a row of bossed rivets which, in addition to their decorative function, serve to connect the upper and lower parts of the amphora. Above the shoulder is a frieze of three bird-barques, set on two rows of smallish bosses; between the birds' heads are pairs of large concentric circle motifs. Below the shoulder is a more elaborate version: four bird-barques each "hold" a large concentric circle motif, with smaller pairs between the boats; above this are three rows of simple bosses. It has been calculated that the number of bosses employed runs well into the thousands. The bird-barques and sun motifs clearly mark this amphora as another example of the symbolic goods of the Urnfield period. Their original function probably went beyond the purely secular. This vase belongs to a small group of similar vessels of the type Gevelinghausen-Vejo-Seddin, whose findspots stretch from Etruria to Denmark. Although their ori-

gin can no longer be determined with certainty, they not only demonstrate the wide-ranging trade relations of the time, but also shared religious practices across regions. A.J./F.V.

Jockenhövel 1974, 16ff

215 CAULDRON AND TWO CUPS

Hajdúsámson, Hajdú Bihar, Hungary
Bronze
Ha A2 / Ha B1, 11th–10th centuries BC
Two handled cauldron Height 15.5 cm, Diameter 22.5 cm; One handled cup Height 6 cm, Diameter 15.5 cm; Cup Height 4.7 cm, Diameter 14.4 cm
Déri Múzeum Debrecen
Inv. Nos. 1909/170; 1909/258; 1909/171

This hoard was found north of the village of Hajdúsámson at a depth of sixty to seventy cm. The three bowls were stacked one inside the other. In the uppermost, smallest bowl were three bronze cups, also stacked one inside the other. The handle was held in place in small sleeves by conical rivets. Just below the mouth is a band incised linear ornament, combined with rows of loops or zigzag lines. Most of the vessels show signs of repeated repair-work, which suggests they were used over a long period.

The hoard is one of the drinking services that were widespread in the Late Bronze Age. They were probably deposited in cult or religious practices, perhaps based on the concept of a symposium in the afterlife. A.J./F.V.

Patay 1990, nos. 9–11

216
CAULDRON

Milkernagh, Granard, Longford County,
Ireland
Bronze
Late Bronze Age / Early Iron Age,
9th–6th centuries BC
Height 32 cm, Diameter 54 cm
National Museum of Ireland, Dublin
Inv. No. 1925:13

This cauldron, which can hold about
forty litres of liquid, was found 1884
under a dozen feet of turf in Milkernagh
Bog, near Granard. It is made up of thin
sheets of bronze in bands: the bottom
piece is single and rounded in profile,
the next row up consists of two strips,
whilst the second and third rows are of
three pieces each. The rim is fashioned
from only two pieces joined together
under the handles and is slightly everted.
To strengthen it, the sheet at the rim is
turned over around a bronze ring. The
handles consist of two bronze rings,
secured on the interior by rings given a
ribbed ornamentation. These rings are
further fastened to the rim by twisted
bronze stays, two inside and two out.
Over thirty bronze cauldrons from this
period have been found in Ireland. The
form is based ultimately upon Greek and
Oriental prototypes, which perhaps suggests long-distance contacts along the
Atlantic seaboard.   A.J./F.V.

Thomas 1899

217 SEAL

Lerna – Settlement III, Phase C, Argolid,
Greece
Steatite
Early Bronze Age, EH II,
middle of 3rd millennium BC
Length 1.8 cm, Width 1.8 cm, Height 1 cm
Archaeological Museum, Argos
Inv. No. L 7.322
Ill. p. 193

Irregular square plaque with rounded
corners of purplish-brown steatite. One
surface has a low crescent-shaped lug
grip, centrally placed. The under-side
bears the engraved motif: three superimposed irregular zigzags with four triangular motifs placed near the corners.
The surface is well polished.
Some parallels have been found at Asine
in the Argolid and at other Early Helladic settlements on the Mainland. These
seals probably ultimately have a Cretan
origin: examples with elementary geometric forms and simple linear decoration are known on Crete in the Early
Minoan Period. The seal from Lerna was
most probably used for securing various
containers of products, such as jars or
boxes, during storage or exchange: it
indicates the high level of economic
organisation at the important Early Helladic settlement of Lerna, especially in
its third phase (Lerna III), with its fortifications and a central, monumental
public building, the House of the Tiles.
A considerable collection of clay sealings
associated with the House of the Tiles
provides clear evidence for the administrative use of seals at Lerna during this
period.
It has been suggested that this kind of
Early Helladic/Early Minoan seals could
also have been used to decorate objects
and materials.   N.D.-V.

Banks 1967, 221–222, no. 428, pl. 9; Heath
1958, 81–121; CMS V.1, 28–29, 36 no. 35

218 SEAL

Lerna – Settlement IV, Phase B, Argolid,
Greece
Clay
Early Bronze Age, EH III, second half of
the 3rd millennium BC
Height 2.5 cm, Diameter base 2.7 cm
Archaeological Museum, Argos
Inv. No. L 4.67
Ill. p. 193

A conical stamp-seal of yellow-brown
clay, grey in places, with a polished surface. A perforation near the apex of the
cone was used for the suspension of the
seal. On the base of the cone the motifs
are incised: irregular, somewhat curvilinear zigzags between two circles. The
inner circle has a round depression with
a small rounded protuberance at its
centre.
This type of conical terracotta seal has
also been found at other Early Bronze
Age settlements of Mainland Greece and
the Aegean area, usually decorated with
simple rectilinear and curvilinear incised
motifs. They were used mainly for
administrative and also for decorative
purposes.   N.D.-V.

Banks 1967, 650–651, no. 1738; CMS V.1,
28–29, 37, no. 36

219 BAR WITH HIEROGLYPHIC SCRIPT

Knossos, Crete, Greece
Clay
Middle Bronze Age, MM II, 18th century BC
Height 2.5 cm, Length 8 cm
Archaeological Museum, Herakleion
Inv. No. 1286
Ill. p. 188

Four-sided bar of clay with suspension
hole, inscribed in the Hieroglyphic script
on all four sides. Ideograms and numbers can be made out.   E.B.

Olivier & Godart 1996, 100–101

tence continues down to LM III A. It is wide-spread throughout Crete – including Ayia Triada, Knossos, Pyrgos, Zakros, Poros, Juktas and Tylissos; and also outside the island at Kea, Thera and Samothrace.

Although the two scripts, A and B, share some of the same phonetic values, Linear A remains so far undeciphered.

E.B.

Caratelli 1957–58, 363–388; Godart & Olivier 1976, 26 (HT 13)

220 BAR WITH HIEROGLYPHIC SCRIPT

Knossos, Crete, Greece

Clay

Middle Bronze Age II, MM II, 18ᵗʰ century BC

Height 6.8 cm, Width 1.1 cm,

Thickness 1.3 cm

Archaeological Museum, Herakleion

Inv. No. 1287

Clay bar, pointed at one end with a suspension hole, and inscribed with the Hieroglyphic script on four sides. The hieroglyphic or pictographic script first appeared in the Middle Minoan I period – probably derived from Egypt. It was used on seals, roundels, bars, tablets and ritual bowls.

E.B.

Evans 1925, 103; Olivier & Godart 1996, 111

221 ROUNDEL WITH HIEROGLYPHIC SCRIPT

Knossos, Crete, Greece

Clay

Middle Bronze Age, MM II, 18ᵗʰ century BC

Height 4.3 cm

Archaeological Museum, Herakleion

Inv. No. 1269

Clay roundel with a suspension hole at its top, inscribed with the Hieroglyphic script on both sides.

E.B.

Evans 1909, 85; Olivier & Godart 1996, 94–95

222 LINEAR A TABLET

Ayia Triada, Crete, Greece

Clay

Late Bronze Age, LM I, 15ᵗʰ century BC

Height 6.1 cm, Width 10.5 cm, Thick 0.8 cm

Archaeological Museum, Herakleion

Inv. No. 7

Ill. p. 189

Page-like tablet reconstructed from four fragments; on the upper right a small piece is missing. The text (seven lines in Linear A script) is inscribed on one side only.

Linear A was so named by Evans to distinguish it from the later Linear B script which has been now deciphered. Linear A was most in use probably in MM III/ LM I times, though evidence for its exis-

223 LINEAR A TABLET

Ayia Triada, Crete, Greece

Clay

Late Bronze Age, LM I, 15ᵗʰ century BC

Height 11 cm, Width 0.67 cm, Thick 0.8 cm

Archaeological Museum, Herakleion

Inv. No. 1364

This page-shaped tablet, reconstructed from two joining pieces, has text in the Linear A script, here continuing on the reverse.

E.B.

Godart & Olivier 1976, 196, HT no. 117

224 LINEAR B TABLET

Pylos, Palace Messenia, Greece
Clay
Late Bronze Age, LH IIIB, 13th century BC
Height 20.5 cm, Width 11 cm, Thick 1.5 cm
National Archaeological Museum Athens
Inv. No. 14351 (Cn 131)
Ill. p. 189

Page-shaped tablet with a Linear B inscription on one of the main surfaces. The inscribed text reads from left to right; the lines are separated by horizontal incisions. Use is made of syllabograms, ideograms and numerical signs. The first line, the heading, gives a summary of the contents of the tablet.
The tablet belongs to the Cn series, the distinguishing feature of which is the presence of ideograms for domesticated animals. It contains a list of flocks of sheep and goats and their herdsmen that are affiliated to the palace and come from a distinct area of the kingdom of Pylos. The animals were mostly male and were raised for their wool, the raw material for the woollen textile industry of the palace at Pylos.
Such clay tablets, the first written documents in the Greek language, come from the archives that were kept at the Mycenaean palaces, which were the administrative, economic and religious centres of large territories. Linear B tablets are also found at Knossos and Chania on Crete and Mycenae, Tiryns and Thebes on the Greek mainland. L.P.-M.

Palmer 1969, 168–170, 487; Bennett &
Olivier 1963; and 1973, 69, 77; Demako-
poulou 1988, 204, no. 182; Ruipérez &
Melena 1996, 163–166, 169–171

225 LINEAR B TABLET

Pylos, Palace Messenia, Greece
Clay
Late Bronze Age, LH IIIB, 13th century BC
Height 3.8 cm, Length 26.5 cm,
Thick 1.4 cm
National Archaeological Museum Athens
Inv. No. 14352 (TA 709-712)

Leaf-shaped tablet reconstructed from three pieces. The different colours of the clay originate from the fact that the tablet was broken and burnt in the fire that destroyed the palace, but under different atmospheric conditions.
The tablet belongs to the TA series, whose subject concerns the vessels, utensils or the furniture used in a household. The text has only three rows and deals with cooking vessels. The name of each vessel is followed by an ideogram. Common Mycenaean functional vessels are distinguished; the Greek names attributed to them in the Linear B script, such as *pi-je-ra* (pan), *ti-ri-po* (tripod) and *e-ka-ra* (portable hearth), give irrefutable evidence that the language of the Mycenaean texts is Greek. L.P.-M.

Palmer 1969, 29–31, fig. 4; Bennett &
Olivier 1973, 230–231; Demakopoulou 1988,
204, no. 183; Ruipérez & Melena 1996, 175

226 INSCRIBED STIRRUP-JAR

Thebes – Old Kadmeion, Boeotia, Greece
Clay
Late Bronze Age, LH IIIA–B,
14th–13th centuries BC
Height 44.5 cm, Diameter 29.5 cm
Archaeological Museum, Thebes
Inv. No. 853
Ill. p. 186

The large, coarse-ware stirrup-jar, with simple linear decoration, was the common trading vessel in Mycenaean times and used for the transportation of oil or wine. Some of them are inscribed on the shoulder or on the belly in the Linear B script.
This stirrup-jar from the palace at Thebes bears an inscription on the belly. A personal name, Eudamos (*e-u-da-mo*) that refers to the producer or the owner, and is also the name of a place in west Crete may be read in the inscription.
The inscribed stirrup-jars of Thebes constitute a large body and their provenance has aroused much discussion. It seems that the majority originated from west Crete, from workshops that are often described in the inscriptions as *wa-na-ka-te-ro* (royal) and may have related to a palatial centre at Chania. Inscribed stirrup-jars have also been found at other important sites on Crete (Knossos and the cemetery of Armenoi) and on the Greek mainland (Mycenae, Tiryns, Thebes, Orchomenos, Kreusis, Eleusis and recently the acropolis of Midea in the Argolid). L.P.-M.

Raison 1968, 61–63, pl. XXXIX; Sacconi
1974, 135; Catling et al. 1980, 49ff, 105.8;
Hallager 1987, 171ff; Demakopoulou 1988,
206, no. 184

227 INSCRIBED STIRRUP-JAR

Knossos – Unexplored Mansion, Crete, Greece

Clay

Late Bronze Age, LM IIIB, 13th century BC

Height 40.3 cm, Diameter 30.5 cm

Archaeological Museum, Herakleion

Inv. No. 18374

This large, coarse stirrup jar for wine or oil is decorated with stylised octopus tentacles and horizontal bands. On its shoulder are three Linear B signs, *wi-na-jo*, interpreted as the name of the owner or the producer of the liquid contents of the jar. The same inscription appears on a similar jar from the cemetery of Armenoi (see Cat. No. 228).

E.B.

Popham 1969, 43 ff; Demakopoulou 1988, 208, no. 186

228 INSCRIBED STIRRUP-JAR

Armenoi – Chamber Tomb 146, Rethymnon, Crete, Greece

Clay

Late Bronze Age, LM IIIB, 13th century BC

Height 31.5 cm, Diameter 22 cm

Archaeological Museum, Rethymnon

Inv. No. 3363

Ill. p. 190

The coarse-ware stirrup-jar, used for the transportation of liquids, is inscribed on the shoulder with three signs in the Linear B script, *wi-na-jo*. This refers to the owner or the producer of its liquid contents. The same inscription appears on a stirrup jar from Knossos (see Cat. No. 227).

A great number of the inscribed stirrup-jars found in Crete (Chania, Armenoi, Knossos) and in mainland Greece, especially in Thebes (see Cat. No. 226), originated from Chania in west Crete, an important administrative centre in Mycenaean Crete.

L.P.-M.

Demakopoulou 1988, 208, no. 187; Tzedakis 1996, 1124

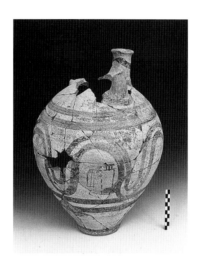

229 INSCRIBED STIRRUP-JAR

Midea – Acropolis, Argolid, Greece

Clay

Late Bronze Age, LH IIIB2, 13th century BC

Height 40 cm, Diameter 28 cm

Archaeological Museum, Nauplion

Inv. No. MI 95AA1

Though mended from numerous fragments, yet large parts of the belly and the shoulder, as well as one handle and false mouth are missing. The linear decoration of the vessel is nonetheless well preserved: on a broad zone at the belly is a double wavy band that resembles stylised octopus tentacles. In one of the open spaces by a tentacle the Linear B inscription *wi-na-jo* is painted.

The name *wi-na-jo* is very common in Linear B inscriptions from Crete. It occurs in the text of many inscribed tablets and on two storage stirrup-jars, one from Knossos and the other from Armenoi. Similar inscribed storage stirrup-jars have been found at most of the palace centres on mainland Greece (Mycenae, Tiryns, Thebes, Orchomenos and Midea) and also at Knossos and Chania on Crete. Recent research has shown that most of the inscribed storage stirrup-jars found in the great Mycenaean centres of the mainland have been imported from west Crete.

K.D.

Demakopoulou & Valakou 1994–1995, 326–327, pl. II; Catling et al. 1980, 88–93

230 SEALING

Monastiraki, Chania, Crete, Greece

Clay

Middle Bronze Age, MM II, 19th–18th centuries BC

Length 12.1 cm, Width 7.6 cm, Thickness 3.3 cm

Archaeological Museum, Rethymnon

Inv. No. MO 11

Near intact sealing of coarse clay of a light red colour, with several inclusions including pieces of straw. The front face has a distinctly convex profile, where were stamped ten impressions of the same seal, as well as one of which only part of the outline is preserved. The rear of the sealing has long, concave profile with an acute-angled depression – the whole having an irregular surface of thin, long depressions. It seems that it must have been used to seal part of the

276

rim of a pithos with a lid of woven reeds or branches of some similar plant.

All the impressions have the same orientation. The periphery in two cases was distorted by that of a neighbour.

The shape of the seal used is flat and circular (lentoid), with a diameter of 1.8 cm. The seal had a central motif in the shape of a cross, the arms of which had flaring ends (a stylised swastika) with the spaces between the arms being occupied by four lozenges (wheel?). The surface of the sealing reveals traces of the finger-nails and fingers of the person who used the seal. A.T.

Unpublished

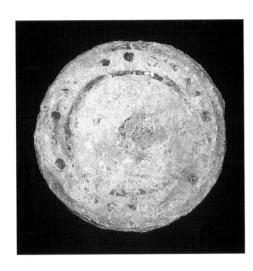

231 WEIGHT

Thorikos – Tholos Tomb III, Attica, Greece

Lead

Late Bronze Age, LH II, 15th century BC

Height 1.2 cm, Weight 1.426 kg,

Diameter 12.5 cm

National Archaeological Museum Athens

Inv. No. 3686

Lead was the standard raw material used for the manufacture of the balance weights that are found in numerous settlement and funerary contexts in the Late Bronze Age Aegean. This piece comes from Thorikos, an important early Mycenaean centre in the area of Laurion, Attica, known in Classical antiquity for its silver mines. It bears a painted decoration in red, a row of dots and concentric circles with a solid circle in the middle. The use of paint is unusual, since linear motives or dots on the balance weights are normally incised or impressed. These signs may be explained as denominational marks, in a weight-measurement system that was in use in Crete (Knossos, Zakros), in the Cyclades (Thera, Kea, Melos) and the Greek mainland (Mycenae, Tiryns, Dendra and Vapheio). L.P.-M.

Servais 1971, 81, figs. 42–43; balance weights see Petruso 1992, 1ff, 56–61

232 KRATER SHERD WITH REPRESENTATION OF A WARSHIP

Kynos, Phthiotis, Lamia, Greece

Clay

Late Bronze Age, LH IIIC, 12th century BC

Height 19 cm, Diameter 14 cm

Archaeological Museum, Lamia

Inv. No. K 8990

Ill. p. 201

Part of the rim and body of a krater mended from two sherds. The rim is everted, flat on top and is painted with a dark brown colour, inside and out. The body has a warship sailing to the right, with two warriors fighting with spears and shields on the deck. In the stern, the helmsman holds the tiller and in the prow a figure wearing a helmet with a billowing crest, and apparently gesticulating strongly, may have been the leader of the attack. The two warriors fighting wear helmets without crests, but with projections that have been interpreted as the hair of unprocessed animal hide. One of them holds a round shield, the other a shield of "Hittite" type.

The ship has a low body line, a curving stern, a tall prow with its top edge in the shape of a (?)horn and a deck. The existence of decks in Mycenaean ships has been disputed, but this Kynos sherd, and others from the same site, demonstrate that warships had one running from stern to prow. This ship had nine oars on each side – an unusual number, and one mentioned in the Homeric poems. The structure in the prow on which the figure is standing may be a ladder, a cabin, or Homer's *ikrion*. Similar structures are known from other scenes of ships from the same period. The Kynos sherd has the earliest certain representation of a warship in the Mycenaean world, and demonstrates that Geometric ships were directly descended from those of the Mycenaean period. Ph.D.

Dakoronia 1987, 117–122

233 BOWL

Eleusis – South Cemetery, grave 11, Attica, Greece

Clay

Geometric Period, MG II, first half of the 8th century BC, c. 770 BC

Height 6.5 cm, Diameter rim 10 cm

Archaeological Museum, Eleusis

Inv. No. 910

Ill. p. 206

An almost intact two-handled bowl (*skyphos*) of the Middle Geometric Phase II, when the first narrative representations in Attic vase-painting appear. On one side of the vase a kneeling archer is shown on a ship aiming towards the left, while the commander steadies the steering oar. The ship has a projecting prow with a bird on it and a tall curving stern. It is not clear whether the ship is approaching or setting out from the shore. At each side of the ship, facing it and probably on land, stands a "Dipylon" warrior with a "figure-of-eight" shield, sword and spears, who is supposed to be taking part in the battle represented.

On the other side of the vase a confrontation is taking place on land: archers and men with spears are engaged in a battle, while two victims lie in the middle of the field with their raised hands overlapping each other. All the figures are rendered in silhouette according to the style of the period, the main concern of the vase-painter being to portray the actions of the human figure and the meaning of the scene depicted. Both scenes on the vase are probably connected and may refer to an adventurous event possibly inspired by the epic poems. Such subject matter would reflect the overseas ventures of the Greeks of this period, of both commercial and warlike character, which culminated in the great colonisation of the 8th century BC throughout the Aegean and the central and east Mediterranean.   N.D.-V.

Coldstream 1968, 26–28; Schweitzer 1969, 36ff, figs. 27–28; Ahlberg 1971, 34ff, figs. 42–43; Sweeney et al. 1988, 62, no. 3

234   PITHOS FRAGMENT

Tenos – Xobourgo, Cyclades, Greece
Clay
Archaic Period, first half of the 7th century BC, 700–650 BC
Preserved Height 65 cm
Archaeological Museum, Tenos
Inv. No. 14
Ill. p. 202

Fragment from the neck of a pithos with relief decoration. In one of the preserved panels a female and a male figure are depicted in profile, confronted, and probably shaking hands. The figures are rendered in quite high relief, and the facial features, hair and clothing details are added by incision – a decorative habit typical of Archaic art during the 7th century BC.

The scene has been interpreted as a representation of Ariadne and Theseus. It might also represent a conversation between Clytemnestra and Aegisthos – a supplication after the murder of Agamemnon. Despite the static quality

and the bold simplicity of line, the figures can be believed to exude a kind of despair after carrying out the murder. The technique of the relief pithos, decorated with pictorial scenes inspired largely by mythology, was widely practised in the Cyclades, and also in mainland Greece (Boeotia, Euboea and Attica). Similar relief pithoi were produced by the Tenian workshops to which this fragment belongs, which flourished in the 8th and 7th centuries BC, and which specialised in the use of compositions with human figures in the decoration of these pithoi. The fragment presented here is arguably inspired by the cycle of the Atreidai, the heroes of which are directly or indirectly connected with the Trojan War.   N.D.-V.

Kontoleon 1969, 227–228, pls. 48–49; Caskey-Ervin 1976, 33 IIIg; Exhibition catalogue Athen 1995, 64, no. 34

235   FRAGMENT OF A KRATER

Argos, Argolid, Greece
Clay
Archaic Period, second quarter of the 7th century BC, c. 670 BC
Preserved Height 24.5 cm,
Width 31 cm
Archaeological Museum, Argos
Inv. No. C 149
Ill. p. 182

On the shoulder-zone of the krater is a panel showing a figured scene depicting the blinding of the Cyclops Polyphemos, inspired by the *Odyssey* IX.387–385. The gigantic Cyclops is half-lying on the rocks of his cave, while two men (the leg of a third is discernible at the broken edge of the piece) – most probably Ulysses and his companions – carry on high a pole, which they are thrusting into the giant's single eye. Their attack is intended to help them to escape from the captivity in which they are held by the one-eyed giant. Polyphemos, taken by surprise, tries to remove the pole with

his hand and puts out his tongue in a grimace that indicates pain or possibly drunkenness, his face and throat are covered by spots and dashes indicating blood. The naked bodies of the figure are rendered in outline with beige paint added within; the hair is long and held with bands on the forehead; the faces are bearded.

The dramatic scene is at once delicate and powerful, the work of an accomplished Argive vase-painter of the period who made use of polychromy and a technique that recalls the Attic workshops. Iconographically, it belongs to the cycle of the adventures of Ulysses crystallised in the Homeric poems, which were a basic source of inspiration for Greek artists from early historical times.   N.D.-V.

Courbin 1955, 1–49, fig. 1–4, pl. I; Sweeney et al. 1988, 97, no. 21; Ahlberg-Cornell 1992, 96, no. 75, fig. 151; Ulisse 1996, 120, no. 2.2

236   SQUAT JUG

Aegina – Sanctuary at Kolonna, Saronic Gulf, Greece
Clay
Archaic Period, second quarter of the 7th century BC, 675–650 BC
Presumed Height 22 cm,
Diameter 25.5 cm
Archaeological Museum, Aegina
Inv. No. 1754
Ill. p. 199

Protoattic oinochoe by the Ram-Jug Painter. On the shoulder zone is a row of three rams with elongated bodies decorated with dense wavy lines indicating their fleece, their heads and muzzles are rendered in outline, the long tails and legs painted solid black. Hanging below each ram is a naked man, the best preserved of which shows bands around his neck, waist and wrists, that are apparently ropes rather than belts. The figure on the left quite clearly holds onto the horns of the ram. The bodies of the heroes are rendered in outline, their faces have heavy eyebrows and pronounced noses, their long hair is painted black. This characteristic scene of the Black-and-White style of the Ram-Jug Painter, named after this vase, is completed with filling motifs, though without crowding the picture.

The scene depicts the famous escape of Ulysses and his companions from the cave of Polyphemos, after they had blinded the drunken giant (see Cat. No. 235), as described in Homer's *Odyssey* IX.437-460. These subjects from the *Odyssey* associated with the Cyclops Polyphemos were popular in the iconography of Early Greek art.

N.D.-V.

Pallaf 1897, 325 ff. figs. 40–41; Kraiker 1951, 87–88, no. 566, pls. 44–45; Sweeney et al. 1988, 97, no. 22; Ahlberg-Cornell 1992, 95, no. 79, fig. 155; Ulisse 1996, 130, No. 2.17

concealed in the body of the animal. Portrayed is the very moment of the escape of Ulysses or of one of his companions from the cave of Polyphemos, the divine-born Cyclops (see Cat. No. 236). This iconographic motif was inspired by the *Odyssey* and popular in Greek Archaic art.

N.D.-V.

Perdrizet 1908, 125–126, no. 680, fig. 469; Ulisse 1996, 130, no. 2.18

237 RELIEF CUT-OUT ORNAMENT

Delphi – Sanctuary of Apollo, Phokis, Greece

Bronze

Archaic Period, second half of the 6th century BC, 540–530 BC

Length 9.1 cm, Height 5 cm,

Thickness 2 cm

Archaeological Museum, Delphi

Inv. No. 2650

Ill. p. 185

A male figure hangs under the body of a ram holding on to the fleece of its shoulders and neck, and is also bound tightly to it by a rope. The face is unbearded; the hair is indicated by horizontal grooves. The ram has a heavy fleece, twisted horns and a pronounced muzzle. The ornament was probably used as an inlay with others such to decorate the surface of some bronze or perhaps wooden object. It was fixed by two nails

Abbreviations

E.B.	Eleni Banou
K.D.	Katie Demakopoulou
Ph.D.	Phanouria Dakoronia
N.D.-V.	Nicoletta Divari-Valakou
C.E.	Christiane Eluère
V.F.	Václav Furmánek
W.F.	Walter Fasnacht
J.J.	Jørgen Jensen
A.J.	Albrecht Jockenhövel
F.K.	Flemming Kaul
S.K.	Sophia Karapanou
Ch.K.-C.	Chaido Koukouli-Chrysanthaki
D.L.	Doina Leahu
J.-P.M.	Jean-Pierre Mohen
L.P.-M.	Lena Papazoglou-Manioudaki
P.Ph.	Pavlos Phlourentzos
C.S.	Christian Servelle
G.T.	George Trohani
A.T.	Anastasia Tsigounaki
F.V.	Frank Verse

Literature

AHLBERG 1971
G. Ahlberg: Fighting on Land and Sea in Greek Geometric Art. Stockholm 1971

AHLBERG-CORNELL 1992
G. Ahlberg-Cornell: Myth and Epos in Early Greek Art. Representation and Interpretation. SIMA 100. Jonsered 1992

ÅKERSTRÖM 1987
Å. Åkerström: Berbati, Vol. 2. The Pictorial Pottery. Stockholm 1987

ALEXIOU 1958
S. Alexiou: Η μινωική θεά μεθ' υψωμένων χειρών, Κρητιά Χρονικά 12, 1958

ALMAGRO BASCH 1966
M. Almagro Basch: Las Estelas Decoradas del Suroeste Peninsular. Madrid 1966

ALMAGRO-GORBEA 1969
M. Almagro-Gorbea: De orfebrería celtica; el deposito de Berzocana y un brazalete del Museo Arcleológico Nacional. Trabajos de Prehistoria 26, 1969

ALMAGRO-GORBEA 1977
M. Almagro-Gorbea: El Bronce Final y el Período Orientalizante en Extremadura. Madrid 1977

ALMAGRO-GORBEA 1993
M. Almagro-Gorbea: Les stèles anthropomorphes de la Péninsule Ibérique. In: Les Représentations Humaines du Néolithique à l'Âge du Fer. Paris 1993

ALMEIDA & OLIVEIRA JORGE 1979
C. A. F. de Almeida, V. Oliveira Jorge: A estátua-menhir de Faioes (Chaves). Porto 1979

ALMGREN
O. Almgren: "Kung Björns Hög" och andra fornlämningar vid Håga. Stockholm 1905

ALTHIN 1945
C. A. Althin: Studien zu den bronzezeitlichen Felszeichnungen von Skåne. Lund 1945

ANER & KERSTEN 1973
E. Aner, K. Kersten: Die Funde der älteren Bronzezeit des nordischen Kreises in Dänemark, Schleswig-Holstein und Niedersachsen. Neumünster 1973ff.

ANNABLE & SIMPSON 1964
F. K. Annable, D. D. A. Simpson: Guide Catalogue of the Neolithic and Bronze Age Collections in the Devizes Museum. Wiltshire Archaeological and Natural History Museum. Devizes 1964

ARCHÉOLOGIE 1989
Archéologie de la France. 30 ans de découvertes. Exhibition Catalogue 1989. Galeries nationales du Grand Palais. Paris 1989

ARMBRUSTER 1996
B. Armbruster: Zu den technologischen Aspekten der Goldfunde von Caldas de Reyes. Madrider Mitteilungen 37, 1996

ARMSTRONG 1909
E. C. R. Armstrong: Prehistoric Shield Found at Clonbrin, Country Longford. PRAI 27, 1909

ARMSTRONG 1920
E. C. R. Armstrong: Guide to the Collection of Irish Antiquities: Catalogue of Irish Gold. Ornaments in the Collection of the Royal Irish Academy. National Museum of Science and Art. Dublin. Dublin 1920

ART DE CHYPRE 1992
Art antique de Chypre au musée du Louvre. Paris 1992

ARTZY 1992
M. Artzy: Incense, Camels and Collared Rim Jars: Desert Trade Routes and Maritime Outlets in the Second Millennium. Oxford Journal of Archaeology 13(2), 1992

ASMUS 1991
W.-D. Asmus: Der Bildstein von Anderlingen und seine Verbindung zu Skandinavien. Die Kunde N. F. 41/42, 1991

AVANT LES CELTES 1988
Avant les Celtes. L'Europe à l'âge du Bronze. 2500–800 avant J-C. Exhibition Catalogue Daoulas 1988

BADER 1990
T. Bader: Bemerkungen über die ägäischen Einflüsse auf die alt- und mittelbronzezeitliche Entwicklung im Donau-Karpatenraum. In: Orientalisch-ägäische Einflüsse in der europäischen Bronzezeit. Mainz 1990

BANKS 1967
E. Banks: The Early and Middle Helladic Small Objects from Lerna. Cincinnati, Ohio, 1967

BARCELÓ 1991
J. A. Barceló: El Bronce del Sudoeste y la cronologia de las estelas alentejanas. Porto 1991

BARFIELD 1991
L. H. Barfield: Wessex with and without Mycenae: New Evidence from Switzerland. Antiquity 65, 1991

BÁRTA 1958
J. Bárta: Majda-Hraškova jaskyňa a jej kultová funkcia v dobe halštatskej. Slovenská Arch. 6, 1958

BASILAKIS 1996
A. Basilakis: Ο χρσός και ο άργυρος στην Κρήτη κατά την πώμη περίοδο του Χαλκού, Heraklion 1996

BASS 1967
G. F. Bass: Cape Gelidonya: A Bronze Age Shipwreck. Philadelphia, Penn., 1967

BASS 1986
G. F. Bass: A Bronze Age Shipwreck at Ulu Burun (Kas): 1984 Campaign. American Journal of Archaeology 90, 1986

BASS 1991
G. F. Bass: Evidence of Trade from Bronze Age Shipwrecks. In: G. H. Gale (ed.): Bronze Age Trade in the Mediterranean. Göteborg 1991

BAURAIN & DARCQUE 1983
Cl. Baurain, P. Darcque: Un triton en pierre à Malia. BCH 107, 1983

BECK, WILBUR & MERET 1964
C. W. Beck, E. Wilbur, S. Meret: Infrared Spectra and the Origin of Amber. Nature 201, 1964

BECK 1974
C. W. Beck: The Provenience of Amber in Bronze Age Greece. The Annual of the British School at Athens 69, 1974

BECKER, JÄGER, KAUFMANN & LITT 1989:
B. Becker, K.-D. Jäger, D. Kaufmann, R. Litt: Dendrochronologische Datierungen von Eichenhölzern aus den frühbronzezeitlichen Hügelgräbern bei Helmsdorf und Leubingen (Aunjetitzer Kultur) und an bronzezeitlichen Flußeichen bei Merseburg. Jahresschrift für mitteldeutsche Vorgeschichte 72, 1989

BEDA 1976
C. Beda: Carul solar antic de la Bujoru, jud. Teleorman. Muzeul National 3, 1976

BEHN 1920
F. Behn: Beiträge zur Urgeschichte des Hauses. Prähistorische Zeitschrift 11/12, 1919/20

BEHRENDS 1993
R.-H. Behrends: Raritäten der späteren Bronzezeit aus dem Rhein bei Karlsruhe. In: E. Sangmeister (ed.): Zeitspuren. Archäologisches aus Baden. Archäologische Nachrichten aus Baden 50, 1993

BELTZ 1910
R. Beltz: Die vorgeschichtlichen Alterthümer des Grossherzogtums Mecklenburg-Schwerin, Schwerin 1910

BENNETT 1958
E. Bennett: Mycenaean Tablets II. Philadelphia, Penn., 1958

BENNETT & OLIVIER 1973
E. L. Bennet, J. P. Olivier: The Pylos Tablets Transcribed, Part 1. Texts and Notes. Incunabula Graeca 51. Rome 1973

BERNABÒ BREA 1964
B. L. Bernabò Brea: Poliochni. Città preistorica nell'Isola di Lemnos I. Rome 1964

BERNABÒ BREA 1976
B. L. Bernabò Brea: Poliochni. Città preistorica nell'Isola di Lemnos II. Rome 1976

BERNABÒ BREA 1955
B. L. Bernabò Brea: A Bronze Age House of Poliokhni (Lemnos). Proceedings of the Prehistoric Society 21, 1955

BETANCOURT 1985
P. P. Betancourt: The History of Minoan Pottery. Princeton, N. J. 1985

BIANCO PERONI 1994
V. Bianco Peroni: I pugnali nell'Italia Continentale. Stuttgart 1994

BIESANTZ 1957
H. Biesantz: Bericht über Ausgrabungen im Gebiet der Gremnos-Magula bei Lavisa im Frühjahr 1958. Archäologischer Anzeiger 72, 1957

BIESANTZ 1959
H. Biesantz: Die Ausgrabung bei der Soufli-Magula. Archäologischer Anzeiger 74, 1959

BLEGEN 1937
C. W. Blegen: Prosymna. The Helladic Settlement Preceeding the Argive Heraeum I–II. Cambridge 1937

BLEGEN ET AL. 1950
C. W. Blegen, J. L. Caskey, M. Rawson, J. Sperling: Troy. Excavations Conducted by the University of Cincinnati 1932–1938. Part I: General Introduction. The First and Second Settlements. Princeton, N. J. 1950

BLEGEN ET AL. 1973
C. W. Blegen, M. Rawson, W. Taylour, W. P. Donovan: The Palace of Nestor at Pylos in Western Messenia, Part III: Acropolis and Lower Town. Tholoi, Grave Circle and Chamber Tombs. Discoveries Outside the Citadel. Cincinnati, Ohio 1973

BÖHM 1930
J. Böhm: Poklad bronzových dýk na Kozích Hřetech. Předběžná zpráva. Památky Archeologické 36, 1928–30

BOUZEK 1985
J. Bouzek: The Aegean, Anatolia and Europe: Cultural Interrelations in the Second Millennium B. C. Göteborg 1985

BORCHHARDT 1972
J. Borchhardt: Homerische Helme. Mainz 1972

BORCHHARDT 1977
J. Borchhardt: Helme. In: Kriegswesen. Archaeologia Homerica 1E. Göttingen 1977

BOYE 1896
V. Boye: Fund af Egekister fra Bronzealderen i Danmark. Copenhagen 1896

BRANIGAN 1975
K. Branigan: The Round Graves of Leukas Reconsidered. BSA 70, 1975

BREUNING-MADSEN 1997
H. Breuning-Madsen: Om Egtvedpigens bevarelse. Nyere undersøgelser vedrørende dannelsen af jernlag omkring egekister i bronzealderhøje. In: Fra Egtvedpigen til Folketinget. Et festskrift til Hendes Majestæt Dronning Margrethe II ved regeringsjubilæet 1997. Det Kongelige Danske Videnskabernes Selskab. Copenhagen 1997

BRIARD 1965
J. Briard: Les dépôts bretons et l'âge du Bronze Atlantique. Rennes 1965

BRIARD 1976
J. Briard: L'âge du bronze en Europe barbare des mégalithes aux Celtes. Toulouse 1976

BRIARD 1984
J. Briard: Les Tumulus d'Armorique. L'Age du Bronze en France 3. Paris 1984

BRIARD 1991
J. Briard: La protohistoire de Bretagne et d'Armorique. N 302b,1. Rennes 1991

BRITISH MUSEUM 1920
British Museum: A Guide to the Antiquities of the Bronze Age in the Department of British and Mediaeval Antiquities. 2nd Ed. London 1920

BROHOLM & HALD 1935
H. C. Broholm, M. Hald: Danske Bronzealders Dragter. Nordiske Fortidsminder II, 5–6. Copenhagen 1935

BROHOLM & HALD 1939
H. C. Broholm, M. Hald: Skrydstrupfundet. Nordiske Fortidsminder III, 2. Copenhagen 1939

BROHOLM & HALD 1940A
H. C. Broholm, M. Hald: Costumes of the Bronze Age in Denmark. Copenhagen 1940

BROHOLM 1940B
H. C. Broholm: Tre kvindegrave fra Gjedsted sogn. Aarbøger for nordisk Oldkyndighed og Historie 1940

BROHOLM 1943
H. C. Broholm: Danmarks Bronzealder I. Copenhagen 1943

BROHOLM 1944
H. C. Broholm: Danmarks Bronzealder II. Copenhagen 1944

BROHOLM 1946
H. C. Broholm: Danmarks Bronzealder III. Copenhagen 1946

BROHOLM 1948
H. C. Broholm: The Midskov Find. Acta Archaologica 19, 1948

BROHOLM 1949
H. C. Broholm: Danmarks Bronzealder IV. Copenhagen 1949

BROHOLM, LARSEN & SKJERNE 1949
H. C. Broholm, W. P. Larsen, G. Skjerne: The Lures of the Bronze Age. Copenhagen 1949

BROHOLM & DJUPEDAL 1952
H. C. Broholm, R. Djupedal: Marcus Schnabel og Bronzealderfundet fra Grevensvænge. Aarbøger for nordisk Oldkyndighed og Historie 1952

BROHOLM 1953
H. C. Broholm: Danske Oldsager. Yngre Bronzealder. Copenhagen 1953

BROHOLM 1958
H. C. Broholm: Bronzelurerne i Nationalmuseet. En arkæologisk undersøgelse. Copenhagen 1958

BRØNDSTED 1958
J. Brøndsted: Danmarks Oldtid II. Bronzealderen. 2nd Ed. Copenhagen 1958

BRØNDSTED 1962
J. Brøndsted: Nordische Vorzeit II. Bronzezeit in Dänemark. Copenhagen 1962

BROODBANK 1992
C. Broodbank: The Spirit is Willing: Review – Article on Colin Renfrew. The Cycladic Spirit (1991). Antiquity 66, 1992

BROWN 1983
A. Brown: Arthur Evans and the Palace of Minos. Oxford 1983

BRUMFIEL & EARLE 1987
E. Brumfiel, T. Earle: Specialization, Exchange and Complex Societies: an Introduction. In: Specialization, Exchange and Complex Societies. Cambridge 1987

BRUNN 1939
W. A. von Brunn: Die Kultur der Hausurnen in Mitteldeutschland. Jahresschrift Vorgeschichte sächsisch-thüringischer Länder 30, 1939

BRUNN 1959
W. A. von Brunn: Bronzezeitliche Hortfunde I. Die Hortfunde der frühen Bronzezeit aus Sachsen-Anhalt, Sachsen und Thüringen. Berlin 1959

BRUNN 1980
W. A. von Brunn: Eine Deutung spätbronzezeitlicher Hortfunde zwischen Elbe und Weichsel. Ber. RGK 61, 1980

281

BUCHHOLZ 1960
H.-G. Buchholz: Die Doppelaxt – eine Leitform auswärtiger Beziehungen des ägäischen Kulturkreises? Prähistorische Zeitschrift 38. 1960

BUCHHOLZ 1974
H.-G. Buchholz: Ägäische Funde und Kultureinflüsse in den Randgebieten des Mittelmeeres. Forschungsbericht über Ausgrabungen und Neufunde 1960–1970. Archäologischer Anzeiger 1974

BUCHHOLZ & KARAGEORGHIS 1973
H.-G. Bucholz. V. Karageorghis: Altägäis und Altkypros. Tübingen 1973

BUCHHOLZ. JÖHRENS & MAULL 1973
H.-G. Buchholz, G. Jöhrens, I. Maull: Jagd und Fischfang. Archaeologia Homerica 1J. Göttingen 1973

BUCK 1979
D.-W. Buck: Die Billendorfer Gruppe. Berlin 1979

BUDAVÁRY 1940
V. Budaváry: Nález starohallstattskej bronzevej spony v Krivokláte (okr. Púchov n/V). Cas. muz. slov. Spolocn. 31. 1940

BURENHULT 1980
G. Burenhult: Götalands hällristningar I. Arlov 1980

BURENHULT 1983
G. Burnehult: Arkeologi i Sverige 2. Stockholm 1983

BURGESS 1980
C. B. Burgess: The Age of Stonehenge. London 1980

BURKERT 1992
W. Burkert: The Orientalizing Revolution: Near Eastern Influence on Greek Culture in the Early Archaic Age. Cambridge. Mass.. 1992

BUTLER & BAKKER 1961
J. J. Butler. J. A. Bakker: A Forgotten Middle Bronze Age Hoard with a Sicilian Razor from Ommerschans (Overijssel). Helinium 1. 1961

BUTLER & SARFATIJ 1971
J. J. Butler. H. Sarfatij: Another Bronze Ceremonial Sword by the Plougrescant-Ommerschans Smith. Berichten van de Rijksdienst voor het oudheidkundig Bodemonderzoek 20–21. 1970–71

BUTLER & WATERBOLK 1974
J. Butler. H. T. Waterbolk: La fouille de A. E. van Giffen á "La Motta". Un tumulus de l'Age du Bronze Ancien à Lannion (Bretagne). Palaeohistoria 16. 1974

CADOGAN 1976
G. Cadogan: Palaces of Minoan Crete. London 1976

CAPELLE 1976
T. Capelle: Holzgefässe vom Neolitikum bis zum späten Mittelalter. Hildesheim 1976

CAPELLE 1980
T. Capelle: Holzschnitzkunst vor der Wikingerzeit. Neumünster 1980

CAPELLE 1995
T. Capelle: Anthropomorphe Holzidole. Lund 1995

CARATELLI 1957–58
P. Caratelli: Nuove epigrafi minoichi di Festos Annuario. 1957–58

CARTER & MORRIS 1995
J. B. Carter. S. P. Morris (ed.): The Ages of Homer. Austin 1995

CASINI 1995
S. Casini (ed.): Le pietre degli dei. Menhir e stele dell'età del Rame in Valcamonica e Valtellina. Bergamo 1995

CASINI. DE MARINIS & PEDROTTI 1996
S. Casini. R. C. de Marinis. A. Pedrotti (eds.): Statue-stele e massi incisi nell'Europa dell'età del Rame. Notizie Archeologiche Bergomensi 3. 1995 (Bergamo 1996)

CASKEY 1964
J. L. Caskey: Investigations in Keos 1963. Hesperia 33. 1964

CASKEY-ERVIN 1976
M. Caskey-Ervin: Notes on Relief Pithoi of the Tenian-Boeotian Group. ASA 80. 1976

CASKEY 1986
M. E. Caskey: The Temple at Ayia Irini. The Statues. Princeton. N. J. 1986

CATLING 1956
H. W. Catling: Bronze Cut-and-Thrust Swords in the East Mediterranean. Proceedings of the Prehistoric Society 22. 1956

CATLING 1961
H. W. Catling: A New Bronze Sword from Cyprus. Antiquity 35. 1961

CATLING ET AL. 1980
H. W. Catling. J. F. Cherry. R. E. Jones. J. T. Kilen: The Linear B Inscribed Stirrup Jars and West Crete. BSA 75. 1980

CAUBET. KARAGEORGHIS & YON
A. Caubet. V. Karageorghis. M. Yon: Les antiquités de Chypre. Paris 1981

CHADWICK 1967
J. Chadwick: The Decipherment of Linear B. 2nd Ed. Cambridge 1967

CHAMPION ET AL. 1984
T. Champion. C. Gamble. S. Shennan. A. Whittle: Prehistoric Europe. London 1984

CHAUNU 1984
P. Chaunu: Conquista y explotación de los nuevos mundos. Barcelona 1984.

CHERRY 1992
J. F. Cherry: Beazley in the Bronze Age? Reflections on Attribution Studies in Aegean Prehistory. In: R. Laffineur, J. L. Crowley (eds.): Eikon: Aegean Bronze Age Iconography: Shaping a methodology. Liège 1992

CHICIDEANU-SANDOR & CHICIDEANU 1990
M. Chicideanu-Sandor & I. Chicideanu: Contributions of the Study of the Gîrla Mare Anthropomorphic Statuettes. Dacia NS 34. 1990

CHILDE 1929
V. G. Childe: The Danube in Prehistory. Oxford 1929

CHROPROVSKY & HERMANN 1982
B. Chroprovsky. J. Hermann (eds.): Beiträge zum bronzezeitlichen Burgenbau in Mitteleuropa. Berlin 1982

CLARKE. COWIE & FOXON 1985
D. C. Clarke. T. G. Cowie. A. Foxon (eds.): Symbols of Power at the Time of Stonehenge. Edinburgh 1985

CLAUSING 1997
C. Clausing: Ein späturnenfelderzeitlicher Grabfund mit Wagenbronzen von Pfullingen. Baden-Württemberg. Archäologisches Korrespondenzblatt 27. 1997

CLINE 1994
E. H. Cline: Sailing the Wine-Dark Sea. International Trade and the Late Bronze Age Aegean. Oxford 1994

CMS I 1964
CMS I: A. Sakellariou: Die minoischen und mykenischen Siegel des Nationalmuseums in Athen. Corpus der minoischen und mykenischen Siegel 1. Berlin 1964

CMS V 1975
CMS V.1: I. Pini (ed.): Kleinere griechische Sammlungen. Part 1: Corpus der minoischen und mykenischen Siegel V.1. Berlin 1975

CMS V 1993
CMS V. Suppl. 1B: I. Pini (ed.): Kleinere griechische Sammlungen: Lamia-Zakynthos und weitere Länder des Ostmittelmeerraums. Corpus der minoischen und mykenischen Siegel. Vol. V. Suppl. 1B. Berlin 1993

COLDSTREAM 1968
J. N. Coldstream: Greek Geometric Pottery. London 1968

COLDSTREAM 1969
J. N. Coldstream: Die geometrische Kunst Griechenlands. Cologne 1969

COLEMAN 1985
J. E. Coleman: "Frying-pans" of the Early Bronze Age Aegean. American Journal of Archaeology 89. 1985

COLES 1962
J. M. Coles: European Bronze Shields. Proceedings of the Prehistoric Society 28, 1962

COLES 1963
J. M. Coles: Irish Bronze Age Horns and their Relations with Northern Europe. Proceedings of the Prehistoric Society 29, 1963

COLES & HARDING 1979
J. M. Coles, A. Harding: The Bronze Age in Europe. London 1979

COURBIN 1956
P. Courbin: Discoveries at Ancient Argos. Archaeology 166–174, 1956

COURBIN 1974
P. Courbin: Tombes géométriques d-'Argos I (1952–1958). École française d'Athènes. Études Péloponnésiennes 7. Paris 1974

COMSA 1966
E. Comsa: Le dépôt de Cioclovina (Carpates Méridionales). Acta Archaeologica Carpathica 8, 1966

COUTIL 1913
L. Coutil: La cachette de fondeur de Larnaud (Jura). In: Congrès Préhistorique de France. Neuvième Session – Lons-le-Saunier. 1913

COUTIL 1914
L. Coutil: L'Âge du Bronze dans le Jura. In: Compte rendu du 9e Congrès préhistorique de France. LeMans 1914

CROUWEL 1981
J. H. Crouwel: Chariots and Other Means of Land Transport in Bronze Age Greece. Amsterdam 1981

DAKORONIA 1987
Ph. Dakoronia: Warships on LH IIIC sherds from Kynos Livanaton. Proceedings of the 2nd International Symposium on Ship Construction in Antiquity. Delphi 1987. Tropis II. Hellenic Institute for the Preservation of Nautical Tradition. 1987

DANI & MOHEN 1996
A. H. Dani, J.-P. Mohen: History of Humanity. Vol. 2. From the Third Millennium to the Seventh Century BC. UNESCO-Routledge. Paris, London 1996

D'ANNA 1977
A. D'Anna: Les Statues-menhirs et Stéles Anthropomorphes du Midi Méditerranéen. Paris 1977

D'ANNA 1998
A. D'Anna: Les Statues-menhirs du Sud de la France. L'Art des Mégalithes Peints et Gravés. Dossiers d'Archéologie no. 230, 1998

DANSGAARD ET AL.1993
W. Dansgaard et al.: Evidence for general instability of past climate from a 250-kyr ice core record. Nature 364, 1993

DAVARAS 1969
C. Davaras: Trois bronzes minoens de Skoteino. BCH 93, 1969

DAVARAS 1976
C. Davaras: A Guide to Cretan Antiquities. Park Ridge, N. J. 1976

DAVIS 1973
E. N. Davis: The Vapheio Cups and Aegean Gold and Silver Ware. New York 1973

DAVIS & SHERIDAN 1993
M. Davis, A. Sheridan: Scottish prehistoric "jet" jewellery: some new work. Proceedings of the Society of Antiquaries of Scotland 123, 1993

DAWKINS 1903–04
R. M. Dawkins: Excavations at Palaikastro III. BSA 10, 1903–04

DEHN 1980
W. Dehn: Zur Beinschiene von Schäfstall bei Donauwörth. Zeitschrift des Historischen Vereins für Schwaben 74, 1980

DEMAKOPOULOU & KONSOLA 1981
K. Demakopoulou, D. Konsola: Archaeological Museum of Thebes. Guide. Athens 1981

DEMAKOPOULOU 1982
K. Demakopoulou: Το Μυκηναϊκό ιερό στο Αμυκλαίο και η ΥΕ ΙΙΙΓ περίοδος στη Λακωνία, Athens 1982

DEMAKOPOULOU 1987
K. Demakopoulou: Πήλινη ζωγραφιστή λάρνακα από τη Βρασέρκα Αργολίδας. In: Studies in Honour of N. Platon. Heraklion 1987

DEMAKOPOULOU 1988A
K. Demakopoulou (ed.): Das mykenische Hellas. Heimat der Helden Homers. Exhibition Catalogue Berlin 1988

DEMAKOPOULOU 1988B
K. Demakopoulou (ed.): Mycenaean World. Five Centuries of Greek Civilization 1600–1100 B. C. Exhibition Catalogue. Athens 1988

DEMAKOPOULOU 1990
K. Demakopoulou (ed.): Troy, Mycenae, Tiryns, Orchomenos. Heinrich Schliemann: The 100th Anniversary of his Death. Exhibition Catalogue. Athens 1990

DEMAKOPOULOU & DIVARI-VALAKOU 1994–95
K. Demakopoulou, N. Divari-Valakou: New Finds with Linear B Inscriptions from Midea. Minos 29–30, 1994–95

DEMAKOPOULOU 1996
K. Demakopoulou (ed.): The Aidonia Treasure. Seals and Jewellery of the Aegean Late Bronze Age. Athens 1996

DEONNA 1934
W. Deonna: Les cuirasses hallstattiennes de Fillinges au Musée d'art et d'Histoire de Genéve. Préhistoire 3, 1934

DICKINSON 1977
O. Dickinson: The Origins of Mycenaean Civilisation. In: Studies in Mediterranean Archaeogy 49. Göteborg 1977

DICKINSON 1994
O. Dickinson: The Aegean Bronze Age. Cambridge 1994

DONDER 1980
H. Donder: Zaumzeug in Griechenland und Cypern. Munich 1980

DONLAND 1989
W. Donland: The Pre-State Community in Greece. Symbolae Osloenses 64, 1989

DÖRPFELD 1902
W. Dörpfeld: Troja und Ilion. Athens 1902

DÖRPFELD 1927
W. Dörpfeld: Alt-Ithaka. Munich 1927

DOUMAS 1965
Chr. Doumas: Κορφή τ' Αρωνιού. Μικρή ανασκαφική έρευνα εν Νάξωι. ADelt 20, 1965

DOUMAS 1977
C. Doumas: Early Bronze Age Burials in the Cyclades. In: Studies in Mediterranean Archaeogy 49. Göteborg 1977

DOUMAS 1983
C. Doumas: Cycladic Art: Ancient Sculpture and Pottery from the N. P. Gourlandris Collection. London 1983

DOUMAS 1995
C. Doumas: Die Wandmalereien von Thera. German Ed. Munich 1995

DRAGONA-LATSOUDI 1977
A. Dragona-Latsoudi: Μυκηναϊκός κιθαρωδός απο την Ναυπλία. Aephem 1977

DRESCHER 1958
H. Drescher: Der Überfangguß. Mainz 1958

DREWS 1993
R. Drews: The End of the Bronze Age. Changes in Warfare and the Catastrophe ca. 1200 B. C. Princeton, N. J., 1993

DUCHÊNE 1997
H. Duchêne: L'or de Troie ou le rêve de Schliemann. Découvertes Gallimard Nr. 250. Paris 1997

DUMITRESCU 1961
V. Dumitrescu: Necropola de incineratie din epoca bronzului de la Cîrna. Bucarest 1961

283

DUMITRESCU 1974
V. Dumitrescu: Arta preistorica în România. Bucarest 1974

EDWARDS & RALSTON 1997
K. J. Edwards, I. B. Ralston (eds.): Scotland, Environment and Archaeology 8000 BC – 1000 AD. Chichester, New York, Weinheim 1997

EGGERS 1936
H. J. Eggers: Das Fürstengrab von Bahn und die germanische Landnahme in Pommern. Erstes Beiheft zum Erwerbungs- und Forschungsbericht. Baltische Studien NF 38. Stettin 1936

ELUÈRE 1982
C. Eluère: Les ors préhistoriques. L'âge du bronze en France 2. Paris 1982

ELUÈRE 1987
C. Eluère: L'or des Celtes. Bibliothèque des Arts, Fribourg 1987

ELUÈRE & MOHEN 1991
C. Eluère, J.-P. Mohen (eds.): Découverte du metal. Paris 1991

EMLYN-JONES, HARDWICK & PURKIS 1992
C. Emlyn-Jones, L. Hardwick, J. Purkis, J. (eds.): Homer, Readings and Images. Duckworth in association with the Open University, London 1992

EMÖDI 1978
I. Emödi: Noi date privind depozitul de la Cioclovina. Studii şi Cercetări de Istorie Veche şi Archeologie 29, 1978

ENGELHARDT 1871
C. Engelhardt: Romerske Statuetter og andre Kunstgjenstande fra den tidlige nordiske Jernalder. Aarbøger for nordisk Oldkyndighed og Historie, 1871

EOGAN 1994
G. Eogan: The Accomplished Art. Gold and Gold-working in Britain and Ireland during the Bronze Age (ca. 2300 – 650 BC). Oxford 1994

EIWANGER 1989
J. Eiwanger: Ein bronzezeitlicher Goldstandard zwischen Ägäis und Mitteleuropa. Germania 67, 1989

EVANS 1909
A. Evans: A Scripta Minoa I. Oxford 1909

EVANS 1928–35
A. Evans: The Palace of Minos at Knossos I–IV. London 1928–35

EVELY 1992
D. Evely: Ground Stone, Stone Vases and Other Objects. Well Built Mycenae 27. Oxford 1992

EXHIBITION CATALOGUE ATHENS 1995
Exhibition Catalogue Athens: Από τη Μήδεια στη Σαπφώ. Athens 1995

FADDA 1991
M. A. Fadda: Il Museo Speleo-Archaeologico di Nuoro. Guide e Itinerari 17. Gallizzi 1991

FADDA & LO SCHIAVO 1992
M. A. Fadda, F. Lo Schiavo: Su Tempiesu di Orune. Fonte sacra nuragica. Quaderni 18. Ozieri 1992

FEDELE 1995
F. Fedele: Ossimo I. Il contesto rituale delle stele calcolitiche e notizie sugli scavi 1988–95. Gianico 1995

FERRARESE CERUTI 1985
M. L. Ferrarese Ceruti: Un bronzetto nuragico da Ossi (Sassari). In: Studi in onore di G. Lilliu. Cagliari 1985

FILIP 1966
J. Filip: Enzyklopädisches Handbuch zur Ur- und Frühgeschichte Europas, 2 Vols. Prag 1966–69

FINLEY 1970
M. I. Finley: Early Greece. The Bronze and Archaic Ages. New York, 1970

FINLEY 1972
M. I. Finley: The World of Ulysses. London 1972.

FISCHER 1993
C. Fischer: Zinnachweis auf Keramik der Spätbronzezeit. Archäologie der Schweiz 16, 1993

FISCHER 1956
U. Fischer: Die Gräber der Steinzeit im Saalegebiet. Vorgeschichtliche Forschungen 15. Berlin 1956

FLORESCU, DAICOVICIU & ROSU 1980
R. Florescu, H. Daicoviciu, L. Rosu: Dictionar enciclopedic de arta veche a României. Bucarest 1980

FOGOLARI 1943
G. Fogolari: Beinschienen der Hallstattzeit von Pergine (Valsugana). Wiener Prähistorische Zeitschrift 30, 1943

FOLCH 1986
J. Folch (ed.): Historia de la Farmacia. Madrid 1986

FORBES 1964–1972
R. J. Forbes: Studies in Ancient Technology I–X. Leiden 1964–1972

FORSSANDER 1942
J. E. Forssander: Koban und Hallstatt. Meddelanden från Lunds Universitets Historiska Museum, 1942

FORTES 1905–08
J. Fortes: A Sepultura da Quinta da Aqua Branca. Portugalia 2, 1905–08

FOSTER 1979
K. P. Foster: Aegean Faience of the Bronze Age. New Haven, Conn., 1979

FRAQUET 1987
H. Fraquet: Amber. London 1987

FRENCH 1971
E. B. French: The Development of Mycenaean Terracotta Figurines. The Annual of the British School at Athens, 66, 1971

FURMÁNEK 1979
V. Furmánek: Svedectvo Bronzového Veku. Bratislava 1979

FURMÁNEK, RUTTKAY & SISKA 1991
V. Furmánek, A. Ruttkay, S. Šiška: Dejiny Dávnovekého Slovenska. Bratislava 1991

GAGE 1936
I. Gage: An Account of a Gold British Corselet now in the British Museum. Archaeologia 26, 1936

GAIMSTER 1991
M. Gaimster: Money and Media in Viking Age Scandinavia. In: R. Samson (ed.): Social Approaches to Viking Studies. Glasgow 1991

GALÁN DOMINGO 1993
E. Galán Domingo: Estelas, Paisaje y Territorio en el Bronce Final del Suroeste de la Península Ibérica. Complutum extra no. 3. Madrid 1993

GALE & STOS-GALE 1986
N. H. Gale, Z. A. Stos-Gale: Oxhide Copper Ingots in Crete and Cyprus and the Bronze Age Metal Trade. The Annual of the British School at Athens 81, 1986

GALE 1991
N. H. Gale (ed.): Bronze Age Trade in the Mediterranean. Studies in Mediterranean Archaeology 90. Göteborg 1991

GALLAY 1995
A. Gallay (ed.): Dans les Alpes à l'aube du métal. Archéologie et bande dessinée. Sion 1995

GALLIS 1992
K. Gallis. Ατλας Προϊστορικών Οικισμών της Ανατολικής Θεσαλικής Πεδιάδας. Larisa 1992

GEDIGA 1970
B. Gediga: Motywy figuralne w sztuce ludności kultury łużyckiej. Wrocław 1970

GEDL 1980
M. Gedl: Die Dolche und Stabdolche in Polen. Munich 1980

GELLING & DAVIDSON 1969
P. Gelling, H. E. Davidson: The Chariot of the Sun and Other Rites and Symbols of the Northern Bronze Age. 1969

GERLOFF 1975
S. Gerloff: The Early Bronze Age Daggers in Great Britain and a Reconsideration of the Wessex Culture. Prähistorische Bronzefunde VI.2. Munich 1975

GERLOFF 1995
S. Gerloff: Bronzezeitliche Goldblechkronen aus Westeuropa. Betrachtungen zur Funktion der Goldblechkegel vom Typ Schifferstadt und
der atlantischen "Goldschalen" der
Form Devil's Bit und Atroxi. In: A. Jockenhövel (ed.). Festschrift für Hermann
Müller-Karpe zum 70. Geburtstag. Bonn
1995

GETZ-GENTLE 1996
P. Getz-Gentle: Stone Vases of the
Cyclades in the Early Bronze Age. _
1996

GETZ-PREZIOSI 1987A
P. Getz-Preziosi: Sculptors of the
Cyclades: Individual and Tradition in
the Third Millennium B. C. Ann Arbor,
Mich., 1987

GETZ-PREZIOSI 1987B
P. Getz-Preziosi: Early Cycladic Art in
North American Collections. Richmond,
Va., 1987

GIARDINO 1995
C. Giardino: The West Mediterranean
Between the 14th and 8th Centuries
B. C. Oxford 1995

GILL & CHIPPINDALE 1993
D. W. J. Gill, C. Chippindale: Material
and Intellectual Consequenses of
Esteem for Cycladic Figures. American
Journal of Archaeology 97, 1993

GIMBUTAS 1965
M. Gimbutas: Bronze Age Cultures in
Central and Eastern Europe. Paris, Den
Haag, London 1965

GIOT, BRIARD & PAPE 1979
P. R. Giot, J. Briard, L. Pape: Protohistoire de la Bretagne. Rennes 1979

GLOB 1952
P. V. Glob: Danske Oldsager II. Yngre
Stenalder. Copenhagen 1952

GLOB 1969
P. V. Glob: Helleristninger i Danmark.
Aarhus 1969

GLOB 1974
P. V. Glob: The Mound People. Danish
Bronze Age Man Preserved. Ithaca, N.Y.,
1974

GODART, L. & OLIVIER 1969
L. Godart, J. P. Olivier: Receuil des
inscriptions de Lineaire A. Paris 1969

GOETZE 1984
B.-R. Goetze: Die frühesten europäis-
chen Schutzwaffen. Bayerische
Vorgeschichtsblätter 49, 1984

GOMES & MONTEIRO 1977
M. V. Gomes, J. P. Monteiro: As estelas
decoradas da Herdade de Pomar
(Ervidel-Beja). Estudo comparado.
Setúbal Arqueológica 2–3, 1976–77

GOMES 1994
M. V. Gomes: A necrópole de Alfar-
robeira (S. Bartolomeu de Messines) e a
Idade do Bronze no concelho de Silves.
Xelb 2, 1994

GOMES 1995
M. V. Gomes: As denominadas "estelas
alentejanas". A Idade do Bronze em
Portugal. Lisbon 1995

GOODISON 1989
L. Goodison: Death, Women and the
Sun. Bulletin Supplement 53. London
1989

GÖTTLICHER 1978
A. Göttlicher: Materialien für ein Cor-
pus der Schiffsmodelle im Altertum.
Mainz 1978

GRAHAM 1987
J. W. Graham: The Palaces of Crete.
Princeton, N. J., 1987

GRÄSLUND 1967
B. Gräslund: The Herzsprung Shield
Type and its Origin. Acta Archaeologica
38, 1967

GRAZIADIO 1991
G. Graziadio: The Process of Social
Stratification at Mycenae in the Shaft
Grave Period: A Comparative Examina-
tion of the Evidence. American Journal
of Archaeology 95, 1991

GRIMALDI 1996
D. A. Grimaldi: Amber. Window to the
Past. New York 1996

GRÖSSLER 1908
H. Grössler: Das Fürstengrab im
Großen Galgenhügel am Paulsschacht
bei Helmsdorf (in Mansfelder
Seekreise). Jahresschrift Halle 6/7,
1908

GUARDUCCI 1939–40
M. Guarducci: Missione archaeologica
italiana in Creta (anno 1939). Annuario
I–II, 1939–40

HACHMANN 1972
R. Hachmann: Aunjetitzer Kultur. In:
Reallexikon der germanischen Alter-
tumskunde. 2nd Ed. Vol. 1. Berlin 1972

HAGEN 1954
A. Hagen: Europeiske impulser i øst-
norsk bronzealder. Viking 18, 1954

HALLAGER 1987
E. Hallager: The Inscribed Stirrup Jars:
Implications for Late Minoan IIIB Crete.
American Journal of Archaeology 91,
1987

HAMPE & SIMON
E. Hampe, R. Simon: Tausend Jahre
frühgriechische Kunst. Munich 1980

HAMPEL 1886
J. Hampel: A Bronzkor emlékei
Magyarhonban. Budapest 1886

HAMPEL 1887
J. Hampel: Alterthümer der Bronzezeit
in Ungarn. Budapest 1887

HÄNSEL 1995
B. Hänsel (ed.): Handel, Tausch und
Verkehr in bronze- und früheisen-
zeitlichen Südosteuropa. Südosteuropa-
Schriften 17. Munich 1995

A. HÄNSEL & B. HÄNSEL 1997
A. Hänsel, B. Hänsel: Gaben an die Göt-
ter. Schätze der Bronzezeit Europas.
Berlin 1997

HARDING 1984
A. F. Harding: The Mycenaeans and
Europe. London 1984

HARDMEYER & BÜRGI 1975
B. Hardmeyer, J. Bürgi: Der Goldbecher
von Eschenz. Zeitschrift für Schweiz-
erische Archäologie und Kunst-
geschichte 32, 1975

HARTMANN 1970
A. Hartmann: Prähistorische Goldfunde
aus Europa. Spektralanalytische Untersuchungen und deren Auswertung. Studien zu den Anfängen der Metallurgie 3.
Berlin 1970

HÄSSLER 1991
H. J. Hässler (ed.): Ur- und
Frühgeschichte in Niedersachsen.
Stuttgart 1991

HAUSSOULIER 1878
B. Haussoulier: Catalogue déscriptif des
objets découverts à Sparta. Bulletin de
Correspondance Hellénique 1878

HAWKES 1955
C. F. C. Hawkes: Grave-groups of the
British Bronze Age. Inventaria Archaeo-
logica (Great Britain 1). London 1955

HAWKES & SMITH 1955
C. F. C. Hawkes, M. A. Smith: Bronze
Age Hoards in the British Museum.
Inventaria Archaeologica (Great Britain
2). London 1955

HAWKES 1957
C. F. C. Hawkes (ed. M. A. Smith):
Bronze Age Hoards and Grave-groups
from the N. E. Midlands. Inventaria
Archaeologica. Great Britain 1957

HAWKES & SMITH 1957
C. F. C. Hawkes, M. A. Smith: Buckets
and Cauldrons. On some Buckets and
Cauldrons of the Bronze and Iron Age.
The Antiquaries Journal 37, 1957

HEATH 1958
M. C. Heath: Early Helladic Clay Seal-
ings from the House of the Tiles at
Lerna. Hesperia 27, 1958

HELENO 1935
M. Heleno: Joyas pré-romanas. Ethnos
1, 1935

HELMS 1988

M. Helms: Ulysses' Sail. An Ethno-graphical Odyssey of Power. Knowledge and Geographical Distance. Princeton, N.J., 1988

HENCKEN 1959

H. Hencken: Herzsprung Shields and Greek Trade. American Journal of Archaeology 54, 1959

HENCKEN 1971

H. Hencken: The Earliest European Helmets. Harvard University Bulletin 28, 1971

HERMET 1893

F. Hermet: Sculptures préhistoriques dans les deux cantons de Saint-Affrique et de Saint-Sernin, Aveyron. Mémoires de la Société des Lettres, Sciences et Arts de l'Aveyron 14, 1893

HIGGINS 1961

R. A. Higgins: Greek and Roman Jew-ellery. London 1961

HÖFER 1906

P. Höfer: Der Leubinger Grabhügel. Jahresschrift Halle 5, 1906

HOOD 1978

S. Hood: The Arts in Prehistoric Greece. The Pelican History of Art. H-armondsworth 1978

HOOPS REALLEXIKON DER GERMANISCHEN ALTERTUMSKUNDE 1997

Hoops Reallexikon der germanischen Altertumskunde, Vol. 10: Fürstengräber. Berlin 1997

HUGHES-BROCK 1985

H. Hughes-Brock: Amber and the Myce-naeans. Journal of Baltic Studies 16, 1985

HUNDT 1953

H.-J. Hundt: Über Tüllenhaken und -gabeln. Germania 31, 1953

HUNDT 1955

H.-J. Hundt: Versuch zur Deutung der Depotfunde der nordischen jüngeren Bronzezeit. Jahrbuch RGZM 2, 1955

HÜTTEL 1981

H.-G. Hüttel: Bronzezeitliche Trensen in Mittel- und Osteuropa. Munich 1981

HÜTTEL 1982

H.-G. Hüttel: Zur Abkunft des danubi-schen Pferd-Wagen-Komplexes der Alt-bronzezeit. In: B. Hänsel (ed.): Südost-europa zwischen 1600 und 1000 v. Chr. Prähistorische Archäologie in Südost-europa I. Berlin 1982

IAKOVIDIS 1969–1970

Sp. Iakovidis: Περατή, Το Νεκροταφείο, Α, Β, Γ 1969–70

IAKOVIDIS 1983

S. E. Iakovidis: Late Helladic Citadels on Mainland Greece. Leiden 1983

IMMERWAHR 1990

S. A. Immerwahr: Aegean Painting in the Bronze Age. Pennsylvania 1990

INGSTAD 1961

A. S. Ingstad: Votivfunnene i nordisk bronzealder. Viking 25, 1961

INNERHOFER 1997

F. Innerhofer: Frühbronzezeitliche Barrenhortfunde – Die Schätze aus dem Boden kehren zurück. In: A. Hänsel, B. Hänsel (eds.): Gaben an die Götter. Schätze der Bronzezeit Europas. Berlin 1997

IRISCHE KUNST 1983

Irische Kunst aus drei Jahrtausenden. Exhibition Catalogue. Köln 1983.

JACOB 1995

C. Jacob: Metallgefässe der Bronze- und Hallstattzeit in Nordwest, West- und Süddeutschland. Stuttgart 1995

JACOB-FRIESEN 1963

G. Jacob-Friesen: Einführung in Nieder-sachsens Urgeschichte, Part 2: Bronzezeit. Hildesheim 1963

JACOB-FRIESEN 1967

G. Jacob-Friesen: Bronzezeitliche Lanzenspitzen Norddeutschlands und Skandinaviens. Hildesheim 1967

JACOB-FRIESEN 1970

G. Jacob-Friesen: Die Kupferäxte vom Typ Eschollbrücken. Die Kunde NF 21, 1970

JAHN 1950

M. Jahn: Ein kultureller Mittelpunkt bei Halle/Saale während der frühen Bronzezeit. _ 1950

JAHNSEN ET AL. 1992

S. J. Jahnsen et al.: Irregular Glacial Interstadials Record in a New Greenland Ice Core. Nature 359, 1992

JENSEN 1978

J. Jensen: Kultøkser fra bronzealderen. Nationalmuseets Arbejdsmark. Copenhagen 1978

JENSEN 1979

J. Jensen: Bronzealderen 1–2. Sesams Danmarkshistorie. Copenhagen 1979

JENSEN 1981

J. Jensen: Et rigdomscenter fra yngre bronzealder på Sjælland. Aarbøger for nordisk Oldkyndighed og Historie 1981

JENSEN 1982A

J. Jensen: Nordens Guld. Gyldendal. Copenhagen 1982

JENSEN 1982B

J. Jensen: A Votive Axe from North Zealand and New Gold Finds from South Western Zealand. Journal of Dan-ish Archaeology 1, 1982

JENSEN 1988

J. Jensen: I begyndelsen. Politiken/ Gyldendals Danmarkshistorie. Copen-hagen 1988

JENSEN 1992

J. Jensen: Thomsens Museum. Historien om Nationalmuseet. Copenhagen 1992

JENSEN 1995

J. Jensen: The Prehistory of Denmark. 2nd. Ed. London 1995

JENSEN 1997

J. Jensen: Fra Bronze-til Jernalder. En kronologisk undersøgelse. Nordiske Fortidsminder 15, 1997

JENSEN 1998A

J. Jensen: De forsvundne bronzealder-lurer. Nationalmuseets Arbejdsmark. Copenhagen 1998

JENSEN 1998B

J. Jensen: Manden i kisten. Hvad bronzealderens gravhøje gemte. Copen-hagen 1998

JENSEN & CHRISTENSEN 1991

J. Jensen, K. Christensen: Egtvedpigens alder. Nationalmuseets Arbejdsmark. Copenhagen 1991

JOCKENHÖVEL 1974

A. Jockenhövel: Eine Bronzeamphore des 8. Jahrhunderts v. Chr. von Gevel-inghausen, Kr. Meschede (Sauerland). Germania 52/1, 1974

JOCKENHÖVEL 1974

A. Jockenhövel: Fleischhaken von den Britischen Inseln. Archäologisches Kor-respondenzblatt 4, 1974

JOCKENHÖVEL 1986

A. Jockenhövel: Struktur und Organisa-tion der Metallverarbeitung in urnen-felderzeitlichen Siedlungen Süddeutsch-lands. Veröffentlichung des Museums für Ur- und Frühgeschichte Potsdam 20, 1986

JOCKENHÖVEL 1990

A. Jockenhövel: Bronzezeitlicher Burg-enbau in Mitteleuropa. Untersuchun-gen zur Struktur frühmetallzeitlicher Gesellschaften. In: Orientalisch-ägäische Einflüsse in der europäischen Bronzezeit. Mainz 1990

JOCKENHÖVEL & KUBACH 1994

A. Jockenhövel, W. Kubach (eds.): Bronzezeit in Deutschland. Archäologie in Deutschland. Sonderheft. Stuttgart 1994

JOCKENHÖVEL 1997

A. Jockenhövel: Europäische Bronzezeit. In: Von der Höhlenkunst zur Pyramide. Brockhaus – Die Bibliothek, vol. 2. Leipzig-Mannheim 1997

JØRGENSEN 1975

Jørgensen, M. Schou (ed.): Guld fra Nordvestsjælland. Holbæk 1975

JUNG 1968

C. G. Jung: Theoretische Überlegungen zum Wesen des Psychischen. Olten, Freiburg i. Br. 1968

KARO 1930–33

G. Karo: Die Schachtgräber von Mykenai. Munich 1930–33

KAUL 1998

F. Kaul: Ships on Bronzes. In: The Ship as Symbol in Prehistoric and Medieval Scandinavia. Studies in Archaeology & History. Vol. 3. Copenhagen 1998

KAUS 1988/89

M. Kaus: Kimmerischer Pferdeschmuck im Karpatenbecken – das Stillfrieder Depot aus neuer Sicht. MAGW 118/119, 1988/89

KELLY 1983

E.-P. Kelly: _. In: M. Ryan: Treasures of Ireland. Irish Art 3000 BC – 1500 AD. Dublin 1983

KIBBERT 1980

K. Kibbert: Die Äxte und Beile im mittleren Westdeutschland I. Munich 1980

KILIAN 1993

I. Kilian: Überlegungen zum spätbronzezeitlichen Schiffswrack von Ulu Burun (Kas). Jahrbuch RGZM 40, 1993

KILIAN 1978

K. Kilian: Ausgrabungen in Tiryns 1976. Archäologischer Anzeiger 1978

KILIAN 1981

K. Kilian: Zeugnisse mykenischer Kultausübung in Tiryns. In: R. Hägg, N. Marinatos (eds.): Sanctuaries and Cults in the Aegean Bronze Age. Proceedings of the First International Symposium of the Swedish Institute in Athens. Stockholm 1981

KILIAN 1987

K. Kilian: Zur Funktion der mykenischen Residenzen auf dem griechischen Festland. In: R. Hägg, N. Marinatos (eds.): The Function of the Minoan Palaces. Stockholm 1987

KILIAN 1988

K. Kilian: Mycenaean Architecture. In: K. Demakopoulou (ed.): Mycenaean World. Five Centuries of Greek Civilization 1600–1100 B. C. Exhibition Catalogue. Athens 1988

KILIAN-DIRLMEIER 1993

I. Kilian-Dirlmeier: Die Schwerter in Griechenland (außerhalb der Peloponnes), Bulgarien und Albanien. Stuttgart 1993

KJÆR 1927

H. Kjær: To Votivfund fra yngre Bronzealder fra Fyen og Jylland. Aarbøger for nordisk Oldkyndighed og Historie 1927

KJÆRUM & OLSEN 1990

P. Kjærum, R. A. Olsen (eds.): Oldtidens Ansigt. Århus 1990

KNAPE & NORDSTRÖM 1994

A. Knape, H.-Å. Nordström: Der Kultgegenstand von Balkåkra. Stockholm 1994

KOEHL 1981

R. Koehl: The Function of Aegean Bronze Age Rhytae. In: R. Hägg, N. Marinatos (eds.): Sanctuaries and Cults in the Aegean Bronze Age. Proceedings of the First International Symposium of the Swedish Institute in Athens. Stockholm 1981

KOLLING 1968

A. Kolling: Späte Bronzezeit an Saar und Mosel. Saarbrücken 1968

KOLONAS 1989

L. Kolonas: in: ArchDelt 44. B1 Chron., 1989

KONTOLEON 1969

N. Kontoleon: Die frühgriechische Reliefkunst. ArchEphem. 1969

KOSSACK 1974

G. Kossack: Prunkgräber. Studien zur vor- und frühgeschichtlichen Archäologie. In: Festschrift für Joachim Werner 1. Munich 1974

KOSSACK 1990

G. Kossack: Kultgerät, Weihgabe und Amulett aus spätbronzezeitlichen Seeufersiedlungen. Archäologie der Schweiz 13, 1990

KOUKOULI-CHRYSANTHAKI 1987–1990

Ch. Koukouli-Chrysanthaki: Οικισμός της Πρώιμης Εποχής του Χαλκού στη Σκάλα Σωτήρος Θάσου, Το Αρχαιολογικό Έργο στη Μακεδονία και Θράκη. Vol. 1–3, 1987–90

KOVACS 1977

T. Kovacs: L'Age du Bronze en Hongrie. Budapest 1977

KOVACS & STANCZIK 1988

T. Kovacs, I. Stanczik (eds.): Bronze Age Tell Settlements of the Great Hungarian Plain I. Budapest 1988

KOWIANSKA-PIASZYKOWA & KURNATOWSKI 1953

M. Kowianska-Piaszykowa, S. Kurnatowski: Kurkan kultury unietyckiej w Łękach Małych, pow. Kóscian. FontAPos 4, 1953

KOWIANSKA-PIASZYKOWA 1956

M. Kowianska-Piaszykowa: Wyniki badán archeologicznych kurhanu III kultury unietyckiej w Łękach Małych, w pow. kósciańskim. FontAPos 7, 1956

KOWIANSKA-PIASZYKOWA 1968

M. Kowianska-Piaszykowa: Wyniki badán archeologicznych kurhanu IV kultury unietychiej w Łękach Małych, pow. Kóscian. FontAPos. 19, 1968

KRAHE 1981

G. Krahe: Beinschiene der Urnenfelderzeit von Schäfstall, Stadt Donauwörth, Landkreis Donau-Ries, Schwaben. In: R. Christlein (ed.): Das archäologische Jahr in Bayern 1980. Stuttgart 1981

KRAIKER 1951

W. Kraiker: Aigina. Die Vasen des 10. bis 7. Jahrhunderts v. Chr. Berlin 1951

KRITSELLI-PROVIDI 1982

I. Kritselli-Providi: Τοιχογραφίες του Θρησκευτικού Κέντρου των Μυκηνών. Athens 1982

KRUTA 1992

V. Kruta: L'Europe des origines. Paris 1992

LA VALLE D'AOSTA

La Valle d'Aosta nel quadro della preistoria e protostoria dell'arco alpino centro-occidentale. Atti della XXXI Riunione Scientifica I. I. P. P. Florence 1997

LACROIX 1957

B. Lacroix: La nécropole protohistorique de La Colombine, d'apres les fouilles de G. Bolnat. Soc. des fouilles de l'Yonne, Cahier no. 2, 1957

LAFFINEUR 1987

R. Laffineur (ed.): Thanatos. Les coutumes funéraires en Egée à l'Âge du Bronze. Liège 1987

LAMPE 1982

W. Lampe: Ückeritz. Ein jungbronzezeitlicher Hortfund von der Insel Usedom. Berlin 1982

LANDAU 1977

J. Landau: Les representations anthrophomorphes de la région méditerraneenne (3me au 1er millénaire). Paris 1977

LATACZ 1996

J. Latacz: Homer: His Art and His World. Ann Arbor, Mich., 1996

LAUX 1971

F. Laux: Die Bronzezeit in der Lüneburger Heide. Hildesheim 1971

LAWLER 1940

L. B. Lawler: The Dancing Figures from Palaikastro. A New Interpretation. American Journal of Archaeology 44, 1940

LEAHU 1988

V. Leahu: Obiecte de metal si marturii ale practicarii metalurgiei in aria culturii Tei. In: SCIVA 39, 1988

LENERZ-DE WILDE 1995

M. Lenerz-de Wilde: Prämonetäre Zahlungsmittel der Bronzezeit aus Baden-Württemberg. Fundberichte aus Baden-Württemberg 20, 1995

LETICA 1973

Z. Letica: Antropomorfne figurine bronzanog doba u Jugoslaviji. Belgrade 1973

LEVI & POHL 1970
F. Levi, I. Pohl: Ostia. Notiziedegli Scavi. Serie 8, Vol. 24. Rome 1970

LEVY 1982
J. E. Levy: Social and Religious Organization in Bronze Age Denmark. An Analysis of Ritual Hoard Finds. B.A.R. Oxford 1982

LINDENSCHMIT 1864
L. Lindenschmit: Die Alterthümer unserer heidnischen Vorzeit I,10. Mainz 1864

LINDQVIST 1942
S. Lindqvist: The Boat Models from Roos Carr. Acta Archaeologica 13, 1942

LOMBORG 1973
E. Lomborg: Die Flintdolche Dänemarks. Copenhagen 1973

LO SCHIAVO 1991
F. Lo Schiavo: La Sardaigne et ses relations avec le Bronze final Atlantique. In: C. Chevillot, A. Coffyn (eds.): L'Âge du Bronze Atlantique. Actes du 1er Colloque du Parc Archéologique de Beynac. Beynac-et-Cazenac 1991

LO SCHIAVO 1994
F. Lo Schiavo: Doro Levi e i bronzi nuragici. In: Omaggio a Doro Levi. Quaderni 18. Ozieri 1994

LO SCHIAVO 1996A
F. Lo Schiavo: Bronzi nuragici nelle tombe della prima età del Ferro di Pontecagnano. In: La presenza etrusca nella Campania meridionale. Atti delle Giornate di Studio. Salerno-Pontecagnano, 16–18 nov. 1990. Florence 1996

LO SCHIAVO 1996B
F. Lo Schiavo: Voce "Sardinia". In: J. Turner (ed.): The Dictionary of Art 27, 1996

LO SCHIAVO 1997
F. Lo Schiavo: La navigazione nel Mediterraneo dai Micenei ai Fenici. In: PHOINIKES B SHRDN. Fenici in Sardegna. Nuove acquisizioni. Exhibition Catalogue. Oristano 1997

LO SCHIAVO
F. Lo Schiavo: La Sardegna nell'età del Bronzeo Finale e nella prima èta del Ferro. In: F. De Lanfranchi (ed.): La Sardegna e la Corsica nell'età del Bronzo e del Ferro (in course of publication)

LO SCHIAVO, MACNAMARA & VAGNETTI 1985
F. Lo Schiavo, E. Macnamara, L. Vagnetti: Late Cypriot Imports to Italy and their Influence on Local Bronzework. PBSA 53, 1985

LOWLER 1940
L. Lowler: The Dancing Figures from Palaikastro. A New Interpretation. American Journal of Archaeology 44, 1940

LUND 1986
C. Lund (ed.): The Bronze Lurs. Second Conference of the ICTM Study Group on Music Archaeology. Stockholm November 19–23, 1984, Vol. 2. Stockholm 1986

LULL 1983
V. Lull: La "cultura" de El Agrar. Madrid 1983

MACHNIK 1977
J. Machnik: Frühbronzezeit Polens. Übersicht über die Kulturen und Kulturgruppen. Wroclaw, Warsaw, Cracow, Gdansk 1977

MADDIN 1988
R. Maddin: The Beginning of the Use of Metals and Alloys. Cambridge, London 1988

MARANGOU 1990
L. Marangou (ed.): Cycladic Culture, Naxos in the 3rd Millennium BC. Athens 1990

MARINATOS
S. Marinatos: Excavations at Thera V. Athens 1972

MARINATOS 1935
S. Marinatos: Ανασχαφαί εν Κρήτη. PAE, 1935

MARINATOS 1937
S. Marinatos: Αι μινωιχαί θεαί του Γάζι AEpem., 1937

MARINATOS 1962
S. Marinatos: Zur Frage der Grotte von Archalochori. Kadmos 1962

MARINATOS & HIRMER 1973
S. Marinatos, M. Hirmer: Kreta, Thera und das mykenische Hellas. Munich 1973

MARSTRANDER 1979
S. Marstrander: Zur Holzschnitzkunst im bronzezeitlichen Norwegen. Acta Archaeologica 50, 1979

MÁTHÉ 1997
M. Sz. Máthé: The "Missing" Axe of the Hajdúsámson treasure. In: T. Kovács (ed.): Studien zur Metallindustrie im Karpatenbecken und den benachbarten Regionen. Festschrift für Amália Mozsolics zum 85. Geburtstag. Budapest 1997

MATHARI 1987
M. Mathari: The Local Pottery Wares with Painted Decoration from the Volcanic Destruction Level of Akrotiri, Thera. Archäologischer Anzeiger 1987

MATHIASSEN 1952
Th. Mathiassen: Et krumsværd fra Bronzealderen. Aarbøger for nordisk Oldkyndighed og Historie 1952

MATHIASSEN 1957
Th. Mathiassen: Endnu et krumsværd. Aarbøger for nordisk Oldkyndighed og Historie 1957

MATTHÄUS 1978
H. Matthäus: Neues zur Bronzetasse von Dohnsen, Kr. Celle. Die Kunde NF 28/29, 1978

MATTHÄUS 1980
H. Matthäus: Die Bronzegefässe der kretisch-mykenischen Kultur. Munich 1980

MATTHÄUS 1985
H. Matthäus: Metallgefässe und Gefässuntersätze der Bronzezeit, der geometrischen und archaischen Periode auf Cypern mit einem Anhang der bronzezeitlichen Schwertfunde auf Cypern. Munich 1985

MATTHIAS 1976
W. Matthias: Die Salzproduktion. Ein bedeutender Faktor in der Wirtschaft der frühbronzezeitlichen Bevölkerung an der mittleren Saale. Jahresschrift für mitteldeutsche Vorgeschichte 60, 1976

MATZ & BIESANTZ 1964
F. Matz, H. Biesantz: Corpus der minoischen und mykenischen Siegel. Berlin 1964

MEE 1984
C. B. Mee: The Mycenaeans and Troy. In: L. Foxhall, J. Davies (eds.): The Trojan War. Its Historicity and Context. Bristol 1984

MEIER-ARENDT 1992
W. Meier-Arendt, (ed.): Bronzezeit in Ungarn. Forschungen in Tell-Siedlungen an Donau und Theiss. Frankfurt/Main 1992

MENDONI 1997
L. Mendoni: Poliochni. On Smoke-Shround Lemnos. An Early Bronze Age Centre in the North Aegean. Athens, Thessaloniki 1997

MENGHIN 1997
W. Menghin: Der Berliner Goldhut. Ein Zeremonienhut der späten Bronzezeit. In: MuseumJournal 11, Heft 2, 1997

MENGHIN & SCHAUER 1977
W. Menghin, P. Schauer: Magisches Gold. Kultgerät der späten Bronzezeit. Exhibition Catalogue. Nürnberg 1977

MENGHIN & SCHAUER 1983
W. Menghin, P. Schauer: Der Goldkegel von Ezelsdorf. Kultgerät der späten Bronzezeit. Die vor- und frühgeschichtlichen Altertümer im Germanischen Nationalmuseum 3. Nürnberg, Stuttgart 1983

MENKE 1972
M. Menke: Die jüngere Bronzezeit in Holstein. Neumünster 1972

MERHART 1969
G. von Merhart: Panzer-Studien. In: G. Kossack (ed.): Hallstatt und Italien. Gesammelte Aufsätze zur Frühen Eisenzeit in Italien und Mitteleuropa. Mainz 1969

MERHART 1941
G. von Merhart: Zu den ersten Metallhelmen Europas. 30. Bericht der Römisch-Germanischen Kommission, 1941

MILLOTTE 1963
J. P. Millotte: Le Jura et les Plaines de Saône aux âges des métaux. Paris 1963

MOBERG 1975
C. A. Moberg: Kiviksgraven. Uddevalla 1975

MOHEN ET AL. 1972
J.-P. Mohen et al.: Société Préhistorique Française, Typologie des objects de l'Âge du Bronze en France. Paris 1972ff.

MOHEN 1977
J.-P. Mohen: Broches à rôtir articulées de l'Âge du Bronze. Antiquités Nationales 9, 1977

MOHEN 1987
J.-P. Mohen: Marmesse. In: Trésors des Princes Celtes. Exhibition Catalogue. Galéries Nationales du Grand Palais. Paris 1987

MOHEN 1990
J.-P. Mohen: Métallurgie préhistorique. Introduction à la Paléométallurgie. Paris, Milan, Barcelona, Mexico 1990

MOHEN 1991
J.-P. Mohen: Les sépultures de métallurgistes du début des âges des métaux en Europe. In: C. Eluère, J.-P. Mohen (eds.): Découverte du métal. Paris 1991

MORDANT & MOHEN 1996
D. Mordant, J.-P. Mohen: La vie préhistorique. Dijon 1996

MORRIS & POWELL 1997
I. Morris, B. Powell, (eds.): A New Companion to Homer. Leiden 1997

MORTEANI AND NORTHOVER 1995
G. Morteani, J. P. Northover (eds.): Prehistoric Gold in Europe. Mines, Metallurgy and Manufacture. Dordrecht 1995

MOTTIER 1971
Y. Mottier: Bestattungssitten und weitere Belege zur geistigen Kultur. In: W. Drack (ed.): Ur- und frühgeschichtliche Archäeologie der Schweiz, Vol. 3: Die Bronzezeit. Basel 1971.

MOSCALU & BEDA 1988
E. Moscalu, C. Beda: Bujoru, un tumul cu en car-cazan votiv apartinând culturii Basarabi. Thraco-Dacia 9, 1988

MOUNTJOY 1984
P. A. Mountjoy: The Marine Stile Pottery of LM IB/LH IIA. The Annual of the British School at Athens 79, 1984

MOUNTJOY 1993
P. A. Mountjoy: Mycenaean Pottery. An Introduction. Oxford 1993

MOZSOLICS 1967
A. Mozsolics: Bronzefunde des Karpatenbeckens. Budapest 1967

MUCKELROY 1981
K. Muckelroy: Middle Bronze Age Trade between Britain and Europe: a Maritime Perspective. Proceedings of the Prehistoric Society 47, 1981

MUHLY, MADDIN, KARAGEORGHIS 1981
J. D. Muhly, R. Maddin, V. Karageorghis (eds.): Early Metallurgy in Cyprus, 4000–500 B. C. Larnaka 1981

MUHLY 1973
J. D. Muhly: Copper and Tin. Transactions. New Haven, Conn., 1973

MÜLLER 1982
D. W. Müller: Die späte Aunjetitzer Kultur des Saalegebietes im Spannungsfeld des Südostens Europas. Jahresschrift für mitteldeutsche Vorgeschichte 65, 1982

MÜLLER 1903
S. Müller: Solbilledet fra Trundholm. Copenhagen 1903

MÜLLER-KARPE 1980
H. Müller-Karpe: Handbuch der Vorgeschichte IV. Bronzezeit. Munich 1980

MUNKSGÅRD 1974
E. Munksgård: Oldtidsdragter. Copenhagen 1974.

MURRAY 19932
O. Murray: Early Greece. Cambridge, Mass., 1993

MYLONAS 1966
G. E. Mylonas: Mycenae and the Mycenaean Age. Princeton, N. J., 1966

MYLONAS 1983
G. E. Mylonas: Mycenae, Rich in Gold. Athens 1983

NAGY 1979
G. Nagy: The Best of the Achaeans: Concepts of the Hero in Archaic Greek Poetry. Baltimore, Md., 1979

NAGY 1996
G. Nagy: Homeric Questions. Austin 1996

NEEDHAM 1979
S. Needham: Two Recent British Shield Finds and their Continental Parallels. Proceedings of the Prehistoric Society 45, 1979

NEUMANN 1953
E. Neumann: Zur psychologischen Bedeutung des Ritus, Kulturentwicklung und Religion. Zurich 1953

NIEMEIER 1980
W.-D. Niemeier: Die Katastrophe von Thera und die spätminoische Chronologie. Jahrbuch des Deutschen Archäologischen Instituts 95, 1980

NORLING-CHRISTENSEN 1943
H. Norling-Christensen: Bronzealderhjælmene fra Viksø. Copenhagen 1943

NOVOTNÁ 1970
M. Novotná: Die Bronzehortfunde in der Slovakei. Bratislava 1970

OELMANN 1959
F. Oelmann: Pfahlhausurnen. Germania 37, 1959

OLIVEIRA 1995
J. Oliveira: A estela decorada da Tapada da Moita. In: A Idade do Bronze em Portugal. Lisbon 1995

OLIVEIRA JORGE 1995
S. Oliveira Jorge: Introducao. A Idade do Bronze em Portugal. Discursos de Poder. Lisbon 1995

OLIVEIRA JORGE 1996
S. Oliveira Jorge: Regional diversity in the Iberian Bronze Age. On the Visibility and Opacity of the Archaeological Record. Porto 1996

OLIVEIRA JORGE & ALMEIDA 1980
S. Oliveira Jorge, C. A. F. de Almeida: A estátua-menhir fálica de Chaves. Porto 1980

OLIVEIRA JORGE & OLIVEIRA JORGE 1983
V. Oliveira Jorge, S. Oliveira Jorge: Nótula preliminar sobre uma estátua-menhir do Norte de Portugal. Porto 1983

OLIVEIRA JORGE & OLIVEIRA JORGE 1993
V. Oliveira Jorge, S. Oliveira Jorge: Statues-menhirs et stèles du Nord du Portugal. In: Les représentations humaines du Néolitique à l'Âge du Fer. Paris 1993

OLIVIER 1986
J.-P. Olivier: Cretan Writing in the Second Millennium B. C. World Archaeology 17, 1986

OLIVIER & GODART 1996
J.-P. Olivier, L. Godart: Corpus hieroglyphicarum Inscriptionum Cretae, Et Cretoises 31 (CHIC), 1996

OTTO 1958
K.-H. Otto: Soziologisches zur Leubinger Gruppe der Aunjetitzer Kultur. Ausgrabungen und Funde 3, 1958

PALLAF 1897
L. Pallaf: Ein Vasenfund aus Aegina. Archäologische Mitteilungen, 1897

PALMER 1969
L. R. Palmer: The Interpretation of Mycenaean Greek Texts. Oxford 1969

PAPATHANASSOPOULOS 1961/62
G. Papathanassopoulos: Κυκλαδικά Νάξου. ADelt 17, 1961/62

PAPATHANASSOPOULOS. VICHOS & LOLOS 1995
G. Papathanassopoulos, Y. Vichos, Y. Lolos: Dokos: 1991 campaign. ENALIA. Annual 1991, Hellenic Institute of Marine Archaeology 3, 1995

PAPAZOGLOU-MANIOUDAKI 1994
L. Papazoglou-Manioudaki: A Mycenaean Warrior's Tomb at Krini near Patras. The Annual of the British School at Athens 89, 1994

PARE 1987
C. F. E. Pare: Der Zeremonialwagen der Bronze- und Urnenfelderzeit. Seine Entstehung. Form und Verbreitung. In: Vierrädrige Wagen der Hallstattzeit. Untersuchungen zur Geschichte und Technik. Mainz 1987

PARE 1992
C. F. E. Pare: Wagons and Wagon-Graves of the Early Iron Age in Central Europe. Oxford 1992

PARLAMA 1994
L. Parlama: Το τέλος της πρώϊμης Χαλκοκρατίας στο Παλαμάρι Σκύρου. Σχέσεις και προβλήματα χρονολογήσεως. ADelt 42 (1987). publ. 1994

PATAY 1968
P. Patay: Urnenfelderzeitliche Bronzeschilde im Karpatenbecken. Germania 46, 1968

PATAY 1990
J. Patay: Die Bronzegefäße in Ungarn. Munich 1990

PATZEK 1992
B. Patzek: Homer und Mykene. Munich 1992

PAULÍK 1968
J. Paulík: Panzer der jüngeren Bronzezeit aus der Slowakei. Bericht RGK 49, 1968

PEACHEY 1996
C. Peachey: Continuing Study of the Uluburun Shipwreck Artifacts. Spring 1996

PELON 1976
O. Pelon: Tholoi. tumuli et cercles funéraires. Paris 1976

PENDLEBURY 1939
J. D. S. Pendlebury: The Archaeology of Crete. London 1939

PENHALLURICK 1986
R. D. Penhallurick: Tin in Antiquity. Its Mining and Trade Throughout the Ancient World With Particular Reference to Cornwall. London 1986

PENNAS. VICHOS, LOLOS 1995
Ch. Pennas, Y. Vichos, Y. Lolos: The 1991 Underwater Survey of the Late Bronze Age Wreck at Point Iria. ENALIA. Annual 1991. Hellenic Institute of Marine Archaeology 3, 4–15, 1995

PERDRIZET 1908
P. Perdrizet: Fouilles de Delphes V. Monuments Figurés. Petits Bronzes. Terres-Cuites, Antiquités Diverses. Paris 1908

PERONI 1978
R. Peroni: in: L. Fasani (ed.): Illustrierte Weltgeschichte der Archäologie. Munich 1978

PERSSON 1931
A. Persson: The Royal Tombs at Dendra near Midea. Lund 1931

PERSSON 1942
A. Persson: New Tombs at Dendra near Midea. _ 1942

PETRESCU-DÎMBOVITA 1977
M. Petrescu-Dîmbovita: Depozitele de bronzuri din România. Bucarest 1977

PETRESCU-DÎMBOVITA 1978
M. Petrescu-Dîmbovita: Die Sicheln in Rumänien mit Corpus der jung- und spätbronzezeitlichen Horte Rumäniens. Munich 1978

PETRESCU-DÎMBOVITA ET AL. 1995
M. Petrescu-Dîmbovita et al. (eds.): Treasures of the Bronze Age in Romania. Bucarest 1995

PETRUSO 1992
K. M. Petruso: Ayia Irini. The Balance Weights. An analysis of weight measurements in prehistoric Crete and the Cycladic Islands. Keos 8. Mainz 1992

PIGGOTT 1938
S. Piggott: The Early Bronze Age in Wessex. Proceedings of the Prehistoric Society 4, 1938

PIGGOTT 1983
S. Piggott: The Earliest Wheeled Transport. From the Atlantic Coast to the Caspian Sea. London 1983

PIGGOTT 1992
S. Piggott: Wagon. Chariot and Carriage: Symbol and Status in the History of Transport. London 1992

PINGEL 1974
V. Pingel: Bemerkungen zu den ritzverzierten Stelen und zur beginnenden Eisenzeit im Südwesten der Iberischen Halbinsel. Hamburger Beiträge zur Archäologie 4, 1974

PINGEL 1992
V. Pingel: Die vorgeschichtlichen Goldfunde der Iberischen Halbinsel. Berlin 1992

PLATON 1964
N. Platon: Oriental Seals from the Palace of Cadmus. Illustrated London News. Nov. 28, 1964

PLATON 1981
E. Platon: The Cylinder Seals from Thebes. Archiv für Orientalische Forschung 1981

PODZUWEIT 1979
C. Podzuweit: Trojanische Gefäßformen der Frühbronzezeit in Anatolien, der Agäis und angrenzenden Gebieten. Mainz 1979

POPESCU 1956
D. Popescu: Prelucrarea aurului în Transilvania înainte de cucerirea romană. Materiale si cercetari arheologice 2, 1956

POPHAM 1969
M. R. Popham: A LM IIIB Inscription from Knossos. Kadmos 8, 1969

POPHAM 1984
M. R. Popham: The Minoan Unexplored Mansion at Knossos. Oxford 1984

PORADA 1981–82
E. Porada: The Cylinder Seals found at Thebes in Boeotia. Archiv für Orientforschung 28, 1981–82

POURSAT 1977A
J. C. Poursat: Les ivoires mycéniens. Paris 1977

POURSAT 1977B
J. C. Poursat: Catalogue des ivoires mycéniens du Musée National d'Athenes. Paris 1977

POWELL 1953
T. G. E. Powell: The Gold Ornament from Mold, Flintshire, North Wales. Proceedings of the Prehistoric Society 19, 1953

PRIMAS & RUOFF 1981
M. Primas, U. Ruoff: Die urnenfelderzeitliche Inselsiedlung "Großer Hafner" im Zürichsee (Schweiz). Tauchausgrabung 1978–1979. Germania 59, 1981

RAAFLAUB 1997A
K. A. Raaflaub: Homeric Society. In: I. Morris, B. Powell (eds.): A New Companion to Homer. Leiden 1997

RAAFLAUB 1997B
K. A. Raaflaub: Politics and Interstate Relations in the World of Greek Poleis: Homer and Beyond. Antichthon 31, 1997

RAAFLAUB 1997C
K. A. Raaflaub: Soldiers, Citizens, and the Evolution of the Early Greek Polis. In: L. Mitchell, P. J. Rhodes (eds.): The Development of the Polis in Archaic Greece. London 1997

RAAFLAUB 1998
K. A. Raaflaub: A Historian's Headache: How to Read "Homeric Society"? In: N. Fischer. H. van Wees (eds.): Archic Greece: New Evidence and New Approaches. Cardiff & London 1998

RAFTERY 1980
J. Raftery: Artists and Craftsmen. Irish Art Treasures. Dublin 1980

RAISON 1968

J. Raison: Les vases a inscriptions peintes de l'âge mycénien et leur contexte archéologique. Incunabula Graeca XIX. Rome 1968

RAISON 1969

J. Raison: Le Grand Palais de Knossos. Rome 1969

RANDSBORG 1967

K. Randsborg: "Aegean" Bronzes in a Grave in Jutland. Acta Archaeologica 38, 1967

RANDSBORG 1968

K. Randsborg: Von Periode II zu III. Acta Archaeologica 39, 1968

RANDSBORG 1993

K. Randsborg: Kivik. Archaeology and Iconography. Acta Archaeologica 64, 1993

RANDSBORG 1996

K. Randsborg: Absolute Chronology. Archaeological Europe, 2500–500 BC. Acta Archaeologica 67. Acta Archaeologica Supplementa 1. Copenhagen 1996

RASCHKE 1954

G. Raschke: Ein Goldfund der Bronzezeit von Etzelsdorf-Buch bei Nürnberg. Germania 32, 1954

RATTI 1994

M. Ratti, (ed.): Antenati di pietra. Statue-stele della Lunigiana e archeologia del territorio. Genova 1994

REDFIELD 1975

J. Redfield: Nature and Culture in the Iliad: The Tragedy of Hector. Chicago, Ill., 1975

RENFREW 1969

C. Renfrew: The Development and Chronology of the Early Cycladic Figurines. American Journal of Archaeology 73, 1969

RENFREW & WAGSTAFF 1982

C. Renfrew, M. Wagstaff, (eds.): An Island Polity. The Archaeology of Exploitation in Melos. Cambridge 1982

RENFREW 1985

C. Renfrew: The Archaeology of cult. The Sanctuary at Phylacopi. London 1985

RENFREW 1991

C. Renfrew: The Cycladic Spirit: Masterpieces from the Nicholas P. Gourlandris Collection. New York 1981

RENFREW & BAHN 1996

C. Renfrew, P. Bahn: Archaeology. Theories, Methods and Practice. 2nd Ed. London 1996

RETHEMIOTAKIS 1990

G. Rethemiotakis: Ανθρωπομορφική πλαστική στην Κρήτη: Από την νεοανακτορική μέχρι την υπομινωική περίοδο, δ. δ. Rethymnon 990

RIECKHOFF 1990

S. Rieckhoff: Faszination Archäologie. Regensburg 1990

ROVINA 1986/1990

D. Rovina: Il santuario nuragico di Serra Niedda (Sorso). NBAS 3, 1986/1990

ROWLANDS 1980

M. Rowlands: Kinship, alliance and exchange in the European Bronze Age. In: J. Barret, R. Bradley (eds.): Settlement and Society in the British Later Bronze Age. London 1980

RUIPÉREZ & MELENA 1996

M. Ruipérez, J. Melena: Οι Μυκηναίοι Έλληνες (Los Griegos micénicos). Athens 1996

RUSU 1993

M. Rusu: Chars de combat hallstattiens chez les Thraces nord-danubiens. In: The Early Hallstatt period (1200–700 B. C.) in south-eastern Europe. Proceedings of the International Symposium. Alba Iulia 1993

RUTKOWSKI 1991

B. Rutkowski: Petsofas. A Cretan Peak Sanctuary. Warsaw 1991

RØNNE

P. Rønne: Fattigmands sværd. Skalk, 1986

SACCONI 1974

A. Sacconi: Corpus delle inscrizioni vascolari in Lineare B. Rome 1974

SAKELLARIOU 1964

A. Sakellariou: Die minoischen und mykenischen Siegel des Nationalmuseums in Athen. Berlin 1964

SAKELLARIOU-XENAKI 1985

A. Sakellariou-Xenaki: Οι θαλαμωτοί τάφοι των Μυκηνών. Ανασκαφής Χρ. Τσούντα. Paris 1985

SAKELLARIOU-XENAKI 1989

A. Sakellariou-Xenaki: Techniques et evolution de la bague-cachet dans l'art crétomycenien. Fragen und Probleme der bronzezeitlichen ägäischen Glyptik. Beiträge zum 3. Internationalen Marburger Siegel-Symposium, 5.–7. September 1985. Berlin 1989

SAKELLARAKIS 1976

J. Sakellarakis: Mycenaean Stone Vases. Studi micenei ed egeo-anatolici 17, 1976

SAMBIN 1989

C. Sambin: Génie minoen et génie égyptien. Un emprunt raisonné. BCH 113, 1989

SANCHES & OLIVEIRA JORGE 1987

M. Sanches, V. Oliveira Jorge: A "estátua-menhir" da Bouca (Mirandela). Porto 1987

SANDARS 1961

N. K. Sandars: The First Aegean Swords and their Ancestry. American Journal of Archaeology 65, 1961

SANDARS 1985

N. K. Sandars: The Sea Peoples. Warriors of the Ancient Mediterranean. London 1985

SAPOUNA-SAKELLARAKIS 1984

E. Sapouna-Sakellarakis: Η Ευβοϊή Κύμη της εποχής των αποικισμών. AEphem, 1984

SAPOUNA-SAKELLERAKIS 1995

E. Sapouna-Sakellerakis: Die frühen Menschenfiguren auf Kreta und in der Ägäis. Stuttgart 1995

SAVORY 1968

H. N. Savory: Spain and Portugal. London 1968

SCHAAF 1984

U. Schaaf: Ein bronzezeitliches Sistrum aus Rheinhessen. Jahrbuch RGZM 31, 1984

SCHACHERMEYR 1980

F. Schachermeyr: Die Ägäische Frühzeit IV. Griechenland im Zeitalter der Wanderungen. Vienna 1980

SCHAUER 1971

P. Schauer: Die Schwerter in Süddeutschland, Österreich und der Schweiz. Munich 1971

SCHAUER 1975

P. Schauer: Die Bewaffnung der "Adelskrieger" während der späten Bronze- und frühen Eisenzeit. In: Ausgrabungen in Deutschland. Mainz 1975

SCHAUER 1978

P. Schauer: Die urnenfelderzeitlichen Bronzepanzer von Fillinges, Dép. Haute-Savoie, Frankreich. Jahrbuch RGZM 25, 1978

SCHAUER 1980

P. Schauer: Der Rundschild der Bronze- und frühen Eisenzeit. Jahrbuch RGZM 27, 1980

SCHAUER 1982

P. Schauer: Die Beinscheinen der späten Bronze- und frühen Eisenzeit. Jahrbuch RGZM 29, 1982

SCHAUER 1983

P. Schauer: Orient im spätbronze- und früheisenzeitlichen Occident. Jahrbuch RGZM 30, 1983

SCHAUER 1984A

P. Schauer: Überregionale Gemeinsamkeiten bei Waffengräbern der ausgehenden Bronzezeit und älteren Urnenfelderzeit des Voralpenraumes. Jahrbuch RGZM 31, 1984

SCHAUER 1984B

P. Schauer: Spuren minoisch-mykenischen und orientalischen Einflusses im

atlantischen Westeuropa. Jahrbuch
RGZM 31, 1984

SCHAUER 1986A
P. Schauer: Die kegel- und glockenför-
migen Helme mit gegossenem Scheitelk-
nauf der jüngeren Bronzezeit Alteu-
ropas. In: Antike Helme. Mainz 1986

SCHAUER 1986B
P. Schauer: Die Goldblechkegel der
Bronzezeit. Ein Beitrag zur Kul-
turverbindung zwischen Orient und
Mitteleuropa. Mainz 1986

SCHLIEMANN 1874
H. Schliemann: Atlas Trojanischer
Altertümer. Leipzig 1874

SCHLIEMANN 1878
H. Schliemann: Bericht über meine
Forschungen und Entdeckungen in
Mykenae und Tiryns. Leipzig 1878

SCHLIEMANN 1878
H. Schliemann: Mycenae. A Narrative of
Researches and Discoveries at Mycenae
and Tiryns. London, New York 1878

SCHLIEMANN 1881
H. Schliemann: Ilios. Leipzig 1881

SCHMIDT 1915
H. Schmidt: Die Luren von Daberkow.
Kr. Demmin. Prähistorische Zeitschrift
7, 1915

SCHMIDT 1993
J.-P. Schmidt: Holzschalenbeschläge aus
Schuby, Kr. Schleswig-Flensburg. Zu
den Holzschalen der älteren Bronzezeit
in Norddeutschland und Dänemark.
Hammaburg NF 10, 1993

SCHÖNBÄCK & SOFKA 1970
B. Schönbäck, V. Sofka (eds.): Guld-
skatter från Karpaterne. Stockholm
1970

SCHUBART 1972
H. Schubart: Die Funde der älteren
Bronzezeit in Mecklenburg. Neumünster
1972

SCHÜLE 1976
W. Schüle: Der bronzezeitliche Schatz-
fund von Villena (Prov. Alicante).
Madrider Mitteilungen 17, 1976

SCHULZ 1993
R. Schulz: Die natürlichen Vorkommen
von Bernstein in Nordbrandenburg und
die Besiedlung der Bronzezeit. Veröf-
fentl. d. Brandenburg. Landesmuseum
für Ur- und Frühgeschichte 27, 1993

SCHÜTZ-TILLMANN 1995
C. Schütz-Tillmann: (K)ein neues
Wagengrab in Zuchering. Stadt Ingol-
stadt, Obb. In: Ausgrabungen und
Funde in Altbayern 1992–1994. Exhi-
bition Catalogue. Gäubodenmuseum
Straubing, 1995

SCHÜTZ-TILLMANN 1997
C. Schütz-Tillmann: Das urnen-
felderzeitliche Grabdepot von
Münchsmünster, Lkr. Pfaffenhofen a. d.
Ilm. Germania 75, 1997

SCHWEINGRUBER 1983
F. H. Schweingruber: Der Jahrring.
Standort, Methodik, Zeit und Klima in
der Dendrochronologie. Bern, Stuttgart
1983

SCHWEINGRUBER 1987
F. H. Schweingruber: Tree Rings. Basics
and Applications of Dendrochronology.
Dordrecht 1987

SCHUBART 1973
H. Schubart: Mediterrane Beziehungen
der El Agrar-Kultur. Madrider Mitteilungen 14, 1973

SCHUMACHER-MATTHÄUS 1985
G. Schumacher-Matthäus: Studien zu
bronzezeitlichen Schmucktrachten im
Karpatenbecken. Mainz 1985

SCHMIDT & NITZSCHKE 1980
B. Schmidt, W. Nitzschke: Ein früh-
bronzezeitlicher "Fürstenhügel" bei
Dieskau im Saalkreis. Ausgrabungen
und Funde 25, 1980

SCHWANTES 1939
G. Schwantes: Geschichte Schleswig-
Holsteins 1. Neumünster 1939

SCHWEITZER 1969
B. Schweitzer: Die geometrische Kunst
Griechenlands. Cologne 1969

SCULLY 1990
S. Scully: Homer and the Sacred City.
Ithaca, N. Y., 1990

SEAGER 1912
R. Seager: Exploration in the Island of
Mochlos. Boston, New York 1912

SERVAIS 1971
J. Servais: Thoricos V (1968), Objects
trouvés dans la tholos. _ 1971

SHAY 1995
J. Shay: Achilles in Vietnam. New York
1995

SHENNAN 1982
S. J. Shennan: Exchange and Ranking:
the Role of Amber in the Earlier Bronze
Age of Europe. In: C. Renfrew,
S. J. Shennan (red.): Ranking,
Resources and Exchange. Cambridge
1982

SHENNAN 1993
S. J. Shennan: Settlement and Social
Change in Central Europe 3500–1500
BC. Journal of World Prehistory 7.2,
1993

SHENNAN 1994
S. J. Shennan: Commodities, Transactions and Growth in the Central European Early Bronze Age. Journal of
European Archaeology 1(2), 1994

SHEPHERD 1981
I. A. G. Shepherd: Bronze Age Jet Working in North Britain. In: J. Kenworthy
(ed.): Early Technology in North
Britain. Edinburgh 1981

SHERRATT & TAYLOR 1989
A. Sherratt, T. Taylor: Metal Vessels in
Bronze Age Europe and the Context of
Vulcitrun. In: J. G. P. Best, N. M. W. de
Vries (eds.): Thracians and Mycenaeans.
Leiden 1989

SHERRATT & SHERRATT 1991
A. Sherratt, S. Sherratt: From Luxuries
to Commodities. The Nature of Mediterranean Bronze Age Trading Systems. In:
N. H. Gale (ed.): Bronze Age Trade in
the Mediterranean. Jonsered 1991

SHERRATT 1992
A. Sherratt: Sacred and Profane Substances: The Ritual Use of Narcotics in
Later Neolithic Europe. In: P. Garwood
et al. (ed.): Sacred and Profane. Oxford
1992

SHERRATT 1993
A. Sherratt: What Would a Bronze Age
World System Look Like? Relations
between Temperate Europe and the
Mediterranean in Later Prehistory. Journal of European Archaeology 1 (2),
1993

SILVA ET AL. 1984
A. C. F. Silva et al.: Deposito de fundi-
dor do final da Idade do Bronze do
Castro da Senhora da Guia (Baiões,
S. Pedro do Sul, Viseu). Porto 1984

SIMON 1990
K. Simon: Höhensiedlungen der älteren
Bronzezeit im Elbsaalegebiet. Jarhress-
chrift für mitteldeutsche Vorgeschichte
73, 1990

SIRET 1887
E. Siret, L. Siret: Les premiers âges du
métal dans le Sud-est de l'Espagne.
Anvers 1887

SOPRONI 1956
S. Soproni: in: Banner, J. : Die Péceler
Kultur. Budapest 1956

SOROCEANU 1995
T. Soroceanu: Der Bronzefund von Gir-
bau, Kr. Cluj. In: T. Soroceanu (ed.):
Bronzefunde aus Rumänien. Berlin
1995

SOTO 1991
J. G. de Soto: Le Fondeur, le Trafiquant
et les Cuisiniers. La Broche d'Amath-
onte de Cypre et la Chronologie Absolue
du Bronze final Atlantique. In: C.
Chevillot, A. Coffyn (eds.): L'Âge du
Bronze Atlantique. Actes du 1er Colloque du Parc Archéologique de Beynac.
Saladais 1991

SPADEA 1996
R. Spadea: Il Tesoro di Hera. Bolletino d'Arte 88, 1996

SPECK 1981
J. Speck: Schloss und Schlüssel zur späten Pfahlbauzeit. Helvetia Archaeologica 12, 1981

SPINDLER 1992
K. Spindler: Der Mann im Eis, Vol. 1. Innsbruck 1992. Der Mann im Eis. Vol. 2. (in course of publication)

SPINDLER 1994
K. Spindler: The Man in the Ice. London 1994

SPROCKHOFF 1938
E. Sprockhoff: Die germanischen Vollgriffschwerter. Berlin 1938

SPROCKHOFF 1955
E. Sprockhoff: Das bronzene Zierband von Kronshagen bei Kiel. Offa 14, 1955

SPROCKHOFF 1956
E. Sprockhoff: Jungbronzezeitliche Hortfunde der Südzone des nordischen Kreises (Periode V). Vol. 1–2. Mainz 1956

SPROCKHOFF & HÖCKMANN 1979
E. Sprockhoff, O. Höckmann: Die gegossenen Bronzebecken der jüngeren nordischen Bronzezeit. Mainz 1979

SPYROPOULOS 1967
Th. Spyropoulos: Ergon 1967

SPYROPOULOS 1969
Th. Spyropoulos: Praktika 1969

SPYROPOULOS 1972
Th. Spyropoulos: Υστερομυκηναϊκοί Ελλαδικοί Θησαυροί. Athens 1972

STARY 1980
P. F. Stary: Das spätbronzezeitliche Häuptlingsgrab von Hagenau. In: K. Spindler (ed.): Vorzeit zwischen Main und Donau. Erlangen 1980

STENBERGER 1979
M. Stenberger: Det forntidna Sverige. Stockholm 1979

STEWART 1962
J. Stewart: Finds and Results of the Excavations in Cypres 1927–31. In: The Swedish Cyprus Expedition IV, 1 A, 1962

STJERNQUIST 1958
B. Stjernquist: Ornementation métallique sur vases d'argile. Meddelanden från Lunds Universitets Historiska Museum 1958

STJERNQUIST 1961
B. Stjernquist: Simris II. Bronze Age Problems in the Light of the Simris Excavations. Bonn, Lund 1961

STRAHM 1966
Ch. Strahm: Renzenbühl und Ringoldswil. Jahrbuch des Bernisches Historisches Museum 45–46, 1965–66

STRAHM 1972
Ch. Strahm: Das Beil von Thun-Renzenbühl. Helvetica Antiqua 3, 1972

SWEENEY ET AL. 1988
J. Sweeney, T. Curry, Y. Tzedakis (eds.): The Human Figure in Early Greek Art. Athens, Washington 1988

SVORONOS 1906
J. N. Svoronos: Pelékeis kai emipéleaka. Journal International d' Archeologie Numismatic 9, 1906

SZYDLOWSKA 1965
E. Szydlowska: L'instrument de musique de la culture lusacienne trouvé á Przeczyce, distr. Zawiercie. Archaeologia Polona 8, 1965

SZYDLOWSKA 1972
E. Szydlowska: Cmentarzysko kultury luzyckiej w Przeczycach, pow. Zawiercie 1968–72, 4 Vols. Bytom 1972

TASIC 1984
N. Tasic, (ed.): Kulturen der Frühbronzezeit des Karpatenbeckens und Nordbalkans. Belgrade 1984

TAYLOR 1980
J. Taylor: Bronze Age Goldwork of the British Isles. Cambridge 1980

THEOCHARIS 1958
D. Theocharis: Εκ της Προκεραμεικής Θεσσαλίας, Θεσσαλικά Α', 1958

THEOCHARIS 1960
D. Theocharis: ArchDelt Chron. 16, 1960

THEVENOT 1984
J. P. Thevenot: Le dépôt de Jonchères à Blanot (Côte-d'Or). 10e Congrès National des Sociétés Savantes, Archeologie II. Dijon 1984

THEVENOT 1991
J. P. Thevenot: L'Âge du Bronze en Bourgogne. Le dépôt de Blanot (Côte-d'Or). Dijon 1991

THIMME 1977
J. Thimme (ed.): Art and Culture of the Cyclades (Engl. Ed.). Karlsruhe 1977

THOMAS 1990
G. Thomas, Palaima (ed.): Aegean Seals, Sealings and Administration. Aegaeum 5, 1990

THOMAS 1899
W. J. Thomas: Bronze Cauldron found at Milkernagh Bog, near Granard, Co. Longford. The Journal of the Royal Society of Antiquaries of Ireland 9, 1899

THOMSEN 1929
T. Thomsen: Egekistefundet fra Egtved fra den ældre Bronzealder. Copenhagen 1929

THRANE 1965A
H. Thrane: Dänische Funde fremder Bronzegefäße. Acta Archaeologica 36, 1965

THRANE 1965B
H. Thrane: Hoards of the Danish Bronze Age (Mont. IV). Inventaria Archaeologica, DK 3. Bonn 1965

THRANE 1966
H. Thrane: Dänische Funde fremder Bronzegefäße der jüngeren Bronzezeit (Periode IV). Acta Archaeologica 36, 1966

THRANE 1975
H. Thrane: Europæiske forbindelser. Copenhagen 1975

THRANE 1984
H. Thrane: Lusehøj ved Voldtofte – en sydvestfynsk storhøj fra yngre broncealder. Odense 1984

THRANE 1994
H. Thrane: Centres of Wealth in Northern Europe. In: K. Kristiansen, J. Jensen (eds.): Europe in the First Millennium B. C. Sheffield 1994

THRANE 1995
H. Thrane: Placing the Bronze Age "lurer" in their proper context. In: A. Jockenhövel (ed.): Festschrift für Hermann Müller-Karpe zum 70. Geburtstag. Bonn 1995

TITE 1972
M. S. Tite: Methods of Physical Examination in Archaeology. London, New York 1972

TOCIK 1981
A. Tocik: Nitriansky Hrádok-Zámeček. Nitra 1981

TREUE 1986
W. Treue (ed.): Achse, Rad und Wagen. Fünftausend Jahre Kultur- und Technikgeschichte. Göttingen 1986

TRONCHETTI 1986
C. Tronchetti: Nuragic Statuary from Monte Prama. In: Sardinia in the Mediterranean. Ann Arbor, Mich., 1986

TSOUNTAS 1898
C. Tsountas: Κυκλαδικά. AEphem 1898

TYLECOTE 1987
R. F. Tylecote: The Early History of Metallurgy in Europe. London, New York 1987

TZEDAKIS 1969
Y. Tzedakis: Ανασκαφαί ΥΜ ΙΙΙΑ/Β νεκροταφείου εις περιοχήν Καλαμίου Χανίων AAA 2, 1969

TZEDAKIS 1970
Y. Tzedakis: Μινωϊκός κιθαρωδός, AAA 3, 1970

293

TZEDAKIS 1996
Y. Tzedakis: La nécropole d'Armenoi. In: E. Miro, L. Godart, A. Sacconi (eds.): Atti e Memorie del Secondo Congresso Internazionale di Micenologia. Roma, Napoli 1991. Incunabula Graeca 98, 1996

UGAS & LUCIA 1987
G. Ugas, G. Lucia: Primi scavi nel sepolcreto nuragico di Antas. In: La Sardegna nel Mediterraneo tra il II e il I Millennio. Selargius-Cagliari 1987

ULISSE 1996
Ulisse, il mito e la memoria. Progretti Museali Editore, Roma. Exhibition Catalogue. Palazzo delle Esposizioni. Rome 1996

USLAR 1955
R. von Uslar: Der Goldbecher von Fritzdorf bei Bonn. Germania 33, 1955

VANDKILDE 1996
H. Vandkilde: From Stone to Bronze. The Metalwork of the Late Neolithic and Earliest Bronze Age in Denmark. Aarhus 1996

VANDKILDE, RAHBEK & RASMUSSEN 1996
H. Vandkilde, U. Rahbek, K. L. Rasmussen: Radiocarbon Dating and the Chronology of Bronze Age Southern Scandinavia. Acta Archaeologica 67, 1996

VENTRIS, CHADWICK 1973
M. Ventris, J. Chadwick: Documents in Mycenaean Greek. 2nd Ed. Cambridge 1973

VERLINDEN 1984
C. Verlinden: Les statuettes anthropomorphes crétoises en bronze et en plomb, du 3e millenaire au 7e siecle av. J. C. Louvain-la-Neuve 1984

VERMEULE 1964
E. Vermeule: Greece in the Bronze Age. Chicago, London 1964

VERMEULE & KARAGEORGHIS 1982
E. Vermeule, V. Karageorghis: Mycenaean Pictorial Vase Painting. Cambridge, Mass., 1982

VIZDAL 1972
J. Vizdal: Erste bildliche Darstellung eines zweirädrigen Wagens vom Ende der mittleren Bronzezeit in der Slowakei. Slovenská Arch. 20, 1972

VOLLGRAFF 1904
W. Vollgraff: Fouilles d'Argos. Bulletin de correspondance Hellénique 28, 1904

VULPE 1970
A. Vulpe: Die Äxte und Beile in Rumänien. Munich 1970

VULPE 1977
A. Vulpe: Kritische Anmerkungen zu den karpatenländischen Kulturzeugnissen der Altbronzezeit. Jahresbericht des Instituts für Vorgeschichte der Universität Frankfurt/Main 1977

VULPE 1985
A. Vulpe: Der Goldschatz von Radeni. Jud. Neamt. Prähistorische Zeitschrift 60, 1985

VULPE 1995
A. Vulpe: Der Schatz von Persinari in Südrumänien. In: A. Jockenhövel (ed.): Festschrift für Hermann Müller-Karpe zum 70. Geburtstag. 1995

V. V. A. A. 1957
V. V. A. A.: New Larousse Encyclopedia of Mythology. New York 1957

WACE 1932
A. G. B. Wace: Chamber Tombs at Mycenae. Archaeologia 82, 1932

WARREN 1969
P. Warren: Minoan Stone Vases. Cambridge 1969

WEES 1992
H. van Wees: Status Warriors: War, Violence, and Society in Homer and History. Amsterdam 1992

WEGNER 1996
G. Wegner (red.): Leben-Glauben-Sterben vor 3000 Jahren. Bronzezeit in Niedersachsen. Exhibition Catalogue. Hanover 1996

WELS-WEYRAUCH 1978
U. Wels-Weyrauch: Die Anhänger und Halsringe in Südwestdeutschland und Nordbayern. Munich 1978

WEST 1997
M. L. West: The East Face of Helicon: West Asiatic Elements in Greek Poetry and Myth. Oxford 1997

WHITE 1945
E. Mc. White: Irish Bronze Age Instruments. Journal of the Royal Society of Antiquaries of Ireland 75, 1945

WILDE 1862
W. R. Wilde: A Descriptive Catalogue of the Antiquities of Gold in the Museum of the Royal Irish Academy. Dublin 1862

WILLIS 1994
R. Willis (ed.): Mythologies du monde entier. Paris 1994

WILSON
D. M. Wilson (ed.): The Collections of the British Museum. 3rd Ed. London 1991

WINGHART 1993
S. Winghart: Das Wagengrab von Poing. Lkr. Ebersberg, und der Beginn der Urnenfelderzeit in Südbayern. In: H. Dannheimer, R. Gebhard (eds.): Das keltische Jahrtausend. Exhibition Catalogue. Prähistorische Staatssammlung. Munich 1993

WININGER 1995
J. Wininger: Die Bekleidung des Eismannes und die Anfänge der Weberei nördlich der Alpen. In: K. Spindler et al. (ed.): Der Mann im Eis, Vol. 2: Neue Funde und Ergebnisse. Vienna, New York 1995

WÜSTEMANN 1974
H. Wüstemann: Zur Sozialstruktur im Seddiner Kulturgebiet. Zeitschrift für Archäologie 8, 1974

WYSS 1981
R. Wyss: Kostbare Perlenkette als Zeuge ältesten Fernhandels in Zürich. Helvetia Archaeologica 12, 1981

XANTHOUDIDES 1924
St. Xanthoudides: The Vaulted Tombs of Mesara. London 1924

XENAKI-SAKELLARIOU 1985
A. Xenaki-Sakellariou: Οι Θαλαμωτοί Τάφοι των Μυκηνών. Athens 1985

YOUNGER 1991
J. G. Younger: A Bibliography for Aegean Glyptic in the Bronze Age. CMS Beiheft 4. Berlin 1991

ZAHARIA & ILIESCU 1968
E. Zaharia, O. Iliescu: in: Fasti Archaeologici 18–19, 1968

ZERVOS 1954
C. Zervos: Einleitung. In: G. Pesce (ed.): Prähistorische Bronzen aus Sardinien. Exhibition Catalogue. Kunsthaus Zürich 1954. Zürich 1954

ZERVOS 1956
C. Zervos: L'art de la Crète néolithique et minoenne. Paris 1956

ZERVOS 1957
C. Zervos: L'art des Cyclades du début à la fin du l'âge de Bronze. 2500–1100 avant notre ère. Paris 1957

ZICH 1996
B. Zich: Studien zur regionalen und chronologischen Gliederung der nördlichen Aunjetitzer Kultur. Berlin, New York 1996

ZIDDA 1997
G. Zidda: Aspetti iconografici delle stele antropomorfe di Aosta. La valle d'Aosta nel quadro della preistoria e protostoria dell'arco alpino centro-occidentale. In: Atti della 31. Riunione Scientifica. Florence 1997

ZUMTHOR 1994
P. Zumthor: La medida del Mundo. Madrid 1994

Photo Credits

Archäologisches Institut, Nitra – Marta Novotnà: Cat. No. 125

Archäologisches Landesmuseum der Christian-Albrecht-Universität, Schleswig: Cat. No. 167

Archäologisches Landesmuseum – Landesamt für Bodendenkmalpflege Mecklenburg-Vorpommern: p. 6, Cat. Nos. 178, 185, 212

Archäologisches Museum Donauwörth – F. Meitinger: Cat. No. 157

Archivo Nacional de Fotografia – José Pessoa: pp. 118 left, center, right, 119 left, center, right

Avant les Celtes. L'Europe à l'âge du Bronze. 2500–800 avant J-C. Exhibition Catalogue Daoulas 1988: Cat. No. 165

Bernisches Historisches Museum – Stefan Rebsamen: Cat. No. 161

Kjeld Christensen: pp. 112, 113

A. S. Coixao: p. 61

Complexual Muzeal Judeteamt Neamt – G. Dumitriu: p. 170 left, center and right, Cat. No. 191

Katie Demakopoulou: pp. 68, 98, 100

Pierre et Maurice Chuzeville: Cat. No. 22

Katie Demakopoulou (ed.): Troy, Mycenae, Tiryns, Orchomenos. Heinrich Schliemann: The 100th Anniversary of his Death. Exhibition Catalogue. Athens 1990: p. 90

Dorset Natural History and Archaeological Society at the Dorset County Museum: p. 102, Cat. No. 160

Etnografické Mùzeum Zilina, Martin – Marta Novotnà: Cat. No. 186

Stefano Flore: p. 123

Geowissenschaftliche Sammlungen der Bergakademie Freiberg – Michael Knopfe: Cat. No. 87

Germanisches Nationalmuseum Nürnberg – Jürgen Musolf: pp. 176, 177 above and below, 178, 180, Cat. No. 205

Hamburger Museum für Archäologie und die Geschichte Harburgs Helms-Museum: Cat. No. 107

Antony F. Harding: pp. 38 left and right, 39 left, 42

Hellenic Ministry of Culture – I. Iliades: pp. 10, 12, 57, 67 left and right, 188, 189 left, 190, Cat. Nos. 7, 10, 28, 67, 71, 73, 74, 76, 219, 220, 221, 222, 223, 227, 228; S. Mavrommatis: pp. 202, 234; National Archeological Museum, Athens, Photographic Archive: pp. 1, 201 (Lamia), Cat. Nos. 6, 8, 9, 30, 31, 33, 37, 41, 42, 43, 51, 54, 55 (Patras), 56, 60 (Larissa),

61 (Thasos), 63, 64, 65, 229 (Nauplin), 230 (Lamia), 233, 236; The National Hellenic Committee (I.C.O.M): pp. 88, 99, 101, 125 left and right, 182, 186, Cat. Nos. 2, 26, 38, 44, 49, 52, 53, 57, 58, 59, 66, 226, 233, 235, 236; The National Hellenic Committee (I.C.O.M.), S. Mavrommatis: p. 133, Cat. Nos. 68, 234; The National Hellenic Committee (I.C.O.M.), Photographic Archive: pp. 199, 206 left and right; I. Papadakis: Cat. No. 230; R. Parisis: Cat. No. 5; Y. Patrikianos: p. 193 right, Cat. Nos. 217, 218; St. Stournaras: pp. 18, 37, 54 left and right, 55, 185, 189 right, Cat. Nos. 3, 4, 11, 12, 13, 14, 15, 16, 17, 18, 19, 27, 48, 70, 224, 225, 231, 237; D. Tamviskos: pp. 52, 194, 195, 196, Cat. Nos. 1, 29, 34, 39, 46, 47, 50, 69, 84

Hirmer Verlag, München: p. 66

Historisches Museum der Pfalz, Speyer: p. 173

I. Iliades: Cat. Nos. 32, 35–36, 40, 45, 62

Albrecht Jockenhövel: pp. 71 above and below, 143, 144

Piet de Jong: p. 69 left

G. Karo: Greifen am Thron. Erinnerungen an Knossos. Baden-Baden 1959: p. 9

Kulturhistorisches Museum Stralsund: Cat. No. 129

A. Knape, H.-Å. Nordström: Der Kultgegenstand von Balkåkra. Stockholm 1994: Cat. No. 131

Landesamt für Archäologie Sachsen-Anhalt – A. Hörentrup: Cat. No. 142

Landesamt für Archäologie Sachsen mit Landesamt für Vorgeschichte. Japanisches Palais, Dresden: p. 45, Cat. No. 210

Landesdenkmalamt Baden-Württemberg. Dept. Archäologische Denkmalpflege, Karlsruhe: p. 85, Cat. No. 109

Landesmuseum Mainz – U. Rudischer: Cat. Nos. 138, 181

Walter Leitner: pp. 24 left, 24 right, 26

Raffaele C. de Marinis: pp. 146, 147, 148, 149, 150, 151 left and right

Martina Marthari: pp. 159, 162 left and right

K. P. Martinek: pp. 49 left and right, 50

Xenophon Michael: Cat. Nos. 20, 23, 24, 25

Jean-Pierre Mohen: p. 156

Musée d'Art et d'Histoire, Geneva – N. Sabato: Cat. No. 148

Musée Denon, Section Archéologie, Chalon-sur-Saône: p. 32, Cat. No. 102

Musée des Antiquités Nationales, Saint-Germain-en-Laye – RMN: Cat. No. 196; J. G. Berizzi: p. 179, Cat. Nos. 101, 200, 202, 203, 204; G. Blot: pp. 95, 171, Cat. No. 196; Loïc Hamon: p. 91, Cat. Nos. 88, 89, 95, 96, 97, 117, 118, 146, 147, 155, 163, 164, 203; H. Lewandowski: p. 80, Cat. No. 110

Musée du Donjon, Niort – Ph. B. Renaud: Cat. No. 128

Musée du Louvre, Departement des Antiquités Orientales: Cat. Nos. 21, 72; Jean-Pierre Chuzeville: Cat. No. 179

Musée Fenaille, Rodez – André Méravilles: Cat. No. 171

Museo archeologico di Aosta, Italy – L'Image – Courmayer: Cat. Nos. 169, 170

Museo Civico di Storia Naturale, Verona – Photographic Archive of the Natural History Museum: Cat. No. 100

Museo Arqueológico Nacional, Madrid: Cat. No. 173

Museu Nacional da Arqueologia, Lisbon – José Pessoa: Cat. Nos. 162, 1991

Museu "Rainha D. Leonor", Beya, Portugal – A. Cunha: Cat. No. 174

Museum Debrezen – Kàroly Kozma: p. 89, Cat. No. 104

Museum der Stadt Regensburg, Historisches Museum, Presse und Informationstelle der Stadt Regensburg – Peter Ferstl: p. 106, Cat. No. 168

Museum of Natural History and Archaeology, Institute of Archaeology, Trondheim – P. E. Fredriksen: Cat. No. 187

Museum Schwab, Bienne (Biehl) – Daniel Mueller: Cat. No. 114

Muzeul national de istorie al Romaniei, Bucarest: p. 79 right, Cat. Nos. 94, 99, 111, 177, 192; Marius Amariei: Cat. No. 83

Muzeum Gòrnoslaskie, Bytom: Cat. No. 137

Nàrodni muzeum, Prague – Vlasta Dvoràkovà: p. 103, Cat. No. 103

National Museum of Ireland, Dublin – Valerie Dowling: Cat. Nos. 134, 135, 152, 193, 194, 197, 216

National Museum of Wales: Cat. No. 79

Nationalmuseet Copenhagen: p. 8 left, 58, Cat. Nos. 77, 78, 81, 91, 92, 105, 113, 120, 182, 184, 189, 190, 209, 226; Kit Weiss: pp. 13, 58 right, 59 left and right, 86, 94, 97, 108 right, 109, 130, 135, 136, 169, 193 left, Cat. Nos. 81, 90, 106, 119, 132, 133, 136, 143, 145, 149, 150, 166, 175, 180, 183, 213

Nationalmuseum Budapest: Cat. No. 112

Naturhistorisches Museum Wien: p. 134, Cat. No. 176

Niedersächsiches Landesmuseum Hannover – Karl-Heinz Uhe: p. 105

S. Oliveira Jorge: pp. 62, 63

Giovanni Pittalis: p. 124

Poznan Archaeological Museum: p. 58, Cat. Nos. 141, 159

Prähistorische Staatssammlung, Munich – Michael Berger: Cat. No. 93

Provincia di Trento, Servizio Beni Culturali. Ufficio Beni Archeologici – Archivo fotografico, Ufficio Beni Archeologici

European Advisory Committee

Portugal
Susana Oliviera Jorge, Universidade do Porto, Porto

Rumania
George Trohani, Muzeul National de Istorie a României, Bucarest

Russia
Iuri Piotrovski, The State Hermitage Museum, St. Petersburg

Slovak Republic
Václav Furmánek, Archologický ústav SAV, Nitra

Spain
María Luisa Ruiz-Gálvez Priego, Universidad Complutense, Facultad de Geografía e Historia, Madrid

Switzerland
Walter Fasnacht, Schweizerisches Landesmuseum, Zürich

Turkey
Nilüfer Turkan Atakan, Istanbul Arkeoloji Müzerleri, Istanbul

Supervision

Irène Bizot, General Administrator of the Réunion des musées nationaux
Jean Digne, Director of the Association Française d'Action Artistique/Ministère des Affaires étrangères
Wenzel Jacob, Director of the Kunst- und Ausstellungshalle der Bundesrepublik Deutschland, Bonn
Jette Sandahl, Director of Exhibitions and Public Programmes, National Museum of Denmark
Daniel Tarschys, Secretary General of the Council of Europe
Yannis Tzedakis, Director General of Antiquities, Ministry of Culture, Athens

Scientific Committee

Sappho Athanassopoulou, Department of Exhibitions of the Ministry of Culture, Athens
Katie Demakopoulou, Director Emeritus of the National Archaeological Museum, Athens
Christiane Eluère, Chief Curator of the Research Laboratory of the Museums of France
Jørgen Jensen, Curator, National Museum of Denmark, Copenhagen
Albrecht Jockenhövel, Professor, Westfälische Wilhelms-Universität, Seminar für Ur- und Frühgeschichte, Münster
Niels-Knud Liebgott, Director, De danske Kongers kronologiske Samling, Rosenborg, Copenhagen
Jean-Pierre Mohen, Director of the Research Laboratory of the Museums of France, Paris

Acknowledgements

Austria
Naturhistorisches Museum, Prähistorische Abteilung,
    Wien

Cyprus
Cyprus Museum, Department of Antiquities, Nicosia

Czech Republic
Národni muzeum, Praha

Denmark
National Museum of Denmark, Copenhagen
Moesgaard Museum, Aarhus

France
Musée Archéologique, Chalon-sur-Saône
Musée Bernard d'Agesci, Niort
Musée du Louvre, département des Antiquités grecques,
    étrusques et romaines, Paris
Musée du Louvre, département des Antiquités orientales,
    Paris
Musée Fenaille, Rodez
Musée des Antiquités Nationales, Château de
    Saint-Germain-en-Laye

Germany
Römisches Museum der Städtischen Kunstsammlungen
    Augsburg, Augsburg
Stiftung Preußischer Kulturbesitz, Staatliche Museen zu
    Berlin, Museum für Vor- und Frühgeschichte,
    Berlin
Rheinisches Landesmuseum, Bonn
Erich Bäcker, Donauwörth
Landesamt für Archäologie mit Landesmuseum für
    Vorgeschichte, Dresden
Technische Universität Bergakademie Freiberg,
    Geowissenschaftliche Sammlungen, Freiberg
Landesamt für Archäologie Sachsen-Anhalt, Landes-
    museum für Vorgeschichte, Halle (Saale)

Hamburger Museum für Archäologie und die Geschichte
    Harburgs, Helms-Museum, Hamburg
Niedersächsisches Landesmuseum, Abt. Ur- und
    Frühgeschichte, Hannover
Landesdenkmalamt Baden-Württemberg, Archäolo-
    gische Denkmalpflege Außenstelle Karlsruhe,
    Karlsruhe
Staatliche Museen Kassel, Kassel
Landesamt für Bodendenkmalpflege Mecklenburg-
    Vorpommern, Archäologisches Landesmuseum,
    Lübsdorf
Mittelrheinisches Landesmuseum, Mainz
Prähistorische Staatssammlung, Museum für Vor- und
    Frühgeschichte, München
Westfälisches Museum für Archäologie, Münster
Germanisches Nationalmuseum, Nürnberg
Museen der Stadt Regensburg, Kunst- und Kultur-
    historische Sammlungen, Regensburg
Archäologisches Landesmuseum der Christian-
    Albrechts-Universität, Schloß Gottorf, Schleswig
Historisches Museum der Pfalz, Speyer
Schwedenspeicher-Museum Stade, Regionalmuseum
    im Elbe-Weser-Raum, Stade

Great Britain
Royal Pavilion, Libraries & Museums Brighton & Hove,
    Brighton
National Museums & Galleries of Wales, Dep. of
    Archaeology and Numismatics, Cardiff
Dorset County Museum, Dorset
Royal Museum of Scotland, Department of Archaeology,
    Edinburgh
Hull and East Riding Museum, Kingston-upon-Hull

Greece
Ministry of Culture, Department of Prehistoric and
    Classical Antiquities, Athens
National Archaeological Museum, Athens
Numismatic Museum, Athens

Archaeological Museum, Aegina
Archaeological Collection of Apeiranthos, Naxos,
    Cyclades
Archaeological Museum, Argos, Argolid
Archaeological Museum, Chania, Crete
Archaeological Museum, Delphi, Phokis
Archaeological Museum, Eleusis, Attica
Archaeological Museum, Herakleion, Crete
Archaeological Museum, Kea, Cyclades
Archaeological Museum, Lamia, Phthiotis
Archaeological Museum, Larisa, Thessalia
Archaeological Museum, Melos, Cyclades
Archaeological Museum, Nauplion, Argolid
Archaeological Museum, Patras, Achaia
Archaeological Museum, Rethymnon, Crete
Archaeological Museum, Tenos, Cyclades
Archaeological Museum, Thasos
Archaeological Museum, Thebes, Boeotia

Hungary
Magyar Nemzeti Múzeum, Budapest
Soproni Muzeum, Sopron
Déri Múzeum Debrecen

Ireland
National Museum of Ireland, Dublin

Italy
Museo Civico, Bolzano
Museo Civico di Storia Naturale, Sez. Preistoria, Verona
Servizio Beni Culturali, Ufficio Beni Archeologici, Trento
Servizio Archeologica e Diagnostica, Aosta

Norway
Vitenskapmuseet, Norges teknisk-naturvitenskapelige
    universitet, Trondheim

Poland
Muzeum Górnoslaskie, Bytom
Muzeum Archeologiczne, Poznan

Portugal
Museu Rainha D. Leonor, Beja
Museu Nacional de Arqueologia, Lisboa

Rumania
Muzeul National de Istorie a României, Bucarest
Complexul muzeal judetean Neamt, Piatra Neamt

Russia
The State Hermitage Museum, St. Petersburg

Slovak Republic
Slovenské múzeum ochrany prírody a jaskyniarstva,
    Liptovský Mikulás
Slovenské národné múzeum, Martin
Zemplínske múzeum, Michalovce
Archeologický ústav SAV, Nitra

Spain
Museo Arqueológico Nacional, Madrid

Sweden
Statens Historiska Museum, Stockholm

Switzerland
Bernisches Historisches Museum, Bern
Museum Schwab, Biel
Musée d'Art et d'Histoire, Département de
    Pré- et Protohistoire, Genève
Schweizerisches Landesmuseum, Zürich

Colophon

This catalogue is published to accompany the exhibition
Guder og Helte i Bronzealderen. Europa på Odysseus' tid
from December 19, 1998, to April 5, 1999, at the National Museum of Denmark, Copenhagen.
Götter und Helden der Bronzezeit. Europa im Zeitalter des Odysseus
from May 7 to August 8, 1999, at the Kunst- und Ausstellungshalle der Bundesrepublik Deutschland, Bonn, Germany
L'Europe au temps d'Ulysse. Dieux et Héros à l'Age du bronze
from September 28, 1999, to January 9, 2000, at the Galeries nationales du Grand Palais, Paris, and
Θεοί και Ήρωες της Εποχής του Χαλκού. Η Ευρώπη στις ρίζες του Οδυσσέα.
(Gods and Heroes of Bronze Age Europe. The roots of Ulysses)
from February 11 to May 7, 2000, at the National Archaeological Museum, Athens

Issued by
National Museum of Denmark, Copenhagen, Denmark, Kunst- und Ausstellungshalle der Bundesrepublik Deutschland, Bonn, Germany, Réunion des Musées nationaux, Paris, France, Association Française d'Action Artistique / Ministère des Affaires étrangères, Paris, France, Hellenic Ministry of Culture, General Directorate of Antiquities, Athens, Greece

Concept
Katie Demakopoulou, Christiane Eluère, Jorgen Jensen, Albrecht Jockenhövel, Jean-Pierre Mohen

Supervising Editor
Jorgen Jensen

Managing Editor
Petra Kruse

Associate Editor
Helga Willinghöfer

Subject Editor
Doniert Evely

Assistant Editor
Michael Koch

Editorial Coordinator
Christine Traber

Translations
Melissa Thorson Hause, Steven Lindberg, John S. Southard

Graphic Design
Konnertz Buchgestaltung Köln

Production Coordinator
Heiko Seitz

Typesetting
Weyhing Digital, Stuttgart

Lithography
C+S Repro, Filderstadt

Printed by
Dr. Cantz'sche Druckerei, Ostfildern-Ruit

Cover Illustration
The Chariot of the Sun, from Trundholm
(Cat. No. 175)